T0331853

Promoting Global Competencies Through Media Literacy

Melda N. Yildiz
New York Institute of Technology, USA

Steven S. Funk
Montana State University – Billings, USA

Belinha S. De Abreu
National Telemedia Council, USA

A volume in the Advances in Media,
Entertainment, and the Arts (AMEA) Book Series

Published in the United States of America by
    IGI Global
    Information Science Reference (an imprint of IGI Global)
    701 E. Chocolate Avenue
    Hershey PA, USA 17033
    Tel: 717-533-8845
    Fax: 717-533-8661
    E-mail: cust@igi-global.com
    Web site: http://www.igi-global.com

Copyright © 2018 by IGI Global. All rights reserved. No part of this publication may be reproduced, stored or distributed in any form or by any means, electronic or mechanical, including photocopying, without written permission from the publisher. Product or company names used in this set are for identification purposes only. Inclusion of the names of the products or companies does not indicate a claim of ownership by IGI Global of the trademark or registered trademark.

Library of Congress Cataloging-in-Publication Data

Names: Yildiz, Melda N., 1969- editor.
Title: Promoting global competencies through media literacy / Melda N.
  Yildiz, Steven S. Funk, and Belinha S. De Abreu, editors.
Description: Hershey PA : Information Science Reference, [2018]
Identifiers: LCCN 2017013844| ISBN 9781522530824 (hardcover) | ISBN
  9781522530831 (ebook)
Subjects: LCSH: Media literacy--Study and teaching. | Digital media--Study
  and teaching.
Classification: LCC P96.M4 P76 2018 | DDC 302.23071--dc23 LC record available at https://lccn.loc.gov/2017013844

This book is published in the IGI Global book series Advances in Media, Entertainment, and the Arts (AMEA) (ISSN: 2475-6814; eISSN: 2475-6830)

British Cataloguing in Publication Data
A Cataloguing in Publication record for this book is available from the British Library.

All work contributed to this book is new, previously-unpublished material. The views expressed in this book are those of the authors, but not necessarily of the publisher.

For electronic access to this publication, please contact: eresources@igi-global.com.

Advances in Media, Entertainment, and the Arts (AMEA) Book Series

Giuseppe Amoruso
Politecnico di Milano, Italy

ISSN:2475-6814
EISSN:2475-6830

Mission

Throughout time, technical and artistic cultures have integrated creative expression and innovation into industrial and craft processes. Art, entertainment and the media have provided means for societal self-expression and for economic and technical growth through creative processes.

The **Advances in Media, Entertainment, and the Arts (AMEA)** book series aims to explore current academic research in the field of artistic and design methodologies, applied arts, music, film, television, and news industries, as well as popular culture. Encompassing titles which focus on the latest research surrounding different design areas, services and strategies for communication and social innovation, cultural heritage, digital and print media, journalism, data visualization, gaming, design representation, television and film, as well as both the fine applied and performing arts, the AMEA book series is ideally suited for researchers, students, cultural theorists, and media professionals.

Coverage

- Music & Performing Arts
- Products, Strategies and Services
- Visual Computing
- Drawing
- Design Tools
- Cultural Heritage
- New Media Art
- Humanities Design
- Sports & Entertainment
- Popular Culture

IGI Global is currently accepting manuscripts for publication within this series. To submit a proposal for a volume in this series, please contact our Acquisition Editors at Acquisitions@igi-global.com or visit: http://www.igi-global.com/publish/.

The Advances in Media, Entertainment, and the Arts (AMEA) Book Series (ISSN 2475-6814) is published by IGI Global, 701 E. Chocolate Avenue, Hershey, PA 17033-1240, USA, www.igi-global.com. This series is composed of titles available for purchase individually; each title is edited to be contextually exclusive from any other title within the series. For pricing and ordering information please visit http://www.igi-global.com/book-series/advances-media-entertainment-arts/102257. Postmaster: Send all address changes to above address. Copyright © 2018 IGI Global. All rights, including translation in other languages reserved by the publisher. No part of this series may be reproduced or used in any form or by any means – graphics, electronic, or mechanical, including photocopying, recording, taping, or information and retrieval systems – without written permission from the publisher, except for non commercial, educational use, including classroom teaching purposes. The views expressed in this series are those of the authors, but not necessarily of IGI Global.

Titles in this Series

For a list of additional titles in this series, please visit: www.igi-global.com/book-series

Exploring Journalism Practice and Perception in Developing Countries
Abiodun Salawu (North-West University, South Africa) and Toyosi Olugbenga Samson Owolabi (Lagos State University, Nigeria)
Information Science Reference • copyright 2018 • 339pp • H/C (ISBN: 9781522533764) • US $185.00 (our price)

Digital Innovations in Architectural Heritage Conservation Emerging Research and Opportunities
Stefano Brusaporci (University of L'Aquila, Italy)
Engineering Science Reference • copyright 2017 • 152pp • H/C (ISBN: 9781522524342) • US $115.00 (our price)

Music as a Platform for Political Communication
Uche Onyebadi (Texas Christian University, USA)
Information Science Reference • copyright 2017 • 309pp • H/C (ISBN: 9781522519867) • US $195.00 (our price)

Media Law, Ethics, and Policy in the Digital Age
Nhamo A. Mhiripiri (Midlands State University, Zimbabwe & St. Augustine University, Tanzania) and Tendai Chari (University of Venda, South Africa)
Information Science Reference • copyright 2017 • 330pp • H/C (ISBN: 9781522520955) • US $195.00 (our price)

Handbook of Research on the Facilitation of Civic Engagement through Community Art
Leigh Nanney Hersey (University of Louisiana Monroe, USA) and Bryna Bobick (University of Memphis, USA)
Information Science Reference • copyright 2017 • 672pp • H/C (ISBN: 9781522517276) • US $275.00 (our price)

Convergence of Contemporary Art, Visual Culture, and Global Civic Engagement
Ryan Shin (University of Arizona, USA)
Information Science Reference • copyright 2017 • 390pp • H/C (ISBN: 9781522516651) • US $195.00 (our price)

Cultural Influences on Architecture
Gülşah Koç (Yıldız Technical University, Turkey) Marie-Therese Claes (Louvain School of Management, Belgium) and Bryan Christiansen (PryMarke, LLC, USA)
Information Science Reference • copyright 2017 • 352pp • H/C (ISBN: 9781522517443) • US $180.00 (our price)

Design Innovations for Contemporary Interiors and Civic Art
Luciano Crespi (Politecnico di Milano, Scuola del Design, Italy)
Information Science Reference • copyright 2017 • 427pp • H/C (ISBN: 9781522506669) • US $205.00 (our price)

701 East Chocolate Avenue, Hershey, PA 17033, USA
Tel: 717-533-8845 x100 • Fax: 717-533-8661
E-Mail: cust@igi-global.com • www.igi-global.com

Editorial Advisory Board

Mustafa Serkan Abdusselam, *Giresun University, Turkey*
Smadar Bar-Tal, *Levinsky College of Education, Israel*
Victoria Brown, *Florida Atlantic University, USA*
Flory Dieck-Assad, *Tecnologico de Monterrey, Mexico*
Hui-Yin Hsu, *New York Institute of Technology, USA*
Sevinj Iskandarova, *James Madison University, USA*
Lala Jabbarova, *Baku State University, Azerbaijan*
Matthew Lewerenz, *Walden University, USA*
Kelly McNeal, *William Paterson University, USA*
Ann-Marie Parkes, *New York Institute of Technology, UAE*
Tami Seifert, *Kibutzim College of Education, Israel*
Aakanksha Sharma, *Indira Gandhi National Open University, India*
Sujatha Sosale, *The University of Iowa, USA*
Shaing-Kwei Wang, *New York Institute of Technology, USA*

Table of Contents

Section 3
Global Projects Around the World: Digital and World Savvy Curriculum

Section 4
Theory to Practice for the Digital Age: Current Research and Transdisciplinary
Approaches

Detailed Table of Contents

Section 1
Assessment and Media Education Framework, Theory, Background, and Brief History

The twenty-first century citizens must develop their media literacy competence at several levels such as technique, reflective and creative, auto-regulation, social participation and pedagogical. Even though the citizens' empowerment is a general society responsibility, school plays a crucial role, especially if school is able to respond to a set of challenges, namely breaking the traditional resistance to change, integrating formal and informal learning, educating for the media beyond the technical dimension, overcoming the digital divides, protecting citizens' data, and training teachers. This chapter focuses on this last challenge, presenting three research projects which involved in-service teacher training (2007-2011; 2012-2015; 2016-2018). Results showed that K-12 teachers are able to develop media literacy activities with their pupils, using traditional and/or digital technologies, during in-service teacher training courses. As such, they are also able to overcome the lack of technologies in their classrooms by using their own devices or pupils' devices.

Chapter 2

Technology to learn the digital literacy skills required to attend postsecondary institutions or to access distance learning courses. Three groups of students are impacted by the lack of access to technology: (a) without broadband access, (b) students' low socioeconomic status, and (c) students' primary language is not English. Without digital literacy skills, selecting, applying, and fully participating in a postsecondary education is difficult. This chapter will outline the challenges these three groups of students have in accessing broadband, the impact the lack of access created in Florida, and solutions that were suggested to address lack of high speed broadband.

Chapter 3

This chapter is to challenge the research opportunity of media literacy in the twenty-first-century learning environment. Different technologies with human-computer interaction are addressed in this section as two different main structures. The relationships between these two structures are constructed as matrices. One of these structures is constituted by the educational technologies of the twenty-first century. The second is the learning framework of the twenty-first century. The research will be done using content analysis of the technologies used and learning frameworks. Based on the data obtained, this study will attempt to demonstrate that teachers can provide more effective and productive instruction using human-computer interaction. This section will hopefully provide information to teachers and students about suitable learning environments designed for the use of and in conformance with twenty-first-century skills with the use of innovative technologies, and technologies they should use in these environments.

Section 2
Best Practices, Assessment Strategies, and Teachable Moments From the Field

Digital Storytelling is an effective tool to develop Media Literacy skills in educational settings. This chapter will analyze and present current research/literature on Media Literacy through Digital Storytelling in regard to developing and assessing media literacy skills. Authors have been implementing an instructional project called Digital Storytelling Contests (DISTCO) since 2008. DISTCO reached out to more than 10000 K-16 students and teachers over the years. The goal is to relay the experiences on how media literacy has been developed through Digital Storytelling activities with DISTCO. In addition, the current DISTCO rubric for assessing digital storytelling projects is modified to include a version assessing Media Literacy through digital storytelling.

Chapter 5

This book chapter summarizes an extensive literature review on gaming literacies and learning. It carefully examines the definition of gaming literacies from both message consumption and production perspectives, stemming from the definition of foundational literacies and information communication and technology (ICT) literacies. We establish a framework based on Bloom's taxonomy to explore the role of gaming literacies on learners' cognitive, affective and psychomotor domains. We discuss the implications for teachers to adopt games in the classroom, possible problems and concerns to have learners play games, synthesize practices for using games in educational context, and provide suggestions for future research.

Chapter 6

The use of Web 2.0 environments and social media in teaching and learning facilitates the provision of participatory and creative, learner-oriented teaching. The proposed chapter describes the role of social media in teaching and learning in colleges of higher education and suggests possible uses and applications for a variety of social media environments in education, especially the environments of Facebook, Twitter, WhatsApp, and Instagram. Social networks facilitate activities that promote involvement, collaboration and engagement. Modeling of best practices using social networks enhances its usage by students, increases student confidence as to its implementation and creates a paradigm shift to a more personalized, participatory and collaborative learning and a more positive attitude towards its implementation.

Chapter 7

As many educational institutions become more globally competitive, and the number of diverse teachers increases, it becomes even more imperative to avoid what some cultures might deem as inappropriate and unprofessional verbal and non-verbal forms of communication. Those behaviors are sometimes interpreted in different ways, depending on the cultural perspective. Any unwanted verbal and non-verbal actions often increase stress, unwelcomed job pressures, and hinder a positive work environment. At the institutional level where teachers are very diverse, understanding verbal and nonverbal behaviors must be addressed. The researchers propose a methodology which will help multilingual, multicultural teachers' communication styles within the workplace and how to improve cross-cultural team collaborations. Additionally, the information provided in this study allows educational leaders to make inferences about their teachers' team performance and expectations based on their motivation, experiences, and skills used when working with a multicultural team.

Section 3
Global Projects Around the World: Digital and World Savvy Curriculum

Media literacy is the raison d'être of journalism and media education in universities. With the advent of digital technologies and generational online developments such as Web 2.0, media literacy has now turned into multimedia literacy, where future media professionals learn to write, produce video and audio, edit, link, curate, and disseminate the content produced as individual communicators rather than members of a production team where each member specializes in one or two of these aspects to media production. Simultaneously there has been an increase in efforts to globalize educational experiences for students. These developments raise questions about new elements to media literacy, pedagogy, assessment, and learning the ethics of responsible communication about foreign cultures in the media. This chapter tackles these questions by reflecting on a Study Abroad course experience where students in a US university traveled to South India, and created content in the field about specific experiences related to development.

Establishment of the Shluvim network in 2010 responded to the Israeli education profession's need to introduce innovative pedagogical challenges. This social-professional network provides a virtual space for its members, empowering them through discussion on different aspects of education. The article describes a case study, employing both qualitative and quantitative methodology (questionnaires and interviews), to identify the dynamics of quantitative components involved in the evolvement of the network and to elicit members' experiences in the communication process. Findings reveal challenges involved in informed use of social networking in education and show how participation in the professional network can assist members' professional development, although it is necessary to adapt to changes in usage patterns and competition with alternative social networks. The research enhances understanding of the social-professional network's role as an empowering environment for the Israeli education system in general and for teachers' education and professional development in particular.

The Organization for Economic Co-operation and Development (OECD) defines global competence as the capacity to analyze global and intercultural issues critically and to engage in open, appropriate and effective interactions. Since media forms the basis for attaining and sharing information, formulating ideas and opinions about people, events and situations, exploring different cultures, perspectives, rejecting notions as well as accepting truths, media and information literacy (MIL) is an effective and essential way to attain this global competence. As MIL competencies are closely aligned with global competencies, interlinking the two helps in attaining true global citizenship. This chapter explains the problems, prospects and possibilities for MIL training in India. The history and evolution of media and its regulatory structure in India and how this has impacted and continues to influence the spectrum of media and information literacy is the core of this study.

Chapter 11

The media is one of the main resources from which people derive information about events surrounding them. The media tries to mirror realities, transmit various events, including cases of aggression and violence; however, lack of control on quality and quantity of information may result in perilous outcomes. This chapter offers a psychological analysis of the influence of media on crime in society, as well as the relation of crime levels with information about aggression and violence. The results of the research suggest that frequent, overstated, and embellished media disseminations of information of an aggressive character, without considering its possible psychological outcomes, increases viewers' levels of aggression and violence. In order to prevent this increase, it is crucial not to eliminate aggressive information from media completely, but instead to present it while taking into account its psychological effects.

Section 4
Theory to Practice for the Digital Age: Current Research and Transdisciplinary Approaches

Chapter 12

The U.S. and many countries across Europe and around the world are currently experiencing increased cultural tensions and xenophobia, particularly against those whose ethnic, religious, or linguistic orientations make them a minority or an otherwise vulnerable group. This comes despite the fact that we are a more interconnected global society than perhaps ever before in our history. Communication is central to overcoming this obstacle, and language instruction can be an integral locus for directly confronting perceptions and prejudices. Creating practical learning applications and assessments that foster critical thinking and utilize ontological, ethical, and educational practices rooted in the Tao Te Ching, integrated with a critical pedagogical framework, can effect positive social change and help foster global unity through mutual linguistic and ontological identification.

Chapter 13

Teachers and professors are searching for the best academic strategy to support an educational process that could provide an effective digital learning experience. After the evaluation of Learning Management Systems (LMS's), this chapter proposes the hypotheses that through the use of Microsoft OneNote Class Notebook (MONCN) as a teaching innovation in undergraduate Finance courses, the student's learning process is enhanced, and the students themselves perceive this LMS as a tool that enriches their education and improves their academic experience. The smart way to implement intelligent technology such as the use of MONCN will be to create an evolution through innovation, not a revolution; but the impact of this digital notebook could prove to be revolutionary if applied wisely. MONCN will enable faculty and students to survive the current challenges of media literacy and to thrive in the years to come; it could be replicated with great success in any university.

Chapter 14

Of the many identity markers that students claim and encounter throughout their educational journeys, none might be more salient than gender. While much of the European Union seems to be sloughing off the gender binary as a vestige of the 20th century, many educators and students in the U.S. continue to reinforce the binary through explicit and implicit strategies that normalize the cisgender condition while othering those who are trans*+. The purpose of this chapter is to explore the entrenchment of the gender binary in the American post-secondary system, to analyze the media frenzy currently addressing trans*+ identities, and to offer a theoretical framework of Trans*+ Media Literacy, borne of Critical Media Literacy, to address specifically how post-secondary educators and students can create gender expansive and inclusive spaces that might foster the growth of students prepared to think of gender representation and media production that challenge the binary and encourage gender expansiveness to flourish.

As technology increasingly becomes a part of our day-to-day lives in the United States and throughout the globe, there is a greater push for students to develop the digital and media literacy skills necessary for the twenty-first century. In the United States, students learning these skills often come from a wide range of linguistic and cultural backgrounds. The diversity of the U.S. is one of its greatest strengths, but with this diversity come cultural differences in access to technology and how it is used across different cultural contexts. This chapter analyzes the constructs of digital and media literacy, the ways in which culture can be defined and how that can affect the intersectional identities performed in the social and participatory world of Web 2.0. It also examines access to technology and how technology is used for communication and accessing information in Russia, Germany, and Azerbaijan, and how approaching digital and media literacy through the lens of cross-cultural communication can help teachers to better meet the needs of learners from diverse backgrounds.

Coming from Azerbaijan to America as a Fulbright Scholar, I packed as many assumptions as I did suitcases. After conducting my research, I realized that everything I learned while visiting the United States should be shared with my students, to prevent them from some culture shock and to prepare them to be globally-minded, thinking of mediated messages about foreign countries in a critical manner. This chapter is a result of this endeavor, a sort of auto-ethnographical tour through the America that I saw through my positionality as an Azerbaijani woman.

Foreword

To see, where others have not yet begun to look

This is my personal definition of the artist. It was also my father's definition of the scientist. Both are inextricably connected through their common bonds of learning, testing that knowledge and actively contributing to new knowledge and insight. "The backbone of learning," he maintained, "is Interest—which means, in its Latin origin, *inter esse*—to be present with one's heart. Such learning is a combination of the creative process and hard and detailed work."

The ability to "see where others have not yet begun to look" is a natural gift, but it can be taught. It is in essence critical thinking; and that is media literacy. It is also the essence of scientific research. To be media literate is to "see" with a critical eye; it can also be an awakening of the artistic soul within. And for the scientist, it poses the challenge of how to measure such an experience. The goal of media literacy education is to reform traditional education into a new way of "seeing" and the goal of research within this field is to validate that premise.

We have, in this twenty-first century, the prospect of creating entirely new approaches to education; approaches that open students to their own more deeply reflective pace and creative energy, learning from their inner vision and discovery rather than from the outside in. We can give them the opportunities to discover through their own adventures, and by teaching them to think, reflect, and act, we can lead them "to see where others have not yet begun to look."

As parents, teachers, and as a society, we can teach our children to "know and improve the changing waters in which they swim" (S.I. Hayakawa). It is the *Ecology of Childhood* at work. It is our privilege to nurture our children and help them navigate through their ever-changing environment, both natural and mediated. We have the opportunity to send them into this new future with their backpacks filled to the brim with the tools to discover, to create, and to climb their own highest mountains. The challenge for education in this new millennium is possibly the most exhilarating new frontier at our door!

Yet none of these lofty goals can succeed or remain alive without a foundation of appropriate documented research. These ideas must be validated, tested and retested, assessed with the tools of scientific research and within the realities of their time. The research must be rigorous, yet flexible, evolving within the culture, both locally and globally. We must draw upon all of the amazing new research being done about the brain that has implications for learning and literacy. Such research is essential. It will lead to new learning and assessment that is meaningful and authentic.

Solid scientific research about the "art" of teaching media literacy is also key to establishing our field. Valid assessment can provide the long-sought credibility for media literacy to take its own place as a recognized legitimate department of knowledge and study in the Academy. Thus, the creation of this academic discipline will transform the way literacy is seen by all.

Marieli Rowe
National Telemedia Council, USA

Foreword

The need to teach university students the skills of critical media and digital literacies in a global world, and empowering future teachers to teach K-12 students multiple literacies, are more pressing that ever today. As students immerse themselves in worlds of texting, Facebook, Instagram, Twitter, YouTube, and social networking, on-line games, and new forms of digital and virtual media, they continue to consume vast amounts of television, film, popular music, and varied sources of news and information. Yet, contrary to popular belief, the majority of students entering university lack basic digital and critical media literacy skills and are hardly the savvy digital natives they are so widely claimed to be.

In fact, there are numerous pedagogical experts and reliable studies that demonstrate that there is an escalating racial, ethnic, gender and class divide, or digital inequality, in relation to new media and technological literacies, including computer science, especially between disenfranchised and affluent youth, and the richer and poorer nations. This is associated with, but not exclusive to, the global position and levels of the schools they attend, and their family's educational background, class, and lifestyle, which clearly dispels the problematic, widely publicized fallacy that the "new generation" is especially adept at employing new digital technologies, and do not require instruction in this regard.

And for even those students seemingly literate in new media, further study often reveals that it is the social, entertainment, gaming, gambling and interactive dimensions of the Internet and new media with which they are particularly familiar. In actuality, these same students often lack the abilities to be able to critically assess the media and virtual realities which occupy so much of their everyday lives and relationships, as well as to make informed decisions regarding the credibility of the information which they access.

Hence, the need for such studies as are produced in the book *Promoting Global Competencies Through Media Literacy* and conversations about the need for assessment of media education on a comparative and global scale. The studies collected in this book encompass a diverse range of important topics including in Section 1 studies involving "Assessment and Media Education Framework, Theory, Background, and Brief History" and encompassing "Assessing Media Literacy in Teacher Education," "Technology Access Gap for Postsecondary Education," "Teaching Digital and Media Literacy as Cross-Cultural Communication," and "Global Media Literacy: Innovative Learning Technologies."

Section 2 engages "Best Practices, Assessment Strategies, and Teachable Moments From the Field," including studies of "Developing and Assessing Media Literacy Through Digital Storytelling," "Children and Games," "Gaming Literacy," "Digital Media and Social Network in the Training of Pre-Service Teachers," "Teaching Technology and Media as Cross-Cultural Communication," and "A Counterpoint on American Education and Media: One Fulbright Scholar's Quest to Prepare Students for Travel to America." The titles signal the broad range of technologies and pedagogical practices utilized in media education and the need for imagination and creativity in this emerging field.

As befits a project engaging assessment of media and digital literacies in a global context, contributors from different parts of the world present in Section 3 "Assessment Projects Around the World: Digital and World Savvy Curriculum." These studies include "The Psychological Effects of Violence-Related Information from Media," "Learning Content Creation in the Field," "Assessing Multilingual Multicultural Teachers' Communication Styles," "Media Literacy and Competency Mapping in India," "A Study on the Effectiveness of Visual in E-Learning Content for School Children in India," and "The Shluvim Social-Professional Network."

Section 4 focuses on "Assessment From Theory to Practice for the Digital Age: Current Research and Transdisciplinary Approaches." Studies here also engage a wide range of approaches and pedagogies from different global perspectives including "Learning to Unlearn: Using Taoism and Critical Pedagogy in Language Education to Foster Global Unity," "An Analytical Study on the Impact and Effectiveness of Visuals in E-learning Method Among School Children," "Teaching Undergraduate Finance via a Digital Literacy Platform," and "Trans*+ Media Literacy Framework: On Navigating the Dynamically Shifting Terrain of Gender in Media and Considering the Assessment of Key Competencies." Together, the studies in this volume highlight the variety of pedagogical approaches and creative thinking in media education throughout the world.

The need for new thinking and conversations about media literacy assessment is all the more pressing given revelations in 2017 about the ubiquity of local and global production of fake news and the escalation of cyber-bullying, as well as the social and political conflicts and tensions that are mediated through new and older media which, in turn, strongly influence politics, culture, and society in the contemporary global arena.

Since postsecondary students are often unable to reflect upon their use of web-based technologies and to discern between legitimate and illegitimate sources of information, media literacy education is increasingly crucial. For example, 2006 study, supported by the Pew Charitable Trust, revealed that 50% of college seniors were unable to understand the basic arguments put forward in newspaper editorials or even compare credit card offers (Nemko, 2008). Further, student literacies in this regard have hardly improved since then, according to the findings of a 2016 Stanford Graduate School of Education assessment study of high school and college students' "on-line reasoning skills" and ability to evaluate Information drawn from a diversity of Internet sources.

Indeed, in one of the assessment studies, 80% of the 203 students surveyed could not distinguish between advertisements and news stories, on a popular online magazine, even though these were what are commonly referred to as "native ads" with clearly identified "sponsored content!" (Donald, 2016). In fact, the overall findings of this in-depth research study, which is hardly the first of its kind, are especially alarming and speak to a serious lacuna at all levels of U.S education. As they put it in the Executive Summary of this 2016 "Evaluating Information: The Cornerstone of Civic Online Reasoning" report:

When thousands of students respond to dozens of tasks there are endless variations. That was certainly the case in our experience. However, at each level—middle school, high school, and college—these variations paled in comparison to a stunning and dismaying consistency. Overall, young people's ability to reason about the information on the Internet can be summed up in one word: bleak.

The Brexit campaign, the 2016 U.S. presidential election, and recent elections from France to Kenya have all clearly demonstrated is that it is even more crucial that citizens become literate in media culture, emergent new media, and related technological, computer and web 2.0 digital forms. It is within this context that many experts argue that critical media literacy courses should be a part of required curricula within all elementary, secondary and post-secondary educational institutions, and that discussion of media education assessment should be a crucial part of contemporary education theory and practice.

Further, the need for conversations about new media, new literacies, and education today on a local and global scale is especially urgent in view of the escalating amount of time students engage with multiple forms of media (which is conservatively estimated at 9 hours a day). Since many members of an entire generation are dedicating more time to entertainment and media/digital interaction than to their studies, or to a full-time job, it would seem to be commonsense that schools should be aggressively educating students in media and digital literacies. Moreover, they should also be developing curricula to assist students to better understand and navigate media and digital culture, produced by some of the most powerful and influential societal institutions and multi-billion-dollar industries, which mediate our everyday experiences, material relations and perceptions of the world. And critical news media literacies need to be developed so that students can critically assess news and information, and distinguish between information and propaganda.

Hence, readers, teachers, and scholars should join the educators whose work is collected in this volume to participate in an emerging global effort to educate and empower students and citizens to meet the challenges of the contemporary era.

Rhonda Hammer
UCLA, USA

Douglas Kellner
UCLA, USA

REFERENCES

Donald, B. (2016). Stanford researchers find students have trouble judging the credibility of information on-line. *Stanford Graduate School of Education News*. Retrieved from https://ed.stanford.edu/news/stanford-researchers-find-students-have-trouble-judging-credibility-information-online

Nemko, M. (2008). America's most overrated product: The Bachelor's degree. *Chronicle of Higher Education*. Retrieved from http://www.chronicle.com/article/americas-most-overrated/19869

Preface

We are a global society. This fact has been evident since the Internet became a voice for the world through its many connections, but more prominently through social networks.

As Dr. Neil DeGrass Tyson said, "We are all connected. To each other, biologically. To the earth, chemically. To the rest of the universe atomically" (Miejan, 2010). To the global communities with the new media and technologies and social media, we may add, "electronically.

The high-speed development of technologies has captured our societies like no other. It asks us to question how we receive, interact, and put forth information. It creates possibilities for engagement at every age level. By the same token, it asks us to consider some of the drawbacks of interacting online, as behaviors correlate with development. There are many positive, ethical, and constructive questions being considered and analyzed:

- Are sites appropriate for students?
- What does it mean to be a digital citizen?
- How can we rely on online information when there is a clear message of misinformation?
- What does it mean to be an online learner?
- Have we lost site of the purpose and nature of what we engage in while online? Can we even distinguish it?
- Where are the gaps? Potentials? Needed Theoretical Thinking?

In participating in this book, *Promoting Global Competencies through Media Literacy,* authors tackled a wide assortment of questions. Further, they analyzed the issues presented to them by acknowledging who they were in their research, where they lived in many cases, or what they were teaching.

The compilation of chapters provides a scope of how people are engaging with all these dynamics at play in a very much a global sense. From India, Mexico, Portugal, Turkey, and the United States, just to name a few countries, academics grappled with idea of competencies within their work and through the consideration of how media literacy education is a part of the process of learning.

One of our own co-editors had her own experience with this through her Fulbright experience in Azerbaijan. As a Fulbright scholar, Yildiz spent four months in the Fall of 2016 working as a visiting scholar at Azerbaijan State Pedagogical University (http://adpu.edu.az/), conducting participatory action research among educators. During her amazing and enriching scholarly experience, which she shared with her 13-year-old son, she spent the semester co-teaching, co-presenting, and conducting research. Her son's experience was just as invaluable as he participated in the school and community. A global education opportunity was afforded to him as he attended an Azerbaijani school and took courses on Russian, German, French and Azerbaijani languages.

Yildiz not only participated in scholarly activities, she also hosted events and projects to introduce U.S./American culture, people, politics, and education. One of those events took place when Yildiz hosted a Thanksgiving potluck dinner for over 120 guests at her home to share the experiences of this American with her Azerbaijani and American colleagues, students, and neighbors. Her Thanksgiving dinner was featured on local television and the U.S. Embassy website. It provided dialog and cultural exchange among Azerbaijani and US Scholars.

Global scholar experiences are shared throughout this book by various contributors. In this book, some of our colleagues wrote chapters sharing their autoethnographical pieces. These pieces stemmed out of Yildiz's Fulbright experiences.

Additionally, this edited book promotes global competencies and new media and technologies as a powerful tool to further teacher education, media education, social justice education, and global education. What role does media education play in preparing new generations for this media saturated world? How can we harness the dynamism and connectivity of media to rethink how we assess student competencies to transform education in the digital age? This edited book serves to answer many of these questions by providing a four-part look at the role of global competencies, media literacy, and assessment and evaluation in K-16 education.

As Celot and Perez Tornero (2009) explain, the ultimate focus of media literacy is to empower people to participate in civic life. Moreover, media literacy can provide the framework of analysis through which students begin to challenge dominant myths that seem "normal" or "natural," but in fact serve to subject marginalized populations to second-class citizenry (Funk, Kellner, & Share, 2016). While media literacy, and critical media literacy have gained much traction as the subject of articles, teacher education courses, and conferences, to date, few scholarly studies have investigated how assessment is conducted within the context of media literacy. This text provides a comprehensive overview of the assessment practices of instructors engaging students through media literacy pedagogy from K through university-level curricula.

This book proposes to outline transdisciplinary and transformative assessment practices. It researches the conflicting perspectives on assessment as a device often used punitively towards educators, but a tool that can also have an emancipatory effect on students and educators who interact through assessment methods designed to "celebrate learning" (Broadfoot, 1991). Our goals are to:

1. Review the often-conflicting views on assessment while outlining key terminology of and practices in assessment and how these can be contextualized within a media literacy framework;
2. Showcase the assessment practices of educators working in K-12, Humanities, STEM, and Teacher Education departments; and
3. Demonstrate creative strategies and possibilities for engaging educators and students in utilizing a wide array of assessment strategies that highlight the emancipatory work being done with media literacy in educational settings from kindergarten through graduate school.

Situated within the context of teaching and learning media literacy within the global classroom, this book aims to advance scientific knowledge of innovative technologies and participatory learning practices as a means to promote the assessment of media literacy while advancing students' civic engagement, global competencies (http://asiasociety.org/node/8875), and 21st Century Skills (http://www.p21.org).

As such, this book is divided into four sections, "Assessment and Media Education Framework, Theory, Background, and Brief History"; "Best Practices, Assessment Strategies, and Teachable Moments From the Field"; "Global Projects Around the World: Digital and World Savvy Curriculum"; "Theory to Practice for the Digital Age: Current Research and Trandisciplinary Approaches."

In Section 1, "Assessment and Media Education Framework, Theory, Background, and Brief History," scholars from Portugal, the U.S., and Turkey share their empirical and theoretical research to deepen the dialogue of assessment. In "Assessing Media Literacy in Teacher Education," Vitor Tomé shares the findings of two studies that he has co-authored and, bravely shares the preliminary findings of an ongoing study while revealing these studies' shortcomings and making timely recommendations. Moreover, Tomé reflects on the qualitative data gathered from these studies to offer practical recommendations for media literacy education teachers and trainers. Tomé highlights the critical role of media literacy in teacher education and the urgent need for media literacy educators to acknowledge the ubiquitous use of media by children before they enter primary school. Tomé's work reminds educators that media literacy does not require large financial expenditures, and, more importantly, that media literacy bridges the gap between home and school while empowering students to learn social responsibility and critical thinking.

This chapter is followed by Brown's "Technology Access Gap for Postsecondary Education: A Statewide Case Study," which provides an in-depth analysis of postsecondary students' access to technology and their digital literacy skills. The findings of this research describe what students are affected by a lack of access to technology, and in what specific ways this lack affects their digital literacy. More importantly, Brown explains how this lack of digital literacy skills makes participating fully in the college experience difficult for these students. The chapter concludes by offering practical and timely solutions for educators seeking to improve students' access to technology in order to increase their digital literacy and improve their college experience.

This section is concluded with "Global Media Literacy: Innovative Technologies," which offers an analysis of various technologies used in classrooms to facilitate human-computer interaction. Examining the different technologies with human-computer interaction, the relationships among them are categorized as matrices. This chapter organizes these matrices into two main structures, the educational technologies of the twenty-first century, and the learning framework of the 21st century. By dividing these matrices and frameworks into clusters, Serkan Abdusselam offers educators a detailed overview of the various educational technologies and their potential roles in increasing media literacy.

Section 2, "Best Practices, Assessment Strategies, and Teachable Moments From the Field," features scholars from the U.S. and Israel sharing their empirical research to offer practical tools for educators seeking to incorporate media in the classroom. "Developing and Assessing Media Literacy Through Digital Storytelling" introduces readers to the media literacy assessment work being done in Digital Storytelling Contests (DISTCO), developed by media scholars at the University of Houston and North American University. Since its inaugural event in 2008, DISTCO has encouraged more than 10,000 K-12 students to critically and creatively engage in producing digital stories. The rubrics introduced by Dogan and Almus in this chapter offer educators a much-needed assessment tool that promotes active media participation while fostering students' academic responsibility and criticality through creative multi-media narrative production.

In "Gaming Literacy: Exploring the Potential of Using Games for K-12 Teaching and Learning," readers are treated to an extensive literature review on gaming literacies and learning. This chapter carefully examines the definition of gaming literacies from both message consumption and production perspectives, stemming from the definition of foundational literacies and information communication and technology (ICT) literacies. Hsu and Wang establish a framework based on Bloom's taxonomy to explore the role of gaming literacies on learners' cognitive, affective and psychomotor domains. As they discuss the implications for teachers to adopt games in the classroom, possible problems and concerns to have learners play games, synthesize practices for using games in educational context, and provide suggestions for future research, they add an exciting new thread to the discourse of gaming in educational settings.

Describing the establishment of the Shluvim network in 2010 and its response to the Israeli education profession's need to introduce innovative pedagogical challenges, is the empirical piece, Chapter 6, titled "Digital Media and Social Network in the Training of Pre-Service Teachers." It describes a mixed-methods case study to identify the dynamics of quantitative components involved in the evolvement of the Shluvim and to elicit members' experiences in the communication process. This social-professional network provides a virtual space for its members, empowering them through discussion on different aspects of education. Seifert's research enhances understanding of the social-professional network's role as an empowering environment for the Israeli education system in general and for teachers' education and professional development in particular.

Section 3, "Global Projects Around the World: Digital and World Savvy Curriculum," offers readers a glimpse at media assessment methods through a global perspective as scholars from the Azerbaijan, India, Israel, and the U.S. share their research and experiences. In Chapter 8, Sosale brings global perspectives in her article, "Learning Content Creation in the Field: Reflections on Multimedia Literacy in Global Context." She discusses a multimedia literacy course as part of a Study Abroad program. The article addresses the media production as the platform for learning multimedia literacy to communicate responsibly about unfamiliar cultures. Chapter 9, "The Shluvim Social-Professional Network: A Bridge for Educational Challenges and Trailblazers in Education," is by Bar-Tal and Seifert from the Kibbutzim College of Education, Israel.

Sharma, from Indira Gandhi National Open University, contributed Chapter 10, "Promoting Global Competencies in India: Media and Information Literacy as Stepping Stone." This chapter provides readers an in-depth examination of the ways in which media literacy is being used to improve educational outcomes. In Chapter 11, Jabbarova from Baku State University shares her research on "The Psychological Effects of Violence-Related Information From Media." This piece explores the effects of violence portrayed in media and reminds educators of their important role in mitigating potentially negative effects of media.

In Section 4, "Theory to Practice for the Digital Age: Current Research and Transdisciplinary Approaches," scholars from Azerbaijan, Mexico, and the U.S. grapple with what it means to utilize trans-discplinary pedagogies with the context of mediated classrooms to promote global citizenship. In this theoretical meandering that mimics the very Taoist practice, it explores "Learning to Unlearn: Using Taoism and Critical Pedagogy in Language Education to Foster Global Unity" and makes pleasantly surprising connections among Taoism, Buddhism, Islam, and Christianity and Critical Pedagogy. Lewerenz reminds us that, despite the hard work of Freire, Giroux, McLaren, and other educational activists and radicals, little regarding the Western concept of educational "banking" has changed. Modeling the critical pedagogy of the language it seeks to foster, this chapter reminds educators to remain "fluid," to invite the chaos of unknowing into our classrooms, and to remember that an ancient tradition may inform the most modern of practices.

In "Teaching Undergraduate Finance via a Digital Literacy Platform," Dieck-Assad presents the findings of a mixed-method study aimed at assessing the effectiveness of an online learning platform for Finance students. The data revealed that students using the online platform demonstrated a higher level of engagement and satisfaction with their course. Moreover, as the author underscores, the students also began to gain digital and technical literacies that will help them not only to develop more marketable skills for the workforce, but more nuanced critical thinking skills to better prepare them to meet the demands and rewards of global citizenship.

Chapter, 14, "Trans*+ Media Literacy Framework: On Navigating the Dynamically Shifting Terrain of Gender in Media and Considering the Assessment of Key Competencies," co-editor Steven Funk explores the entrenchment of the gender binary in the American post-secondary system, analyzes the media frenzy currently addressing trans*+ identities, and offers the Trans*+ Media Literacy Framework. Contextualizing his work with the framework of Critical Media Literacy, Funk offers this new framework to address specifically gender expansiveness and gender equity in the college classroom within the context of media literacy.

Funk underscores the importance of considering gender identity equity as a major, yet often ignored, facet of global citizenship in discourses relating to media literacy. Having experienced hardships and prejudice, as well as privilege and power, revolving around gender identity and gender presentation in academic settings, Funk is personally invested in exploring gender identity and mediated gender representations as they challenge and/or reinforce profit, privilege, and power. In this book, he introduces the Trans*+ Media Literacy framework, a product of his research in Critical Media Literacy and his commitment to gender expansiveness and gender equity.

The final chapters are auto-ethnographical pieces highlighting their global scholar experiences. Mary Catherine Boehmer wrote Chapter 15, "Teaching Digital and Media Literacy as Cross-Cultural Communication," highlighting about her experiences as an English teaching fellow in Azerbaijan. In Chapter 16, Shahla Naghiyeva Shnagiyeva shared her experiences as a Fulbright scholar in the United States in her chapter, "A Counterpoint on American Education and Media: One Fulbright Scholar's Quest to Prepare Students for Travel to America."

Chapter 15 reveals a scholar struggling to grapple with the concepts of media and digital literacy while moving across the globe for various teaching appointments. This chapter details Boehmer's rich and detailed exploration of personal experiences and makes recommendations to educators about how we can remind ourselves of the often implicit and habitual communicative behaviors informed through our sense of cultural (un)belonging. Boehmer poignantly reminds readers to remember how culture, intersectionality, and gender inform our mediated practices and to meet students where they are, rather than to risk focusing on developing students' discrete skill sets.

OBJECTIVES

The purpose of this book is to provide K-16 educators assessment tools and strategies that are transformational and transdisciplinary while highlighting best practices for twenty-first century classrooms. Each chapter emphasizes the current issues, theories, perspectives, and challenges faced in global media literacy education.

Interest in the field of global media literacy education has been not only intense but also critical. There is increasing worldwide attention and focus on developing media literacy and information literacy skills to effectively serve the needs of new generations by preparing them for the global civic and economic demands of twenty-first century. There are also growing numbers of non-profit and nongovernmental organizations that offer curricula that are in media literacy focused. This global movement connects schools to local, national, and global projects and organizations and leads to sustainable collaborations.

Educational institutions and policymakers are constantly pressed to find innovative, creative, and cost-effective ways to enhance student learning. Focusing on transformative research on global education that affects learning is also a game changer in media education. This text explores the multiple concepts of building a bridge from data to information and knowledge to wisdom through a global education framework that is transdisciplinary, innovative, and inclusive.

The book provides a wide range of strategies and frameworks to empower educators, teacher candidates, and educational researchers to examine the benefits, challenges, and opportunities of integrating educational assessment and evaluation into media literacy education. This comprehensive and timely book aims to be an essential resource for identifying transdisciplinary approaches to research and practice in the media literacy education field.

KEY FEATURES

- An historical overview of the ways in which the term "educational assessment," and "global literacies and competencies" have been interpreted in media education and integrated into educational settings and research.
- The theoretical and empirical interpretation of media literacy education in the educational assessment and evaluation context.
- Media Literacy Education in practice: exploration of the issues, theories, research and best practices in terms of students, curricula, assessment, and pedagogies.
- Conceptual challenges and opportunities for educational assessment and evaluation for preparing new generation for the second half of the twenty-first century.
- Assessment in practice: exploration of the issues, theories, research and best practices in terms of students, curricula, and pedagogies.
- Conceptual challenges and opportunities for assessment for preparing the new generation for the second half of the twenty-first century.
- Innovative practices in assessment and accreditation integrating new media and technologies.
- Assessment and identity: examination of testing for media literacy competencies while increasing cultural responsiveness and gender inclusivity.

TARGET AUDIENCE

This book is designed for a global audience and an essential collection for teacher educators, pre- and in-service teachers, academicians, researchers, parents, and librarians who seek to integrate innovative assessment strategies in the twenty-first-century classroom. Further, this book benefits school administrators, higher education faculty, classroom teachers, government and private curriculum development agencies, educational technology specialists, directors of Teaching and Learning centers, and other stakeholders interested in various types of current and emerging issues in educational assessment, theory, research, and best practices in the field of media education. Underpinned by the heutagogical teaching model (Hase & Kenyon, 2000; Blaschke, 2012), this book is intended for the next generations of transformative and visionary educational leaders, whose interest is in media literacy education for the digital age.

In conclusion, the main aim of this handbook is to draw on the connections between media literacy and global education, and their crucial role in preparing our students for the global economy. Each contributing author has explored how a critical approach to the study of new media combines knowledge, reflection, social justice and action; promotes culturally and linguistically responsive pedagogy; and prepares a new generation to be socially responsible members of a multicultural, democratic society.

Melda N. Yildiz
New York Institute of Technology, USA

Steven Seth Funk
Montana State University – Billings, USA

Belinha De Abreu
National Telemedia Council, USA

REFERENCES

Blaschke, L. M. (2012). *Heutagogy and lifelong learning: A review of heutagogical practice and self-determined learning*. Retrieved from http://www.irrodl.org/index.php/irrodl/article/view/1076/2087

Broadfoot, P. (1991). *Assessment: a celebration of learning*. Australian Curriculum Studies Association.

Celot, P., & Pérez Tornero, J. M. (2009). *Study on assessment criteria for media literacy levels*. Retrieved from http://ec.europa.eu/culture/media/literacy/studies/index_en.htm

Funk, S. S., Kellner, D., & Share, J. (2016). Critical media literacy as transformative pedagogy. In M. N. Yildiz & J. Keengwe (Eds.), *Handbook of research on media literacy in the digital age*. Hershey, PA: IGI Global. doi:10.4018/978-1-4666-9667-9.ch001

Hase, S., & Kenyon, C. (2000). *From andragogy to heutagogy*. Ultibase, RMIT. Retrieved from http://ultibase.rmit.edu.au/Articles/dec00/hase2.htm

Miejan, T. (2010). Just how connected are we? *Edge Magazine*. Retrieved from http://www.edgemagazine.net/2010/04/just-how-connected-are-we/

Section 1
Assessment and Media Education Framework, Theory, Background, and Brief History

Chapter 1
Assessing Media Literacy in Teacher Education

Vitor Tomé
Algarve University, Portugal

ABSTRACT

The twenty-first century citizens must develop their media literacy competence at several levels such as technique, reflective and creative, auto-regulation, social participation and pedagogical. Even though the citizens' empowerment is a general society responsibility, school plays a crucial role, especially if school is able to respond to a set of challenges, namely breaking the traditional resistance to change, integrating formal and informal learning, educating for the media beyond the technical dimension, overcoming the digital divides, protecting citizens' data, and training teachers. This chapter focuses on this last challenge, presenting three research projects which involved in-service teacher training (2007-2011; 2012-2015; 2016-2018). Results showed that K-12 teachers are able to develop media literacy activities with their pupils, using traditional and/or digital technologies, during in-service teacher training courses. As such, they are also able to overcome the lack of technologies in their classrooms by using their own devices or pupils' devices.

INTRODUCTION

Between 2008 and 2011 the Portuguese Government implemented a 'one laptop per child program' at the Primary School level, consisting of the distribution of 750 personal computers to children, which would reduce the student-computer ratio from 15/1, in 2006/07, to 1/1 in 2010 (GEPE, 2011). The program, titled 'e-escolinha,' was presented as revolutionary at the pedagogical level, but the assessment results showed a completely different scenario: it had no significant effect on the classroom pedagogical practice, mainly due to the lack of previous teacher training, even though teachers also pointed out difficulties on work organization and management as well as on logistical aspects (Pereira, Pereira, & Melro, 2015). An independent study also concluded that "media education or media literacy could have provided a conceptual framework" for the 'e-escolinha' program, but "digital media literacy objectives were completely marginalized" (*idem*, p. 88).

DOI: 10.4018/978-1-5225-3082-4.ch001

Copyright © 2018, IGI Global. Copying or distributing in print or electronic forms without written permission of IGI Global is prohibited.

The 'e-escolinha' case study showed that technology does not change pedagogy by itself, and pointed out the need of an ecological approach when designing technology-based pedagogical programs. One the one hand, technology and the media boost the integration of formal learning environments, non-formal and informal, which is understandable, because "the mediatic-educational question is not only a school issue but also a family issue and an issue for all educators who work in the territory" (Rivoltella, 2012, p. 25). On the other hand, the articulation of formal and informal learning requires the enlargement of the concept of literacy, which keeps the traditional logic, based on reading, writing, listening, and speaking, but includes "digital literacy," which is "create, work, share, socialize, research, play, collaborate, communicate and learn" (Meyers, Erickson, & Small, 2013, p. 356).

We are living in the era of "digital and media literacy," which encompasses "the full range of cognitive, emotional, and social competencies that include the use of text, tools and technologies; the skills of critical thinking and analysis; the practice of messaging composition and creativity; the ability to engage in reflection and ethical thinking; as well as active participation through teamwork and collaboration" (Hobbs, 2010, p. 17). Media literacy "relates to the ability to access the media, to understand and critically evaluate different aspects of the media and media content and to create communications in a variety of contexts" (Commission of the European Communities, 2009, p. 10). These different terminologies are used to refer media literacy, and include digital literacy, information literacy, visual literacy, Internet literacy or news literacy. UNESCO (2011) generally defines media literacy as, "competencies that emphasize the development of enquiry-based skills and the ability to engage meaningfully with media and information channels in whatever form and technologies they are using" (p. 18). We may consider Media Education as the process aiming to develop the competencies, whereby media literacy is the outcome (Buckingham, 2003).

Thus, the 21st century citizens must develop media literacy competences at five levels:

1. Techniques for dealing with digital technologies, which implies capabilities in terms of hardware, software, programming, and security monitoring (UNESCO, 2014);
2. Reflective and creative, to achieve the critical analysis and production of media messages (Buckingham, 2009; UNESCO, 2011), which implies the ability to evaluate content, reflect on the political and economic influence in the media, and know how to deal with risks and opportunities (UNESCO, 2014);
3. Self-regulation. (subject-media), which is the use of technology and media in a personal logic, exercising rights such as being connected or not, deleting the digital footprint, using media innovatively and creatively whether for entertainment, learning or work. (UNESCO, 2014).
4. Social or general, crucial to an effective participation in contextualized practices that only make sense together with the aforementioned, in a holistic way, since "the skills cannot be understood out of context". (2013). (p. 361). Meyers et al.
5. Pedagogical, which consists of knowing how to use the media in learning situations, not just "to know its potential and its risks," but rather "to know and know how to use their languages and codes in the critical perspective of a broad learning that today is an essential part of the learning experience" (Fantin, 2012, pp. 71–72).

This citizens' empowerment, which implies transliteracy (Thomas, 2008) and transmedia (Alper & Herr-Stephenson, 2013) skills, should begin in the cradle (Gonnet, 1999) and continue on a lifelong basis (Rivoltella, 2012). Media Literacy, as has been advocated in UNESCO documents (1982, 2007, 2014), the European Union (Commission of the European Communities, 2001, 2007, 2009; European Commission, 2007, 2008) and governments of various countries in Europe, including Portugal (Ministério da Educação e Ciência, 2011). In order to develop media literacy, at the school level, there are several challenges to which we must respond (Tomé, 2015), namely: to break the traditional school resistance to change, to integrate formal and informal learning, to educate for the media engagement beyond the technical dimension, to fight the digital divides, to protect citizens' data, and to train teachers. This chapter focuses on this last challenge.

TEACHER TRAINING IN MEDIA LITERACY AND CITIZENSHIP IN THE DIGITAL ERA

The need for teacher training in media literacy was early pointed out by the Grünwald Declaration (UNESCO, 1982) but despite all the efforts made since then, the celebration of the 25th anniversary of the Declaration, from which resulted the Paris Declaration (UNESCO, 2007), showed that the global landscape did not change significantly. The weak or non-existing pre-service and in-service teacher training in media literacy was one of the main problems identified by Pinto, Pereira, Pereira & Ferreira (2011) during a national research study on media literacy developed in Portugal. The authors recommended a huge investment on teacher training, from Preschool to Secondary School, especially in Higher Education (pre-service) and in in-service teacher training centers. Focusing on digital media and social networks, de Abreu (2011) states that "the greater issue for many teachers is that they do not actually know how to use social networking sites and furthermore they do not understand how to tie it in their already full curriculum" (p. 52). Or, they are not able to operate the digital devices and prefer not to use them in order to hide their difficulties from the students (UNESCO, 2015). Even the Council of the European Union (2012) agrees that "the pedagogical competences of primary school teachers in the teaching of reading and writing, for instance in the pedagogical use of ICT, need to be strengthened," besides "supporting teachers in secondary schools to teach literacy across all subjects and, where relevant, promoting access to expert advice for all teachers" (p. 2).

Among teachers, the question is not to use or not digital media. An Australian research study involving teachers and students from Preschool to Year 12 revealed that "screen content is now a part of the seamless flow of a lesson, with YouTube being the far most used resource," but teachers have little time to spend identifying and adapting YouTube content for the classroom, and they need specific help in this task (Cunningham, Dezzuani, Goldsmith, Burns, Miles, Henkel, Ryan & Murphy, 2016).

Apart from the lack of teacher training, there is a lack of research in school contexts involving collaboration among researchers, teachers, media representatives and political decision-makers (Rivoltella, 2007), the lack of educational resources validated by specialists, teachers and students (Tomé, 2008), and an insufficient curricular development as well (Frau-Meigs & Torrent, 2009).

This chapter presents three research projects that involved teacher training activities, from which two are already finished (2007-2011; 2012-2015) and one is still ongoing (2016-2018). All of them aimed to contribute to overcome the problems identified above and focused on teachers training.

MEDIA EDUCATION IN CASTELO BRANCO

The research project Media Education in Castelo Branco - Portugal (2007-2011) had as its main focus the development of media literacy skills by students and teachers, through the production of printed and/or online school newspapers. Educational resources (DVD "Let´s produce school newspapers", an on-line school newspaper platform and a support manual) were produced, validated, tested, and made available to the 24 public schools of the region after a presentation to the school boards and to teachers. The work developed by teachers and their students (in classes, journalism club or other) was always supported by members of the research team; however, they were not enough since during the first year of the project it became clear that teachers were not prepared to use those resources with students. To tackle this problem, the authors organized a certified in-service teacher training course in media literacy.

Teachers' interest was greater than expected. A total of 192 enrolled, but only 150 were accepted (due to legal and time limitations, since only six classes of 25 were organized), namely: eight from Pre-school, eight from Primary School, 36 from Middle School, and 76 from Secondary School. Regarding Middle and Secondary School, most teachers were teaching Portuguese (56), followed by English teachers (15), Art and Visual Technology (12). Only 15 taught Mathematics, Sciences or Physics and Chemistry.

The course, developed between January and July 2009, was successfully completed by 128 teachers. Eighty-seven pieces of work were handed in (teachers worked in groups, developed activities with their students, documented them with student productions and organized a final report). The developed activities could be put into four different groups:

- Analyzing newspaper articles and/or the production of different journalistic forms for a school newspaper (on paper, on-line or on a notice-board)
- Critical analysis and/or the production of images (photographs, drawings, cartoons, posters, advertising)
- Critical analysis of the advantages and problems associated with media consumption and publication
- Analysis and production of multimedia messages (film animation, debates recorded on video, advertising)

The themes that were most dealt with in activities with students were based on environmental questions (protecting the planet, recycling), historical facts (e.g.: the Portuguese Revolution in 1974, the Centenary of the Portuguese Republic), positive and negative features of the media (traditional and digital) and advertising, health education (prevention of AIDS and H1N1) and citizenship education (regional traditions, being a citizen at home, at school and outside).

Some teachers, bearing in mind the subject they teach, opted for more specific themes, such as analysis of the labels of different products (chemistry), the representation of the human being on paper, video or photography (visual arts), the death penalty (moral and religious education and civic education), the effects of advertising on the choice of food (primary school), Astronomy Day (physics and chemistry), using Word, Power Point, and Paint (pre-school), and using on-line resources as tools for work (information technology).

TRAINERS' ASSESSMENT

Except one Physical Education teacher, everyone was able to successfully incorporate Media Education activities into their previous pedagogical plans. The great majority of the teachers arranged their activities in terms of critical analysis and output responding to media messages by using different platforms, but only 5% were able to produce multimedia messages, in most cases with some problems with the sound and image quality. An interdisciplinary approach for Media Education was put in practice since more than 90% of the reports clearly referred it, not only among scientific areas but also between educational levels and age-groups. About 2,000 students, from Pre-school to Secondary School were involved.

According to teachers' perception, students showed a greater motivation in performing activities related to the use of media which requires searching, critical analysis and production. They clearly preferred to look for information using computers rather than using printed material. Concerns about authorial rights were raised by more than half the teachers, who wanted the students to be aware of this issue. Although many students knew about disrespecting an author's rights, generally, they continued to disregard them. A large majority of teachers' reports showed significant omissions when they considered the finished project. Some teachers did not present any opinion, while others chose to give very superficial thoughts. The authors had asked for a consideration of the long-term effects of the project, as well as difficulties encountered and surprises. Our analysis of the retrospective reports showed that the difficulty most often mentioned was lack of time, while the surprises were in the increased motivation and commitment, even of students who were normally the least interested in educational activities. The authors concluded that it was crucial to provide more training in the area.

A PESTALOZZI TRAINING MODULE ON SOCIAL MEDIA

Between 2012 and 2015, the author helped to develop a research project aimed at understanding how Portuguese youth (aged from 9 to 16), their teachers and parents, use online social networks (OSN); the practices and interactions they develop in that environment; how they perceive the risks, opportunities, and learning on these platforms. The research followed the design of mixed methods and data were collected, in 2013, from 549 students, 267 of their parents/caregivers, and 150 of their teachers.

In 2012, during the Pestalozzi training module, "The importance of social media for democratic participation", the authors developed an in-service teacher training unit/course titled "Participation of teachers and young people on social media: is it democratic?" which was tested in Portugal from 10th December 2012 to 18th February 2013, and attended by 14 teachers, five from Primary School and nine from Middle School (teaching History, Geography, English, Portuguese, Arts and Music). Twelve of the 14 teachers were using social networks), namely Facebook (12), YouTube (8) or Google+ (6).

Training was developed over six sessions, three in attendance and lasting three hours (two at the beginning and one at the end), and three other using Skype (with a minimum duration of one hour and three hours maximum). The training planning, the objectives and the type of work that should be developed by the trainees, together with their students, were introduced in the first session. In the second session, the trainees were asked to organize themselves into working groups to implement the activities with their students. Skype sessions were intended to support the activities of the graduates with their students, but only two trainees attended. The others preferred the contact via email or even personally. The final session consisted of presenting the works developed by trainees.

WORK DONE BY TRAINEES

Three of the trainees worked individually, because there were no school peers attending the training. The remaining organized into four groups: three of three elements and one of two. In total 264 students of seven groups of schools were involved: 22 from Primary School and 242 from Middle School. The developed activities are presented in Table 1.

Through the activities developed during the training course, teachers knew better how their students used Internet and social networks, or not, and what they knew about:

1. The digital divides persist, since 10% of the students had no Internet access. However, even those without Internet access and OSN had a clear perception of what their friends were doing on OSN and reported that they would like to do the same (communicate, play ...);
2. Children did not report situations where they have witnessed hate speech, but in all these activities they mentioned bullying through social media;
3. Students had a clear understanding that they cannot publish whatever they want on the Internet and even argue that there are limits. Some of them even mention the possibility of being punished by the authorities if they publish inappropriate content;
4. Among children's fears that clearly stood out is the fear of being kidnapped, and of strangers entering their account or publishing confidential information, so they are unanimous in saying that they should not talk to strangers;

Table 1. Activities developed during the training course (2012/2013)

Group	Participants	Activity
1	1 teacher, 64 students aged 11/12, and 28 aged 13/14	Reflection on the use of OSN, namely on the role of two Facebook groups run by the Musical Education teacher, in which they were taking part. Groups were considered essential to student-student and teacher-student effective contacts
2	3 teachers, 67 students aged 11/12	Reflection on situations in OSN that made them feel bad. A video was produced with the sentences selected (e.g.: "I've already been hurt by what has been written and I was really bad. It was someone I liked")
3	3 teachers, 57 students aged 10/12	Discussion on "The two faces of Facebook". A questionnaire was applied and videos on the students' opinions were produced
4	3 teachers, 23 children aged 12/13	Children answered a questionnaire on OSN use and attended a lecture conducted by an expert from the National Guard. After, they answered the questionnaire again and many students, particularly girls, expressed the intention of changing attitudes (e.g.: being more careful of what they publish)
5	1 teacher, 3 students aged 12	Reflection on OSN, their potentialities and risks. The students produced a set of advice to minimize the risks of using social networks, with the support of a website. The text produced was published in the school newspaper
6	1 teacher, three children aged 9	Approaching the OSN topic, the teacher found out that it was the first time the students had a discussion on it. She asked the students how they would like to use social media. A student wanted to "ask the prime minister to open more factories for the unemployed that are so many. My mother is one of them"
7	2 teachers, 19 children aged 8/9	In a rural and poor area, only eight students had Internet access at home, but each student debated and drew his/her opinion about OSN. Students' opinions were recorded (in audio support) and a video was produced

5. For children, the advantages of the network are to communicate with family (some in other countries) and friends (especially the closest in real life), to play games and to publish information;
6. The discussion on the subject of social networking was something that interested students, regardless their academic success and having or not having Internet access.

TRAINERS' ASSESSMENT

The action complied with the initial planning and the objectives were achieved. The great asset of this training was the opportunity teachers had to discuss the use of social networking with students, to understand attitudes, benefits and fears of students towards social media. Teachers completed a self-reflection about their use of social networks and the potential that social media has in terms of teaching and developing relationships with students. They focused much on the risks of using social media, but the activities were also important to address the advantages of networks in students' daily lives.

The products of the activities were less important than the processes, but they were of high quality, respected copyright and allowed trainers to perceive the kind of work done with students. Not only has there been interdisciplinarity between Primary and Middle School teachers and between subject areas (e.g. Portuguese and Music Education), but also between curricular and non-curricular subjects (Portuguese / Civics and Study Support).

In the Skype sessions only two teachers participated, those who lived outside the city, because the remaining clearly preferred using email to contact the trainer. When using Skype, it is important to support teachers from the beginning because the study demonstrated that some teachers did not use Skype because they had no account or did not know how to use these tools. Some teachers used social media to talk about social media and even to publish the results, as was the case of three groups, who produced videos available on YouTube. However, the results showed that more teacher training is needs, as they need to feel comfortable in using social media in an educational context, and they need more time to allow them to deepen their themes. Trainees requested more media literacy trainings and more trainings focused on the technical aspects of using digital media.

DIGITAL CITIZENSHIP EDUCATION

Final core results from the project developed from 2012 to 2015 showed that:

1. 90% of students, 75% of teachers and 66% of parents use social media
2. 100% of all groups prefer to share others' content instead of publishing their own content
3. 35% of students say they have already felt uncomfortable using social media
4. teachers and parents are more concerned about the risks than the opportunities of students in social media
5. Teachers and students consider learning in social media but they do not face the formal and informal contexts like two sides of a coin, which would be the learning
6. 90% of the students started using social media before 13, and 40% started using it at the age of 8 or before

The study concluded that there was an urgent need to follow two main guidelines: to empower citizens on digital citizenship with a focus on children aged 8 years old and younger, and to achieve this task, it is important to research school, family and community contexts (de Abreu & Tomé, 2016).

In 2015, de Abreu and Tomé started the project 'Digital Citizenship Education for Democratic Participation' in Odivelas (Lisbon neighborhood), which aimed to answer the following question: To what extent can a local, and replicable project, in school and out-of-school contexts, empower Preschool and Primary School age children to become active and effective citizens in the digital era? The methodological approach of this exploratory project is founded on action research; it has undergone frequent improvements, and the authors are following a research model developed by Sefton-Green, Marsh, Erstad & Flewitt (2016).

The field work started with an in-service teacher training attended by 10 Preschool teachers and 15 Primary School teachers. The training course (25 hours, eight sessions) started on January 4th 2016 and ended on February 29th 2016. It focused on technical competences, cultural competences (critical analysis, reflexive and creative production of media messages), intercultural issues, human rights, and children's rights.

Teachers organized themselves in 10 groups and developed digital literacy activities with 366 of their students (147 preschoolers and 219 primary schoolers). The activities were embedded in the work that had been previously planned, were to use the media as a resource, but with an ecological perspective, traditional and/or digital. Participants always had the support of the trainer and the resources available through a course blog. Each group established a duly justified topic, its objectives and the development of the activity. They presented the results and produced a final report. The activities and the participants involved are presented in Table 2.

In the developed activities, teachers showed an evident concern to better know the media diet of their students. In one case, amongst 77 students, between ages 4 and 8, 67 had a personal tablet and 15 had a smartphone. In another disadvantaged socio-economic school, amongst approximately 51 students, between ages 6 and 7, 39 had a computer at home, 38 had tablet and 24 used a smartphone, although the device wasn't their own.

The use of media raised mainly two types of questions to teachers. Firstly the safe use of the Internet. Secondly, the lack of resources at schools. In many schools, there are usually computers and a projector in the library, but not in the classroom, and no tablets or smartphones. The following was the resulting distribution:

1. Two Preschool teachers asked parents to authorize their children to take tablets to school, but most were reticent, fearing that the tablets could be damaged.
2. Two Preschool teachers asked parents who used the tablets at home, to work together with the children in order to help them to draw, complete word association assignments, and perform numerical assignments. According to the teachers, this activity was very important, as parents and children found that the tablet can be used for more than entertainment purposes.
3. Not having the means to do online research or the delivery of daily newspapers, at school, two teachers created an assignment for students to complete at home, asking them to get news on the decision of the Government to eliminate the 4th year exams.

The teachers were able to integrate the activities in the pedagogical plans organized at the beginning of the school year without changing them.

Table 2. Activities developed during the training course (2016)

Group	Participants	Activity Core Objective
1	Three teachers (2 Preschool, 1 Primary); 77 children: 51 aged 4-6; 26 aged 7-8.	Address risks and opportunities on the Internet and use the tablet in an educational context
2	Two Preschool teachers; 11 children aged 5/6	Promote the safe and creative use of media for teaching pedagogy and involving the educational caregivers
3	Three Preschool teachers; 70 children aged 4-6	Produce a book of illustrated rhymes and develop phonological awareness
4	Two teachers; 20 children aged 9-10	Analyze online newspapers on the government's decision to terminate the national exams in Grade 1
5	Two teachers; 26 children aged 8-9	Increase the interest in the present role of the media in reporting on what is happening in the world
6	Three teachers; 20 children aged 7/8 and 24 aged 9/10	Analyze the issue of the refugee crisis from images of newspapers and online surveys
7	Three teachers; 25 students aged 5/6.	Raise awareness among students of diverse learning contexts, including the media
8	Three teachers; 15 students aged 4/5	Explore the printed newspaper, its role in society, the role of news and images
9	Two teachers; 27 students aged 7/9	Address the concept of bullying through visualization, analysis, and discussion of videos
10	Two teachers; 51 students aged 6/7	Identify advertisements, analyzing their message and purpose

Students debated current issues by analyzing news stories, in particular news issues that concerned them such as: the government's decision to terminate the tests on the 4th of the 1st Cycle Year; the question of Zika virus; domestic violence; the refugee crisis in the Mediterranean Sea; and a bomb threat at Faro Airport. However, when dealing with current issues, many children did not go beyond the headlines to understand the news. In terms of distinguishing advertising from news, the teachers concluded that students of 6/7 years of age have a hard time making the separation and were too influenced by ads.

The teachers organized themselves into groups. This was important to realize that as some teachers belonged to different schools, it narrowed previous opportunities for working together. Even when it was possible to gather Preschool teachers with 1st Cycle teachers, it only occurred in one group.

TRAINERS' ASSESSMENT

Even though Preschool and Primary School teachers recognize great teaching potential to using the media, either in formal or informal contexts, there is a lack of media literacy practices in their classrooms, mainly due to two reasons:

1. The lack of teacher training: most teachers point to the lack of training or professional development in the area of media and technology in the classroom, which is consistent with the international literature (De Abreu, 2011; Redecker, Ala-Mukta & Punie, 2010; UNESCO, 2015).
2. Lack of resources and legal limitations: teachers stated that the use of mobile phones is forbidden to students, as is the use of tablets. That is, the use of digital equipment most preferred by children is not available in schools (Chaudron, 2016). Nevertheless, after in-service teacher training, teachers were able to develop digital literacy activities with children using traditional and digital media.

Poor use of digital media in the classroom can be attributed to an erroneous perception by teachers (Chaudron, 2015, 2016; Marsh, 2014). This is supported by the teacher training reflections, which stated how surprised they were by the increased use of digital technologies by children. Although the use of digital media in the prescribed activities was not a condition, two teacher groups developed activities using tablets involving children and parents. This inclusion was important because many of the parents of young children do not know whether their children should use this form of media or not. At the same time, parents believe schools should use these technologies (Palaiologou, 2016).

The teachers organized educational activities aimed at bringing students to analyze and produce media content, which means developing skills of critical analysis, reflective and creative production. They analyzed media content focused on current themes. In some cases, themes were chosen and researched by students, thus linking popular culture and school. Students reflected on communication in different media and the media function in society, i.e., the teachers did not use only the media to teach, but also to teach about media. The authors therefore recommend more teacher training and professional development be held.

CONCLUSION

K-12 teachers are able to develop media literacy activities with their pupils, using traditional and/or digital technologies, especially during in-service teacher training courses and benefit from guidance from a trainer. It is also important to offer them certified in-service teacher training, not only because it attracts them (because they need to attend training courses do progress in their professional careers), but also because pre-service teacher training in media literacy is residual or poor, as it happens in Portugal.

Teachers also lack specific training on the technical use of media in classrooms, especially on digital media. These technologies must be used in teacher training courses in order to help them find new ways to promote the efficiency of available resources in an educational context. Moreover, during training courses, teachers should be invited to present the activities developed with students, because this is an effective way to share knowledge and practices among them.

Teachers are able to overcome the lack of technologies in their classrooms by using their own devices or pupils' devices. But, technology does not change pedagogy by itself. Media literacy activities become richer and more effective if they are developed by small groups of teachers, preferably from several school levels and/or several scientific areas, that is, on an interdisciplinary basis.

The project 'Media Education in Castelo Branco' accomplished these conditions. However, after it ended, most teachers stop developing media literacy activities. That is, the project failed on its sustainability objectives. That is why in the third project, 'Digital Citizenship Education for Democratic Participation' the authors decided to start a community-based project from the early beginning.

During the project 'Social Networks and New Media Literacy,' the authors decided to run a deep characterization on the context, collecting quantitative and qualitative data from teachers, students, and parents. At the same time, the authors offered a teacher training course to understand both if teachers were prepared to develop media literacy digital activities with their students, and how the authors could improve the training course having in mind the research results.

The initial idea was to start, by the end of the second project, a new and longitudinal one, offering an improved in-service teacher training to Middle School teachers, and then continuing to work with them in the following years, giving them support and resources so they would be able to develop media literacy activities with their students on a sustainable manner, involving families and the community. But in the meantime, technology use evolved exponentially.

Young children's online practices had been largely ignored over the last decade by policymakers in most countries (Holloway, Green & Livingstone, 2013) but they are now on the spot. The tablet became the most popular device among young children and all the families use smartphones. Children are living in rich digital environments even those from under privileged families (Chaudron, 2016). Over half of the 3-4 year-olds in the United Kingdom use tablets as well as a third of the children under five-years-old (Marsh, 2014). In the UK, by the age of two, most children are using a tablet or a laptop (Sefton-Green et al., 2016). A study in four European countries showed that among under five-year-old children, 60% use digital technologies and 23% simultaneously use television, computers and Internet (Palaiologou, 2016).

It would be a huge mistake to ignore this new reality. At the field level, the project was organized in seven phases:

1. Presentation of the project to Odivelas City Hall Education Department and ask them to be logistical partners
2. Production and validation of data collection instruments (questionnaires do teachers and parents, interview guides to children)
3. In-service teacher training course (Jan-Feb 2016)
4. Longitudinal study with teachers who volunteered after the training course (Mar 2016-Feb 2018)
5. Data collection from parents, children and out-of-school entities in order to characterize context (Apr-Jun 2016)
6. Share results with participants and involve them on a digital citizenship education
7. Improved intervention plan (Sep 2016-Feb 2018)

After the course, the authors started working with 10 of the 25 teachers (three Preschool, five Primary teachers, a teacher of Special Education and a teacher librarian), belonging to the same Primary school, in the development of activities with their students. Data were collected from 38 parents/caregivers and their children, as well as from teachers and local community (especially Social Services and Health Services).

In December 2016, the school published the first edition on its newspaper, giving notice of the activities developed on citizenship in the digital era. A week after, the school board of the school grouping (who manages a Secondary School, a Middle School, four Primary Schools and four Preschools) asked us to stretch the project to all Preschools and all Primary Schools, and the authors agreed. Currently the authors are working with 40 teachers and about 800 children of a same community.

In January 2017, Odivelas City Hall decided to organize a candidacy to European funds in order to stretch the project to the nine public schools groups of the municipality, involving about 1,500 teachers and 19,000 students from K-12. The stretching will be done gradually in the following years, having always the in-service teacher training as a priority as well as its sustainability.

Table 3. Questions to assess media literacy approaches in schools

Organization	1. Were the teachers able to:
	    a. Organize media literacy activities with their students?
	    b. Organize themselves in small working groups?
	    c. Organize groups involving teachers from different educational levels, scientific areas (interdisciplinary/ transdisciplinary)?
	    d. Ask for the trainer's advice during the activities development (e.g.: in person or through digital media)?
	2. Was the trainer able to:
	    a. Answer to teachers' requests in due time?

Development	1. Were the teachers able to:
	    a. Develop media literacy activities with their students?
	    b. Overcome the lack of resources (if it was the case)?
	    c. Integrate those activities in their previous pedagogical plans without major changes?
	    e. Ask for the trainer's advice during the activities development (e.g.: in person or through digital media)?
	    d. Involve other people in the activities (e.g.: parents, local community…)?
	2. Was the trainer able to:
	    a. Answer to teachers' requests in due time?

Evaluation	1. Were the teachers able to:
	    a. Produce a thorough report on the activity (structure: activity name, time used, objectives, data on students involved, procedure, results and outputs)?
	    b. Critically evaluate the weaknesses and strengths of the procedure, identifying remediation strategies?
	    c. Critically evaluate the in-service teacher training course?
	2. Was the trainer able to:
	    a. Improve the in-service teacher training course having in mind the teachers' evaluation?
	    b. Produce a leaflet or handbook based on the teachers' reports in order to disseminate the practices developed? Are the practices replicable?
	    c. Produce a thorough report on the in-service teacher training course?

Recommendations

Having in mind these studies' findings, it is crucial to assess media literacy approaches in schools, especially during and after in-service teacher training courses, as shown in Table 3.

Answering these questions, the trainer should be able to improve his/her courses and to report on them. This is crucial, especially as this report should be shared with the teachers who have attended the course through a blog, a website or other digital platform, where all the resources used during the training course must be available too.

REFERENCES

Alper, M., & Herr-Stephenson, R. (2013). Transmedia Play: Literacy Across Media. *Journal of Media Literacy Education*, *5*(2), 366–369.

Buckingham, D. (2003). *Media Education: Literacy, Learning and Contemporary Culture*. Cambridge: Polity Press and Blackwell Publishing.

Buckingham, D. (2009). Media Education Policy: The future of Media Literacy in the Digital Age: some challenges for policy and practice. In *Euromeduc – Media Literacy in Europe*. Brussels: Euromeduc.

Chaudron, S. (2015). *Young Children & Digital Technology: A qualitative exploratory study across seven countries*. Luxembourg: Publications Office of the European Union.

Chaudron, S. (2016). Young Children, Parents and Digital Technology in the Home Context Across Europe: The Findings of the Extension of the Young Children (0-8) and Digital Technology Pilot Study to 17 European Countries (oral presentation). *Presented at DigiLitEY Project Meeting 3*, Larnaca, Cyprus, May 17-18.

Commission of the European Communities. (2001). Comunicação da Comissão ao Conselho e ao Parlamento Europeu Plano de acção eLearning -Pensar o futuro da educação. Retrieved from http://eur-lex.europa.eu/LexUriServ/LexUriServ.do?uri=CELEX:52001DC0172:PT:HTML

Commission of the European Communities. (2007). Comunicação da Comissão ao Parlamento Europeu, ao Conselho, ao Comité Económico e Social Europeu e ao Comité das Regiões - Uma abordagem europeia da literacia mediática no ambiente digital. Retrieved from http://ec.europa.eu/avpolicy/media_literacy/ec_com/index_en.htm

Commission of the European Communities. (2009). Commission Recommendation on media literacy in the digital environment for a more competitive audiovisual and content industry and an inclusive knowledge society. Retrieved from http://eur-lex.europa.eu/LexUriServ/LexUriServ.do?uri=OJ:L:2009:227:0009:0012:EN:PDF

Council of the European Union. (2012, 19 December). Council conclusions of 26 November 2012 on literacy. Official Journal of the European Union. Retrieved from http://eur-lex.europa.eu/legal-content/EN/TXT/PDF/?uri=OJ:C:2012:393:FULL&from=EN

Cunningham, S., Dezzuani, M., Goldsmith, B., Burns, M., Miles, P., Henkel, C., & Murphy, K. et al. (2016). *Screen Content in Australian Education: Digital Promise and Pitfalls*. Brisbane: Digital Media Research Centre.

de Abreu, B. (2011). *Media Literacy, Social Networking and the Web 2.0 Environment for the K-12 Educator*. New York: Peter Lang Publishing.

de Abreu & Tomé. V. 2017. Mobile Learning through Digital Media Literacy. New York: Peter Lang.

European Commission. (2007). Report on the results of the public consultation on Media Literacy. Retrieved from http://ec.europa.eu/avpolicy/media_literacy/docs/report_on_ml_2007.pdf

European Commission. (2008). B-Brussels: study on criteria to assess media literacy levels - SMART 2008/0005. Retrieved from http://ted.europa.eu/Exec?DataFlow=ShowPage.dfl&Template=TED/N_one_result_detail_curr.htm&docnumber=89657-2008&docId=89657-2008&StatLang=EN

Fantin, M. (2012). Mídia-educação no currículo e na formação inicial de professores. In *Mónica Fantin e Pier Cesare Rivoltella, orgs, Cultura Digital e Escola: pesquisa e formação de professores*. Campinas, SP: Papirus Editora.

Frau-Meigs, D., & Torrent, J. (2009). *Mapping Media Education Policies in the World – Visions, Programmes and Challenges*. New York: UN – Alliance of Civilizations.

GEPE – Gabinete de Estatísticas e Planeamento da Educação & Direção de Serviços de Estatística. (2011). *Educação em Números – Portugal 2011*. Lisboa: GEPE.

Gonnet, J. (1999). *Éducation et Médias*. Paris: PUF.

Hobbs, R. (2010). *Digital Media Literacy – A Plan of Action*. Washington: The Aspen Institute.

Holloway, D., Green, L., & Livingstone, S. (2013). *Zero to eight. Young children and their internet use. LSE*. London: EU Kids Online.

Marsh, J. (2014). Young Children's Online Practices: Past, Present and Future. *Paper presented at the Literacy Research Association Conference*, Marco Island, December 3-6. Retrieved from https://www.academia.edu/9799081/Young_Childrens_Online_Practices_Past_Present_and_Future

Meyers, E., Erickson, I., & Small, R. (2013). Digital literacy and informal learning environments: An introduction. *Learning, Media and Technology, 38*(4), 355–367. doi:10.1080/17439884.2013.783597

Ministério da Educação e Ciência. (2011). Recomendação no 6/2011 sobre Educação para a Literacia Mediática. Retrieved from http://dre.pt/pdf2s/2011/12/250000000/5094250947.pdf

Palaiologou, I. (2016). Children under five and digital technologies: Implications for early years pedagogy. *European Early Childhood Education Research Journal, 24*(1), 5–24. doi:10.1080/1350293X.2014.929876

Pereira, S., Pereira, L. & Melro, A. (2015). The Portuguese programme one laptop per child: Political, educational and social impact. In *Digital Literacy, Technology and Social Inclusion – Making sense of one-to-one computer programmes around the world* (pp. 29-100). Vila Nova de Famalicão: Edições Húmus.

Pinto, M., Pereira, S., Pereira, L., & Ferreira, T. (2011). *Educação para os Media em Portugal: experiências, actores e contextos*. Lisboa: ERC.

Redecker, C., Ala-Mukta, K., & Punie, Y. (2010). *Learning 2.0 – The impact of Social Media on Learning in Europe*. Luxembourg: Office for the Official Publications of the European Communities.

Rivoltella, P. (2007). Realidad y desafíos de la educación en medios en Italia. *Comunicar, 28*, 17–24.

Rivoltella, P. (2012). Retrospectivas e tendências da pesquisa em mídia-educação no contexto internacional. In *Cultura Digital e Escola: pesquisa e formação de professores, org. Mónica Fantin e Pier Cesare Rivoltella*. Campinas, SP: Papirus Editora.

Sefton-Green, J., Marsh, J., Erstad, O., & Flewitt, R. (2016). Establishing a Research Agenda for the Digital Literacy Practices of Young Children: A White Paper for COST Action IS1410. Retrieved from http://digilitey.eu

Thomas, S. (2008). Transliteracy and new media, In Randy Adams, Steve Gibson e Steffan Füller Arisona, eds., Transdisciplinary Digital Art: Sound, Vision and the New Screen (pp. 101-109). Berlin: Springer-Verlag Berlin Heidelberg.

Tomé, V. (2008). CD-Rom "Vamos fazer jornais escolares": um contributo para o desenvolvimento da Educação para os Média em Portugal [PhD Thesis]. Faculdade de Psicologia e de Ciências da Educação da Universidade de Lisboa, Portugal.

Tomé, V. (2015). Redes sociais online: práticas e percepções de jovens (9-16), seus professores e encarregados de educação. In E. Bévort & V. Reia-Baptista (Eds.), Research on social media: a glocal view. Vitor Tomé (pp. 127-335). Lisbon: RVJ-Editores.

UNESCO. (1982). Declaração de Grünwald. Retrieved from http://www.UNESCO.org/education/pdf/MEDIA_E.PDF

UNESCO. (2007). Paris Agenda or 12 recommendations for media education. Retrieved from http://www.diplomatie.gouv.fr/fr/IMG/pdf/Parisagendafin_en.pdf

UNESCO. (2011). *Media and Information Literacy: curriculum for teachers*. Paris: UNESCO.

UNESCO. (2013). *Alfabetização midiática e informacional: currículo para formação de professores / Carolyn Wilson, Alton Grizzle, Ramon Tuazon, Kwame Akyempong e Chi-Kim Cheung*. Brasília: UNESCO, UFTM.

UNESCO. (2014). Declaration on Augmented Media and Information Literacy (MIL) in the Digital era. Paris: Unesco. Retrieved from http://www.unesco.org/new/en/communication-and-information/resources/news-and-in-focus-articles/in-focus-articles/2014/paris-declaration-on-media-and-information-literacy-adopted/

UNESCO. (2015). Keystones to foster inclusive Knowledge Societies - Access to information and knowledge, Freedom of Expression, Privacy, and Ethics on a Global Internet- Paris: UNESCO. Retrieved from http://www.unesco.org/new/fileadmin/MULTIMEDIA/HQ/CI/CI/pdf/internet_draft_study.pdf

ADDITIONAL READING

Assessment made incredibly easy! (2013). 5th ed.). Philadelphia, PA: Wolters Kluwer Health/Lippincott Williams & Wilkins.

Banta, T. W., & Kinzie, J. (2015). *Assessment essentials: Planning, implementing, and improving assessment in higher education*. San Francisco, CA: Jossey-Bass, a Wiley Brand.

Barkley, E. F., & Major, C. H. (2016). *Learning assessment techniques: A handbook for college faculty*. San Francisco, CA: Jossey-Bass & Pfeiffer.

Barrett, H. (2010). Balancing the two faces of e-portfolios. *Educação, Formação & Tecnologias, 3*(1), 6–14. Retrieved from http://eft.educom.pt

Barrett, H. (2010). Balancing the Two Faces of ePortfolios. Educação, Formação & Tecnologias, 3(1), 6-14. Retrieved from http://eft.educom.pt

Barrett, H. (2004–8) My online portfolio adventure. Retrieved from http://electronicportfolios.org/myportfolio/versions.html

Barrett, H. (2008). My Online Portfolio Adventure (2004-2008). Retrieved from http://electronicportfolios.org/myportfolio/versions.html

Beck, R., & Bear, S. (2009). Teacher's self-assessment of reflection skills as an outcome of e-folios. In P. Adamy & N. B. Milman (Eds.), *Evaluating electronic portfolios in teacher education*. Charlotte, NC: Information Age Publishers.

Beck, R., & Bear, S. (2009). *Teacher's Self-Assessment of Reflection Skills as an Outcome of E-Folios. In Adamy & Milman (Eds.), Evaluating Electronic Portfolios in Teacher Education.* Charlotte: Information Age Publishers.

Black, P., & William, D. (1998, November). Inside the black box: Raising standards through classroom assessment. *Phi Delta Kappan, 80*(2), 139–148.

Brookhart, S. M., Association for Supervision and Curriculum Development., & Ebook Library. (2013). How to create and use rubrics for formative assessment and grading. Alexandra, VA. ASCD.

CAST. (2016). *Universal design for learning.* Retrieved from http://www.cast.org

Chouinard, J. A., & Cousins, J. B. (2009). A review and synthesis of current research on cross-cultural evaluation. *The American Journal of Evaluation, 30*(4), 457–494. doi:10.1177/1098214009349865

Contandriopoulos, D., & Brousselle, A. (2012). Evaluation models and evaluation use. *Evaluation, 18*(1), 61–77. doi:10.1177/1356389011430371 PMID:23526460

Cooksy, L. J., & Mark, M. M. (2012). Influences on evaluation quality. *The American Journal of Evaluation, 33*(1), 79–84. doi:10.1177/1098214011426470

Crooks, T. J. (1988). The impact of classroom evaluation practices on students. *Review of Educational Research, 58*(4), 438–481. Retrieved from http://search.proquest.com/docview/214114484?accountid=14872 doi:10.3102/00346543058004438

Dweck, C. S. (2007). *Mindset: The new psychology of success.* New York, NY: Random House.

EdPuzzle. (2016). Retrieved from https://edpuzzle.com/

Ellis, A. K. (2001). *Teaching, learning, and assessment together: The reflective classroom.* Larchmont, N.Y: Eye on Education.

Fairbairn, S. B., & Fox, J. (2009). Inclusive achievement testing for linguistically and culturally diverse test takers: Essential considerations for test developers and decision makers. *Educational Measurement: Issues and Practice, 28*(1), 10–24. doi:10.1111/j.1745-3992.2009.01133.x

Feuer, M. J. (2011). Politics, economics, and testing: Some reflections. *Mid-Western Educational Researcher, 24*(1), 25–29.

Fink, L. D. (2013). *Creating significant learning experiences: An integrated approach to designing college courses.* San Francisco, CA: Jossey-Bass.

Fleischer, D. N., & Christie, C. A. (2009). Evaluation use: Results from a survey of U.S. American Evaluation Association members. *The American Journal of Evaluation, 30*(2), 158–175. doi:10.1177/1098214008331009

Goldstein, J., & Behuniak, P. (2011). Assumptions in alternate assessment: An argument-based approach to validation. *Assessment for Effective Intervention, 36*(3), 179–191. doi:10.1177/1534508410392208

Hinton, K. (2012). *A practical guide to strategic planning in higher education.* Society for College and University Planning.

Hollowell, D., Middaugh, M., & Sibolski, E. (2006). *Integrating Higher Education, Planning and Assessment: A Practical Guide.* Society for College and University Planning.

JISC. (2008). *Effective Practice with e-Portfolios.* Retrieved from http://www.jisc.ac.uk/whatwedo/themes/elearning/eportfolios/effectivepracticeeportfolios.aspx

Kahoot. (2016) Retrieved from https://kahoot.it/

Kelly, M. A., & Kaczynski, D. (2008). Teaching evaluation from an experiential framework: Connecting theory and organizational development with grant making. *The American Journal of Evaluation, 29*(4), 547–554. doi:10.1177/1098214008324181

Kirkhart, K. E. (2010). Eyes on the prize: Multicultural validity and evaluation theory. *The American Journal of Evaluation, 31*(3), 400–413. doi:10.1177/1098214010373645

Kohn, A. (2015). Rescuing our schools from "tougher standards." Retrieved from http://www.alfiekohn.org/standards-testing/

Kuh, G. D., Ikenberry, S. O., Jankowski, N., Cain, T. R., Ewell, P. T., Hutchings, P., & Kinzie, J. (2014). *Using Evidence of Student Learning to Improve Higher Education.* New York, NY: John Wiley & Sons.

Kukla-Acevedo, S., Streams, M. E., & Toma, E. (2012). Can a single performance metric do it all? A case study in education accountability. *American Review of Public Administration, 42*(3), 303–319. doi:10.1177/0275074011399120

LaVelle, J. M., & Donaldson, S. I. (2010). University-based evaluation training programs in the United States 1980–2008: An empirical examination. *The American Journal of Evaluation, 31*(1), 9–23. doi:10.1177/1098214009356022

Looney, J. W. (2009). Assessment and innovation in education. *OECD Education Working Papers, 24.* Retrieved from doi:10.1787/222814543073

Metzger, M. J., Flanagin, A. J., & Medders, R. B. (2010). Social and heuristic approaches to credibility evaluation online. *Journal of Communication, 60*(3), 413–439. doi:10.1111/j.1460-2466.2010.01488.x

Middaugh, M. (2009). *(n.d.). Planning and assessment in higher education: Demonstrating institutional effectiveness.* Josey-Bass. doi:10.1002/9781118269572

Padlet.com. (2016). Retrieved from https://padlet.com/

Petersen, N. Center for Teaching, Learning, & Technology, Washington State University (2008). "Case Studies of Electronic Portfolios for Learning" Retrieved from: http://wsuctlt.wordpress.com/2008/03/14/case-studies-of-electronic-portfolios-for-learning/

Petersen, N. (2008). Case studies of electronic portfolios for learning. Retrieved from http://wsuctlt. wordpress.com/2008/03/14/case-studies-of-electronic-portfolios-for-learning/

Piotrowski, S. J., & Ansah, E. (2010). Organizational assessment tools: Report cards and scorecards of the federal agencies. *Public Administration Quarterly, 34*(1), 109–142.

Programme for International Student Assessment (PISA). (2012). PISA 2012 results. Retrieved from http://www.oecd.org/pisa/keyfindings/pisa-2012-results.htm

Richardson, R. D., Hawken, L. S., & Kircher, J. (2012). Bias using Maze to predict high-stakes test performance among Hispanic and Spanish-speaking students. *Assessment for Effective Intervention, 37*(3), 159–170. doi:10.1177/1534508411430320

Robinson, K. (2006, February). Do schools kill creativity? [Video]. Retrieved from http://www.ted.com/talks/ken_robinson_says_schools_kill_creativity.html

Samuels, M., & Ryan, K. (2011). Grounding evaluations in culture. *The American Journal of Evaluation, 32*(2), 183–198. doi:10.1177/1098214010387657

Smith, N. L. (2010). Characterizing the evaluand in evaluating theory. *The American Journal of Evaluation, 31*(3), 383–389. doi:10.1177/1098214010371820

Smith, N. L., Brandon, P. R., Hwalek, M., Kistler, S. J., Labin, S. N., Rugh, J., & Yarnall, L. et al. (2011). Special section: Looking ahead: The future of evaluation. *The American Journal of Evaluation, 32*(4), 565–599. doi:10.1177/1098214011421412

Socrative. (2016). Retrieved from http://www.socrative.com/

Sriranganathan, G., Jaworsky, D., Larkin, J., Flicker, S., Campbell, L., Flynn, S., & Erlich, L. et al. (2012). Peer sexual health education: Interventions for effective programme evaluation. *Health Education Journal, 71*(1), 62–71. doi:10.1177/0017896910386266

Suskie, L. (2009). *Assessing student learning: A common sense guide* (2nd ed.). San Francisco, CA: Jossey-Bass.

Suskie, L., & Banta, T. W. (2010). *Assessing Student Learning: A Common Sense Guide.* New York, NY: John Wiley & Sons.

Suskie, L. A. (2015). *Five dimensions of quality: A common sense guide to accreditation and accountability.* San Francisco, CA: Jossey-Bass, a Wiley brand.

Techrepublic. (2016). *Use google forms to create a self grading quiz.* Retrieved from http://www.techrepublic.com/blog/google-in-the-enterprise/use-google-forms-to-create-a-self-grading-quiz/

The Gordon Commission. (2013). To assess, to teach, to learn: A vision for the future of assessment (Technical Report). Retrieved from http://www.cse.ucla.edu/colloquium/GC_Report030513_Report.pdf

Tucker, M. S. (2011). *Surpassing Shanghai: An agenda for American education built on the world's leading systems.* Cambridge, MA: Harvard Education Press.

UNESCO. (2013). Global media and information literacy assessment framework: Country readiness and competencies. Retrieved from http://unesdoc.unesco.org/images/0022/002246/224655e.pdf

Vanhoof, J., & Van Petegem, P. (2011). Designing and evaluating the process of school self-evaluations. *Improving Schools, 14*(2), 200–212. doi:10.1177/1365480211406881

Walvoord, B. (2010). *Assessment clear and simple: A practical guide for institutions, departments, and general education* (2nd ed.). San Francisco, CA: Jossey-Bass.

Walvoord, B. E., & Anderson, V. J. (2013). *Effective grading: A tool for learning and assessment in college*. San Francisco, Calif: Jossey-Bass.

Western and Northern Canadian Protocol for Collaboration in Education. (2006). Rethinking classroom assessment with purpose in mind. Retrieved from http://www.wncp.ca/media/40539/rethink.pdf

Worsnop, C. (1997). *Assessing Media Work*. Mississauga, Canada: Wright Communications.

KEY TERMS AND DEFINITIONS

Castelo Branco: Portuguese region (6.675 km^2) located in the central Portugal countryside, near Spain, with 196.000 inhabitants, representing one of the lowest population densities in the country (34 inhabitants/km^2).

Community-Based Project: A concerted approach within the family, school and out-of-school contexts aiming to empower children to exercise an active and effective citizenship in the digital era.

E-Escolinha: Program implemented by the Portuguese Government (2008-2011) following the 'one laptop per child' strategy, and consisting of the distribution of 750 personal computers to Primary School children.

Media Education/Media Literacy: Media Education as the process aiming to develop the competencies, whereby Media Literacy is the outcome.

Media Literacy Competences: Set of values, attitudes, skills, knowledge and critical understanding that the 21st century citizens must be able to mobilize when dealing with media in each specific contexts and particular situations.

Odivelas: Portuguese municipality (27 km^2) located in Lisbon neighborhood, with 145.000 inhabitants, representing the second highest population density in the country (5424 inhabitants/km^2).

Teacher Training: A 25-hour course offered to in-service teachers, focused on media literacy, during which the teachers organize and develop media literacy activities with their students (k-12).

Chapter 2
Technology Access Gap for Postsecondary Education:
A Statewide Case Study

Victoria Brown
Florida Atlantic University, USA

ABSTRACT

Technology to learn the digital literacy skills required to attend postsecondary institutions or to access distance learning courses. Three groups of students are impacted by the lack of access to technology: (a) without broadband access, (b) students' low socioeconomic status, and (c) students' primary language is not English. Without digital literacy skills, selecting, applying, and fully participating in a postsecondary education is difficult. This chapter will outline the challenges these three groups of students have in accessing broadband, the impact the lack of access created in Florida, and solutions that were suggested to address lack of high speed broadband.

INTRODUCTION

Accessing and analyzing digital information, creating products, sharing new information, and communicating ideas are digital literacy skills considered important for employability and life skills (MediaSmarts, n. d.). Digital literacy skills are so important that the Partnership for 21st Century Learning (P21) stated that "all learners need and deserve 21st century learning opportunities to thrive as tomorrow's leaders, workers, and citizens" (P21, n. d.). Within the Framework for 21st Century Learning are the digital literacy skills of information, media, and technology (P21, 2007). The framework represents the skills and the knowledge that teachers, educational experts, and business leaders view as important to be successful in work, life, and citizenship.

DOI: 10.4018/978-1-5225-3082-4.ch002

Copyright © 2018, IGI Global. Copying or distributing in print or electronic forms without written permission of IGI Global is prohibited.

Lack of access to technology creates a technology divide that begins at the elementary educational level and impacts students' postsecondary educational careers. A relationship exists between the use of digital media and student academic achievement. The time that students spend using computers correlates with higher scores on the Program for International Student Assessment which scores on the mathematics assessment section (Organization for Economic Co-Operation and Development, 2005). . The same variable of time spent using informational technology also correlates with better grades and grade point averages (Jackson et al., 2008). The more time students spend using technology leads to a greater diversity in activities in which students engaged while on the computer. The increased diversity of activities created more opportunities to engage in self-selected academic activities, including reading websites and writing about their experiences (Jackson et al., 2008).

The impact of an inadequate access to technology extends beyond high school and leads to a cycle of continual lack of access (See Figure 1). Lack of access at the K-12 educational system translates into implications for postsecondary institutions as admission decisions are based upon standardized assessments, grades, and grade point averages. It is possible that students without technology are not developing the skills that will allow them to be admitted to a university. Furthermore, the lack of access promotes a continual digital divide in which 90% of college graduates compared with 37% of non-high school graduates have high-speed Internet access in their homes (Zickuhr & Smith, 2013).

Broadband serves as a gateway to a highly connective world. Individuals with low socioeconomic status (SES) do not have the resources to either own a computer or to pay for broadband in order to access the full range of educational resources. Individuals whose primary language is not English often place ownership of the technology as a low priority. This paper will explore these three contributing factors to the lack of access to technology for distance learning both at a national and a state level and the proposed solutions to access to the university system in Florida.

Figure 1. Cycle generated by lack of access

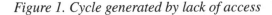

ISSUES, CONTROVERSIES, PROBLEMS

The Aspen Institute published a report that resulted from a partnership with the MacArthur Foundation titled "The Aspen Institute Task Force on Learning and the Internet: Learner at the Center of a Networked World" (2014). The thought leaders who created the report saw technology as the driving force to advance every sector of society. For this reason, technology should be reshaped to match these changes within the educational system. In the K-12 system, students need to begin using the network to obtain information and apply that knowledge for a lifetime of learning. As students move into the college system, they need to use the knowledge about connecting through networks to think critically, analyze data, and create new information. Not having early access and knowledge of the network can impact these students' ability to develop the digital literacy skills described in the Framework for 21st Century Learning (P21, 2007).

As with other forms of technology, distance learning was believed to be the answer to many problems in the distribution of educational opportunity. For example, Massive open online courses (MOOCs) were to provide free or low cost educational opportunities through open platforms for online courses which would lead to massive enrollment. Sixty-five percent of the participants in the HarvardX project had bachelor's degrees or above (Ho et al., 2015). The major reason for the exclusion from distance learning continues to be the digital divide. As a side note, the next technology believed to increase access is mobile technology.

The State University System of Florida Board of Governors began grappling with many distance learning issues in 2012. At that time, the Board of Governors began the first exploratory study, which provided the first recommendations to the Board as the next steps in advancing distance learning. A task force was formed with members from the Florida College System (FCS) and the State University Systems (SUS). The task force was charged with recommending strategies for better coordinating services and online programs within both systems to ensure that both state economic development needs and student demands were met in an effective and cost-efficient manner (SUS of Florida Board of Governors, 2013).

In 2015, a group of public university presidents and provosts from across the state were identified to recommend a plan to advance distance education. This collaborative effort resulted in the Online Education 2025 Strategic Plan for the SUS. The plan had 9 goals, 15 strategies, and 49 tactics across three areas of quality, access, and affordability to increase the distance education credits to 3.48 million. To reach that goal, 75% of the undergraduate and 50% of the graduate student body will need to be taking online courses by 2025 (SUS of Florida Board of Governors, 2015).

The Online Education 2025 Strategic Plan was designed to address another concern by the Board of Governors. In the first joint address to Congress in 2009, President Barack Obama set a goal to have the highest proportion of college graduates in the world by year 2020 (U.S. Department of Education, 2011). Florida legislators also believed in increasing the number of college graduates as an important goal. In 2009, Florida graduated 839,048 students (O'Conner, 2012). To meet the national goals, Florida would need to graduate 1,480,000 to 1,630,000 students in 2020 (U.S. Department of Education, 2011).

To achieve the increased enrollment goals, Florida would need to do two things. First, increase capacity at the post-secondary institutions. If the online education plan works, the enrollment would increase. However, the university leaders wanted to ensure that enrollment was not increased without thinking about the quality of the education provided. As the universities increased online enrollment, classroom space requirements could be repurposed into modern student gathering spaces or collaborative classrooms. The use of online had the potential to make the campuses sustainable through lower energy consumption. Second, the system would need to recruit over 500,000 new students into both the colleges and universities. The Complete Florida (2015) initiative was charged with assisting adults who had started their postsecondary education but had not finished. These students could take advantage of the many distance learning degrees offered 100% online by Florida institutions. Distance learning was viewed as one of the conduits to a post-secondary education because of the flexibility of the delivery mode increased the potential to reach students who may be place bound or working.

To move the Online Education 2025 Strategic Plan forward, two committees were formed. The first was the Steering Committee whose membership consisted of five provosts from the public universities in Florida. The second was an Implementation Committee with distance learning leaders. The distance learning leaders chaired nine workgroups to work on 49 tactics is support of the 15 strategies. The Implementation Committee developed a schedule and action steps for the tactics. The Student Services Workgroup was to address four of the tactics, of which one of them was about student access to technology. This tactic was to address the previous concerns about increasing access to a postsecondary education by Floridians (SUS Florida Board of Governors, 2016).

- **Tactic Access 2.1.4.:** Secure student support resources to ensure students have access to technology required for online education.
- **Timeline Action Item Due December 2016:** Student Services Workgroup to make recommendations on resources needed with the respective costs to the Implementation Committee and Steering Committee.
- **Timeline Action Item Due January 2017:** A report will be delivered to the Implementation Committee and the Steering Committee for its discussion at its January 2017 meeting. Future action steps will be identified (p. 15).

In response to the implementation schedule, the Student Services Workgroup was formed consisting of distance learning and student support leaders from both the public colleges and the universities. Florida Completes and Florida Virtual Campus provide a variety of statewide services for students searching for a postsecondary institution in Florida to complete a previously started degree. Representatives from both initiatives were consulted to determine the present level of services provided statewide. The workgroup met over a period of nine months to identify the resources available to students and other student needs. The result of the meetings was a white paper, portions of which are presented here. The white paper identified the challenges within the state and recommendations to address access issues. The first step of this process was to understand the scope of the challenges students experience as they access technology. The group identified three contributing causes in accessing technology: (a) lack of broadband, (b) low socioeconomic status, (c) English as a second language. (See Figure 2) The second step was to identify solutions that could be implemented at the state and institutional levels to improve the access.

ACCESS CHALLENGES

Lack of Broadband

In 2013, President Barack Obama launched the ConnectED initiative with the goal of connecting 99% of K-12 students in America with access to broadband Internet in the classroom by 2018 (Meyer, 2015).

Figure 2. Contributors to access challenges

Since ConnetED was launched, 20 million more students have gained access to broadband at school, according to Joseph South, Director of the Office of Educational Technology of the United States Department of Education. However, access in K-12 has not expanded to all Americans. Nearly 1 in 5 Americans have no options of accessing broadband services. Another 45% of Americans have access to only one provider of broadband services from home (State of Tennessee v. Federal Communications Commission and United States of America, 2015). Achieving access objectives nationally and in the state of Florida continues to be a challenge.

A closer look at the national landscape indicates that broadband deployment in the United States has failed to keep pace with today's Internet content consisting of advanced, high-quality voice, data, graphics, and video. With the advancement of technology, the Federal Communications Commission (FCC) in 2015 voted to change the definition of broadband to a minimum of 25 megabits per second (Mbps) download speeds with 3 Mbps upload speeds. The change in definition tripled the number of U.S. households without high-speed broadband access (Singleton, 2015). The Federal Communications Commission (2016) found that 34 million Americans, a full 10% of the population in the United States, lacked access to 25 Mbps/3 Mbps service. This failure is especially acute in rural communities where 39% of rural Americans (23 million people) lack access to 25 Mbps/3 Mbps. On tribal lands and in U.S. territories, nearly two-thirds of residents lack broadband services (FCC, 2016).

Florida is ranked ninth as the most connected state in the United States (BroadBandNow, 2016). However, throughout Florida, areas exist that have no broadband, no wireless access, or inadequate access. For students to participate in a basic online course with textual or web-based instruction, a minimum access to broadband needs to be 25 Mbps. To access course material with video streaming or recorded video, students should have access to 75 to 100 Mbps of speed. The average statewide broadband speed in Florida is 35.8 Mbps (BroadBandNow, 2016). Per BroadBandNow (2016), 1.2 million Floridians are without access to a wired connection capable of 25 Mbps download speeds. Three counties in Florida have no access to 25 Mbps broadband: (a) Union, (b) Gilchrist, and (c) Dixie. With these numbers, many

Floridians do not have the basic access to broadband to interact successfully in an online course much less video based classes.

Low Socioeconomic Status

The least educated and underprivileged people still lagged in Internet access, usage, and scope (Zhang, 2013) than other segments of the U.S. population. The latest Pew Research (2016) analysis indicated that Internet nonadoption correlated with socioeconomic and demographic variables, including age, educational attainment, household income, race and ethnicity, and community type. Of U.S. adults, 15% do not use the Internet (Anderson & Perrin, 2015). One-third of individuals or families making less than $20,000 a year have no access to the Internet. Another third go online, but do not have Internet access at home. Roughly one-third (31.4%) of households whose incomes fall below $50,000 and with children ages 6 to 17 do not have a high-speed Internet connection at home (Horrigan, 2015). Forty-five percent of mobile Internet users go online primarily with their cellphones.

Students who do not have access to adequate technology can be disadvantaged academically, socially, and financially (Domonell, 2014). This disparity in adequate home Internet service has led to what is now referred to as the homework gap (Meyer, 2015). Low SES students who lack home access to high-speed Internet and computers struggle with doing homework given in K-12 classrooms on the small screens, including research papers (Fleming, 2012). Roughly 7 in 10 of K-12 teachers assign homework requiring broadband access at home; however, 1/3 of those students' lack home Internet access, per the Federal Communications Commission (n. d.). The homework gap impacts numerous school-age children when accessing instructional materials and prevents these children from developing robust digital literacy skills. Students need to know how to complete online forms, search library databases, and edit term papers. All skills difficult to accomplish using a smartphone thereby making these mobile devices poor replacements for all computer functions (Farkas, 2016). From an academic perspective, no access to broadband technologies prohibits basic multimedia communication, working on research projects, and participating in online class discussions.

Differences in access to technology can have direct effects on K-12 classroom instruction (Chapman, Masters, & Pedulla, 2010). Typical students attending high needs (HN) and non-high needs (NHN) schools differed in access to technology. Teachers in HN schools continued to have less technical abilities than those in NHN schools. Lack of technical ability prevents these important educators from demonstrating how technology can be used to support learning or encouraging the development of digital literacy skills. Continued uneven distribution of resources in schools is one of the most prevalent problems in education today. Wealthier students benefit from schools with higher-paid teachers, better facilities, and newer materials. Poorer kids are left behind with less access to similar resources. The steady growth of digital technology in teaching has widened that resource imbalance (Ferreira, 2014).

Students from the lower SES are overcoming the barriers to enrolling into a public university. Across Florida in the 2013-2014 academic year, 188,590 undergraduate students received some form of grant aid. Of that number, 102,288 received grant aid from Pell, and another 111,115 were awarded a federal student loan to apply to the cost of their education (National Center for Education Statistics, n.d.). This number does not represent those that may have attempted to apply but did not have the technology know-how and the digital literacy skills to select or to complete the application process or who may have enrolled in a college rather than a university.

English as a Second Language

For English language learners (ELL), access has become a multifaceted issue. For this segment of the population, the digital divide exists due to language barriers. Language proficiency is one of the most powerful predictors of Internet use, even controlling for other demographic factors (Smith, 2010). Seven thousand languages are currently spoken around the world; however, websites are written in only a few of the most commonly used languages. Further, 80% of websites are in English even though less than 1 in 10 people in the world speak that language (Dubey, 2011). Because the Internet is not in their primary language, many non-English speakers do not value the technology, reducing the likelihood of owning a computer or access to high-speed Internet in the home. With limited access, individuals from this segment of the population are not aware of services available through the school or library, or they may be unable to get to the library on a regular basis (Robertson, 2013). Robertson accentuated the fact that English language learner (ELL) students may be particularly susceptible to believing information they receive electronically because they may come from a culture where very little information is printed; therefore, written information is usually considered reliable.

Historically, Hispanics have had lower levels of Internet use than their peers. While the gap has narrowed to some extent, Hispanics consistently reported the lowest levels of Internet use of any racial or ethnic group (Morris, 2015). Twenty-four percent of Latinos are not online versus 14% of Whites and 15% of African Americans (Caumont, 2013). While 75.4% of White non-Hispanics, 75.3% of Asian American non-Hispanics, and 64% of African American non-Hispanics reported using the Internet in 2013, only 61% of Hispanics were online (Morris, 2015). Most low- and moderate-income families have some form of Internet connection, but many are under connected, with mobile-only access and inconsistent connectivity. Families headed by Hispanic immigrants are less connected than other low- and moderate-income families (Rideout & Katz, 2016). In addition, 1 in 10 (10%) immigrant Hispanic families have no Internet access at all compared with 7% of U.S.-born Hispanics, 5% of Whites, and 1% of Blacks. Families headed by Hispanic immigrants are less connected than other low- and moderate-income families. Rideout and Katz (2016) also reported that the main reason some families do not have home computers or Internet access is because they cannot afford either to purchase a computer or broadband and discounted Internet programs are reaching very few.

The relative share of cyberspace which is English has shrunk to around 30%, while French, German, Spanish, and Chinese have all pushed into the top 10 languages online (Young, 2013). One in 10 U.S. public school students is an ELL (Mead, 2012). Mead also observed that in the past 2 decades, the population of ELL students has both grown rapidly and has expanded beyond traditional "border" states to communities in all parts of the country. Florida's ELL population totals over 265,000 which is third in the nation per the Florida Department of Education (2016). In Fall 2014, 77,633 Hispanic students enrolled in Florida's public universities, approximately 24% of the total student population. A portion of these students had a level of English language skills that allowed them to be successful in an academic setting. Others struggled with accessing post-secondary education due to the lack of English skills. Many of these students came from homes where Spanish was the primary language with the potential of limited access to the Internet.

To make the most of instructional technology, ELLs need to have the language skills and the vocabulary necessary to understand how to use the technology. The need to implement instructional strategies to help ELL students build technical skills and digital literacy is crucial and is an important part of the process (Robertson, 2013). Providing ELLs handouts with visuals of the computer screen so that they can follow along and develop skills to access online resources should be part of any instructional technology settings and libraries where access is available. Improvement of cultural and language services, including digital recordings in the native languages and computer stations for digital research, should be implemented for a population that suffers a massive achievement gap compared with their non-ELL peers (Mead, 2012). For the growing population of students whose first language is not English, learning to speak and to write English fluently is essential to access online information to succeed in college and in a career.

SPECIFIC DIGITAL CHALLENGES

Regardless of which of the above issues leads to the lack of access, these individuals struggle as they begin the pre-enrollment processes at any postsecondary institution due to their lack of digital literacy skills. High-achieving, low-income students often fail to enroll in a postsecondary institution that is comparable to their level of achievement. Of this group, 15% to 40% do not enroll in college after acceptance. Overestimating the cost of attending the institutions, difficulty in filling out the complex financial aid forms and lack of guidance through the application process are cited as common reasons for this failure (Knight, 2016).

To navigate the pre-enrollment process requires digital literacy skills developed over time using Internet resources. For example, being able to locate digital resources with advice about applying to a post-secondary institution and navigating college-search websites can pose a challenge for a student with few digital competencies. Without extensive knowledge in evaluating information provided on the Internet, these students also struggle in determining the credibility of the information they are viewing (Fleming, 2012). No access to technology prohibits basic online communications within online courses and participation in class discussion (Domonell, 2014). This digital struggle results in a continuous cycle with the students not obtaining a post-secondary degree and lower salaries.

Mobile Device Challenges

Another challenge occurs in accessing distance learning content using smartphones. Although course materials can be produced in pdf formats or by using responsive web designs, the smartphones have limitations. Increasingly, websites and educational applications are becoming more readily available for smartphones. The ownership of mobile devices is providing wider accessibility by students to instructional materials outside the classroom. In 2014, 98% of 18-29-year-olds and 97% of 30- 49-year-olds owned a cellphone (Pew Research Center, 2016). However, students, using mobile phones to access information, experience numerous challenges which lead to abandoning of Internet searches. Smartphones are good for handling short messages, reading documents, and watching short videos. However, students are challenged as they read lengthy content such as a textbook or writing long documents.

As an example of the challenges student may experience as they use one of the learning management systems app for coursework is the Canvas mobile app. The Canvas mobile app has different challenges depending on the operating systems of the mobile device. In general, students have access to Canvas from any browsers on a computer; however, mobile browsers are not supported leading to features not functioning as anticipated. The app for Android does not allow attachments to be uploaded, view peer reviews, schedule assignment reminders, view collaborations or conferences, upload group files, group collaborations, or group conferences. iOS users are unable to create calendar events, view bookmarks, view profile bios, change languages, view peer reviews, view collaborations, view conferences, edit discussion topics, view what-if scores, view notifications, view outcomes, view group collaborations, group conferences, or group notifications (Canvas by Instructure, 2016).

Students who are using mobile devices as the only means to access course content can miss critical aspects of the course at the same time are not practicing digital literacy skills. These students may be unaware of the peer reviews given to them on projects or assignments. They are not able to participate in group meetings leading to not receiving credit for group assignments or not feeling connected to the other class members because of no access to the class members' bio information. Assignments to create documents or presentations are difficult to complete using a mobile app and cannot be turned in due to the lack of an attachment function. Finally, students may not be able to edit their calendar to establish their own project deadlines. The instructional content delivered to a mobile device also looks different from content viewed using a computer screen. The Canvas app will strip out images and digital media to ensure the content is downloadable to the mobile device (Canvas by Instructure, 2016). Those instructional elements could be crucial in understanding the content.

The Blackboard Learn mobile app provides many tools that can enhance the learning experience. The mobile app provides an activity stream which prioritizes events and actions the students need to do within their classes. Students can also view, complete, and submit assignments and text. Synchronous learning tools are available to communicate with fellow classmates (Blackboard, 2017). However, the app has similar problems as the Canvas app. The app does not provide full functionality. Students who are attempting to write lengthy research papers or projects would find it difficult to do this on a small screen. A full-size computer screen makes these tasks easier.

DIGITAL ACCESS FOR RESEARCH

Lack of access to technology impacts students' ability in utilizing databases in libraries, organizing the information, and writing about research. Accessing electronic resources through databases has expanded over the past few years. Libraries have been gradually converting the paper-based products to digital resources, increasing the access to a wide variety of scientific journals. Large providers with library content have also been converting the journals into digital formats. However, searching library databases can still be difficult on a smartphone due to search websites that may not be mobile responsive (Farkas, 2016).

To understand the impact lack of access due to the slow conversion of library resources to responsive websites, the Members Council on Library Services Executive Board was consulted. The Executive Board described variability across the different colleges and universities in the accessibility of the library websites or pages in providing library services by mobile devices (Members Council on Library Services Executive Board, 2016). The variability across institutions ranged from just beginning to explore new mobile responsive web design products to full conversions to mobile responsive pages for the library websites. Although the large journal providers EBSCO and ProQuest are mobile friendly, the highly specialized discipline-specific databases may not be mobile responsive. Even with apps or mobile-designed websites, the navigation of electronic databases remains cumbersome or the licensed resources purchased by libraries are not mobile friendly (Farkas, 2016).

Not all library resources are available in a digital format. Many resources in the library remain paper-based. To check-out those types of library materials, students often drive to a campus to access the resources quickly. Ordering books or converting paper-based content to digital when requested through the library takes time for library staff to convert and to deliver the material to the students' mailing addresses. The time lag in receiving required materials can be frustrating for students who are meeting assignment due dates. Additionally, the conversion process costs libraries time and money. Due to budget constraints, it is difficult to provide every library item to a distance learning student.

An ongoing challenge facing libraries as described by the Members Council on Library Services Executive Board (2016) is ensuring that all video is captioned. The advantage of captioned video is not only accessibility by students with a disability, the transcripts created through the captioning process can be utilized with low bandwidth as text downloads faster than video. Even though most purchased videos are captioned, small independent producers of educational videos in some content areas are expensive to purchase and frequently are not captioned. The digitized rights for these videos can cost as much as $400.00 per semester plus the additional cost to make the captions for delivery of the video an expensive additional cost per course. Libraries also own or manage many older videos, DVD or video tapes that are not captioned.

Libraries and computer labs are becoming central location points for students to supplement technology available at their homes or in their dorm rooms. For example, students will drive to a campus to access high-speed Internet connections to watch streamed video files, download large document files, or search library databases. The students with older computers or laptops are unable to load the appropriate software programs required for class. To compensate, the students will go to on-campus computer labs or libraries where the computers have the required software programs. Many libraries allow laptops or tablets to be checked out for use while in the library as another approach for addressing the lack of technology or ownership of older technology by the students (Members Council on Library Services, 2016).

Internet access through the college and university library system is unreliable for students attending campuses in other regions of Florida. In those regions within the state of Florida where broadband access is limited, students often go to the nearest college or university campus to gain access to their online courses. Once on the campus, access may or may not be available. Colleges and universities in these regions view open access to support the community. For example, one college allowed guest access to the Internet because of the number of people in the community without access to the Internet. Another university addressed the Internet access issue through an access partnership program. This approach is a formal agreement between institutions which allows Internet access to students from specific institutions in the region. Other post-secondary institutions are unable to provide the access to the public for security and financial reasons. At these institutions, students are required to use their student ID to access computers or the Internet (Members Council on Library Services, 2016).

Florida's Members Council on Library Services (2016) has worked to increase the access of electronic collections statewide. Whenever possible, electronic databases of materials are bought as shared state resources. Several challenges exist in purchasing additional shared digital content. The institutions participating in the shared resources often have different missions. K-12 students should not be able to obtain all materials in the state shared resources as some resources will be inappropriate for that age group, while those same are required for doctorate or graduate programs. Also universities need different types of resources than colleges.

To further compound the sharing of resources are the tracking mechanisms the content publishers put in place at the institution. For example, if a resource is requested through the library loan program, the content owner can request additional funds for the extra requests or insist the requesting institution subscribe to the database. To protect the databases, the licenses are available for specific IP addresses associated with the campus. Students must use a remote proxy service with an institutional identification to access the electronic databases off campus. To provide wider access to the databases is extremely costly to the institution (Hixson, 2016).

Librarians have encountered other issues as students from other institutions attempt to use the Internet connections (Members Council on Library Services, 2016). The information technology departments are protecting the network and student data by blocking access to specific types of websites. Blocked websites include learning management systems and access to courses from outside institutions. Other websites students may not be able to access include potential "cheating sites." These are websites that students may use during testing to locate answers to exam questions but are often used by faculty to support improved study habits for exams as homework.

Public libraries and other public available hotspots are often cited as alternatives for accessing technology for distance learning courses. However, access to the technology can be hindered if the student does not have transportation to the library, computer lab, or hotspot. For successful completion of one online class, the student needs access to technology for 3 to 10 hours per week. Demand for the computers in public libraries often exceeds stations available, resulting in signing up for 30-minute increments of computer usage which is not enough time to complete assignments (Kasperkevic, 2014). Other limitations include closing as early as 6 p.m., making those technology hubs unsuitable substitutions for an accessible location such as the home (Kasperkevic). Other access points, coffee shops or fast-food restaurants, require ownership of a laptop or a tablet.

Accessing the research resources is just one barrier; another barrier is the type of device being used to organize and to create new ideas. The linkage to the library resources is only as good as the learning management system in accessing mobile content. The mobile devices also have small screens, making the reading of lengthy research documents challenging. Editing a research paper on a smartphone is not an adequate replacement for the editing features and viewing capabilities of a computer for research papers or projects (Domonell, 2014; Farkas, 2016).

Challenges in Accessing Technology

Several myths exist as to methods students can use to access technology when they do not have access from their homes. Another barrier that students must overcome is the demand for higher levels of bandwidth when taking video streaming courses. Students also need to be assured of extended access over several years to successfully complete their degree programs. Students often start taking classes believing that using a neighbor's or grandparent's computer which again limits time they can spend on the computer interacting with course materials. Therefore, solutions for this group of students need to be long-term.

Myth 1: Students can use their financial aid money to purchase computer equipment and Internet access. Economic socially disadvantaged students often do not have the luxury to spend their financial aid money on technology. The money is often spent on transportation, housing, and food. These students often forgo the purchase of textbooks to meet basic needs.

Myth 2: Students can go to a public library to complete their homework. This solution is not viable due to the limited resources at public libraries. The computers available often are unable to meet the demands of the local community. Thus, the computer usage is limited to 30 minutes. The limited time is compounded by the limited hours. Another challenge in the use of public libraries is the lack of transportation or the students' neighborhoods are unsafe for walking or bicycling to the library.

Myth 3: Students can use the campus library. This assumption is counterintuitive to taking courses online. Using the library does not work for students who live off campus or some distance from the campus.

Myth 4: Most students own a smartphone so they can access course material. This assumption has two flaws. First, the students must own an updated smartphone to benefit from the fastest available connection speeds. In some cases, students own a handed-down family phone or an older model due the expense associated with upgrading. Second, the course material accessible by the smartphone is inadequate for the learning experience.

SOLUTIONS AND RECOMMENDATIONS

In recent years, policymakers and advocates have pushed to make it easier for low-income households with school-age children to have broadband, arguing that low-income students are at a disadvantage without online access to do schoolwork (Horrigan, 2015). The federal initiatives expand the access to broadband from a variety of different angles.

Several federal programs are being implemented to address low bandwidth access for students and communities locally, statewide, and at the national level. The National Education Technology Plan (U.S. Department of Education, 2016) had a vision of equity, active use, and collaborative leadership to make everywhere, all-the-time learning possible. National Education Technology Plan proposed the establishment of a robust technology infrastructure that meets current connectivity goals and augmented to future demand in K-12 classrooms (U.S. Department of Education, 2016). One of these programs ConnectHome is an initiative to help provide high-speed Internet access, technical assistance, digital literacy programs, and devices to K-12 students living in public and assisted housing (Meyer, 2015). This pilot program will initially reach more than 200,000 children in 27 cities and one tribal nation. Finally, Connect2Compete, through partnerships with local Internet service providers, provides low-cost broadband, computers, training, and content solutions for disadvantaged communities across the United States (EveryoneOn, 2016).

Partnering school districts with local businesses to provide Wi-Fi access for learning are making the most of existing school district assets. As part of an effort to bridge the digital divide, the state of Washington's Kent School District installed Wi-Fi kiosks in public housing developments so that students and their parents can get online with state provided tablets or laptops (Monahan, 2014). The state of California's Coachella Valley District's outfitted school buses with Wi-Fi hotspots. The school buses are then parked in nearby trailer parks so students can have access outside the classroom (Clapman, 2016).

The federal initiatives reach beyond classes and students through two other programs. The FCC began an initiative that subsidizes telephone subscriptions for low-income households that also covers broadband (Horrigan, 2015). Lifeline Broadband expanded the Lifeline Assistance free government cellphone program to include broadband. The program is offered either as fixed broadband (cable or DSL) or mobile (on phone or tablet). Lifeline service providers who offer the FCC Lifeline subsidy provides 150GB of data usage per month with 10 Mbps download and 1 Mbps upload speed to eligible households. Through the Mobile Lifeline Broadband, eligible individuals receive 500 MB of Internet data usage per month with an increase to 2GB by the end of 2018. To qualify, the individuals must be participants in a federal, state, or local assistance program such as food stamps, public housing, Medicaid, Section 8 housing, Supplemental Security Income, Home Energy Assistance Programs, or National School Lunch (CheapInternet.com, n. d.).

Extending broadband access at the university level has taken a slightly different approach. The University Corporation for Advanced Internet Development is a nationwide project designed to interconnect research and educational networks to create a dedicated 100-200 Gbpsnationwide fiber backbone with 3.2 Tbps total capacity (BroadbandUSA, 2010). The networks are often referred to as Internet2. The goal of the project is to create a 50-state network with 121,000 community anchors with 100 to 200 Gbps nationwide fiber backbone with 3.2 Tbps total capacity. The network will include colleges, universities, libraries, and other government organizations (National Telecommunications and Information Administration, n.d).

Federal Programs to Improve Floridians' Broadband Access

Within the federal programs are local implementations. The local programs are designed to increase broadband access to low-income families. Comcast has two of these programs. Comcast's Internet Essentials program connected 274,000 low-income families in Florida to online access at home for $9.95 per month. The program includes an Internet-ready laptop for under $150, Internet speed at 10 Mbps, and a free Wi-Fi router. To participate, eligible families need at least one child in the National School Lunch Program (Dahlberg, 2015). Comcast Corporation is piloting a local program in partnership with HUD's ConnectHome initiative for public housing residents in Miami-Dade County, Florida. This program provides Comcast's existing Internet Essentials low-cost broadband access to low-income families in that region.

Other companies also developed consumer products to lower the cost of access for qualifying families. AT&T offers high-speed Internet services at $5 per month for low-income households at 3 Mbps download speed. For an additional $5, the speed increases from 5 to 10 Mbps per month. AT&T waives all activation fees and includes a wireless router. A computer for $149.99 is available for qualifying families (CheapInternet.com, n. d.). CenturyLinks offers Internet Basics with 1.5 Mpbs in the service areas, at $9.95 (CheapInternet.com, n. d.). In partnership with Connect2Compete, Bright House Networks and Mediacom offer households with a child eligible for the National School Lunch program high-speed Internet at $9.95 per month (CheapInternet.com, n. d.). Cox Low-Income Internet offers $9.95 to low-income families that participate in several federal programs such as Supplemental National Assistance Program, Temporary Assistance for Needy Family, National School Lunch program, or live in HUD-assisted housing (CheapInternet.com, n. d.).

In Florida, two other projects are working to improve the broadband connections though infrastructure improvements. Florida LambdaRail (FLR), also known as Florida's 1000 Gigabit Research and Education Network, is an independent statewide fiber optical network owned and operated on behalf of 12 universities, both public and private, across Florida. The 1,540 miles of dark fiber connected the 12 institutions with transmission ability up to 100 Gbps. The goal is to bring together people, resources, and information to foster innovation and discovery (Florida LambdaRail, n. d.). The Broadband Florida Initiative (2016), housed within the Florida Department of Management Services (DMS), provides programs and staff assistance dedicated to increasing broadband capacity, reducing the digital divide, enhancing Florida's digital economy, and providing resources for continued growth. These initiatives include broadband data collection and mapping, cost-free E-Rate, grants and resource development assistance, and providing digital toolkits for broadband planning and implementation in Florida communities.

Examples of Florida Educational State Solutions

Access to the Internet from home is just one part of the problem. Not having access to broadband leads to other challenges by both low socioeconomic and ELL families. Florida has put in place a series of services to support students with limited access to technology. Florida offers an extensive range of services that are helpful for students with little technology experience in the selecting of a degree or a postsecondary institution.

One of the challenges in selecting the proper institution is knowing what degree to pursue. Currently under development is a tool called FindMyCollegeMajor. This project is supported by a U.S. Department of Labor grant led by Broward College for completion by April 28, 2017. For place-bound nontraditional students selecting the major they want to pursue can be a challenge. FindMyCollegeMajor empowers future students to explore majors, identify majors that fit their interests, capture a one-pager on the program with relevant data, and bring that information to the college's admissions office. In so doing, a barrier to college knowledge is overcome. The first admissions session begins with an informed dialogue, and students enter meta-majors from the start. The expected result of this product is an empowered student based upon an informed dialogue and increased program exposure.

Once the students make the decision as to which institution they want to attend, the FloridaShines offers a variety of helpful tools to promote successful completion of the degree. The first of these tools is a series of tips for students to evaluate readiness for taking online courses from the Get Ready for College Pages as pdf documents. These documents include a college checklist, how to manage your time, note-taking skills, developing study skills, and test-taking strategies. Another tool supports students as they plan their educational careers. The purpose is to support retention and graduation. The Ed Planner allows high school students to develop a 4-year personalized course plan to keep them on track to graduation. Students select any course in the Florida Course Catalog system. The school counselors approve plans electronically. The Florida Course Catalog system allows students to select online courses from the different institutions across the state. FloridaShines acts as a conduit through a transient sign-in process and method to apply the federal aid to multiple institutions tuition and fees.

As classes begin, FloridaShines have a Succeed in College section. In that section are several tools designed to assist students in evaluating their progress toward graduation. Through the transcript tools, students can obtain transcripts for courses taken at any Florida colleges or universities. The Progress to Graduation tool allows currently enrolled students to check progress towards their degree by evaluating courses taken which can be applied to the degree and the courses required to complete their degree. Finally, the Impact of Changing Majors tool allows students to evaluate the impact of changing majors by applying to the new degrees previously taken courses. This way, the student can determine the number of excess hours and identifies the increased cost due to the change in degree.

Complete Florida is another state-sponsored initiative which reaches out to 3 million Floridians who started a degree but did not finish. Complete Florida focuses on the exclusive 100% online programs to provide the flexibility needed to complete the degree. Upon applying to the program, the students are assigned a success coach. The coach supports returning students for both college and university degree programs through the enrollment and admissions processes at the institutions participating in the program. The coach provides information about the different programs the student would qualify for based upon grades and interest. The coach acts as a liaison on behalf of the student with the institution the student selected in which to enroll. A scholarship program, based upon time toward degree completion, was implemented through Florida Completes. Those reentering students with more hours receive better scholarships to complete quickly. Career coaching is also available with access online from 8:00 a.m. to 5:00 p.m., with appointments available afterhours.

Through Florida Virtual Campus and the state library systems work together to provide the best possible service for students. Florida's college and university students search for books, articles, and other eContent from any library at a Florida public postsecondary institution. The Uborrow tools allows students to request library materials located at another college or university library. The Florida Electronic Library allows students to explore all public libraries in Florida. Finally, Ask A Librarian provided Florida students with 24-hours-a-day access to online reference services through email. Sunday through Thursday from 10 a.m. to midnight, either live chat or text messaging are available.

Expanding Broadband Access One Student at a Time

Expanding broadband access is difficult for postsecondary institutions since colleges and universities are unable to influence increasing access into rural areas of Florida to improve economic status of students or the primary language of students. Therefore, expanding access needs to be a process that assists individual students. Informing students of the availability of low-cost Internet services provided through the ConnectHome and Lifeline Broadband partnerships within local communities is an easy first step. The information can be posted to marketing and admissions websites. Another strategy is to finance scholarships or grants for students identified as at-risk through financial aid. Through the scholarships or grants would be a way to purchase broadband service while attending classes. Some institutions are providing short-term laptop or tablet rentals for students. These students can connect to high-speed Internet while on campus to download course material but still have the convenience of completing class work at home or at other convenient locations (Domonell, 2014).

Potential Ways to Support the Development of Digital Literacy Skills

Students who come to the postsecondary institutions without digital literacy skills need support through the student lifecycle. To assist students through the enrollment process, institutions can provide academic coaching programs. The academic coach begins supporting students during the application process through enrollment. In this way students have assistance as they complete the application and the financial aid forms. Coaches also give these students suggestions for how to locate additional funding for their education. The coaches stay with the students into the first semester to ensure they are connected to the resources and support services required to complete their degrees.

Digital literacy skill development often occurs through the library educational services that are available to all students. The libraries are taking steps to ensure the media resources are available from responsive websites for access by mobile devices (Farkas, 2016). Libraries often provide seminars or design lessons for specific courses to teach how to use library resources, research strategies, and search techniques. Providing education opportunities in different formats that enhance the services the library offers can open doors for students with few digital literacy skills. For example, libraries can provide the sessions through live-streaming or recorded events. Students can access the sessions on multiple devices and at a times convenient for them. Another good solution is to embed librarians into the online courses and insert easily accessible navigation to library resources and assistance.

OPPORTUNITIES FOR RESEARCH

Technology is constantly changing and evolving. Because of this perpetual transformation of the technology used in instructional environments, research into the impact and usage of technology within vulnerable populations should continue. The Horizon Report (New Media Consortium, 2017) identifies trends for the next 5 years in the use of technology for higher education. The 2017 Higher Education Edition identified for the next 10 years improving digital literacy as a challenge. "Digital literacy is … developing skills to select the right tool for a particular context to deepen their learning outcomes and engage in creative problem-solving" (New Media Consortium, 2017, p. 24).

The New Media Consortium (2017) tied to the digital literacy the concept of mobile technology enhancing the informal learning experiences such as Lynda.com or YouTube platforms. The exposure to informal learning platforms will give future postsecondary students a broader range of knowledge and experiences before entering college or university classrooms. Without the exposure, students will continue to fall behind in digital literacy skills and the application of those skills to improve their learning.

Another observation of the Consortium that impacts the development of digital learning skills is the use of mobile devices as gateways to personalized working and learning environments (New Media Consortium, 2017). Working adults are returning to postsecondary institutions to further their education and to improve their lives. This segment of the population is more likely to use the mobile devices to access their learning because the use of the devices fits into their daily schedule. Future research should understand how to integrate the devices into the learning environments and continue to evaluate the access by the lower income and non-English, speaking students.

As future students have access to the Internet of Things, they are going to develop an understanding of the interconnection of objects within a system. Affluence is going to gain access to the Internet of things from the wearable technologies to tracking purchases both within and outside store settings. The understanding of the interactions of the objects with broadband will allow students to develop newer ways of connecting objects with one another. Without access, how will students develop this understanding and what impact will this have on their upward mobility?

CONCLUSION

Some type of divide between those in the lower and higher socioeconomic status will continue to occur as technology continues to evolve. However, with the evolution of technology the definition of what digital literacy means will change. As educators, understanding the digital divide as it evolves is important to make sure that students are developing the digital skills they need to be fully functional members of society. As computers first came on the scene in the latter part of the 20th century, technology grants were provided for schools to be connected to the Internet. As society realized that funding of technology was not a one-time event, these funding sources are not as readily available today. Yet, access to the Internet and to update technology is important in K-12 schools as schools may be the only true technology access students have they need to develop the ability to learn how to use that technology. Communities that fund these schools should accept this constant change in technology and create ways to continually fund the upgrades needed in the schools. Educators need continual professional development and training to enhance their skills to provide the best learning experiences using digital literacy in the classrooms.

Postsecondary institutions also need to be aware of the continual advancement of the technology. During the two, four, or six years required for students to receive a high-quality education, technology can change drastically. These institutions need to stay updated in their approaches to how they teach the constantly evolving digital literacy skills they will need as they become full citizens and join the workforce. Educators in postsecondary institutions should continue to evaluate the digital literacy skills that student have or do not have to provide the best educational experiences for those who come from situations in which they may not have had access to technology due to the lack of access because of region, low socioeconomic status, or limited English language.

ACKNOWLEDGMENT

Special thanks to the Student Services Workgroup for the Implementation Committee Florida State Online Education plan for guiding the process in the identification of issues in Florida and resources available to support students which were described in the Technology Access Whitepaper. Thank you also to the staff at the Center for eLearning at Florida Atlantic University who assisted with the background research for this project.

REFERENCES

P21. (2007). Framework for 21st century learning. *Partnership for 21st Century Learning.* Retrieved from http://www.p21.org/our-work/p21-framework

P21. (n. d.). Our vision and mission. *Partnership for 21st Century Learning.* Retrieved from http://www.p21.org/about-us/our-mission

Anderson, M., & Perrin, A. (2015). 15% of Americans don't use the Internet. Who are they? *Pew Research Center.* Retrieved from http://www.pewresearch.org/fact-tank/2015/07/28/15-of-americans-dont-use-the-Internet-who-are-they/

Blackboard. (2017). *Bb student.* Retrieved from http://www.blackboard.com/mobile-learning/bbstudent.aspx

Broadband, U. S. A. (2010). *Connecting America's communities.* Retrieved from http://www2.ntia.doc.gov/files/grantees/ALL_USCAID.pdf

Broadband Florida Initiative. (2016). *Broadband Florida initiative.* Retrieved from http://broadbandfla.com/

BroadBandNow. (2016). *Broadband service in Florida.* Retrieved from http://broadbandnow.com/Florida

Canvas by Instructure. (2016). *Canvas by Instructure mobile features.* Retrieved from https://s3.amazonaws. com/tr-learncanvas/docs/Mobile_CanvasbyInstructure.pdf

Caumont, A. A. (2013). Who's not online? 5 factors tied to the digital divide. *Pew Research Center,* retrieved from http://www.pewresearch.org/fact-tank/2013/11/08/whos-not-online-5-factors-tied-to-the-digital-divide/

Chapman, L., Masters, J., & Pedulla, J. (2010). Do digital divisions still persist in schools? Access to technology and technical skills of teachers in high needs schools in the United States of America. *Journal of Education for Teaching, 36*(2), 239–249. doi:10.1080/02607471003651870

CheapInternet.com. (n. d.). *Inexpensive Internet service for Florida: Low-income qualifications, DSL, cable, mobile Internet.* Retrieved from http://www.cheapInternet.com/states/florida-Internet-service

Clapman, L. (2016). Wi-Fi-enabled school buses leave no child offline. *PBS NewsHour.* Retrieved from http://www.pbs.org/newshour/bb/wi-fi-enabled-school-buses-leave-no-child-offline/

Complete Florida. (2015). *Finish your degree: Let's get started.* Retrieved from https://www.complete-florida.org/

Dahlberg, N. (2015). Comcast expands low-income Internet program. *Miami Herald.* Retrieved from http://www.miamiherald.com/news/business/article29973996.html

Domonell, K. (2014). Bridging the digital divide: How institutions are making iPads and laptops accessible to all students. *University Business.* Retrieved from https://www.universitybusiness.com/article/bridging-digital-divide

Dubey, P. (2011). Overcoming the digital divide through machine translation. *Translation Journal, 15*(1). Retrieved from http://translationjournal.net/journal/55mt_india.htm

EveryoneOn. (2016). *About us.* Retrieved from http://everyoneon.org/about/

Farkas, M. (2016). The new digital divide. *American Libraries Magazines.* Retrieved from https://americanlibrariesmagazine.org/2016/01/04/new-digital-divide-mobile-first-design/

Federal Communications Commission. (2016). *2016 Broadband progress report.* Retrieved from https://www.fcc.gov/reports-research/reports/broadband-progress-reports/2016-broadband-progress-report

Federal Communications Commission. (n. d.). Connecting America: The national broadband plan. *Federal Communication Commission.* Retrieved from http://download.broadband.gov /plan/national-broadband-plan.pdf

Ferreira, J. (2014). *The digital divide and America's achievement gap* [The Knewton Blog.] Retrieved from https://www.knewton.com/resources/blog/ceo-jose-ferreira/the-digital-divide/

Fleming, N. (2012). Digital divide strikes college-admissions process. *Education Week, 32*(13), 14–15.

Fleming, N. (2012). Digital divide strikes college-admissions process: Some students lack hardware, savvy. *Education Week, 32*(13), 14.

Florida Department of Education. (2016). *English language learners*. Retrieved from http://www.fldoe.org/academics/eng-language-learners/

Florida LambdaRail. (n. d.) *About us*. Retrieved from http://www.flrnet.org/?page_id=491

Hixson, C. (2016). Personal interview.

Ho, A., Chuang, H. A., Reich, J., Coleman, C., Whitehill, J., Northcutt, C., . . . Petersen, R. (2015). *HarvardX and MITx: Two years of open online courses* (HarvardX Working Paper No. 10). doi:10.2139/ssrn.2586847

Horrigan, J. B. (2015). The numbers behind the broadband 'homework gap'. *Pew Research Center*. Retrieved from http://www.pewresearch.org/fact-tank/2015/04/20/the-numbers-behind-the-broadband-homework-gap/

Jackson, L. A., Zhao, Y., Kolenic, A. III, Fitzgerald, H. E., Harold, R., & Von Eye, A. (2008). Race, gender, and information technology use: The new digital divide. *Cyberpsychology & Behavior*, *11*(4), 437–442. doi:10.1089/cpb.2007.0157 PMID:18721092

Kasperkevic, J. (2014). Connection failed: Internet still a luxury for many Americans. *The Guardian*. Retrieved from http://www.theguardian.com/money/us-money-log/2014/jan/26/Internet-luxury-low-income-americans

Knight, G. (2016). Could a tweet or a text increase college enrollment or student achievement? *The Conversations*. Retrieved from http://theconversation.com/could-a-tweet-or-a-text-increase-college-enrollment-or-student-achievement-57939

Mack, S. (2013, June). What we mean when we talk about Florida's digital divide. *State Impact Florida*. Retrieved from https://stateimpact.npr.org/florida/2013/06/10/what-we-mean-when-we-talk-about-floridas-digital-divide/

Mead, S. (2012, May). *Sara Mead's policy notebook: Teddy Rice, President and Co-Founder, Ellevation*. Retrieved from http://blogs.edweek.org/edweek/sarameads_policy_notebook/2012/05/teddy_rice_president_and_co-founder_ellevation.html

MediaSmarts. (n. d.). *The intersection of digital and media literacy*. Retrieved from http://mediasmarts.ca/digital-media-literacy/general-information/digital-media-literacy-fundamentals/intersection-digital-media-literacy/

Members Council on Library Services. (2016, November 30). Web conference focus interview at regular meeting at University of Central Florida.

Members Council on Library Services Executive Board Members (2016, September 22). Phone conference call.

Meyer, L. (2015). White House announces ConnectHome initiative to address the homework gap. *THE Journal*. Retrieved from https://thejournal.com/articles/2015/07/15/white-house-announces-connecthome-initiative-to-address-the-homework-gap.aspx

Monahan, R. (2014). What happens when kids don't have Internet at home? *The Atlantic*. Retrieved from http://www.theatlantic.com/education/archive/2014/12/what-happens-when-kids-dont-have-Internet-at-home/383680/

Morris, J. B. (2015). *Language and citizenship may contribute to low Internet use among Hispanics*. U.S. Department of Commerce, National Telecommunications and Information Administration. Retrieved from https://www.ntia.doc.gov/blog/2015/language-and-citizenship-may-contribute-low-Internet-use-among-hispanics

National Center for Education Statistics. (n. d.). *IPEDs Data Center*. Retrieved from https://nces.ed.gov/ipeds/datacenter/

National Telecommunications and Information Administration. (n. d.). University cooperation for advanced Internet development. Retrieved from http://www2.ntia.doc.gov/grantee/university-corporation-for-advanced-Internet-development

New Media Consortium. (2017). *NMC horizon report: 2017 higher education edition*. Retrieved from http://cdn.nmc.org/media/2017-nmc-horizon-report-he-EN.pdf

Organization for Economic Co-Operation and Development. (2005). *Are students ready for a technology-rich world? What PISA studies tell us*. Paris, France: OECD Publications.

Pew Research Center. (2016). *Mobile technology fact sheet*. Retrieved from http://www.pewInternet.org/fact-sheets/mobile-technology-fact-sheet/

Rideout, V. J., & Katz, V. S. (2016). *Opportunity for all? Technology and learning in lower-income families. A report of the Families and Media Project*. New York, NY: The Joan Ganz Cooney Center at Sesame Workshop.

Ritzhaupt, A. D., Liu, F., Dawson, K., & Barron, E. B. (2013). Differences in student information and communication technology literacy based on socioeconomic status, ethnicity, and gender: Evidence of a digital divide in Florida schools. *Journal of Research on Technology in Education*, *45*(4), 291–307. doi:10.1080/15391523.2013.10782607

Robertson, K. (2013). Preparing ELLs to be 21st-century learners. *Colorin Colorado*. Retrieved from http://www.colorincolorado.org/article/preparing-ells-be-21st-century-learners

Singleton, M. (2015, January 29). The FCC has changed the definition of broadband. *The Verge*. Retrieved from http://www.theverge.com/2015/1/29/7932653/fcc-changed-definition-broadband-25Mbps

Smith, A. (2010). Technology trends among people of color. *Pew Internet and American Life Project*. Retrieved from http://www.pewInternet.org/2010/09/17/technology-trends-among-people-of-color/

State of Tennessee v. Federal Communications Commission and United States of America. (2015).

State University System of Florida Board of Governors. (2013). *Task force on postsecondary online education in Florida: Final report*. Retrieved from http://flbog.edu/about/taskforce/_doc/2013_12_09_Online-Task-Force-Final-Report.pdf

State University System of Florida Board of Governors. (2015). *Online education 2025 strategic plan.* Retrieved from http://OnlineStratePlanning%Committee/2015_11_05%20FINAL_StrategicPlan.pdf

State University System of Florida Board of Governors. (2016). *Implementation schedule and action steps for strategic goals and associated tactics for online education: 2025 strategic plan.* Retrieved from http://flbog.edu/board/advisorygroups/_doc/online/2016_07_24_Implementation _Timeline.pdf

The Aspen Institute. (2014). *The Aspen Institution task force on learning and the Internet: Learner at the center of a networked world.* Retrieved from https://assets.aspeninstitute.org/content/uploads/files/content/docs/pubs/Learner-at-the-Center-of-a-Networked-World.pdf

U.S. Department of Education. (2011). *Meeting the nation's 2020 goal: State targets for increasing the number and percentage of college graduates with degrees.* Retrieved from https://www.whitehouse.gov/sites/default/files/completion_state_by_state.pdf

U.S. Department of Education. (2016). Future ready learning: Reimagining the role of technology in education. *2016 National Education Technology Plan.* Retrieved from https://tech.ed.gov/files/2015/12/NETP16.pdf

Young, H. (2013). The digital language divide: How does the language you speak shape your experience of the Internet? *British Academy for the Humanities and Social Sciences.* Retrieved from http://labs.theguardian.com/digital-language-divide/

Zhang, P. H. (2013). *Digital divides and socio-demographic factors: A longitudinal quantitative study of Internet users in U.S. from 2000 to 2010.* Retrieved from ProQuest. (UMI Number: 3556741)

Zickuhr, K., & Smith, A. (2013). Home broadband 2013: Trends and demographic differences in home broadband adoption. *Pew Research Center.* Retrieved from http://www.pewInternet.org/2013/08/26/home-broadband-2013/

KEY TERMS AND DEFINITIONS

Broadband: Broadband is a faster connection to the Internet than dial-up access.

Digital Divide: The lack of access to technology or the Internet that creates an inequality to access based upon on economic or social factors.

English Language Learners: Students who, need to learn English, to participate fully in the educational experience in United States schools.

Homework Gap: This gap is created when teachers assign homework that requires a computer or access to the Internet which some students do not have because of either the inability or the interest to purchase computers or access to broadband.

Low-Socioeconomic Status: Individuals who, based upon the economic and social status, are unable to buy technology tools or Internet access.

Chapter 3
New Media and Learning:
Innovative Learning Technologies

Mustafa Serkan Abdusselam
Giresun University, Turkey

Ebru Turan Guntepe
Giresun University, Turkey

ABSTRACT

This chapter is to challenge the research opportunity of media literacy in the twenty-first-century learning environment. Different technologies with human-computer interaction are addressed in this section as two different main structures. The relationships between these two structures are constructed as matrices. One of these structures is constituted by the educational technologies of the twenty-first century. The second is the learning framework of the twenty-first century. The research will be done using content analysis of the technologies used and learning frameworks. Based on the data obtained, this study will attempt to demonstrate that teachers can provide more effective and productive instruction using human-computer interaction. This section will hopefully provide information to teachers and students about suitable learning environments designed for the use of and in conformance with twenty-first-century skills with the use of innovative technologies, and technologies they should use in these environments.

INTRODUCTION

Human beings have made efforts to communicate since the beginning of history, conveying their feelings and thoughts and passing information to each other using all available opportunities. Technological developments have enabled audio-visual communication tools such as radio, TV, newspaper, and Internet to affect the masses, and consequently different aspects of interpersonal communication have arisen (Walter, 1992). Having facilitated mass communication, these tools rapidly became widespread in the 1980s, and they have gained power over time—coming to be collectively referred to as "the media" (Karataş, 2008). Thus, "the media" is defined as any communication tool that includes all kinds of verbal, written, printed, digitally visual text, and images used to reach the masses. That in turn has led to the emergence of the concept of media literacy: the ability of individuals to access different forms of

DOI: 10.4018/978-1-5225-3082-4.ch003

Copyright © 2018, IGI Global. Copying or distributing in print or electronic forms without written permission of IGI Global is prohibited.

media, to understand the messages the media carry, to create their own messages, and to critically evaluate messages (İnceoğlu, 2006; Kellner & Share, 2005; Buckingham, 2003). Using the media, individuals can now send messages to intended receivers whenever they want (Barut & Koç, 2016); for their part, recipients should analyze and interpret all messages because media messages can be fictionalized and placed strategically for individuals' point of view. Regarding the media, the published literature includes statements such as: messages should be correctly understood and handled from a critical perspective; reality should be distinguished from fiction; it's possible that the world as presented by the media may not be real and the recipient should comprehend that; the directing and governing functions of the media should be taken into account; and the senders may endeavor to impose their own opinions. Media literacy trains persons who can evaluate and properly use information, whatever its origin (RTÜK, 2014).

The concept of literacy has changed along with the necessities and the technological and socioeconomic movements of the age. Literacy has been referred to in various fields throughout history and defined in different ways for its validity at a given time (Odabaşı, 2000). With the invention of writing, literacy was accepted as the ability to analyze written texts (Murray, 2008; Wecker, Kohnlet & Fischer, 2007). Today, literacy has blended with other functions and has introduced new concepts such as information literacy, media literacy, technology literacy, to name a few. These concepts can usually be combined: an individual's ability to code and analyze a message indicates literacy in the field of the message (Potter, 2005; Livingstone, 2004), which can be evaluated through its subject (Waetjen, 1993).

Behrens (1994) defined information literacy as the ability to access information to solve a real-life problem, or through various resources to ensure continuous information and to determine the strategies on how to obtain information. Doyle (1994) stated that individuals evaluate and organize information and integrate it with their existing information. Information literacy also involves ethical and legally acceptable use of information. Information literacy leads to other areas of literacy, and it has been expressed as an umbrella for other areas of literacy (Savolainen, 2002). Media literacy can teach ways to learn and to properly access information to solve the problems people encounter throughout their life. As in a constructivist approach, information literacy requires learners to access and learn the information by themselves. Learners must have good information literacy to sort the correct information from a mass of information (Bruce, 1999). As technology should be used to access the right information, technological literacy is important.

A technologically literate person is one who questions technological processes and innovations from a critical perspective. Technological literacy can be defined as the intellectual process, competence, and order required to understand the relationship between individuals and community through access to technology. Therefore, people should understand why technology and its use are important at the level of countries (Canbaz, 2010). A person who can question technology also can criticize the benefits and disadvantages of technological developments and is aware of their effects on the community because thereby, people affect their immediate relatives or friends and help direct their future.

Today, technology is more pervasive in our lives than it was in the past, and there have been many developments in information and communication technologies. Both of these things have led the concept of media to be transformed into the concept of new media. In the new media environment, individuals can communicate online with each other or with others, cooperate, create online content and share opinions and ideas with each other in addition to having access to stable information (Maloney, 2007). Thus, individuals are provided with a media environment that they can access anytime and anywhere, use to express their opinions easily and get responses from other individuals as well (Bulunmaz, 2011). It is commonly known that the use of media motivates students in the teaching and learning process and attracts their attention as well (Çakır, Koçer & Aydın, 2012; Hobbs, 1998). Then, it is necessary to include in our lives innovative technologies that are both desktop and web-based, have mutual communication and support multiple senses with both written and visual features in accordance with individuals' needs from this environment.

With new technologies being introduced in daily life, computers have gained wearable, portable and faster new forms in response to individual needs rather than limited by their conventional form. These new forms of technology are expected to enable people to use hardware and software efficiently and effectively.

BACKGROUND

Technology affects individuals and communities by providing products that affect the quality of life. Social, political, and economic developments in communities are also considerably affected by technology. In addition, technological developments affect the attitudes, needs, and social or cultural values (Healty, 1990). Social requirements or the need for the improvement of current technology bring with them the development of new technologies. An association is made between a software application and an individual's everyday life, and operations are built upon this software application in every aspect of life (Odabaşı, 2000). Today's individuals play two main roles in digital era: the first is to develop software applications, and the second is to interpret the recorded data and use the data in the desired way through the developed software applications. A programmer at the far end of the world can use the software developed by another programmer at the other end of the world. It should be noted that a software application must have been developed by a programmer to be used. At this point, programmers have an undeniable importance.

The International Society for Technology in Education (ISTE) has determined the National Education Technology Standards, and the crucial skills for teachers and students in relation to these new literacies. The ISTE is not the first organization to determine literacy types; however, it is an organization with good standards that should be implemented. A comprehensive review of ISTE standards shows that they focus on social, ethical and human issues, technology tools and media skills rather than human behaviors. In this age, ISTE has determined that students who are described as digital age learners should meet standards that make them empowered learners, digital citizens, knowledge constructors, innovative designers, computational thinkers, creative communicators and global collaborators.

Today's teachers and students are the members of a digital era; they are the digital natives who produce instead of consuming. Digital natives have emerged with the introduction of new technologies to communities (Prensky, 2001). After the new technologies have earned a greater place in society for both digital locals and digital migrants, the concept of technology literacy began to be considered more than before.

On the other hand, a majority of students in the schools in Turkey belong to the generation Z: the oldest of these students are 16 years old. This generation likes using the Internet and mobile technologies—in other words, they are the natives of today's technologies (Oblinger & Oblinger; Prensky,2001). However, the community has assigned them a significant role. They should be skilled producers instead of just users of the current technology so that they have a voice in the world of the future. In addition, generation Z students should benefit from generation X and Y teachers to acquire a vision. Similarly, it has become a necessity for the teachers of generation X to use these tools in the education and training process considering that generation Z and Y students use new media tools in communication thanks to the internet (Knight & Kim, 2007).

Teachers, using a constructivist approach, should associate new technologies with subjects and concepts and support students' access to these technologies to involve them in learning environments. Technology has an important role in enriching the teaching environment: teachers play the role of a guide, and the students play a role of an explorer searching for information. Teachers should lead the way to integrate significant points with technology and to help students achieve their goals. Self-efficacy is expected to be high when learning is supported by technology. However, students may consider information technology (IT) to be a procedural convenience, rather than understanding how it is also a cognitive advantage (Carbonara, 2005).

With the introduction of technology in classes, environments such as distance-based learning, educational multimedia, human-computer interface, intelligent learning/tutoring, interactive learning, collaborative learning, online education, simulations for learning, and technology-based learning have been included in some curricula. In these environments, teachers and students find opportunities such as unlimited access, primary source material, collecting and recording data; they can then collaborate with students, teachers, and experts around the world and can express understanding via images, sound, and text, easy measurement, and through publishing and presenting new knowledge (Holt, Smissen & Segrave, 2006). Along with these opportunities, students should be provided with an awareness and understanding of what information is and the purposes for which it should be used (Akkoyunlu, 1996). The educational approach should emphasize the place of technology in daily life and raise students' awareness about the integration between technology and modern life using examples from social life. As the students become aware of this integration, social development will accelerate (Trilling & Fadel, 2009). In accordance with social acceleration, innovative technologies will be shaped by twenty-first century skills, and the use of the new media in education will become more popular. Teachers have changed their ways of communication in class with these technologies. In addition, the ways of sharing, cooperation and feedback and the types of learning materials have also changed. Accordingly, the most important point is to use innovative technologies as intended effectively, productively and enjoyably.

MAIN FOCUS OF THE CHAPTER

Issues, Controversies, Problems

People are immersed in the digital environment in the global world. The digital environment has provided all persons with the opportunity to use a common language that consists of 1's and 0's. Living in a digital environment has become the norm; digital devices are the primary tools used by people today. However, multi-digitalization has led an information overload (Eppler & Mengis, 2004). Technology and information should always be addressed together. As technologies change, writing, conveyance, or sharing of information may be different. Technology has existed through the human history, but it has continuously diversified and developed. In other words, the benefits of the use of technology have gained more importance (Markus & Robey, 1988). With the development of the Internet becoming widespread, accessing or sharing information can be achieved rapidly, beyond anyone's imagination. Various hardware and software that have come into use in classes—such as computers, mobile devices, interactive boards, the Internet and web 2.0 tools—are known to facilitate teaching and enrich classes.

This has led a change in teachers' opinions about teaching methods and students' understanding of ways to learn. Teachers should integrate technologies and curricula considering the needs of their students (Hew and Brush, 2007).

Technology aims to solve problems, to think critically, and to understand human-computer interaction (Leu, Kinzer, Coiro and Cammack, 2004). Using computers or another tool people can solve problems, organize and analyze data logically, concretize the abstract situations using simulations, and make analyses by finding solutions for problems using algorithm flows. In this role, Technology will contribute not only to information and communication technologies, but also to students' effective and efficient thinking (Mumtaz, 2000).

The individualization of learning has made the interaction between people and computers compulsory. However, the fact that this individualization is not realized through face-to-face interaction leads to a number of disadvantages, including low interaction between individuals and insufficient feedback (Falowo, 2007; Li, 2009), disappointment in students due to the unsatisfied expectations (Falowo, 2007; Galusha, 1997) and the design of students exercise materials without taking students' needs into consideration (Falowo, 2007). Educational environments should be supported with specific teaching strategies and new technologies appropriate to the curriculum which motivate students, draw their attention and enable them to actively participate in order to eliminate such disadvantages (Hobbs, 1998; Brown, 2006). New technologies allow educational programs and course content to be always accessible and to be reviewed by forming a basis for multi-learning settings. These settings are also interactive environment where students can test themselves through individual tests, receive feedback rapidly, increase their motivation and ensure permanent education thanks to new technologies that support education. Remedial adjustments can also be made for educational environment in line with online measurement and assessment systems and feedback.

The increase in technology in general, facilitate students' adaptation to the developing technologies of the century and turn themselves into productive individuals. Students' gains include experience, analytical thinking, establishing cause and effect relationships, and teamwork. Teachers and students will directly be supported to be innovative; and indirectly, their entrepreneurial abilities will be enhanced. New technology also make contributions such as improving students' reasoning skills, increasing their abilities for independent thinking, decision-making, putting thoughts into action, supporting mental readiness, and increasing their concentration time (Best, 2016). In particular, technology has positive effects such as introduction to mathematical and geometrical thinking, three-dimensional design and imagination, because they allow concretizing abstract situations in education (Danesi, 2016).

With technology accepted in education and training environments, teachers and students have made attempts to learn how to use technology, and the use of technology has become regarded as an objective. As these technologies assume a larger place in life and, among them most importantly perhaps the Internet, have become widespread, people have started to use technology to learn and technology has begun to be used as a tool (Johannesen, Øgrim, & Giæver, 2014). Technology has been assigned with more roles in line with the needs and expectations of the natives of the digital era. Furthermore, the introduction of alternative learning environments has initiated the process of transformative learning with technology (Ledford, 2016).

The curricula should be integrated with the appropriate content for curricula standards and the learning environment to integrate information and communication technologies with education environments, as well as its successful use (Plomp, Anderson & Kontogiannopoulou-Polydorides, 1996). Current standards, evaluations, teaching, professional development, and learning environments should be updated in line with the needs of the students who belong to today's generation and in relation to 21st century skills. The Partnership For 21st Century Skills (P21) determined these skills to be innovation skills, media and technology skills, and life and career skills. To acquire these 21st century skills, basic information should be acquired through fundamental subjects (such as English, reading or language arts, world languages, arts, mathematics, economics, science, geography, history, and government and civics).

P21 defines the learning and innovation skills as those that distinguish students from each other. The organization emphasizes the students' focus on creativity, critical thinking, communication, and cooperation. Considering the current importance of access to information, rapid change of technological devices and cooperation as we live surrounded by technology and media, people should effectively use and evaluate these skills to acquire information media and technology skills. Information, media and information, and communication technology literacy should therefore be addressed. In addition, the importance of life and career skills is also emphasized for the development of students' thinking abilities and social and emotional competence. P21 states that life and career skills include characteristics such as flexibility and adaptability, initiative and self-direction, social and cross-cultural skills, productivity and accountability, and leadership and responsibility. Figure 1 represents the relationship between the learning framework of the 21th century and innovative learning technologies.

Innovative learning technologies (wearable technology, kinect, the brain–computer interface, mobile devices, for example) should be used as tools to access information, as well as for use and communication of information in this century in which information is undergoing a rapid expansion. Then, effectively accessing correct information, critically evaluating that information, and adopting ethical approaches on the uses of information can be included within the scope of information and media literacy. Innovative learning technologies can be a part of teaching about information media and technology skills.

Innovative learning technologies are known to affect communication and cooperation, problem-solving skills, and creativity. It can be concluded that having information, media, and technology skills directly affect learning and innovation skills. Students are expected to prefer and use appropriate innovative technologies to solve their problem (Bates, 1995), to generate original products, to think critically about these products, and to share these products with others (Ellsworth, 1994). Outputs of innovative technologies match the variables of learning and innovation skills.

Figure 1. Relationship between the learning framework of the 21th century and innovative learning technologies

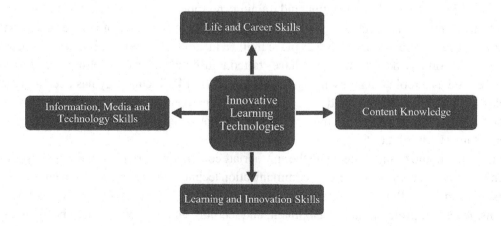

They also affect the variables of life and career skills. Innovative technologies can be used to easily adapt to the technology suitable for the digital age under the flexibility and adaptability variable, to turn toward the learning environments appropriate for people's own needs under the initiative and self-direction variable, to work productively and concertedly with others under the social and cross-cultural variable, to determine objectives and progress in line with these objectives under the productivity and accountability variable, and to use problem solving skills within the scope of aiming at the objectives under the leadership and responsibility variable.

It has been stated that traditional methods and strategies are insufficient to fertilize teaching, and these methods and strategies can be more successful when they are supported by technology (Timmerman, 2000). Students should be taken out from a passive environment by involving innovative technologies in line with the 21th century skills around the fundamental subjects and by re-structuring the standards and assessments, curricula and instruction, professional development, and learning environment; and their cognitive and metacognitive mechanisms should be stimulated. The inclusion of technology in the teaching and learning process has highlighted the concept of media literacy even more. The students are required to have twenty-first century skills, and they aim to have secure and accurate information to access all kinds of information in the media. The innovative technologies that provide unlimited information resources and new instruction methods in information sharing enable teachers and students to access a variety of resources (Atav, Akkoyunlu and Sağlam, 2006). It is necessary to make direct use of the skills included in The 21st Century Student Outcomes & Support Systems (e.g., critical thinking, communication, collaboration and creativity) for the selection of this information. In this context, Figure 2 shows the expansion of media literacy based on the frequency of using innovative technologies.

As Figure 2 shows, the mutuality of information exchange in mobile devices, smart glasses and smart watches within information literacy has popularized these technologies. Regarding technology literacy, these technologies are used more commonly since they have mobile and web support. Regarding media literacy, mobile devices, smart glasses and smart watches are commonly used since they stimulate multiple senses with written and visual features.

These innovative learning technologies has brought with it online learning and blended classrooms (Murphy, Walker & Webb, 2013), project-based activities technology (Istance & Kools, 2013), game-

Figure 2. The relation between technology and information, technology and media literacy

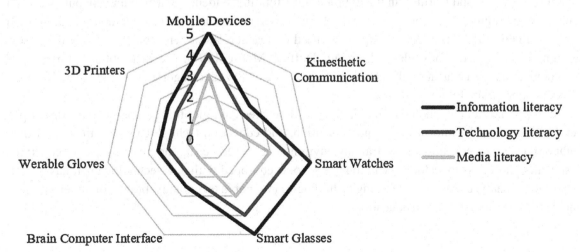

based learning and assessment (Jan, Tan & Chen, 2015), learning with mobile and handheld devices (Liu, Kuo, Shi & Chen, 2015), instructional tools like human-computer interaction (Rogers, 2014) such as RGB-D cameras, brain computer interfaces, wearable technology and kinesthetic communication systems, web-based projects, explorations, and research student-created media, and collaborative online tools to engage students in the learning process. The technologies that are on trial and that have not entirely been integrated with educational and training environments are addressed in the present section, particularly based on innovative equipment. It is important to provide the literacy-level information about a technology before it is integrated in education and training environment (Woodard, 2003).

INNOVATIVE LEARNING TECHNOLOGIES

Easy and rapid access to information in education has become more significant in the present era. Timely and appropriate use of technology by following innovations has become a determining factor for increasing the quality of education. While Hew & Brush (2007) regarded the integration of technology as the use of all kinds of technology to increase students' success in classes; Lim, Teo, Wong, Khine, Chai, & Divaharan (2003) stated that the integration of technology into schools improved students' critical and creative thinking skills.

However, integrating technology with schools alone will be insufficient to increase the quality of education. Brush et al. (2003) stated that although schools have technological tools, teachers very rarely or never use computers in teaching processes. It is important to understand for which purposes information and communication technologies will be used, then select them accordingly, and blend the appropriate teaching and evaluation techniques into education and training processes (Roblyer, 2006; Haşlaman, Mumcu & Usluel 2008). Educational and training environments should be updated to align with the needs of today's students and the skills required in the 21st century. In addition, the 2016 International Society for Technology in Education (ISTE, 2016) standards can be adopted to provide an innovative support system for students and improve their abilities.

Teachers play a primary role in the use of technology in educational institutions and should be trained in accordance with these standards. The ISTE states that teachers should have skills appropriate to the digital era such as designing and developing learning environments, evaluating activities, providing a model for working and learning in the digital era, facilitating students' learning and encouraging their creativity, attending professional development and leadership events, and being a model in digital citizenship (ISTE, 2016). The learning approach used by teachers along with the technology they use in teaching is also a model for students (Lambdin, Duffy & Moore, 1997). The 21st century informational, communication, and educational technologies should be analyzed, categorized, and evaluated in terms of being appropriate for teachers' use.

Teachers and students should be taught the use of new technologies that comply with the developing century, based on the information, communication, and education technologies; and the use of these technologies in the educational and training environment should be supported. Considering generation Z students' closeness to technology in today's schools equipped with new technologies, it has become important to analyze innovative learning technologies (wearable technology, brain–computer interface, and others) and to use them in education.

Wearable Technology Supports Literacy

Wearable technology is defined as devices such as smart watches, smart glasses, or data gloves that users can wear or carry on them, or other devices such as personal computers that can assume the form of clothing items (Conheady, 2014). However, wearable technologies are not limited to hardware: many types of sensors have been developed, which use optics, light, vibration, magnetics, shakes, pressure, power, temperature, chemicals, electricity, and location. These sensors can be transferred to a computer environment through wearable technologies and yield meaningful results (Buğra Kuzu & Demir, 2015). Wearable technology also includes portable, light, and flexible smart devices equipped with sensors that can follow an individual's movements (Pantelopoulos & Bourbakis, 2010). In addition, wearable technology devices allow users free movement and fast and easy access to digital technology, as well as providing time and energy savings (Liu, 2014).

These sensitive technological devices that positively affect human-computer interaction allow easy formation of user data (Amore, 2002). These devices also provide continuous access to various opportunities for information and access (Caon, Tagliabue, Angelini, Perego, Mugellini & Andreoni, 2014). Technology users can safely share their recorded information with others and easily access other people's information through e-mails or blogs, for instance.

Wearable technology, one form of the media, provides its users with a new communication experience. Users have started to be interested in wearable technology and want to have it as a part of their life. This is important for the use of wearable technologies in education. With wearable technologies, a digital interface has been integrated into the conventional structure, aiming to increase the effectiveness of these technologies by analyzing and developing them along with supportive hardware (Vallurupalli, Paydak, Agarwal, Agrawal & Assad-Kottner, 2013).

Currently, people tend toward to wearable technology increasingly more than to portable technology. Because these devices enable information-retrieval processes, such as monitoring physical functions and obtaining biological data, and provide sensor data, using atypical methods compared with devices such as laptops. Generally, wearable technology allows various types of communication, real-time access to information, and storage of information in an internal memory (Seymour, 2008).

Published studies indicate that wearable technologies are preferred by most 21st century learners—in other words, digitally native people who have been born into new technologies and rapidly adopt these technologies (Prensky, 2001). Used in educational environments, these new technologies can facilitate an understanding of the course content by providing supportive materials, thereby enriching the educational environment and reinforcing learning. In addition, wearable technologies can also be used to evaluate learners and providing feedback to them (Buğra Kuzu & Demir, 2015). Only a limited number of studies exist in the literature which examine the use of wearable technologies in education. Yamauchi & Nakasugi (2003) used smart glasses to allow students to see the former (historical) state of a certain region on the smart glasses screen at the same time as they saw the present state of that region on a map. That provided students the opportunity to feel the historic fabric and the sense of history regarding the region being studied. Wu, Dameff & Tully (2014) used smart glasses to prioritize individual experience and to increase empathy in medical education. In the study by Coffman & Klinger (2015), teachers and students used smart glasses to deepen their intellectual interaction with events and to enhance their communication the individuals in the scenario within the scope of the course. In addition, teachers conveyed the images and videos of the events and activities in the scenario at the end of the learning activity, which allowed them to evaluate the course by accessing these records on the Internet.

Smart Watches Supports Literacy

Thanks to smart watches, users always carry the information they want to access on their wrists (Johnson, 2014). These devices operate in connection with smart phones; however, their interaction is simpler and faster compared with smart phones because they are much more accessible on the wrist (Giang, Hoekstra-Atwood & Dönmez, 2014; Forlett, 2014). Students are reminded of course tasks and activities that need to be completed, such as homework and projects, via their smart watch (Yetik & Keskin, 2016). In addition, the hardware of smart watches is enhanced by many sensors that can obtain biological data.

Smart Glasses Supports Literacy

Wearable technology is an interactive interface located on a person's body that has an electronic design basis (Mann, 1997). Smart glasses are wearable technology, bringing the concept of eye-wearable technology into the literature. Although the development of the smart glasses by some companies has been interrupted (Elder & Vakaloudis, 2015), researchers have developed specific hardware to analyze different applications for this technology and to use different sensors. Stated simply, these technologies allow users to perform some commands and processes via an interface. These commands and processes include document transfer, communication, document preparation (Mehdi & Alharby, 2016), rotation of an object around a certain axis, and confirmation and cancellation of a command (Lv, Feng, Feng & Li, 2015). These devices establish a connection between the interface and the computer via Wi-Fi, and can connect to smart phones via a Bluetooth connection. The most significant disadvantage of smart glasses is that users cannot perform touch interactions. Therefore, researchers have tried to find solutions using alternative hardware, including cameras, gloves and wristlets, to allow users to perform touch interactions. Each of these technologies can be used in different ways and are supported by different sensors. Brancati, Caggianese, Frucci, Gallo & Neroni (2015) integrated a RGB+D depth- and color-distinguishing camera into smart glasses and turned users' movements into commands by analyzing their hand gestures and finger locations. The movements then pass to the smart glasses as commands. Although their shapes and functions vary, these hardware types can perceive an individuals' actions, locations, or preferences; these hardware types have been used in virtual reality and augmented reality technologies.

The study by Hicks (2013) also created an environment with smart glasses that enabled students to make a quick review during the lesson by accessing videos on Google+ and have more unique class experiences. Similarly, Schweizer (2014) suggested that students could learn history not only from textbooks, but also by interacting in a three dimensional virtual world where they can navigate freely.

Wearable Gloves Supports Literacy

Wearable gloves are input devices that provide data input to computers via hand gestures and certain hand positions. Hong & Tan (1989) first developed a glove using electronic hardware (fiber guide, optical fiber) and analyzed finger movements. Kadous (1996) supported a wearable glove with more dynamic sensors (gesture sensor, ultrasonic sensor) and a mini-keyboard. Wearable gloves have been developed to detect actions such as brushing teeth, running at a slow pace, standing, wandering, climbing up and down the stairs, and writing on the blackboard, and are integrated into Wi-Fi, Bluetooth, NFC, and RFID communication technologies (Riboni & Bettini, 2011).

Kinesthetic Communication Supports Literacy

The use of educational materials and practices has visibly increased with the rapid development of digital technology, including changes in technologies that convey human gestures to digital environments (Johnson, Smith, Willis, Levine & Haywood, 2011). Kinesthetic technology, which creates an effective environment by enabling students to physically participate in education through movements, does not demand any additional contact. The RGB-D camera on these devices consists of the main components of three-dimensional infrared (IR) sensors, microphones for audio perception, and a motor mechanism that enables the devices to move (Khoshelham, 2011). These technologies are also responsible for a major contribution to the effectiveness of virtual reality.

Movement-based processes rely on controlling computer-aided structures via perception of body movements, mainly detecting movements by sensors and cameras. Kinesthetic devices first begin to ray IR radiation to determine whether there is any human within the field of view. Then, if a human is detected, depth detection is initiated to perceive the information of depth regarding the human and then movement identification process starts. Finally, the devices transfer to the system the patterns that match up with the human movement patterns recorded in the device memory (Jung & Cha, 2010).

Analyses of the application of kinesthetic technology in education reveal that physical applications also create positive effects in education, as well as visual and auditory methods. They increase in-class interaction and stimulate students' creativity (Hui-mei, 2011). This technology has a positive effect on teaching letters during reading and writing learning (Tenekeci, Gümüşçü & Ağırman, 2014), it increases in-class motivation in foreign language teaching (Şahinler-Albayrak, 2015), and provides an entertaining, interactive, and interesting learning experience thanks to physically interactive books (Ayala, Mendívil, Salinas & Rios, 2013).

Brain Computer Interface Supports Literacy

A brain–computer interface (BCI) allows users to communicate and control without connecting to the normal output channels of peripheral nerves and muscles in brain. Considering that everyone deserves equal opportunity, these devices can help individuals who cannot use their motor muscles to move freely, to travel and to control devices. Paralyzed people can perform simple actions—such as turning on and off the lights, television, and other devices—via a BCI (Tiwari & Saini, 2015).

A BCI records mental activity as low-voltage signals and records the brain waves as alpha, beta, and gamma waves. A BCI can be used together with low-cost devices having a biosensor that is used to collect electroencephalographic signals from the surface of the scalp and send them to a computer or to any mobile device connected via Bluetooth technology (Gandyer, Krishnamurthy & Venkatesan, 2015).

In educational environments, BCI technologies are used for self-regulation, learning skills, and cognitive therapeutic or emotional regulation. These technologies can also be used to create and support online laboratories and intelligent tutoring systems (Serrhini, 2015).

Mobile Devices Supports Literacy

Intense use of mobile technologies in daily life and presentation of learning content in a portable form have introduced the concept of mobile learning. Georgieva, Smrikarov & Georgiev (2005) define mobile learning as the use of portable devices that provide the opportunity to access learning materials everywhere and allow the interaction between teachers and students in the educational process.

The most commonly used mobile communication technologies in education are smart cell phones, laptops, tablets, and personal digital assistants. Smart phones, one of the mobile devices most used by students, can be used in education since they provide access to academic papers, digital libraries, all kinds of publications, videos, various sources of information, and lecture notes (Pan & Akay, 2016).

The literature indicates that students consider mobile devices facilitate communication and provide an cooperative environment (Anderson, Franklin, Yinger, Sun & Geist, 2013); that mobile devices are more effective than books in submitting contents (Evans, 2008); that students' academic success and attitudes towards courses improve thanks to mobile learning (Martin & Ertzberger, 2013); that students' curiosity arise with effective use of mobile devices (Çelik, 2012); that mobile devices enable students to feel more confident and make learning more permanent (Ozan, 2013); and that mobile devices make learning of abstract and technical subjects easier and entertaining (Köse, Koç & Yücesoy, 2013)

3D Printer Supports Literacy

Three-dimensional printing is the process of producing three-dimensional solid objects from three-dimensional files prepared in a digital environment (CAD drawings): the machines that carry out these processes are three-dimensional printers that allow the user to obtain, analyze, and turn three dimensional models into three dimensional objects. The three-dimensional objects are created by slicing and layering three-dimensional models and printing them as they overlap using a three-dimensional printer and material melted during the printing process. Three-dimensional printer technologies use the technique to accumulate layers one on the top of the other; however, different methods can be used to create these layers. The most commonly known method is to melt plastic material and then stack the layers to form solid objects (Kruth, Leu, & Nakagawa, 1998). Reverse engineering can also be applied using three-dimensional printers (Singare at all, 2009) to re-model the connectors produced using conventional methods. All known CAD programs are compatible with three-dimensional printers. Users need only save the model designed in any CAD program in stereolithography (STL) format and load it into the three-dimensional printer control program (Qu and Stucker, 2003).

Matrixing has been made to determine which innovative technologies are used with the 21st century skills and guide the readers as well as the future studies to be conducted on the development of media and other types of literacy. Also, the technologies that are currently used in classrooms or regarded necessary to be used in the future have been determined in context of learning and innovation skills. Table 1 shows the matrixing process of the relationship between the 21st century and the innovative learning technologies which prioritize the human-computer interactions.

Table 1 shows that smart watches and glasses, two wearable technology products, are more popular in education than gloves. Similarly, Kinect technology, which is capable of perceiving human movements, is more common in education than the BrainWave Headset or 3D printers. Mobile technology, which is as common in education as it is in other environments, is most commonly used in Android- and IOS-based forms.

Table 1. Matrixing process of the relationship between the 21st century and the innovative learning technologies

21st Century Student Outcomes and Support Systems		Wearable Technology			Kinesthetic	Brain Computer Interface	Additive Manufacturing	Mobile Technology
		Smart Watches	Smart Glasses	Gloves	Kinect (One/360)	BrainWave Headset	3D Printer	
Information, Media, and Technology Skills	Information Literacy	✓	✓	✓	●	✓	✓	●
	Media Literacy	●	●	✓	●	✓	✓	●
	Technology Literacy	✓	✓	✓	●	✓	✓	●
Learning and Innovation Skills	Critical Thinking	●	✓	✓	●	●	●	●
	Communication	●	✓	✓	✓	●	✓	✓
	Collaboration	✓	●	✓	✓	✓	✓	●
	Creativity	●	✓	✓	●	●	●	●
Life and Career Skills	Flexibility & Adaptability	✓	✓	✓	✓	✓	✓	✓
	Initiative & Self Direction	●	✓	✓	●	●	✓	●
	Social & Cross Cultural Skills	●	✓	✓	●	✓	✓	●
	Productivity & Accountability	✓	✓	✓	✓	✓	●	●
	Leadership & Responsibility	✓	✓	✓	✓	✓	✓	●

● Current used technologies
✓ Recommend for future studies

SOLUTIONS AND RECOMMENDATIONS

The entrance of rapidly-developing technology into education has made media literacy more important. The skills of the twenty-first century should be used as guidelines for teaching students to be capable of accurately reading messages that are intended to be given through media literacy, and analyze these messages as well. In accordance with these skills, the use of innovative technologies in learning environments will make the intended message more various and improve effective and productive learning. In this context, smart glasses and watches will make it possible to view lesson content in three dimensional videos and to send posts. Smart gloves will create learning environments for the disabled, and Kinect technology will integrate educational games into the environment without the need for a keyboard or mouse. The brain-computer interface will enable communication and control without connecting to the normal exit channels in the brain. Students will be able to design their own learning objects using 3D printers, and mobile technologies will make learning materials accessible anywhere. With these new technologies, the things that are realized and that are planned to be realized are limited only by the imagination. The expectation from teachers and learners is to shape these technologies with the guidance of the twenty-first century skills.

Being literate in the 21st centuries requires the ability to organize, analyze, and access information using technology. As time has passed, the International Society for Technology in Education (ISTE) has kept pace with this change by updating the National Educational Technology Standards for Students (NETS). The student standards are categorized in 2016 as empowered learner, digital citizen, knowledge constructor, innovative designer, computational thinker, creative communicator, and global collaborator. Individuals should now use the technological tools appropriate for the requirements of the present era and acquire the necessary skills. To achieve this, they should follow the media to find the current technologies and learn how to use them. They should shape their daily life and educational environment in line with these technologies so that their current community can become a producer community.

FUTURE RESEARCH DIRECTIONS

A technologically literate person questions technological processes and innovations from a critical perspective. Individuals can affect their environment and shape their future by that questioning. It is mostly the teacher's responsibility to inspire students to become questioning individuals, and at this point, the teacher's role is associated with 21st century skills.

Using the Internet and software, students can carry out their cooperative works through accessing interactive environments, analyzing problems, finding solutions, and then evaluate the strategies they develop. The technologies explained in this section will play important roles in teaching and learning activities, and particularly with the development of internet technology (Web 3.0 and Web 4.0). Thereby, in-class and out-of-class activities can be richer and can meet the desires and expectations of the individual.

Today, developed countries are the countries that produce and effectively use technology. In this regard, it is suggested that developing countries such as Turkey should produce their own technologies to reach the level of the developed countries (Yıldız, Ilgaz and Seferoğlu, 2010).

An aim of education, then, is to provide students with the 21st century skills and help them to become literate individuals through use of these skills. More focus should be placed on teaching the teachers and students how to design an educational environment appropriate for the 21st century skills and how to support that environment, as well as innovative technologies.

CONCLUSION

Today, the social use of communication tools such as newspaper and radio has been enriched with new media tools that provide more active communication (e.g., wearable technologies and mobile devices) with the development of the digital age. Technology is the most important factor that has led to the increased use of these new media tools by communities. Individuals play a faster, more active, and interactive role using these new tools. Therefore, people should be aware of innovative technologies to be able to access information easily and in different ways; further, they should integrate these technologies with education in 21st century skills for the developments of technologically literate individuals.

With innovative technologies, individuals will create an environment that meets their needs and expectations using alternative communication tools in their daily life and the education environment. Thereby, they can create new learning environments appropriate for individual differences, accurately perceive information, observe from a critical perspective, integrate their own ideas, and evaluate and properly use information, which in turn provides them with the skills necessary in the 21st century. They can shape their own way of learning and structure the information they receive. Because media literacy is based on sending an accurate message to the appropriate target, innovative learning technologies are expected to accelerate and to make this process more proactive.

ACKNOWLEDGMENT

This chapter was supported by the Scientific Research Projects of Giresun University (EĞT-BAP-A-140316-105).

REFERENCES

Akkoyunlu, B. (1996). The influence of computer literacy competencies and existing curriculum programs on student achievement and attitudes. *Hacettepe University Education Faculty Journal, 12*(12), 127–134.

Amore, D. (2002). *Internet future strategies: How pervasive computing services will change the World. Amerika*. Prentice Hall.

Anderson, J., Franklin, T., Yinger, N., Sun, Y., & Geist, G. (2013, September). Going mobile, lessons learned from introducing tablet pcs into the business classroom. In *Proceedings of the Clute Institute International Academic Conference*, Las Vegas, NV.

Atav, E., Akkoyunlu, B., & Sağlam, N. (2006). Prospective teachers' internet access facilities and their internet usage. *Hacettepe University Education Faculty Journal, 30*, 37–44.

Ayala, N. A. R., Mendívil, E. G., Salinas, P., & Rios, H. (2013). Kinesthetic learning applied to mathematics using kinect. *Procedia Computer Science, 25*, 131–135. doi:10.1016/j.procs.2013.11.016

Bates, A. (1995). *Technology, open learning and distance education*. London: Routledge.

Behrens, S. J. (1994). A conceptual analysis and historical overview of information literacy. *College & Research Libraries, 55*(4), 309–322. doi:10.5860/crl_55_04_309

Best, R. A. (2016). An online statistics course from faculty and students' perspectives: A case study, Unpublished doctoral dissertation, University of Walden, United States of America.

Birbaumer, N., Ruiz, S., & Sitaram, R. (2013). Learned regulation of brain metabolism. *Trends in Cognitive Sciences, 17*(6), 295–302. doi:10.1016/j.tics.2013.04.009 PMID:23664452

Brancati, N., Caggianese, G., Frucci, M., Gallo, L., & Neroni, P. (2015). In Intelligent Interactive Multimedia Systems and Services. In E. Damiani, R. Howlett, C. Jain et al. (Eds.), Touchless target selection techniques for wearable augmented reality systems (pp. 1-9). Switzerland: Springer International Publishing.

Brown, J. D. (2006). Media Literacy has Potential to Improve Adolescents Health. *The Journal of Adolescent Health*, *39*(4), 459–460. doi:10.1016/j.jadohealth.2006.07.014 PMID:16982377

Bruce, C. S. (1999). Workplace experiences in information literacy. *International Journal of Information Management*, *19*(1), 33–47. doi:10.1016/S0268-4012(98)00045-0

Brush, T., Glazewski, K., Rutowski, K., Berg, K., Stromfors, C., & Van-Nest, M. et al.. (2003). Integrating technology in a field-based teacher training program: The PT3@ASU Project. *Educational Technology Research and Development*, *51*(2), 57–72. doi:10.1007/BF02504518

Buckingham, D. (2003). Digital literacies: Media education and new media Technologies. In K. Tyner & B. Duncan (Eds.), *Visions/Revisions: Moving forward with media education* (pp. 3–11). Madison, Wisconsin: National Telemedia Council.

Bulunmaz, B. (2011). Otomotiv sektöründe sosyal medyanın kullanımı ve Fiat örneği. *Yeditepe Üniversitesi Global Media Journal*, *2*(3), 19–50.

Çakır, H., & Koçer, M. ve Aydın, H. (2012). Medya okuryazarlığı dersini alan ve almayan ilköğretim öğrencilerinin medya izleme davranışlarındaki farklılıkların belirlenmesi. *Selçuk İletişim Dergisi*, *7*(3), 42–54.

Canbaz, N. (2010). Analysing the technology literacy education needs of female trainees who attend the adult education courses. Unpublished Master Thesis, Çanakkale Onsekiz Mart University, Çanakkale.

Caon, M., Tagliabue, M., Angelini, L., Perego, P., Mugellini, E., & Andreoni, G. (2014, September). Wearable technologies for automotive user interfaces: Danger or opportunity. *Paper presented at 6th International Conference on Automotive User Interfaces and Interactive Vehicular Applications*, Seattle, WA, USA. doi:10.1145/2667239.2667314

Carbonara, D. D. (Ed.). (2005). *Technology literacy applications in learning environments*. Hersey, NJ: IGI Global. doi:10.4018/978-1-59140-479-8

Çelik, A. (2012) The effect of QR code assisted mobile learning environment on productive vocabulary learning in foreign language studies and student reviews: The example of Mobile Dictionary. Unpublished Master Thesis, Gazi University, Institute of Educational Sciences, Ankara.

Childers, S. (2003). Computer literacy: Necessity or buzzword? *Information Technology and Libraries*, *22*(3), 100–105.

Coffman, T., & Klinger, M. B. (2015, March). Google Glass: Using wearable technologies to enhance teaching and learning. *Paper presented at the Society for Information Technology & Teacher Education International Conference*, Las Vegas, NV.

Coiro, J., Knobel, M., Lankshear, C., & Leu, D. J. (Eds.). (2014). *Handbook of research on new literacies*. Routledge.

Conheady, S. (2014). Social engineering in IT security: Tools, tactics, and techniques. Toronto: McGraw-Hill Education.

Danesi, M. (2016). Technology, Society, and Education. In Learning and Teaching Mathematics in The Global Village (pp. 37-73). Springer International Publishing. doi:10.1007/978-3-319-32280-3_2

Doyle, C. S. (1994). *Information literacy in an information society: A concept for the information age.* New York: Diane Publishing.

Elder, S., & Vakaloudis, A. (2015). A technical evaluation of devices for smart glasses applications. Internet Technologies and Applications, 5, 98-103. doi:10.1109/ITechA.2015.7317377

Ellsworth, J. H. (1994). *Education on the internet.* Indianapolis: Sams Publishing.

Eppler, M. J., & Mengis, J. (2004). The concept of information overload: A review of literature from organization science, accounting, marketing, MIS, and related disciplines. *The Information Society, 20*(5), 325–344. doi:10.1080/01972240490507974

Erbaş, Ç., & Demirer, V. (2014). Augmented reality practices in education: Google Glass example. *Journal of Instructional Technologies & Teacher Education, 3*(2), 8–16.

Evans, C. (2008). The effectiveness of m-learning in the form of podcast revision lectures in higher education. *Computers & Education, 50*(2), 491–498. doi:10.1016/j.compedu.2007.09.016

Falowo, R. O. (2007). Factors impeding implementation of web-based distance learning. *AACE Journal, 15*(3), 315–338.

Follett, J. (2014). Fashion with function: Designing for wearables. Designing for emerging technologies. Retrieved from http://www.safaribooksonline.com/library/view/designing-for-emerging/9781449370626/ch01.html

Galusha, J. M. (1997). Barriers to learning in distance education. *Interpersonel Computing and Technology: An Electronic Journal of the 21st Century, 5*(3-4), 6-14.

Gandyer, V. S., Krishnamurthy, M., & Venkatesan, S. (2015, July). *Brain painter: a novel p300-based brain computer interface application for locked-in-syndrome victims.* In *Proceedings of the International Conference on Information Technology and Computer Science* (pp. 88-93).

Georgieva, E., Smrikarov, A., & Georgiev, T. (2005). A general classification of mobile learning systems. *Paper presented at the International Conference on Computer Systems and Technologies*, Varna, Bulgaristan.

Giang, W. C., Hoekstra-Atwood, L., & Donmez, B. (2014). Driver engagement in notifications a comparison of visual-manual interaction between smartwatches and smartphones. *Proceedings of the Human Factors and Ergonomics Society Annual Meeting, 58*(1), 2161-2165.

Haslaman, T., Kuskaya-Mumcu, F., & Kocak-Usluel, Y. (2008). *Integration of ICT Into The Teaching-Learning Process: Toward A Unified Model.* In J. Luca & E. Weippl (Eds.), *Proceedings of World Conference on Educational Multimedia, Hypermedia and Telecommunications 2008* (pp. 2384-2389). Chesapeake, VA: AACE.

Heath, P. (1990). Teaching about Science, Technology, and Society in Social Studies: Education for Citizenship in the 21st Century. *Social Education, 54*(4), 189–193.

Hew, K. F., & Brush, T. (2007). Integrating technology into K-12 teaching and learning: Current knowledge gaps and recommendations for future research. *Educational Technology Research and Development, 55*(3), 223–252. doi:10.1007/s11423-006-9022-5

Hicks, K. (2013). How Google glass can help students make better music. Retrieved from http://edcetera. rafter.com/how-google-glass-can-help-students-make-better-music/

Hobbs, R. (1998). Teaching with and about film and television: Integrating media literacy concepts into management education. *Journal of Management Development, 17*(4), 259–272. doi:10.1108/02621719810210136

Holt, D., Smissen, I., & Segrave, S. (2006, January). New students, new learning, new environments in higher education: Literacies in the digital age. In Who's learning? Whose technology?: *In Proceedings of the 23rd annual conference of the Australasian Society for Computers in Learning in Tertiary Education*, University of Sydney, Sydney, Australia (pp. 327-337). Sydney University Press.

Hong, J., & Tan, X. (1989, May). Calibrating a VPL DataGlove for teleoperating the Utah/MIT hand. In Robotics and Automation. In *Proceedings of 1989 IEEE International Conference* (pp. 1752-1757). IEEE.

Hui-mei, J. H. (2011, July). The Potential of Kinect as Interactive Educational Technology. In *Paper presented at 2nd International Conference on Education and Management Technology*, Singapur.

İnceoğlu, Y. (2006). *Reading the media correctly. I. International Media Literacy*. İstanbul: Marmara University Faculty of Communication Conference Texts.

International Society for Technology in Education. (2016). Retrieved from http://www.iste.org/standards

Istance, D., & Kools, M. (2013). OECD Work on Technology and Education: Innovative learning environments as an integrating framework. *European Journal of Education, 48*(1), 43–57. doi:10.1111/ejed.12017

Jan, M., Tan, E. M., & Chen, V. (2015). Issues and Challenges of Enacting Game-Based Learning in Schools. In T. Lin, V. Chen, & C. Chai (Eds.), *New Media and Learning in the 21st Century* (pp. 67–76). Singapore: Springer. doi:10.1007/978-981-287-326-2_5

Johannesen, M., Øgrim, L., & Giæver, T. H. (2014). Notion in motion: Teachers' digital competence. *Nordic Journal of Digital Literacy, 4*, 300–312.

Johnson, K. M. (2014). An investigation into the smart watch interface and the user driven data requirements for its applications. Retrieved from http://www.cs.ru.ac.za/research/g10j6110/Final%20Proposal%20%20K.%20M.%20Johnson.pdf

Johnson, L., Smith, R., Willis, H., Levine, A., & Haywood, K. (2011). *The 2011 Horizon Report, Texas*. Austin: The New Media Consortium.

Jung, Y., & Cha, B. (2010). Gesture recognition based on motion inertial sensors for ubiquitous interactive game Contents. *IETE Technical Review, 27*(2), 158–166. doi:10.4103/0256-4602.60168

Kadous, M. W. (1996, October). Machine recognition of Auslan signs using PowerGloves: Towards large-lexicon recognition of sign language. In *Proceedings of the Workshop on the Integration of Gesture in Language and Speech* (pp. 165-174).

Karataş, A. (2008). Media literacy levels of the candidate teachers. Unpublished Master Thesis, Afyon Kocatepe University, Social Sciences Institute, Afyon.

Kellner, D., & Share, J. (2005). Toward Critical Media Literacy: Core Concepts, Debates, Organizations, And Policy. *Discourse (Abingdon)*, *26*(3), 369–386. doi:10.1080/01596300500200169

Khoshelham, K. (2011). Accuracy Analysis Of Kinect Depth Data. In *ITC Faculty of Geo-information Science and Earth Observation*. Netherlands: University of Twente.

Knight, D. K., & Kim, E. Y. (2007). Japanese Consumers need for Uniqueness – Effects on Brand Perceptions and Intention. *Journal of Fashion Marketing and Management*, *11*(2), 270–280. doi:10.1108/13612020710751428

Koc, M., & Barut, E. (2016). Development and validation of New Media Literacy Scale (NMLS) for university students. *Computers in Human Behavior*, *63*, 834–843. doi:10.1016/j.chb.2016.06.035

Köse, U., Koç, D., & Yücesoy, S. A. (2013). An augmented reality based mobile software to support learning experiences in computer science courses. *Procedia Computer Science*, *25*, 370–374. doi:10.1016/j.procs.2013.11.045

Kruth, J. P., Leu, M. C., & Nakagawa, T. (1998). Progress in additive manufacturing and rapid prototyping. *Annals of the CIRP*, *47*(2), 525–540. doi:10.1016/S0007-8506(07)63240-5

Küçükyıldz, G., Ocak, H., Şayli, Ö., & Karakaya, S. (2015). Real Time Control of a WheelChair based on EMG and Kinect for the Disabled People. *Paper presented at National Congress of Medical Technologies*, Türkiye, Bodrum. doi:10.1109/TIPTEKNO.2015.7374606

Kuzu, B. Elif., & Demir, K. (2015). Education technology readings 2015. In B. Akkoyunlu, A. İşman ve F. Odabaşı (Eds.), Wearable technology and its use in education (pp. 252-253), Ankara: Pegem Academy.

Lambdin, D. V., Duffy, T. M., & Moore, J. A. (1997). Using an interactive information system to expand preservice teachers' visions of effective mathematics teaching. *Journal of Technology and Teacher Education*, *5*(2), 171–202.

Ledford, D. M. (2016). Development of a Professional Learning Framework to Improve Teacher Practice in Technology Integration [Doctoral dissertation]. Boise State University.

Leu, D. J., Kinzer, C. K., Coiro, J. L., & Cammack, D. W. (2004). Toward a theory of new literacies emerging from the Internet and other information and communication technologies. *Theoretical models and processes of reading*, *5*(1), 1570-1613.

Li, X. (2009). Review of distance education used in higher education in China. *Asian Journal of Distance Education*, *7*(2), 22–27.

Lim, C. P., Teo, Y. H., Wong, P., Khine, M. S., Chai, C. S., & Divaharan, S. (2003). Creating a conducive learning environment for the effective integration of ICT: Classroom management issues. *Journal of Interactive Learning Research, 14*(4), 405–423.

Liu, G. Z., Kuo, F. R., Shi, Y. R., & Chen, Y. W. (2015). Dedicated design and usability of a context-aware ubiquitous learning environment for developing receptive language skills: A case study. *International Journal of Mobile Learning and Organisation, 9*(1), 49–65. doi:10.1504/IJMLO.2015.069717

Liu, Y. (2014). Tangram race mathematical game: Combining wearable technology and traditional games for enhancing mathematics learning. Unpublished doctoral dissertation, Worcester Polytechnic Institute, Worcester, MA, USA.

Livingstone, S. (2004). Media literacy and the challenge of new Information and communication technologies. *Communication Review, 7*(1), 3–14. doi:10.1080/10714420490280152

Lv, Z., Feng, S., Feng, L., & Li, H. (2015, March). Extending touch-less interaction on vision based wearable device. In *Proceedings of the 2015 IEEE Virtual Reality (VR) conference* (pp. 231-232). IEEE.

Maloney, E. J. (2007). What Web 2.0 can teach us about learning. *The Chronicle of Higher Education, 53*(18), B26.

Mann, S. (1997). Wearable computing: A first step toward personal imaging. *Computer, 30*(2), 25–32. doi:10.1109/2.566147

Markus, M. L., & Robey, D. (1988). Information technology and organizational change: Causal structure in theory and research. *Management Science, 34*(5), 583–598. doi:10.1287/mnsc.34.5.583

Marquez, B. Y., Alanis, A., Lopez, M. A., & Magdaleno-Palencia, J. S. (2012). Sport education based technology: Stress measurement in competence. In *Proceedings of the 2012 International Conference one-Learning and e-Technologies in Education (ICEEE)* (pp. 247– 52). IEEE.

Martin, F., & Ertzberger, J. (2013). Here and now mobile learning: An experimental study on the use of mobile technology. *Computers & Education, 68*, 76–85. doi:10.1016/j.compedu.2013.04.021

Mehdi, M., & Alharby, A. (2016). Purpose, Scope, and Technical Considerations of Wearable Technologies. In J. Holland (Ed.), Wearable Technology and Mobile Innovations for Next-Generation Education. doi:10.4018/978-1-5225-0069-8.ch001

Mumtaz, S. (2000). Factors affecting teachers' use of information and communications technology: a review of the literature. *Journal of information technology for teacher education, 9*(3), 319-342.

Murphy, D., Walker, R., & Webb, G. (2013). *Online learning and teaching with technology: case studies, experience and practice.* Routledge.

Murray, J. (2003). Contemporary literacy: Essential skills for the 21st century. *MultiMedia Schools, 10*(2), 14–18.

Murray, J. (2008). Looking at ICT literacy standards through the Big6™ lens. *Library Media Connection, 26*(7), 38–43.

Nantz, K., & Kemmerer, B. (2005).Technology literacy applications in learning environments. In B. Akkoyunlu, & D. D. Carbonara (Eds.), Understanding the Role of Type Preferences in Fostering Technological Literacy (s.107-108), United States of America: Idea Group.

Neill, M. J. (1977). Some thoughts on reasons, definitions and tasks to achieve functional computer literacy. *SIGCSE Bulletin, 9*(1), 175–177. doi:10.1145/382063.803386

Oblinger, D., & Oblinger, J. (2005). Is it age or IT: First steps toward understanding the net generation. *Educating the net generation, 2*(1–2), 20.

Odabaşı, H. F. (2000, May). Social Impact and Technology Literacy. *Paper presented at Education Conference In light of Information Technology (BITE 2000).* Middle East Technical University, Ankara.

Ozan, O. (2013). Scaffolding in connectivist mobile learning environment. Unpublished Master Thesis, Anadolu University, Social Sciences Institute, Eskişehir.

Pan, V. L., & Akay, C. (2016). Prospective teachers' and instructors' opinion on mobile communication technology use for anywhere any time lear. Mustafa Kemal University Journal of Graduate School of Social Sciences, 13(34).

Pantelopoulos, A., & Bourbakis, N. G. (2010). A survey on wearable sensor-based systems for health monitoring and prognosis. *IEEE Transactions on Systems, Man and Cybernetics. Part C, Applications and Reviews, 40*(1), 1–12. doi:10.1109/TSMCC.2009.2032660

Partnership For 21st Century Skills, (P21). Framework For 21st Century Learning. Retrieved from http://www.p21.org/about-us/p21-framework

Plomp, T., Anderson, R. E., & Kontogiannopoulou-Polydorides, G. (Eds.). (1996). *Cross national policies and practices on computers in education.* The Netherlands: Kluwer Academic Publishers. doi:10.1007/978-0-585-32767-9

Potter, J. (2005). Media Literacy (3rd ed.). USA: Sage Pub.

Prensky, M. (2001). Digital natives, digital immigrants. *On the Horizon, 9*(5), 1–6. doi:10.1108/10748120110424816

Qu, X., & Stucker, B. (2003). A 3D surface offset method for STL-format models. *Rapid Prototyping Journal, 9*(3), 133–141. doi:10.1108/13552540310477436

Riboni, D., & Bettini, C. (2011). Hybrid reasoning for context-aware activity recognition. *Personal and Ubiquitous Computing, 15*(3), 271–289. doi:10.1007/s00779-010-0331-7

Roblyer, M. D. (2006). *Integrating educational technology into teaching* (5th ed.). Upper Saddle River, NJ: Pearson Merrill Prentice Hall.

Rogers, Y. (2014, June). New technology, new learning? *In Proceedings of the 2014 conference on Innovation & technology in computer science education* (pp. 1-1). ACM.

RTÜK (Radyo ve Televizyon Üst Kurulu-Radio and Television Supreme Council), Media Literacy Book, Retrieved from https://www.rtuk.gov.tr/duyurular/3788/611/22-09-2014-medya-okuryazarligi-kitabi-sil-bastan.html

Şahinler Albayrak, M. (2015). The impact of Kinect usable 3D virtual reality applications on young learners' vocabulary development in foreign languages vocabulary learning. Unpublished Master Thesis, Fatih University, İstanbul.

Savolainen, R. (2002). Network competence and information seeking on the Internet: From definitions towards a social cognitive model. *The Journal of Documentation*, *58*(2), 211–226. doi:10.1108/00220410210425467

Serrhini, M. (2015). Online Experimentation: Emerging Technologies and IoT, M. T. Restivo, A. Cardoso and A.M. Lopes (Ed.), BCI Sensor as ITS for Controlling Student Attention in Online Experimentation, Spain: International Frequency Sensor Association Publishing.

Seymour, S. (2008). *Fashionable technology: The intersection of design, fashion, science, and technology*. Springer Publishing Company, Incorporated. doi:10.1007/978-3-211-74500-7

Singare, S., Lian, Q., Wang, W. P., Wang, J., Liu, Y., Li, D., & Lu, B. (2009). Rapid prototyping assisted surgery planning. *Rapid Prototyping Journal*, *15*(1), 1923. doi:10.1108/13552540910925027

Stanley, L. D. (2003). Beyond access: psychosocial barriers to computer literacy special issue: ICTs and community networking. *The Information Society*, *19*(5), 407–416. doi:10.1080/715720560

Steakley, L. (2013). Abraham Verghese uses Google Glass to demonstrate how to begin a patient exam. Retrieved from http://scopeblog.stanford.edu/2013/07/25/abraham-verghese-usesgoogle-glass-to-demonstrate-how-to-begin-a-patient-exam/

Stern, M. (2001). Nerds need not apply. *Canadian Business*, *74*(2), 70–74.

Süzen, A. A., & Taşdelen, K. (2013). Home automation for disabilities using kinect technology. *SDU International Technologic Science*, *5*(2), 1–10.

Tenekeci, M. E., Gümüşçü, A., & Ağırman, Ö. (2014, February). Interactive Kinect Application for Letter Training. *Paper presented at Academic Information '14 Academic Information Conference Papers*, Mersin University.

Timmerman, M. A. (2000). Learning in the context of a mathematics teacher education course: Two case studies of elementary teachers' conceptions of mathematics, mathematics teaching and learning, and the teaching of mathematics with technology. *Journal of Technology and Teacher Education*, *8*(3), 247–258.

Tiwari, K., & Saini, S. P. S. (2015). Brain controlled robot using neurosky mindwave. *Journal of Technological Advances & Scientific Research*, *1*(4), 328–331.

Trilling, B., & Fadel, C. (2009). *21st century skills: Learning for life in our times. America*. Jossey –Bass.

Vallurupalli, S., Paydak, H., Agarwal, S. K., Agrawal, M., & Assad-Kottner, C. (2013). Wearable technology to improve education and patient outcomes in a cardiology fellowship program-a feasibility study. *Health Technology*, *3*(4), 267–270. doi:10.1007/s12553-013-0065-4

Waetjen, W. B. (1993). Technological literacy reconsidered. Retrieved from https://scholar.lib.vt.edu/ejournals/JTE/v4n2/waetjen.jte-v4n2.html

Walther, J. B. (1992). Interpersonal effects in computer-mediated interaction a relational perspective. *Communication Research*, *19*(1), 52–90. doi:10.1177/009365092019001003

Wecker, C., Kohnlet, C., & Fischer, F. (2007). Computer Literacy and Inquiry Learning: When Geekslearn Less. *Journal of Computer Assisted Learning*, *23*(2), 133–144. doi:10.1111/j.1365-2729.2006.00218.x

Woodard, B. S. (2003). Technology and the constructivist learning environment: Implications for teaching information literacy skills. *Research Strategies*, *19*(3), 181–192. doi:10.1016/j.resstr.2005.01.001

Wu, T., Dameff, C., & Tully, J. (2014). Integrating Google Glass into simulation-based training: Experiences and future directions. *Journal of Biomedical Graphics and Computing*, *4*(2), 49. doi:10.5430/jbgc.v4n2p49

Yamauchi, Y, & Nakasugi, H. (2003, June). Past Viewer: Development of wearable learning system. *Paper presented at World Conference on Educational Media and Technology*, Honolulu, Hawaii.

Yetik, U. E., & Keskin, N. Ö. (2016). Use of seamless learning approach in open and distance education. *Journal of Research in Education and Teaching*, *5*(1), 98–103.

Yıldız, B., Ilgaz, H., & Seferoğlu, S. S. (2010, February). Science and technology policies in Turkey: An overview of development plans from 1963 to 2013. *Paper presented at Akademic informatic* (pp. 10-12).

KEY TERMS AND DEFINITIONS

Brain Computer Interface: A direct communication pathway between an enhanced or wired brain and an external device.

Digital Era: The definition of what digital means continues to change over time as new technologies.

Human Computer Interaction: Researches the design and use of computer technology, focused on the interfaces between users and computers.

ISTE: International Society for Technology in Education.

Kinesthetic: Physical activities.

NETS: National Educational Technology Standards for Students.

Sensor: An electronic component which detect events or changes in its environment and send the information to other electronics, frequently a computer processor.

Wearable Technology: A smart electronic device with microcontrollers that can be worn on the body as implant or accessories.

Section 2
Best Practices, Assessment Strategies, and Teachable Moments From the Field

Chapter 4
Developing and Assessing Media Literacy Through Digital Storytelling

Bulent Dogan
University of Houston, USA

Kadir Almus
North American University, USA

ABSTRACT

Digital Storytelling is an effective tool to develop Media Literacy skills in educational settings. This chapter will analyze and present current research/literature on Media Literacy through Digital Storytelling in regard to developing and assessing media literacy skills. Authors have been implementing an instructional project called Digital Storytelling Contests (DISTCO) since 2008 (http://www.distco.org). DISTCO reached out to more than 10000 K-16 students and teachers over the years. The goal is to relay the experiences on how media literacy has been developed through Digital Storytelling activities with DISTCO. In addition, the current DISTCO rubric for assessing digital storytelling projects is modified to include a version assessing Media Literacy through digital storytelling.

INTRODUCTION

What Is Media Literacy?

The common definition of media literacy is "the ability to access, analyze, evaluate, and effectively communicate in a variety of forms including print and non-print texts" (Considine, 2009). However, in a world where the means of delivery of information is changing very rapidly, the definition is extended to include all the new media forms including new ways of interactions, and new ways of understanding the information. Some of these new media forms include video-based products, online tools, and social media. The new media formats present enormous opportunities which were not before available. Consumers of media can now reach more information from numerous sources faster and easier than

DOI: 10.4018/978-1-5225-3082-4.ch004

Copyright © 2018, IGI Global. Copying or distributing in print or electronic forms without written permission of IGI Global is prohibited.

ever. However, this may also introduce some risks. For instance, some media formats may have biased, persuasive, and misrepresented information. Also, the variety of media sources can pose a challenge to critically select truthful and accurate content. Media literacy may help people to understand and use all the opportunities presented by the new media forms but also may help them protect themselves and their families from potential risks that come with the new media opportunities (Ofcom, 2017).

Why Is Media Literacy Important?

According to the Center for Media Literacy, there are five main reasons why media literacy is important (Thoman & Jolls, 2003). These include:

1. *The influence of media in our central democratic processes.* In today's world, people need two core skills to be engaged citizens of a democracy: critical thinking and self-expression. Media literacy helps people by instilling these skills and enable them to understand the political messages and participate in by making informed decisions.
2. *The high rate of media consumption and the saturation of society by media.* Owing to all the new forms of media, people are exposed to more variety and a larger amount of media in one day than people were exposed to in one year two generations ago. Media literacy teaches skills so that people can safely navigate through these myriad images and messages.
3. *The media's influence on shaping perceptions, beliefs, and attitudes.* Media experiences create a significant impact on how we understand, interpret, and act on the world. Media education can help us separate ourselves from our dependencies on media influences by helping us to understand them.
4. *The increasing importance of visual communication and information.* Learning to "read" the multiple layers of image-based communication is a necessary addition to traditional print literacy as our lives are increasingly dominated by visual images.
5. *The importance of information in society and the need for lifelong learning.* Even though information processing and information services are very important for the nation's productivity, the growth of global media industries is also challenging independent voices and diverse views. Media education can help people, including teachers and students, understand how to differentiate the information coming from different sources, whose interests may be served and how to find alternative views.

Similarly, Livingstone (2007) argues that media literacy is important for a skilled, creative, and ethical society. It also contributes to a full and meaningful life at a personal level. She stresses that media literacy can contribute to three broad purposes. These are:

-   **Democracy, Participation, and Active Citizenship:** A media and information-literate individual is capable of gaining informed opinions on matters that are relevant to our society and our personal lives and is able to express his/her opinion freely in every domain in a democratic society.
-   **Knowledge Economy, Competitiveness, and Choice:** A media and information-literate individual will be more successful in a market economy increasingly based on information. Such individuals are likely to contribute more, achieve at a higher level, and therefore will make the society more innovative and competitive.

- **Lifelong Learning, Cultural Expression, and Personal Fulfillment:** Media and information literacy is crucial for a full and meaningful life, and for an informed, creative, and ethical society.

TEACHING AND PROMOTING MEDIA LITERACY THROUGH DIGITAL STORYTELLING

Medial literacy education in schools plays an important role for students to gain critical media literacy skills at an early age. It not only helps them to use the media tools creatively and productively, but also encourages students to be active and engaged media consumers and users. We no longer live in the era of Media Literacy 1.0 where people were the consumers of traditional media. Today, in the era of Media Literacy 2.0 where people are creators rather than just consumers, media literacy education becomes even more critical. It increases the role of students in their learning by fostering student-centered learning. Students become more active and they understand by doing rather than just being the passive information receivers when they involve in media literacy education. Digital Storytelling (DST) is one of the prominent tools to teach and promote media literacy as defined in Media Literacy 2.0 where creating is an essential requirement.

What Is Digital Storytelling?

Storytelling is a powerful tool to develop media literacy skills in students. Digital Storytelling allows literacy development in the digital domain. Digital Stories are multimedia products consisting of still images or segments of video containing background music or audio and a voice-over narrative (Hull & Nelson, 2005). In essence, DST is the process of creating a short, purposeful movie with various multimedia components in order to create an engaging presentation. An original script, often in the author's own voice, combined with these components, is an essential part of this process. Topics for digital stories can vary from personal reflections to instructional subjects. A digital story typically runs for three to five minutes (Dogan, 2017). Digital stories are easy to create with readily available tools. A variety of software can be used for creating digital stories, ranging from easy-to-use software such as Microsoft Photostory 3, iMovie, and Windows Movie Maker to more complex programs such as Photoshop Elements and Final Cut Express (Lambert, 2010; Robin & McNeil, 2012).

Even though there are many ways of creating or structuring multimedia stories, the Center for Digital Storytelling (CDS) has identified seven basic elements for digital storytelling (Table 1) (Lambert, 2003).

Process of Creating a Digital Story

Understanding the process of creating a digital story is important because this process has been claimed by digital storytelling researchers to assist with the development of 21st century skills in students (Jakes, 2006; Robin, 2008).

The process of creating digital stories is defined by Jakes and Brannon (2005) in six steps: 1) Writing; 2) Script; 3) Storyboarding; 4) Locating Multimedia; 5) Creating the Digital Story; and 6) Sharing (Figure 1).

Table 1. Seven elements of digital storytelling

Element	Description
Point of View	is the point the story is trying to make and the perspective of the author.
A Dramatic Question	is the underlying question that keeps the audience's attention until the story is over; it is usually addressed at the end.
Emotional Content	is the component that enables the audience to emotionally engage in the story in a personal and powerful way.
The Gift of Your Voice	is using the storyteller's own voice in the story to make the story personal.
The Power of the Soundtrack	is the music played in the background to support the storyline.
Economy	is wise usage of visual and audio in the story to prevent the audience from being overloaded with information.
Pacing	is the rhythm of the story that determines its ultimate success.

Figure 1. The digital storytelling process
Source: Jakes & Brennan, 2005.

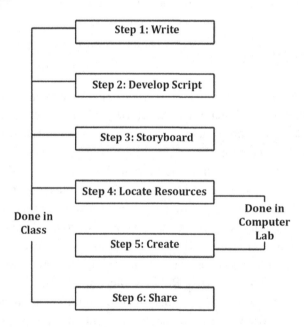

The first step in creating digital stories involves the writing process. This process starts with finding a topic for the story and the author starting to write about the story. A script is developed by the author after the completion of the narrative. The script also defines how the multimedia elements will be used in the story to ensure that they will contribute to the purpose of the story (Jakes & Brennan, 2005). Storyboarding is the process of organizing the flow of the movie. After storyboarding, multimedia that will be used in the story is located, and all components of the story are combined according to the script. In the final step, usually the digital story is shared with an audience (Jakes & Brennan, 2005), and it is seen as an important "public" gathering and acknowledgement of each other's work.

Understanding these specific steps is vital for a true understanding of how DST provides benefits to and helps students to develop skills. The next section will briefly discuss how DST may be used to develop media literacy skills.

MEDIA LITERACY THROUGH DIGITAL STORYTELLING

Digital storytelling and its related activities are known to develop virtually all of the skills students in K-12 are expected to possess in the 21st century (Jakes, 2006). Twenty-first century skills such as Information Literacy, Visual Literacy, Media Literacy, Creativity and Risk Taking can be achieved when students actively participate in the creative process of DST (Jakes & Brennan, 2005; Robin, 2008).

Among these literacy skills, DST has a deep and direct impact on the development of media literacy skills. Digital storytelling helps students to become producers and creators of media content as well as being critical consumers of different media forms. Digital Storytelling helps learners think critically about how to effectively combine multimedia elements such as audio, video, and images within the digital story. Creators of digital stories start with thinking about how the digital media helps to express their story, communicate their emotions and convey feelings through their product.

Digital storytelling provides an interaction between narrative and various media elements. Creating digital stories and media provides many opportunities to engage students in media literacy including how the media influence our perceptions of the world; persuasive techniques used in media; legal, ethical, and, copyright issues with the use of media elements (Ohler, 2013). Students need critical media skills to make sense of and understand the world filled with many forms of media including story-based media, popular video products, and social media. In this digital age, students are expected not only to learn with media, but also to learn and think critically about media. Through DST activities, students can understand the difference between a successful digital story and a purposeful or biased media piece such as an advertisement.

Digital stories provide powerful media literacy learning opportunities as students are involved in the creation and analysis of the media when they actively create digital stories. When students combine a story with technology and media tools to express themselves to others, they learn and experience persuasive nature of the media first hand.

MEDIA LITERACY ASSESSMENT

Measuring media learning outcomes is an underdeveloped area and considered still in its infancy (Fastrez, 2009). One of the main challenges in this area is the lack of clear definitions with media literacy assessment and its criteria. In order to measure the media literacy outcomes, the media literacy term needs to be clearly defined and related competencies need to be developed (Christ, 2004). There is a need for more validity and research instruments to capture media learning outcomes (Martens, 2010).

According to the results of a recent study by Schilder, Lockee, & Saxon (2016), Media Literacy assessment tools need to be instruments measuring higher order thinking skills, critical thinking and student ability to critically analyze, evaluate, and produce media messages. Even though many media literacy researchers desire to move beyond the assessment of lower order thinking skills and content knowledge, it is pedagogically difficult, expensive, and time-consuming to develop assessments measuring higher order thinking skills (Schilder, Lockee, & Saxon, 2016).

In this chapter, the authors present a modified version of DST rubric used in DISTCO studies (Dogan & Robin, 2009; Dogan, 2010; Dogan, 2011; Dogan, 2012; Dogan, 2014; Dogan, 2015). The newly developed rubric is intended to measure media literacy through digital storytelling projects.

Digital Storytelling Contests (DISTCO)

The Digital Storytelling Contests (DISTCO) (2008, 2009, 2010, 2012, 2013, and 2014) are developed by the University of Houston and North American University in order to research how DST is implemented in classrooms by K-12 teachers (Dogan & Robin, 2008). In addition, DISTCO project contributes to educational uses of DST. The DISTCO has two major goals:

- To encourage students and teachers to challenge themselves in an exciting competition where 21st century skills can be enhanced;
- To further current research on the effectiveness of digital storytelling in K-12 education.

The project is designed so that students and teachers from different schools can submit original digital stories within a specified time frame and within contest requirements. The competition is held solely online and original digital stories are submitted through the contest website (http://www.distco.org). Since the first contest in the DISTCO series (2008), there has been a contest held each subsequent year and the research results have been regularly presented at conferences (Dogan & Robin, 2008; Dogan, 2010; Dogan, 2011; Dogan 2012; Dogan, 2014; Dogan, 2015). The latest contest in the series, DISTCO 2016, was open to all K-12 students and teachers on both national and international levels. DISTCO reached out to more than 10,000 K-12 students over the years.

In this chapter, the authors will relay the results and experiences on how media literacy can be developed through DST activities with DISTCO. The DISTCO project uses DISTCO -Digital Storytelling Rubric (Table 2) to evaluate digital stories completed by participants. In addition to current media literacy related rubric categories such as Image Relevancy, Image/Video Quality, Soundtrack Emotion, Copyright Issues in the current rubric, the following new categories are developed for capturing media literacy outcomes: Accuracy/Facts, Persuasion, Media Style, Emotion/Purpose, and Bias.

Media Literacy Related Categories in DISTCO-Digital Storytelling Rubric

Please refer to Table 2 for current DISTCO- Digital Storytelling Rubric. The following categories are related to Media Literacy in this rubric:

Image Relevancy

Image relevancy refers to whether images or videos used in the digital story contribute to the story's message. The description of this category for the top criteria is "Images create a distinct atmosphere or tone that matches different parts of the story. The images communicate symbolism and/or metaphors." Digital Storytellers need to be aware that images chosen in the video product should be relevant to what

Table 2. DISTCO-digital storytelling rubric

Evaluator's Name:			Digital Story ID:		
Category	**4-Excellent**	**3-Good**	**2-Fair**	**1-Poor**	**Score**
Dramatic Question/ Opening Statement	There is an opening statement/question immensely grabbing the attention of the audience in the beginning of the story (Ideally, first 0-15 sec.)	There is an opening statement/question grabbing the attention of the audience in the beginning of the story (Ideally, first 0-15 seconds).	There is an opening statement/question somewhat grabbing the attention of the audience in the beginning of the story (Ideally, first 0-15 seconds).	There is no opening statement/question/ attention grabber in the beginning of the story.	
Purpose	Establishes a purpose early on and maintains a clear focus throughout.	Establishes a purpose early on and maintains focus for most of the presentation.	There are a few lapses in focus, but the purpose is fairly clear.	It is difficult to figure out the purpose of the presentation.	
Script/ Story	The script/story is original and making a contribution to the overall product.	The script/story is somewhat original and making a contribution to the point of the story.	The script/story is somewhat original and making a little contribution to the point of the story.	The script/story is not original, thus not making a contribution to the product.	
Creativity	Overall the work is highly creative.	The work is creative.	The work is somewhat creative.	The work is not creative.	
Economy	The story is told with exactly the right amount of detail throughout. It does not seem too short nor does it seem too long.	The story composition is typically good, though it seems to drag somewhat or need slightly more detail in one or two sections.	The story seems to need more editing. It is noticeably too long or too short in more than one section.	The story needs extensive editing. It is too long or too short to be interesting.	
Duration Of Presentation	Length of presentation is between 3-5 minutes and it feels the right amount of time for the story told.	Length of presentation is between 3-5 minutes but it feels that the story should be longer or shorter in length.	Length of presentation is between 2-3 minutes.	Presentation is less than 2 minutes or more than 6 minutes.	
Image Relevancy	Images create a distinct atmosphere or tone that matches different parts of the story. The images communicate symbolism and/or metaphors.	Images create an atmosphere or tone that matches some parts of the story. The images may communicate symbolism and/or metaphors.	An attempt is made to use images to create an atmosphere/tone but it needs more work. Image choice is somewhat logical.	Little or no attempt to use images to create an appropriate atmosphere/ tone. Image choice is not logical.	
Image /Video Quality	Overall, the picture and video resolution is exceptionally good and within the limit of contest requirements.	Overall, the picture and video resolution is good and within the limit of contest requirements.	Overall, the picture and video resolution is low but within the limit of contest requirements.	Overall, the picture and video resolution is low and not within the limit of contest requirements.	

continued on following page

Table 2. Continued

	Evaluator's Name:		Digital Story ID:		
Category	**4-Excellent**	**3-Good**	**2-Fair**	**1-Poor**	**Score**
Voice - Consistency	Voice quality is clear and consistently audible throughout the presentation.	Voice quality is clear and consistently audible throughout the majority (70-95%) of the presentation.	Voice quality needs more attention.	No Voice is included at all.	
Voice - Pacing	The pace (rhythm and voice punctuation) fits the story line and helps the audience really "get into" the story.	Occasionally speaks too fast or too slowly for the story line. The pacing (rhythm and voice punctuation) is relatively engaging for the audience.	Tries to use pacing (rhythm and voice punctuation), but it is often noticeable that the pacing does not fit the story line. Audience is not consistently engaged.	No Voice is included at all.	
Soundtrack - Originality	All of the music is original (the music is created in a digital storytelling software such as PhotoStory 3 with built-in tools) or an artist's music is used and credited at the end of the story.	Some of the music is original and some of the music belongs to an artist (non-original). The artist's music is credited at the end of the story.	None of the music is original. Only an artist's music (non-original) is used. The artist's music is not credited at the end of the story.	No music (original/non-original) is used at all.	
Soundtrack - Emotion	Music stirs a rich emotional response that matches the story line well.	Music stirs a rich emotional response that somewhat matches the story line.	Music is ok, and not distracting, but it does not add much to the story.	Music is distracting, inappropriate, or is not used.	
Language	Appropriate language is used throughout the story.	Appropriate language is used in majority of the story.	Inappropriate language is frequently used in the story.	No Script/Story/Voice Recording	
Grammar	Grammar and usage are correct and contributed to clarity, style and character development.	Grammar and usage are typically correct and errors do not detract from the story.	Grammar and usage were somewhat correct but errors detract from story.	No Script/Story or Voice Recording	
Copyright Issues	All work used (story, images, and music) seems original and an effort has been made to address copyright issues (e.g. Listing sources of the story and multimedia within the story).	Most of the work used (story, images, and music) seems original and some effort has been made to address copyright issues (e.g. Listing sources of the story and multimedia within the story).	Some of the work used (story, images, and music) seems original and little effort has been made to address copyright issues (e.g. Listing sources of the story and multimedia within the story).	None of the work used (story, images, and music) seems original and no effort has been made to address copyright issues (e.g. Listing sources of the story and multimedia within the story).	
Comments				Total Score	

has been said in a certain scene during the script. When students master these skills, they will be able to critically select images or other visuals representing the concepts or topics they speak about in the project.

Image/Video Quality

Image or video quality refers to physical limitations of the medium, namely its resolution. In any digital product, a certain resolution quality is expected. This category is defined as "Overall, the picture and video resolution is exceptionally good and within the limit of contest requirements in the DISTCO rubric." Learners who create digital stories should pay close attention to the product's visual quality so that the consumer of produced media would have the most benefit from its message and content.

Soundtrack Emotion

There is no denial that soundtrack or background music in a digital story or any other media project may contribute a lot to the emotion of the end product. For instance, a simple image displayed in a project may be interpreted to arouse "sad" feelings if a sad soundtrack is used. The DISTCO rubric intends to measure whether the digital story's soundtrack effect on the audience's emotion with the following category: "Music stirs a rich emotional response that matches the story line well". Media consumers should be cognizant of how music used in media product can manipulate one's feelings either in a positive or negative manner.

Copyright Issues

Copyright issues are a primary concern when working with Digital stories. Media elements used in the projects should either be copyright-free or properly cited if they are copyrighted. The current category on the rubric is as follows: "All work used (story, images, and music) seems original and an effort has been made to address copyright issues (e.g. Listing sources of the story and multimedia within the story)." Project makers are encouraged to carefully select the media elements in their stories so that they are not violating any copyright laws. Critical consumers of media need to be digitally responsible and aware of copyrighted content used in a product.

Newly Developed Rubric Criteria for Media Literacy

Please refer to Table 3 for Media Literacy Rubric for Digital Storytelling. Following categories are developed for this rubric:

Factual Accuracy

The accuracy of information presented in any media product should be one of the primary concerns of the consumers of that media. Thus, storytellers should pay special attention to claims made in digital media products. The new media literacy rubric category is developed as follows: "Multiple factual claims and information are present with clear references to reliable sources"

Table 3. Media literacy rubric for digital storytelling

	Evaluator's Name:		Digital Story ID:		
Category	**4-Excellent**	**3-Good**	**2-Fair**	**1-Poor**	**Score**
Purpose	Establishes a purpose early on and maintains a clear focus throughout.	Establishes a purpose early on and maintains focus for most of the presentation.	There are a few lapses in focus, but the purpose is fairly clear.	It is difficult to figure out the purpose of the presentation.	
Factual Accuracy	Multiple factual claims and information are present with clear references to reliable sources	Multiple claims are present with reference to at least one reliable source.	Presents a limited number of general factual claims with minimal reference to sources.	Presents few or no factual claims.	
Persuasion	Central issue is clearly defined, and the importance of this issue is demonstrated; makes an argument that convinces with logic and evidence; point of view is presented strongly.	Central issue is clearly defined; makes an argument that is logical; point of view is clear.	Central issue is partially defined; makes an argument; point of view is somewhat clear.	Central issue is not identified; makes no argument; the point of view is unclear.	
Media Style	Images, sound clips, music, editing, animations, and transitions are successfully used to communicate ideas and organize complex arguments. Overall media style is powerful and creating a dramatic effect such as amusement or inspiration.	Images, sound clips, music, editing, animations, and transitions are used to communicate ideas and organize ideas into arguments. Overall media style is creating a dramatic effect.	Use of some media elements such as images or sounds contributes to communicating ideas or creates an effect.	Images, sounds, and music does not communicate an idea or create any meaningful effect	
Bias	No Biased information is presented throughout the Digital Story. The information presented is based on facts and objective sources.	Majority of information presented doesn't contain any author bias. The information presented seems to be based on facts and objective sources.	Some of information presented is biased. The information presented is not always based on facts and objective sources.	Biased information presented throughout the Digital Story. The information presented is not verified and is not based on facts and objective sources.	
Image Relevancy	Images create a distinct atmosphere or tone that matches different parts of the story. The images communicate symbolism and/or metaphors.	Images create an atmosphere or tone that matches some parts of the story. The images may communicate symbolism and/or metaphors.	An attempt is made to use images to create an atmosphere/tone but it needs more work. Image choice is somewhat logical.	Little or no attempt to use images to create an appropriate atmosphere/tone. Image choice is not logical.	
Image /Video Quality	Overall, the picture and video resolution is exceptionally good and within the limit of contest requirements.	Overall, the picture and video resolution is good and within the limit of contest requirements.	Overall, the picture and video resolution is low but within the limit of contest requirements.	Overall, the picture and video resolution is low and not within the limit of contest requirements.	

continued on following page

Table 3. Continued

Evaluator's Name:			Digital Story ID:		
Category	**4-Excellent**	**3-Good**	**2-Fair**	**1-Poor**	**Score**
Voice - Consistency	Voice quality is clear and consistently audible throughout the presentation.	Voice quality is clear and consistently audible throughout the majority (70-95%) of the presentation.	Voice quality needs more attention.	No Voice is included at all.	
Voice - Pacing	The pace (rhythm and voice punctuation) fits the story line and helps the audience really "get into" the story.	Occasionally speaks too fast or too slowly for the story line. The pacing (rhythm and voice punctuation) is relatively engaging for the audience.	Tries to use pacing (rhythm and voice punctuation), but it is often noticeable that the pacing does not fit the story line. Audience is not consistently engaged.	No Voice is included at all.	
Soundtrack - Originality	All of the music is original (the music is created in a digital storytelling software such as PhotoStory 3 with built-in tools) or an artist's music is used and credited at the end of the story.	Some of the music is original and some of the music belongs to an artist (non-original). The artist's music is credited at the end of the story.	None of the music is original. Only an artist's music (non-original) is used. The artist's music is not credited at the end of the story.	No music (original/non-original) is used at all.	
Soundtrack - Emotion	Music stirs a rich emotional response that matches the story line well.	Music stirs a rich emotional response that somewhat matches the story line.	Music is ok, and not distracting, but it does not add much to the story.	Music is distracting, inappropriate, or is not used.	
Copyright Issues	All work used (story, images, and music) seems original and an effort has been made to address copyright issues (e.g. Listing sources of the story and multimedia within the story).	Most of the work used (story, images, and music) seems original and some effort has been made to address copyright issues (e.g. Listing sources of the story and multimedia within the story).	Some of the work used (story, images, and music) seems original and little effort has been made to address copyright issues (e.g. Listing sources of the story and multimedia within the story).	None of the work used (story, images, and music) seems original and no effort has been made to address copyright issues (e.g. Listing sources of the story and multimedia within the story).	
Comments				Total Score	

Persuasion

Persuasive techniques are commonly used in media products such as advertisements. It is crucial for media consumers to be aware of either the positive or negative persuasion built in presented media, so that they can critically analyze the information themselves rather than being manipulated by the authors of the media. Thus, a new category is developed for measuring media literacy through digital stories in regard to persuasion: "Central issue is clearly defined, and the importance of this issue is demonstrated; makes an argument that convinces with logic and evidence; the point of view is presented strongly".

Media Style

Media products can be powerful tools to create a dramatic effect such as amusement and inspiration. Users and creators of the media should be able to organize their ideas in a meaningful way and utilize the available technical tools at their proposal. "Media Style" was developed for this purpose: "Images, sound clips, music, editing, animations, and transitions are successfully used to communicate ideas and organize complex arguments. Overall media style is powerful and creating a dramatic effect such as amusement or inspiration."

Bias

Bias can be present in media products but may not be easy to recognize at first. Thus, media users need to be literate in potential bias within the media products they created or they used. Therefore, a new category is added to Media Literacy Rubric through Digital Storytelling, "No Biased information is presented throughout the Digital Story. The information presented is based on facts and objective sources."

CONCLUSION

Media Literacy is a crucial skill that new generations of students, learners, consumers, and creators of media needs to possess in order to make sense of information continuously revolving around them. There is a high need for assessment tools that measure media literacy outcomes. Digital Storytelling can be used to teach and assess media literacy as it involves creating video products comprised of audio, image, and video elements. This chapter presented a modified version of DISTCO Digital Storytelling Rubric for measuring Media Literacy through Digital Storytelling.

REFERENCES

Christ, W. G. (2004). Assessment, media literacy standards, and higher education. *The American Behavioral Scientist*, *48*(1), 92–96. doi:10.1177/0002764204267254

Considine, M., Horton, J., & Moorman, G. (2009, March). Teaching and Reading the Millennial Generation Through Media Literacy. *Journal of Adolescent & Adult Literacy*, *52*(6), 471–481. doi:10.1598/JAAL.52.6.2

Dogan, B. (2010). Educational Use of Digital Storytelling: Research Results of an Online Digital Storytelling Contest. In D. Gibson & B. Dodge (Eds.), *Proceedings of Society for Information Technology & Teacher Education International Conference 2010* (pp. 1061–1066). San Diego, CA: AACE. Retrieved from http://www.editlib.org/p/33494

Dogan, B. (2011). Educational Uses of Digital Storytelling: Results of DISTCO 2010, an Online Digital Storytelling Contest. In M. Koehler & P. Mishra (Eds.), *Proceedings of Society for Information Technology & Teacher Education International Conference 2011* (pp. 1104–1111). Nashville, Tennessee: AACE. Retrieved from http://www.editlib.org/p/36434

Dogan, B. (2012). Educational Uses of Digital Storytelling in K-12: Research Results of Digital Storytelling Contest (DISTCO) 2012. In P. Resta (Ed.), *Proceedings of Society for Information Technology & Teacher Education International Conference 2012* (pp. 1353–1362). Austin, Texas: AACE. Retrieved from http://www.editlib.org/p/39770

Dogan, B. (2014). Educational Uses of Digital Storytelling in K-12: Research Results of a Digital Storytelling Contest (DISTCO) 2013. In M. Searson & M. N. Ochoa (Eds.), *Society for Information Technology & Teacher Education International Conference 2014* (pp. 520–529). Jacksonville, FL: AACE. Retrieved from http://www.editlib.org/p/13080

Dogan, B. (2015). Educational Uses of Digital Storytelling in K-12: Research Results of Digital Storytelling Contest (DISTCO) 2014. In D. Slykhuis & G. Marks (Eds.), *Society for Information Technology & Teacher Education International Conference 2015,* Las Vegas, NV (pp. 595–604). AACE. Retrieved from http://www.editlib.org/p/150056

Dogan, B., & Robin, B. (2008). Implementation of Digital Storytelling in the Classroom by Teachers Trained in a Digital Storytelling Workshop. In K. McFerrin, R. Weber, R. Carlsen, & D. A. Willis (Eds.), *Society for Information Technology & Teacher Education International Conference 2008* (pp. 902–907). Las Vegas, NV: AACE. Retrieved from http://www.editlib.org/p/27287

Fastrez, P. (2009). *Evaluating media literacy as competences: What can we agree on?* Retrieved from http://www.slideshare.net/pfastrez/evaluating-medialiteracy-as-competences-what-can-we-agree-on

Jakes, D. (2006, March). Standards-Proof Your digital storytelling Efforts. *TechLearning*. Retrieved from http://www.techlearning.com/story/showArticle.jhtml?articleID=180204072

Jakes, D. S., & Brennan, J. (2005). Capturing stories, capturing lives: An Introduction to digital storytelling. Retrieved from http://bookstoread.com/etp/earle.pdf

Lambert, J. (2003). *Digital storytelling cookbook and traveling companion.* Berkeley, CA: Digital Diner Press. Retrieved from http://www.storycenter.org/cookbook.pdf

Livingstone, S. (2007). *Internet Literacy: Young People's Negotiation of New Online Opportunities.* The John D. and Catherine T. MacArthur Foundation Series on Digital Media and Learning.

Martens, H. (2010). Evaluating Media Literacy Education: Concepts, Theories and Future Directions. *Journal of Media Literacy Education, 2*(1), 1–22.

Ofcom. (2017). About Media Literacy. Retrieved from https://www.ofcom.org.uk/research-and-data/media-literacy-research/media-literacy

Ohler, J. (2006). The World of Digital Storytelling. *Educational Leadership, 63*(4), 44–47.

Ohler, J. (2013*). Digital Storytelling in the Classroom: New Media Pathways to Literacy, Learning, and Creativity.* Thousand Oaks, CA: Corwin.

Robin, B. (2008). The effective uses of digital storytelling as a teaching and learning tool. In *Handbook of Research on Teaching Literacy Through the Communicative and Visual Arts* (Vol. 2, pp. 429–440). New York, NY: Lawrence Erlbaum Associates.

Schilder, E., Lockee, B., & Saxon, D. P. (2016). The Challenges of Assessing Media Literacy Education. *Journal of Media Literacy Education*, *8*(1), 32–48.

Thoman, E., & Jolls, T. (2003). *Literacy for the 21st Century An Overview & Orientation Guide To Media Literacy Education*. Center for Media Literacy.

KEY TERMS AND DEFINITIONS

Digital Storytelling: A multimedia products consisting of still images or segments of video containing background music or audio and a voice-over narrative.

Media Literacy: The ability to access, analyze, evaluate, and effectively communicate in a variety of forms including print and non-print texts.

Media Literacy Assessment: Measuring learning outcomes through media literacy.

Media Literacy Rubric: Rubric to measure media literacy.

Chapter 5
Gaming Literacies and Learning

Hui-Yin Hsu
New York Institute of Technology, USA

Shiang-Kwei Wang
New York Institute of Technology, USA

ABSTRACT

This book chapter summarizes an extensive literature review on gaming literacies and learning. It carefully examines the definition of gaming literacies from both message consumption and production perspectives, stemming from the definition of foundational literacies and information communication and technology (ICT) literacies. We establish a framework based on Bloom's taxonomy to explore the role of gaming literacies on learners' cognitive, affective and psychomotor domains. We discuss the implications for teachers to adopt games in the classroom, possible problems and concerns to have learners play games, synthesize practices for using games in educational context, and provide suggestions for future research.

INTRODUCTION

In this chapter, we will define gaming literacies in terms of message consumption and production; identify types of knowledge and skills involved through playing and designing games; and establish a framework on how gaming literacies can promote the abovementioned knowledge and skills based on Bloom's taxonomy (cognitive, affective, and psychomotor domains). We will also discuss controversies, concerns and issues about gaming literacies and provide suggestions for future research.

DEFINITION OF GAMING LITERACIES

Foundational Literacy

Literacy has been defined differently throughout the history due to the change of societal demands. Not too long ago, one can be determined as literate if s/he can read and write the basic information about herself or himself. With the change of the complexity in the society and the demand from the job

DOI: 10.4018/978-1-5225-3082-4.ch005

Copyright © 2018, IGI Global. Copying or distributing in print or electronic forms without written permission of IGI Global is prohibited.

market, one needs to have the ability to read, write, speak, listen, and think to be considered literate in order to function properly in their daily life. With new inventions of technologies, literacy, meanwhile, has upgraded and updated to include "the ability to identify, understand, interpret, create, compute, and communicate using visual, audible, and digital materials across disciplines and in any context." (International Reading Association, 2012; Leu, Zawilinski, Forzani & Timbrell, 2014).

Literacy, in general, is a common practice among the public in terms of the purposes of usage in a macro- environment, such as the one defined by what most agree upon due to the necessity for an individual to properly function in a society at large. Literacy is even more powerfully defined as a "situated practice" due to the nature of the language and the communicative purposes involved in a certain culture in a micro-environment. The term "multiple literacies" was used to emphasize different literacy practices among people from different cultural and linguistic backgrounds (Taylor; Bond & Bresler, 2006). It was then expanded to address a broader range of literacy experiences among people who become literate in a world with diverse population and with diverse definitions of being literate (North Central Regional Educational Laboratory, 2001). In the 21st century, technology has raised the intensity and complexity of literate environments, a literate person should possess a wide range of abilities and competencies, many literacies. These literacies—from reading online newspapers to participating in virtual classrooms—are multiple, dynamic, and malleable. (NTCE, 2008)

With profound changes in new technologies such as gaming software, video technologies, Internet, webpages, search engines and many more yet to emerge, the notion of "new literacies" began a different era. Literacy evolves to include a broader set of skills of using information and communication technologies (ICTs) to consume and produce information (Leu et. al, 2004a).

New Literacies: Media Literacy and ICT Literacies

To frame the definition of gaming literacies, we need to discuss media literacy and ICT literacies (some use computer literacy, information technology literacy) since all of which are affected deeply by multimedia, computer technology and the Internet. The changes and the advancement of technologies create new possibilities and ways to enhance comprehension and communication, and has therefore reshaped the meaning of literacy. With the prevalence of ICT tools (WWW, e-mail, weblog, digital video…); its integration in teaching and learning becomes an increasingly important area of focus and bring more opportunities and challenges to the educators and learners. Computer and internet tools become indispensable to a typical student in the information age. A student might need to complete assignments with productivity tools such as word processors and spreadsheets; collaborate with classmates through e-mails, Google Applications, instant messaging, wikis, and weblog; research on the internet using search engine, web browser or even web map (e.g. Google Earth); evaluate and synthesize information; or communicate idea with presentation software or video editing tools.

ICTs are redefining the skills and talents needed in the 21 century (Mehlman, 2003; Hsu, Wang & Runco, 2013). They make tasks easier so learners can place a greater burden on higher-level cognitive skills. In this case, the definition of ICTs should not be limited to the skills to access to hardware, software and network, but to also include the corresponding cognitive skills and general literacy (ICT Literacy Panel, 2002, p. 6). In other words, learners do not just simply apply ICT skills passively, they apply them actively to create and present information needed. Therefore, it is important to include both message consumption and production perspective while defining literacy. For instance, Livingstone (2004) described four essential components of media literacy as the ability to access, analyze, evaluate and create contents in a variety of forms. This ties closely with how Leu and others (2004b) define new literacies:

The new literacies of the Internet and other ICTs include the skills, strategies, and dispositions necessary to successfully use and adapt to the rapidly changing information and communication technologies and contexts that continuously emerge in our world and influence all areas of our personal and professional lives. These new literacies allow us to use the Internet and other ICTs to identify important questions, locate information, critically evaluate the usefulness of that information, synthesize information to answer those questions, and then communicate the answers to others. (Leu et al, 2004, p1572)

ICTs literacies are built on foundational literacy rather than replacing them. (Cesarini, 2004; Leu et al, 2004). Literacy skills are required to respond to content on any forms of media, which is the same with gaming literacies. ICT literacies and gaming literacies share many common features: both require basic knowledge of computer technology and operation skills. In addition, the process of acquiring ICT literacies and gaming literacies are analogous –through practice. The contrasting difference is that gaming literacies exist in particular context while ICTs literacies considered as a broader set of skills that can apply to a wide range of contexts (ICT Literacy Panel, 2002, p. 12). This feature also minimizes the transformative effect of gaming literacies on people's lives.

Characteristics of New Generation

Prensky, in his book Digital Game-Based Learning (2001), described the new generation as games generation. He believes that their mindsets and cognitive processing have been changed due to the influence of the new media and technologies. Prensky used the term "digital natives (2001) to describe this generation. Although more studies with empirical evidences are needed to support the notion that digital natives' learning preference and information processing is differently than previous generations (Foreman, 2003; Wang, Hsu, Campbell, Coster & Longhurst, 2014), there is no doubt that they possess some characteristics that educators should pay attention to. Technology, mobile devices and information and communication technology (ICTs) are pervasive in their digital natives' everyday lives. They have short attention span and pay only attention to things that interest them. They prefer to multi-task and access information in non-linear format. They are attracted to multimedia more than text by itself. They are used to worldwide connectedness through network; fearless to use new technology and new software/hardware (Prensky, 2001, p02-1). These behaviors and learning modalities are observed more often in the games/digital generations than the past generations. Therefore, many educational researchers have urged schools and educators to respond to the changes of digital natives' distinctive experiences with technologies. Teachers should leverage students' already developing capabilities with technologies in ways that will allow them to meet demands of a future workforce in a global information society (Barnes et al. 2007; Brown 2000; Tapscott 2009; Thompson 2013).

Essential Elements of Why Games Engage Players

To help educators or readers unfamiliar with games understand gaming literacies, there is a need to discuss the nature of game before we define gaming literacies. Definition of game can be narrow or broad. Board game and poker are both considered as games because the player needs to achieve the goal (winning) by following the rules and compete with opponents. In this chapter, the term "games" means those required using computer (such as Steam), or a game console such as Play Station, Xbox or Nintendo Wii, or a mobile devices machine such as Play Station Portable, iPhone or Android tablets.

People play games because good games provide them the sense of flow (Csikszentmihalyi 1985, 1998), a process that engages players in activities that challenge their versatile gaming abilities and produce enjoyment. If the task is too easy, players feel bored and stop playing; if the task is too difficult, players give up the attempt to challenge. Good games start with a simple task to let users get familiar with the interface, operation and the game rules. The completion of the task rewards users with scores, advanced skills or objects necessary for completing the task in the next level, and progress player to the next level with more challenging tasks. Players' scores keep adding up, and feel more confident in this game environment while gradually mastering the skills until the ultimate goal is achieved. The balance lies between the task difficulty and the players' skills. Players compete with the computer, with other players, or with themselves. Winning (defeat other players or the computer, attain higher score, or advance to the next level) yields players stronger self-efficacy in the game environment (Craig, Brown, Upright & DeRosier, 2016; Vorderer, Hartmann & Klimmt, 2006) and enjoy themselves becoming an expert of this particular game. That is why "people draw deep pleasure from learning (as gamers' skills progressed) and that such learning keeps people playing" (Gee, 2003), which also concurs with the conclusion Prensky (2001) drew that the following elements are why games engage players:

- Games have rules
- Games have goals
- Games are interactive and provide outcomes and feedback depending on players actions
- Games provide the sense of flow
- Games have winning states and provide player self-efficacy
- Games have conflict/competition/challenge/opposition[1]

Define Gaming Literacies

There are many free games and commercial off-the-shelf games available. These can be divided into nine categories: drill and practice, action game (racing, fighting, platformer), puzzle, simulation, strategy, role play game (RPG), massively multiplayer online games (MMOGs), sandbox, and educational game. It is difficult to develop a definition of gaming literacies that can accommodate all genres. However, there are some similar elements underlying.

Gaming literacies cannot be defined merely as the mastery of game playing skills. According to the definitions of foundational literacy, new literacies and ICT literacies, there is a need to define gaming literacies from two perspectives: message consumption and production. The definition of gaming literacies should broaden to include both "reading" and "writing" levels, one is from player's perspective and the other if from game designer's.

At the "Reading" Level: From Message Consumption Perspective

Here is an example to help us understand how game player begin to develop knowledge and skills about playing games. Diablo is one of the bestselling MMOGs. First time player (who has no MMOGs experience) needs to install Diablo onto the computer and then launch the game. A short story is then presented to give the player background knowledge of the game. The player can choose the avatar to represent him/ her among characters such as Amazon, Assassin or Barbarian, each has its unique strength and skills. Next the player can choose to play as a single player or play with others around the world by entering a remote server. The task at initial level helps player become familiar with the interface, the meaning of various graphics and sounds, and the concept of hometown in which the player can trade objects or receive commissions and rewards. It is through playing at this level, the player learns how to execute actions such as how to kill enemies, find objects or gold, and progresses in experience points and skill levels on the battlefield. The player can ally with other players to fight enemies as a leader or a follower and chat with them while playing. There are many types of spells, armor and weapons available; the player needs to choose the best one for his/her avatar and continue to upgrade the power of these objects. The player has to look for runes and recipes to make crafted items in order to boost the power of an object. Once the value of an object is increased, the player can exchange or trade it with other players within the game or on the auction web site. During the long journey to kill Diablo, the player could research information and strategies of how to survive in this game on the Internet or discuss with other players through chatting or instant message tools.

Literacy is situational in terms of social, cultural and technological contexts. In this case, gaming environment and players' community is the context where gaming literacies constructed. At this level, players are passively receiving information surrounding this game and learning rules constructed by game designers. The skills, knowledge and creativity they developed from a game are restricted and could be applied to the next level of this particular game or similar type of games. There are cases that players may apply what they have learned from educational games and simulation games to a similar situation; however, in general, players are message receiver rather than producer while playing games.

Literacy begins with learning the symbols of the medium (Sherman & Craig, 1995). It is the same for gaming literacies. Players begin to play the game by learning symbols and rules of a game. Beavis (2002a) selected RPG, strategy and shooting games and observed 6 teenager players to play these games, and identified elements entailed reading and playing games. To cover all game genres, we modified these elements as following (Hsu & Wang, 2010):

- **Text:** Players need to be able to read text to understand the information presented in the games. Many games use balloon or dialog box to provide immediate feedback to help players understand game rules or functions of objects, present the narration of the story and conversation among characters. In MMOGs, players need to understand and use the lingos (e.g. lol = laughing out loud) in the game context to communicate with other players so they can come up with solutions to the problems. .
- **Visual Graphical Element:** Players have to be able to identify meanings conveyed through the graphic and animation, and distinguish different player's perspective. Some games present the content in first person perspective (e.g. driving car, shooting) or from God's perspective- place the avatar on the screen and let players take control of it (e.g. Warcraft). Others allow users control most of the objects on the screen (e.g. The Sims). Players have to understand different players' perspective and differentiate objects in 2D or 3D dimensions. The change of color or shapes of objects prompt players to attend to new information with ease.
- **Audio Elements:** Sound elements provide players realistic atmosphere and are sometimes used to signal players to deal with more information.

- **Game Rules:** Rules in a game can be simple as Bejeweled (to achieve highest scores) or complicated as Age of Empires (build a tribe, increase civilization, build military, combat or ally with other players to dominate enemy civilizations, achieve economic victory or build and defend wonders of the world). Players have to explore considerably more effective strategies to achieve goals by complying with the internal game rules. While playing a game, players learn the rules by following the hidden tutorial in the initial level. Players can easily master the gaming literacies by advancing to next levels.
- **Interface:** Players control the game with mouse, keyboard, joystick or other peripheral (e.g. use wireless guitar to play console game Guitar Hero). They have to figure out how to interact with the game by using screen icons or physical peripheral and understand information presented on the interface.

At the "Writing" Level: From Message Production Perspective

At this level, gaming literacies involve higher cognitive skills and stronger social relationship. Until players are motivated to develop their own game, they cannot distinguish themselves from others and move upward to the next level of gaming literacies. A player can still enjoy games without having the experience of designing games; however, a game designer has opportunity to create a unique world with self-made game language and grammar. Players have to be fluent in the first level of gaming literacies before they can advance to the next level as a game designer and be an actively content producer. Williams suggests that computer literacy involves being a part of a community that uses ICTs (2003). The concept is analogous to the gaming literacies. The purpose of designing a game is to engage players; therefore, players' gaming experiences form game designers' decisions and shape the production of the game. In retrospective, Huang (2006) detailed the complexity of social relationship between game designers and players and its influence on the game design.

Pelletier (2005) in her study offered 12 – 13 year old students opportunities to design the screenshot of a RPG game including a sci-fi setting. Students' products demonstrated their abilities to develop unique features of a game and to communicate in text and graphic, as well as in design interface. The design of a real game is far more complicated and requires higher level of cognitive skills. Game design and development involves knowledge and skills in multiple domains: producer, artists, programmers, interactivity designer, sound engineers and testers. Game designers need to decide the unique features and target audience, create game rules, choose interface, develop the prototype for testing, design multimedia elements, conduct evaluation and finalize the game. At this level, game designers have to be proficient with the language and grammar used in computer programming software or multimedia authoring tools. They also need to know the language or jargons used in this community to communicate with other designers. The designer's final decision of developing story, character, event, competition is influenced by the game players' reaction, experts' opinion, and their game playing experience. More and more educators believe that designing games can develop students' learning motivation, literary skills, understanding of subject matter, collaborative skills, and technology skills (Kafai & Burke, 2016; Squire, 2011; Wouters, van Nimwegen, von Oostendorp, & van der Spek, 2013). However, designing games requires many sets of skills and demands a variety of support and scaffold from the educators.

Based on the "reading" and "writing" perspectives, our definition of the gaming literacies is thus generated based on both content consumption and production perspective:

"At the message consumption level, gaming literacies include the knowledge and skills to comprehend information in multimedia format (text, graphic, movie, sound), identify challenges, synthesize and evaluate information in the game, interact with gaming system (including the use of user interface and understanding of game components), communicate and collaborate with players from online community, and apply abovementioned knowledge and skills to achieve the ultimate goal in a game. At the production level, gaming literacies include the knowledge and skills to use media production tools (audio, video, animation) and programming language, design human-computer interface, conduct usability testing, collaborate and communicate with other game developers, apply problem solving and critical thinking skills, research and evaluate information, and design and develop an interactive game with engaging story scripts."

Several Themes of Gaming Literacies

- Gaming literacies is a subset skills of ICT literacies. Players need to acquire certain level of ICT skills in order to play game (Facer, 2003; Hsu & Wang, 2010; Sandford et al, 2006). For example, many games require players to install browser plug-in or other functions such as DirectX. Players have to read the instruction of how to install, how to optimize the computer to accommodate the requirements of playing game, or connect to remote servers to launch games. Players should have certain levels of computer skills to deal with technical issues surfaced while playing games.

- Gaming literacies is situational/contextualized until players become designers. A player can be good at shooting game but knows only a little about MMOGs. Gaming literacies is transferrable if the context is similar. In the Diablo example, once the player knows how to play Diablo, he can immediately play the similar type of game such as Fate without any extra cognitive load. The player still needs go through the basic levels in order to become an expert in Fate. The skills player has learned from Diablo about operation is hardly useful in other types of game such as Grand Theft Auto. Gaming literacies at the player level is not interdisciplinary. Gaming literacies can be understood only in the context in which it is acquired and used. Until fundamental change on gaming technology (e.g. prevalence of artificial intelligence, virtual reality), until it alters the purpose of playing games from "being entertained" to "being educated", the application of gaming literacies at the player level is mostly confined within the game.

- Game players are passively "consuming" message rather than "producing." Mastering ICT literacies enables people to create and develop content. Some may argue that there are games allowing people to express creativity or productivity. We need to take into account that games focus on developing creativity is relatively rare. In addition, the tools players used and the rules they followed to "create" or "assemble" things in games are defined by game designers. Their creativity and productivity are confined within the world of these particular games. Creativity is a complicated concept and is difficult to define. The consensus of various definitions of creativity are that it should be novel, original and should have value (Sternberg, 2001). To explore the potential educational value of games, we need to carefully define the cognitive areas that games can contribute to, rather than maximize and glorify the effects of games on learning.

- Gaming literacies is a preference. Unlike ICT literacies is required and demanded by the societal demand and the workforce, gaming literacies is not a set of skills that all learners should be equipped with. ICT literacies is a new demand and new skills indispensable to succeed in the information age.

Learning Domains That Gaming Literacies Might Contribute to

In this section, we will discuss the potential educational values of games and how fluent gaming literacies might contribute to learning. There are doubts about formal learning taking place in the gaming process. We believe that the possession of gaming literacies will facilitate players' learning in terms of Bloom's Taxonomy in cognitive domain if some premises are established.

Impact of Games on Education

There are two types of games gaining more attention and have been recruited in educational context: simulation and educational games (Gredler, 2004). Some evidence exists that games can effectively contribute to learners' understanding of complex subject matter through simulation games (Randel et al., 1992). Simulations imitate real-world systems and allow users to manipulate and test variables in this system to observe the consequences, explore the underling rules and the cause (input) and effect (output). Players can try different strategies to optimize the system which is not doable or unrealistic to implement in the real world. For example, SimCity series allow players to be the mayor in the virtual city, and the goal is to manage the budget and maximize the ROI (return of investment) to benefit citizens in all perspectives. Educational games are designed to introduce students' knowledge of a specific subject area. Elements of engaging players are incorporated into the design of the games to motivate learners to achieve the learning goals. Studies have confirmed that game features do trigger learners' motivation and attention toward subject matter; however, this does not mean simulation is a panacea to many education problems. There are studies point out that the translation of the "motivation to play the game" to "motivation to learn the subject matter" is not confirmed yet (Garris et al, 2002).

Controversies of Using Games in Educational Context

Negative effects of video gaming are reported in many research studies: greater playing time is correlated with poor grades in school and attention problems, and are more likely to be classified as overweight or obese; violent video game play increases aggression in young players in the short time (Boxer, Groves & Docherty, 2015; Ferguson, 2015; Markey, Markey & French, 2014).

Although some studies report that games have positive effects on learners' motivation, there is a difference between "motivation to play" and "motivation to learn." In a study conducted in UK, teachers work with researchers to incorporate several games in the classroom. The study concluded that teachers do see students' motivation increased; however, they also admitted that the motivation does not help students learn the subject area and does not applied to the learning tasks. Moreover, motivation to play games can also serve as a distraction from the lesson (Goundar, 2014), and even becomes addicted to video game playing (Loton, Borkoles, Lubman & Polman, 2015). Garris and colleagues (2002) asserted that "playing game" is voluntary while "learning" is nonvoluntary, which makes the selection and the design of educational games difficult. Moreover, for learners who do not like the type of games educators adopt, have gender preference, or do not have the acquired gaming literacies; using games may not support their learning (Hamlen, 2015).

How Games Can Contribute to Learning

As educators, we need to carefully choose the appropriate games that can be integrated into curriculum to increase learners' motivation toward a subject matter by introducing content in a game. However, we have to be aware of the potential harm or disadvantages of having learners to play games. Should teachers decide to employ a game to motivate learners, they need to research the knowledge and skills the game can contribute to. Only then a game can be properly introduced to learners, and help them develop appropriate gaming literacies.

If we carefully examine the knowledge and skills learners attain through game playing, we will be able to classify their learning outcomes. We will discuss how mastering these gaming literacies will contribute to cognitive, affective and psychomotor domains proposed by Bloom (Anderson & Krathwohl, 2001; Bloom, 1956). We will use the simulation game SimCity as an example to explain how teachers could use simulation game in the classroom to facilitate their gaming literacies.

Cognitive Domain

- **Knowledge (Remember):** Learners should be able to recall or recognize facts, identify objects or recall the sequence of a game. Teachers could start with a new established virtual city and help students become familiar with the common interaction with the game and get used to the operation, meaning of icons and objects, and how games designers prompt users to continue the next step. Winning is not the priority at this stage. It is important to let learners read contextual clues and cueing systems, including graphics, visuals, multimedia, interactivity, and so on.
- **Comprehension (Understand):** Learner should be able to explain how things work, identify question, and understand symbolic meaning of a gaming system. Teachers should observe if learners can figure out simple gaming rules. Ask them to explain certain perspectives of the games, for example, what phenomenon and rules have they observed and what factors should players be aware when playing SimCity.
- **Application (Apply):** Learners should be able to use limited experience in simple similar situation, and apply skills and knowledge gathered from former levels to the next level. After playing SimCity for a period of time, teachers can ask learners to explain the rules to complete various tasks given in this game, or discuss with peers what challenges a mayor might face running a city.
- **Analysis (Analyzing):** Learner should be able to gather extensive experience and apply it in complex situation. Learners need extensive experiences of playing a complicated game before they can generalize ideas and strategies to succeed in the game. Teachers can interfere and guide them discuss successful strategies and then let them go back to test the strategies discussed. Continue the discussion and implementation until they can make the city population grow and satisfy people's needs. Then teachers could start a city with more difficult challenges and have learners predict what would happen if certain factors are manipulated.
- **Synthesis (Create):** Learner should be able to adapt knowledge and skills to other context. Teachers can introduce learners the criteria to consider a city as a "green city," and have students to power the city with recycle energy and balance the economic growth and the environment protection.

- **Evaluation (Design):** Learner should be able to judge and compare the relevance and useful-ness of information, prepare a list of criteria to evaluate a system, and list rules that are crucial to achieve the goal in a game. Teachers can select a city in which they live, introduce background information of the city (e.g. population, crime rate, facilitates) and identify possible challenges this city have. Have learners apply the rules and strategies they learned from playing Simcity and generate resolution to these problems.

Learning in playing games is hardly occurred without teachers' support. Games may provide teachers opportunities to cultivate higher levels thinking abilities if higher motivation and supportive pedagogies are adopted. Teachers should carefully select games, and make sure learners are comfortable with the op-eration before increasing more challenge tasks to reduce their cognitive load and focus on subject content.

Some learners might show interests in game design and development when they have accumulated several years of game playing experiences. A game designer certainly needs to master skills in all above-mentioned cognitive domains in game design. Teachers could introduce them skills and knowledge they need to master in order to enter the game design career, for example, math, art, or any content areas they show interests. In the design process, they can learn extensive knowledge about interactive story design, artistic expression, and programming skills. Some entry level game design tools are available so novice can start creating simple game. For example, Adventure Game Studio (AGS, http://www.adven-turegamestudio.co.uk/), a free, easy-to-use RPG game development tool. Another one is GameMaker Studio (http://www.yoyogames.com/studio). With these tools, game players can advance from message consumption level to the production level.

Affection Domain

Affection domain refers to emotional learning, or change of learners' value or believe. Many online games allow learners to play collaboratively or complete with each other to achieve goals in games. They might need to form groups and adopt strategies to complete part of a task. The interaction no longer exists only between learner and the game. Player has to interact with other players. Game becomes a tool to mediate certain level of social interaction (Steinkuehler, 2004). Some types of games can be adopted to facilitate learners' understanding of certain issues, such as global warming and poverty. For example, teachers can introduce the game "Ayiti: The Cost of Life (http://www.gamesforchange.org/play/ayiti-the-cost-of-life/)" to learners. It is designed to have students understand about how poverty becomes an obstacle to education, and develop strategies to manage resources to support a family concur the chal-lenge of poverty. After playing this game, teachers should lead discussion or have learners discuss how education can play a vital means of human development.

Psychomotor Domain

Psychomotor domain refers to physical skills. Many types of games can be used to train learners' physi-cal skills such as hand-eyes coordination, speed, use of instruments or tools through the interaction with the game, or perform a set of procedure. Psychomotor skills can be simple action from click and drag to complex sets of skills such as piloting aircraft (Microsoft Flight Simulator provides players near real pilot training environment) or combat training (American's Army provides authentic military experience).

IMPLICATIONS

Although games have positive impact on some learning domains, as educators, we must recognize that gaming technologies only benefit learners when we use them appropriately. When considering adopts games into learning, teacher should consider the following issues.

Consider the needs to adopt games in the classroom. Will other alternative media or easy to access materials achieve the same learning goals? Is the value of using game worth the budget purchasing games, spend time solving technical issues, or risk distracting learners, exposing learners to violent content, and adding to play games?

Select games that are appropriate for most learners. For example, exclude games reward near real violent behaviors, or consider gender difference and preference (Garris, Ahlers, & Driskell, 2002; Games Hartmann & Klimmt, 2006). Also consider the need of learners who are fluent with print materials but unfamiliar with game operation (Beavis, 2002b).

To effectively transfer learners' motivation from playing to learning, teachers have to spent great amount of time on playing game to unveil the layers of the game design, elements that matched with curriculum standards and underlying complexity, especially when the design of most game is to entertain and engage players, not to educate players. This makes it difficult to align game playing with curriculum standards.

Since gaming literacies (for players who do not become designer) is contextual and situational, therefore, if the teacher decides to integrate a game into a subject area, then the teacher may want to reinforce the learning domains we discussed in the previous section.

Use game to trigger learners' motivation toward a subject area. However, teachers should be aware of the difficulty to divert learners' motivation from playing to learning.

Choose and explore appropriate pedagogies to support learning through games. Facer stated that in their research in using games in educational context, "Exploring ways to engage, stimulate, and motivate learners has become the main focus of the research as well as trying to develop digital environments that support new forms of learning (Facer, 2003)." Learning occurs in the game playing environment if appropriate instructional support is provided (i.e. debriefing and scaffolding) (Hsu & Wang, 2010; Ma et al, 2007). There are successful stories such as combining cooperative learning, using computer games to improve learners' math performance (Ke & Grabowski, 2007), and motivate learners to use games to complement and extend students' understanding of the fantasy genre in English class (Beavis, 2002b).

Divert learners' interests toward playing or addicting to games to game design. Teachers can encourage learners who are massive game players to explore the field of game design, which requires extensive knowledge and cognitive skills in various cognitive domains. Their gaming playing experiences will also add benefit to the design process.

Explore the possibilities to improve learners' gaming literacies and help them transfer knowledge and skills learned through playing game to real life context. This strategy is especially important for playing simulation games.

FUTURE RESEARCH OPPORTUNITIES

Questions remained and emerged while we explored the definition and implication of gaming literacies that needs researchers' attention and efforts.

- How can educators transform gaming literacies beyond the gaming context in which it exists? What is the value of gaming literacies to real life challenges? How can learners transfer and apply gaming literacies to resolve problems encountered in everyday life? For example, some believe that collaboration occurred in MMOGs can help players learn the strategies to collaborate with others in real life. However, collaboration in MMGOs is limited to a certain level such as fighting, trading objects. There is a need to study the degree of the knowledge and skills transfer from playing MMGOS to real life collaboration to resolve problems before the conclusion can be made.
- Is there a correlation between gaming literacies and ICT literacies? How improve gaming literacies can contribute to the improvement of ICT literacies?
- If gaming literacies has value to education, how can we assess gaming literacies?
- Explore the possibility to examine the comprehension semiotic system in playing games. It is a system of social convention for giving and taking meaning of certain type. Language has structure property that allow for a great deal for emergence and expressive creativity. It would be interesting to interrogate the "grammars" of different game types to see (and how much) emergence and player creativity/expression is allowed.

CONCLUSION

In summary, at this stage, educators can consider possibilities to adopt simulation and educational games in the classroom to encourage learning. Learning outcomes exist on the following assumptions: teachers facilitate learners to achieve certain degree of gaming literacies to avoid cognitive load, resolve technical issues relating to playing games, adopt pedagogies to support learning through playing game, and consider issues such as gender preference and media preference.

REFERENCES

Anderson, L. W., & Krathwohl, D. R. (Eds.). (2001). *A taxonomy for learning, teaching, and assessing: A revision of Bloom's taxonomy of educational objectives*. New York, NY: Longman.

Barnes, K., Marateo, R., & Pixy Ferris, S. (2007). Teaching and learning with the Net Generation. *Innovate*, *3*(4). Retrieved from http://csdtechpd.org/pluginfile.php/1622/mod_glossary/attachment/25/Teaching_and_Learning_ with_the_Net_Generation.pdf

Beavis, C. (2002a). *RTS and RPGs: New Literacies and Multiplayer Computer Games*, Paper presented at the Annual Conference of the Australian Association For Research in Education, University of Queensland, December 1-5. Retrieved from http://www.aare.edu.au/02pap/bea02658.htm

Beavis, C. (2002b). Reading, writing and role-playing computer games. In L. Snyder (Ed.), Silicon literacies: Communication, innovation and education in the electronic age (pp. 47-61). London: Routledge.

Bloom, B. S. (1956). *Taxonomy of educational objectives, handbook I: The cognitive domain*. New York: David McKay Co Inc.

Boxer, P., Groves, C. L., & Docherty, M. (2015). Video games do indeed influence children and adolescents aggression, prosocial behavior, and academic performance: A clearer reading of Ferguson (2015). *Perspectives on Psychological Science, 10*(5), 671–673. doi:10.1177/1745691615592239 PMID:26386004

Brown, J. S. (2000). Growing up digital: How the Web changes work, education, and the ways people learn. *Change, 32*(2), 10–20. doi:10.1080/00091380009601719

Cesarini, P. (2004). Computers, technology, and literacies. *The Journal of Literacy and Technology, 4*(1). http://www.literacyandtechnology.org/v4/cesarini.htm Retrieved June 10, 2007

Craig, A. B., Brown, E. R., Upright, J., & DeRosier, M. E. (2016). Enhancing children's social emotional functioning through virtual game-based delivery of social skills training. *Journal of Child and Family Studies, 25*(3), 959–968. doi:10.1007/s10826-015-0274-8

Csikszentmihalyi, M. (1985). Emergent motivation and the evolution of the self. In D. A. Kleiber & M. Maehr (Eds.), *Advances in motivation and achievement* (Vol. 4, pp. 93–119). Greenwich, CT: JAI Press.

Csikszentmihalyi, M. (1998). *Finding flow: The psychology of engagement with everyday life.* New York: Basic.

Facer, K. (2003). Computer games and learning: Why do we think it's worth talking about computer games and learning in the same breath? Retrieved June 12, 2007, from http://www.futurelab.org.uk/resources/publications_reports_articles/discussion_papers/Discussion_Paper261/

Ferguson, C. J. (2015). Do angry birds make for angry children? A meta-analysis of video game influences on children's and adolescent's aggression, mental health, prosocial behavior, and academic performance. *Perspectives on Psychological Science, 10*(5), 646–666. doi:10.1177/1745691615592234 PMID:26386002

Foreman, J. (2003). Next-generation: Educational technology versus the lecture. *EDUCAUSE,* (July/August), 13-22, Retrieved May 25, 2007 from http://www.educause.edu/ir/library/pdf/erm0340.pdf

Garris, R., Ahlers, R., & Driskell, J. E. (2002). Games, motivation, and learning: A research and practice model. *Simulation & Gaming, 33*(4), 441–467. doi:10.1177/1046878102238607

Gee, J. P. (2003). Learning about learning from a video game: Rise of Nations. Retrieved from http://simworkshop.stanford.edu/05_0125/reading_docs/Rise%20of%20Nations.pdf

Gentile, D. A., & Anderson, C. A. (2003). Violent video games: The newest media violence hazard. In D. A. Gentile (Ed.), *Media violence and children.* Westport, CT: Praeger Publishing.

Gentile, D. A., Lynch, P. J., Linder, J. R., & Walsh, D. A. (2004). The effects of violent video game habits on adolescent aggressive attitudes and behaviors. *Journal of Adolescence, 27,* 5–22. doi:10.1016/j.adolescence.2003.10.002 PMID:15013257

Goundar, S. (2014). The distraction of technology in the classroom. *Journal of Education & Human Development, 3*(1), 211–229.

Gredler, M. E. (2004). Games and simulations and their relationships to learning. In D. H. Jonassen (Ed.), *Handbook of research for educational communications and Technology* (pp. 571–581). New York: Simon & Schuster Macmillan.

Hamlen, K. R. (2015). Understanding Children's Choices and Cognition in Video Game Play. *Zeitschrift fur Psychologie mit Zeitschrift fur Angewandte Psychologie*.

Hartmann, T., & Klimmt, C. (2006). Gender and computer games: Exploring female's dislikes. *Journal of Computer-Mediated Communication, 11*(4), 910–931. Retrieved from http://jcmc.indiana.edu/vol11/issue4/hartmann.html doi:10.1111/j.1083-6101.2006.00301.x

Hsu, H.-Y., & Wang, S.-K. (2010). Using gaming literacies to cultivate new literacies. *Simulation & Gaming, 41*(3), 400–417. doi:10.1177/1046878109355361

Hsu, H.-Y., Wang, S.-K., & Runco, L. (2013). Middle school science teachers confidence and pedagogical practice of new literacies. *Journal of Science Education and Technology, 22*(3), 314–324. doi:10.1007/s10956-012-9395-7

Huang, A. (2006), Remembering Blizzard North and Diablo II. Retrieved from http://www.diabloii.net/columnists/a-memories-blizzard.shtml

International Information and Communication Technologies (ICT) Literacy Panel. (2002). *Digital transformation: A framework for ICT Literacy*. Princeton, NJ: Educational Testing Services (ETS). Retrieved from http://www.ets.org/Media/Research/pdf/ICTREPORT.pdf

International Reading Association. (2012). *Standards for English Language Arts*. Retrieved from http://www.reading.org/downloads/publications/books/bk889.pdf

Kafai, Y. B., & Burke, Q. (2015). Constructionist gaming: Understanding the benefits of making games for learning. *Educational Psychologist, 50*(4), 313–334. doi:10.1080/00461520.2015.1124022 PMID:27019536

Ke, F., & Grabowski, B. (2007). Gameplaying for maths learning: Cooperative or not? *British Journal of Educational Technology, 38*(2), 249–259. doi:10.1111/j.1467-8535.2006.00593.x

Leu, D. J., Kinzer, C. K., Coiro, J. L., & Cammack, D. W. (2004a). *Toward a theory of new literacies emerging from the internet and other information and communication technologies*. Retrieved from http://www.readingonline.org/newliteracies/leu/

Leu, D. J., Kinzer, C. K., Coiro, J. L., & Cammack, D. W. (2004b). Toward a theory of new literacies emerging from the internet and other information and communication technologies. In R. B. Ruddell & N. J. Unrau (Eds.), *Theoretical models and processes of reading* (5th ed., pp. 1570–1613). Newark, DE: International Reading Association. (Original work published 2000)

Leu, D. J., Zawilinski, L., Forzani, E., & Timbrell, N. (2014). Best practices in teaching the new literacies of online research and comprehension. Retrieved from http://www.orca.uconn.edu/orca/assets/File/Best%20Practices%20in%20new%20literacies.pdf

Livingstone, S. (2004). Media literacy and the challenge of new information and communication technologies. *Communication Review, 7*(1), 3–14. doi:10.1080/10714420490280152

Loton, D., Borkoles, E., Lubman, D., & Polman, R. (2016). Video game addiction, engagement and symptoms of stress, depression and anxiety: The mediating role of coping. *International Journal of Mental Health and Addiction, 14*(4), 565–578. doi:10.1007/s11469-015-9578-6

Ma, Y., Williams, D., Prejean, L., & Richard, C. (2007). A research agenda for developing and implementing educational computer games. *British Journal of Educational Technology, 38*(3), 513–518. doi:10.1111/j.1467-8535.2007.00714.x

Markey, P. M., Markey, C. N., & French, J. E. (2014). Violent video games and real-world violence: Rhetoric versus data. *Psychology of Popular Media Culture, 4*(4), 277–295. doi:10.1037/ppm0000030

Mehlman, B. P. (2003). Technology administration ICT literacy: Preparing the digital generation for the age of innovation. Retrieved from http://www.technology.gov/Speeches/p_BPM_030124-DigGen.htm

National Council of Teachers of English. (2008). The definition of 21st Century Literacies. Retrieved from http://www.ncte.org/governance/literacies

North Central Regional Educational Laboratory. (2001). *Critical Issue: Using Technology to Enhance Literacy Instruction*. Retrieved from http://www.ncrel.org/sdrs/areas/issues/content/cntareas/reading/li300.htm#contacts

Pelletier, C. (2005). The uses of literacy in studying computer games: Comparing students' oral and visual representations of games. *English Teaching, 4*(1), 40–59. Retrieved from http://education.waikato.ac.nz/journal/english_journal/uploads/files/2005v4n1art3.pdf

Prensky, M. (2001). *Digital game-based learning*. New York, NY: McGraw-Hill.

Randel, J. M., Morris, B. A., Wetzel, C. D., & Whitehill, B. V. (1992). The effectiveness of games for educational purposes: A review of recent research. *Simulation & Gaming, 23*(3), 261–276. doi:10.1177/1046878192233001

Salen, K. (2006). Everywhere now: Three dialogues on kids, games, and learning. Retrieved from http://spotlight.macfound.org/images/uploads-participants/everywhere_now_dialogues_salen.pdf

Sherman, W. R., & Craig, A. B. (1995). Literacy in virtual reality: A new medium. *Computer Graphics, 29*(4), 37–42. Retrieved from http://portal.acm.org/citation.cfm?id=216887 doi:10.1145/216876.216887

Squire, K. (2011). *Video games and learning: Teaching and participatory culture in the digital age*. New York, NY: Teachers College Press.

Steinkuehler, C. A. (2004b). Learning in massively multiplayer online games. In Y. B. Kafai, W. A. Sandoval, N. Enyedy, A. S. Nixon, & F. Herrera (Eds.), *Proceedings of the Sixth International Conference of the Learning Sciences* (pp. 521-528). Mahwah, NJ: Erlbaum.

Sternberg, R. J. (2001). What is the Common Thread of Creativity? Its Dialectical Relation to Intelligence and Wisdom. *The American Psychologist, 56*(4), 360–362. doi:10.1037/0003-066X.56.4.360 PMID:11330237

Tapscott, D. (2009). *Grown up digital: How the net generation is changing your world*. New York, NY: McGraw-Hill.

Thompson, P. (2013). The digital natives as learners: Technology use patterns and approaches to learning. *Computers & Education, 65*, 12–33. doi:10.1016/j.compedu.2012.12.022

Tierney, R. J., Bond, E., & Bresler, J. (2006). Examining literate lives as students engage with multiple literacies. *Theory into Practice, 45*(4), 359–367. doi:10.1207/s15430421tip4504_10

Vorderer, P., Hartmann, T., & Klimmt, C. (2003). Explaining the enjoyment of playing video games. In *Proceedings of the ACM International Conference Proceeding Series*. Pittsburgh: Carnegie Mellon University.

Wang, S.-K., Hsu, H.-Y., Campbell, T., Coster, D., & Longhurst, M. (2014). An Investigation of Middle School Science Teachers and Students Use of Technology Inside and Outside of Classrooms: Considering whether digital natives are more technology savvy than their teachers. *Educational Technology Research and Development, 62*(6), 637–662. doi:10.1007/s11423-014-9355-4

Williams, K. (2003). Literacy and computer literacy: Analyzing the NRC's being fluent with information technology. *The Journal of Literacy and Technology, 3*(1). Retrieved from http://www.literacyandtechnology.org/v3n1/williams.htm

Wouters, P., van Nimwegen, C., von Oostendorp, H., & van der Spek, E. D. (2013). A meta-analysis of the cognitive and motivational effects of serious games. *Journal of Educational Psychology, 105*(2), 249–265. doi:10.1037/a0031311

KEY TERMS AND DEFINITIONS

Affection Domain in Bloom's Taxonomy: In this category, learning occurs with change of values and behaviors: receiving, responding, valuing, and organizing.

Bloom's Taxonomy: Bloom's Taxonomy describes learning types, learning behaviors and intellectual skills in three major categories as follows.

Cognitive Domain in Bloom's Taxonomy: In this category, learning occurs in six levels with increasing complexity: knowledge (remember), comprehension (understand), application (apply), analysis (analyzing), synthesis (create), and evaluation (design). At each level, learning involves different level of cognitive processing.

Flow: A process that engages players in activities that challenge their abilities and produce enjoyment. If the task is too easy, players feel bored and stop playing; if the task is too difficult, players give up the attempt to challenge.

Gaming Literacies: At the message consumption level, gaming literacies means the abilities to comprehend multimedia format content, interact with the system, identify and overcome challenges in the game through research or communication with other players. At the message production level, gaming literacies refers to the ability to use media production tools and programming language, apply design principles, collaborate with other game developers, design interactive story, apply problem solving skills to design and develop a game that can engage players.

Information Communication Technologies (ICTs): Information Communication Technologies.

New Literacies: Apply skills, strategies to adopt ICTs to identify questions, locate and evaluation information to answer these questions, and then communicate the answers with others (Leu et al, 2004).

Psychomotor Domain in Bloom's Taxonomy: In this category, learning occurs with development and perfection on motor skills.

ENDNOTE

[1]   Prensky proposed twelve elements in the original text (Prensky, 2001, p5-1).

Chapter 6
Digital Media and Social Network in the Training of Pre–Service Teachers

Tami Seifert
Kibutzim College of Education, Israel

ABSTRACT

The use of Web 2.0 environments and social media in teaching and learning facilitates the provision of participatory and creative, learner-oriented teaching. The proposed chapter describes the role of social media in teaching and learning in colleges of higher education and suggests possible uses and applications for a variety of social media environments in education, especially the environments of Facebook, Twitter, WhatsApp, and Instagram. Social networks facilitate activities that promote involvement, collaboration and engagement. Modeling of best practices using social networks enhances its usage by students, increases student confidence as to its implementation and creates a paradigm shift to a more personalized, participatory and collaborative learning and a more positive attitude towards its implementation.

INTRODUCTION

The last three decades have witnessed a technological revolution influencing the ways in which we create knowledge, communicate, learn and teach. The Internet is 45 years old, and for almost half that time has been available to the general public. Already in 1998, the British scientist Timothy Berners-Lee (2000), who was considered the inventor of the Internet, predicted that the Internet would be a space where anyone could have immediate access not only to surf but also to create contents. In the era of Web 1.0 (1992-2000) it was possible to consume information but only a very few could publish contents, the division between those who created, distributed and consumed information was clear.

During this era, Web 2.0 - also known as "Reading-Writing Internet" - evolved (Price, 2006; Richardson, 2006). Bruns (2008) a social media researcher called this the Produsage era, combining the concepts of production and usage. This new era produced Cloud-based technology making information accessible

DOI: 10.4018/978-1-5225-3082-4.ch006

Copyright © 2018, IGI Global. Copying or distributing in print or electronic forms without written permission of IGI Global is prohibited.

and available in any time and place, changing the way people transmit information and allowing social media to flourish (Johnson, Adams & Cummins, 2012; Siemens, 2005). Although social media were not initially intended for use in education, educators saw the media as having immense potential to implement and advance constructivist learning theory that promotes collective wisdom, allowing access to a wide range of data, sharing surfers' content, and promoting self-expression and a sense of ownership of written materials (Reilly, 2005). King (1993) noted that the perception of the lecturer changed, instead of being the "sage on the stage" he became a guide and the teacher-focused teaching paradigm was replaced by a paradigm of teaching focused on the learning process (Barr & Tagg, 1995); the learner became involved in the construction of knowledge and contributed to it being remembered (Mayer, 1984). Social media anchored in the Web 2.0 world, offers a teaching model involving collaboration, interactions on the web between participants, allowing learners to be independent and using a variety of types of communication and cooperation (Rogers et al., 2007; Sheely, 2006). The Internet is no longer one-directional and controlled by a limited number of content creators, rather it is open and democratic and anyone with Internet and a browser can participate, create, work in collaboration, manage and share knowledge.

The social network characteristics necessitate renewed thinking about interactions between teachers, learners and learning materials and innovative methods should be explored to harness technological means in favor of meaningful teaching and learning processes. As someone who has worked for more than a decade in the implementation of Web 2.0 environments and social media in teaching and learning, I have experienced rich collaborative and creative learner-oriented teaching practices that enable the learners to become engaged and involved through the learning process (Seifert, 2015).

THE WORLD OF WEB 2.0: SOCIAL MEDIA, AND SOCIAL NETWORKS

Social media tools bring about profound changes in educational settings, supporting a social-constructivist paradigm of learning by promoting creative and collaborative engagement of learners with the digital content and tools (Mâță, 2013). Several scholars have theorized the pedagogical potential of using social media, such as social network sites for learning and emphasized the technology's potential for supporting collaborative knowledge construction (Dede 2008; Greenhow 2011; Siemens, 2005). Yet, pre-service students performing practicum in schools saw little evidence of teaching with SNSs in their classes; where this was reported, they perceived these efforts as primarily reinforcing traditional pedagogies and assessments (Greenhow & Askari, 2017). The various digital media tools that can be employed in school classes can be sorted into four categories: (1) tools for experiential writing and shared resources (blog, Twitter); (2) tools for sharing media and tagging (Flicker, Instagram and Youtube); (3) social media applications that permit creation of a semantic network (Facebook and LinkedIn). (4) Synchronic and a-synchronic communication tools (electronic mail, Skype and WhatsApp) (Dabbagh & Reo, 2011).

The Horizon 2014 report summarizes research identifying and describing trends and technologies that will have a greater influence on education teaching and research in the future, the authors note changes in interpersonal communication means in recent years (Johnson, Adams, Becker, Estrada & Freeman, 2014). Among the facts identified: more than 1.2 billion people use Facebook regularly, 2.7 billion people (almost 40% of world population) use social networks, and on 25 leading social media platforms, 6.3 billion people have accounts (including teachers, students, pupils, scientists etc.).

TEACHER PREPARATION IN THE WEB 2.0 AND SOCIAL MEDIA ERA

Present-day students learn in informal ways from various sources and can choose different learning means and methods suited to their personal needs, in contrast to traditional frontal or group learning. Access to education is enabled by a choice of contents, levels of learning, learning methods and at different times, places and paces. Learning environments such as TED Talks, academic materials Khan Academy and MOOC style courses use social media for communication and create collaboration between learners. Communication and collaboration during learning allow learners to learn from the Internet community, creating knowledge and contributing knowledge to the community.

Prensky (2001) notes that it is important for teachers to learn to recognize the language and different ways of thinking of their students, since they are "digital natives" and can be helped by technological means for their learning needs. Insufficient familiarity with the students' world and ways of thinking, may mean that studies may not be relevant or adequate to prepare students to assimilate in the work market (Windham, 2005). The current work market requires a learner with knowledge, skills and talents, able to make important complex decisions, personally oriented to life-long learning and familiar with the use of communication networks both as a producer and participant (Bruns, 2008). The personal learning process is seen as a broad participatory process fed by interaction with the world net community (Scardamalia & Bereiter, 2006).

Teacher preparation can be enhanced by creating opportunities for pre-service teachers in training to experience and effectively model lessons that use different social media tools for their future classrooms, so they understand the usage of social media, develop their professional identity, and rethink their attitudes towards its implementation (Mâţă, 2013). Higher education teacher educators need to seriously examine the potential of these environments for teaching to plan and use them intentionally to provide an optimal response to students' needs and to increase the chances for their learning success.

EMPOWERING THE PRE-SERVICE TEACHER IN THE WEB 2.0 ERA

Online social networks allow the sharing of ideas, attitudes, opinions, suggestions etc., with a broad population. These networks allow to interact with a large group of people in accordance with different needs and areas of knowledge. For example, Kennelly (2009) describes an application of the Myspace social network used for learning about rocks and minerals. On this network members "adopt an image" and represent rocks and minerals that interact one with another. Kennelly suggests that the decision to use a social network should be based on two criteria: a sense of comfort with the learning environment and adaptation of the environment for activities for which it is intended. Adaptation of the environment for activities can be expressed for example in the formation of a participants' group as a unique application for the social network environment, in order to ensure optimal communication and possibilities for learning, and sharing and support for learning. The wide variety of learning environments that are available to the pre-service teacher means that he needs to be familiar with each of them and understand their advantages and disadvantages, challenges and limitations, in order to intelligently choose which to use for a specific goal in teaching.

EXAMPLES OF IMPLEMENTATION OF SOCIAL MEDIA WITH PRE-SERVICE TEACHERS

Social media applications are used widely in academic teaching. A survey that examined the use of social media among a representative sample (whose representativeness is explained in detail in the article) of teaching staff from all USA academic institutes (Moran, Seaman & Tinti-Kane, 2011) found that at least two-thirds of the teaching staff integrated social media in their teaching. This was expressed during the lesson by reading online materials, publication on a blog or forum, publication of answers to questions or in discussions on the social media site etc. The most prevalent uses (reported by 80% of the staff members) included watching film clips during lessons, publishing films after the lessons or presenting them as a viewing assignment in preparation for a lesson. The use of social media has many advantages for learning. For example, it has been found to increase understanding of economics concepts, improves memorization over time and increases students' interest and involvement (Al-Bahrani & Patel, 2015). The use of social media can lead to creativity and involvement of quiet learners those who tend not to participate in lessons and encourage discussions in and outside lessons (Blankenship, 2011; Joosten, 2012; Wang, Sandhu, Wittich, Mandrekar, & Beckman, 2012). Students can use social media to deepen learning after the lesson (Wang, 2012), to form social connections lacking in online teaching (Blankenship, 2011) and to expand the discussion beyond the lesson boundaries (Joosten, 2012; Wang, 2012). Below are the detailed proposals on ways to promote learning by teaching with some social media applications, many of which have been implemented by the pre-service teaching students during the learning process: Facebook, Twitter, WhatsApp and Instagram.

Facebook (https://www.facebook.com) is the largest world social network. It opened to the public in 2006 and constitutes an accessible learning environment that creates user involvement and a sense of identity and belonging to a network citizenship. The use of Facebook allows the individual user to add friends through the sending of a request for friendship (the maximum number allowed is 5,000). Each Facebook user can create personal pages whose popularity can be measured through "likes" by friends which can reach tens of millions. On Facebook, it is possible to search for friends, to tag people in a picture or post, and to invite friends and add a "like" to their personal page or a planned event. It is also possible to build a gallery of pictures, a video gallery or share music. Facebook includes a variety of applications that can be added to a personal page. These characteristics mean that Facebook is an environment that is likely to assist learning and develop the learners' sense of responsibility for their learning and a high level of investment (Kent & Leaver, 2014). Facebook can supplement teaching with various activities characterized by instant publication. An experiment conducted regarding use of this environment over two academic semesters with the Moodle learning management system, showed that this environment is effective when accompanying a course for enrichment and participation and the presentation of materials and/or activities in real time (Seifert, 2016). Possibilities for learning activities on Facebook include:

1. Proffering questions and subjects for discussion.
2. Uploading films and visual materials such as maps so that the student can keep up to date with their friends and share different mappings, such as mapping their professional network (Personal Learning Network), and regular updating.
3. Presentation of surveys that require voting, or choice of a suitable possibility, or publication of an event and request for confirmation of participation. The survey can be shared with a few friends, with all friends or with a defined group, and it is even possible to create a public survey.

4. Sharing materials during and after lessons.
5. Creating a shared timeline, including the possible creation of a personal timeline (e.g. Inventions of the 20th century https://www.facebook.com/20thCenturyInventions/timeline). A timeline is a function that exists on personal pages in Facebook and allows the individual to present a profile of events that occurred over time. This function can be harnessed for teaching purposes. Each individual in a group (or each group) can contribute to the construction of part of the timeline, since there is a uniform user name and code for everyone. For example, activity performed in a lesson by two students that choose to focus on the figure of James Naismith – who invented basketball. The students were asked to draft a collective Google.docs file describing the aspect that they wished to research. Then on Facebook a timeline was presented and at the next stage students attempted creating a collective timeline, sharing different viewpoints that each of the students had investigated. Thus, online information was produced on the chosen figure.
6. Group Work: It is possible to work in a group that is open for all network users or in a group that is closed only including course participants. Alternatively, there might be a covert work group only known to its members. Advantages of a closed or covert group are that there would be freedom of expression for members unthreatened by broader exposure (Seifert, 2016). Advantages of an open group are the accessibility or a discussion or debate in a broad, global context. Using a foreign text is clearly advantageous in an open group when foreign global views are sought.

Twitter (https://twitter.com/) – this is a microblog created in 2006, limited to writing 140 characters (letters and punctuation marks) in a post (tweet), which is suitable for activities where condensed, sharp messages are advantageous, for example in knowledge fields where precise writing is intended for a specific target audience. Twitter allows follow-up by users, who can ask and answer questions, expand discussions beyond lessons and learn to write in a concise more concentrated and sharper manner. For example, it was found that writing short messages on Twitter helped economics students to write better (Kassens).

Examples of learning activities on Twitter include:

1. Discussion on Twitter while watching video during lesson.
2. Accompanying the lecturer's discussion during the lesson by broadcasting students' tweets expressing remarks, questions and comments on the discussion.
3. Creating links to relevant reading materials, presenting students' questions before the lesson and presenting pictures and posters relevant for the lesson.
4. Following Twitter accounts of leading people in the course's knowledge field and discussions relevant to them.
5. Exercises in concise writing when required for the courses.

Hashtags should be defined for use of Twitter in a course. These are keywords that allow tweets to be tagged for future follow-up. For example, in an experiment in an online lesson we set aside an hour for discussion on Twitter and defined a keyword for the discussion. During that hour, the lecturer defined five issues for debate, and time was allotted between these issues for students' consideration. At the end of the activity the documentation of this activity remained as a contribution to those who did not participate and as a goal for future study of the session products.

WhatsApp (https://web.whatsapp.com/) this is an application for immediate announcements existing since 2010 and has attracted many users. It allows users to transmit messages between different trainees without use of SMS messages and free of charge. On WhatsApp messages can be written and received. Similar to Facebook, the messages and groups on WhatsApp are under users' full control. Examples of learning activities include:

1. Construction of a learning environment serving students as a creative contact group, interest group or learning group.
2. Receiving updates and immediate responses to questions or comfortable easy distribution of information through the group.
3. Communication between students in activities, for example "find the treasure"-type activities at different stations across the campus. Different groups of students try to find the treasure, and this environment, empowers access, enabling continuous contact between the student groups and sharing of locations on the campus distributing photographs of stations on WhatsApp to groups having difficulty finding them. If necessary sharing information with oral instructions.
4. Managing short discussions on a subject. These can be distinguished from regular discussion with an icon.
5. Posing clarifying questions during a lesson, sending pictures or sketches for consideration, sending messages.

Instagram (https://instagram.com) an application existing since 2010, allows photography and sharing photographs and films of up to 15 seconds. The application allows graphic filters to be applied to pictures to produce professional finish, addition of labels, editing video and distributing video pictures on social networks. Users can define private accounts or collective groups for a particular activity. Similar to Twitter and other networks, Hashtags can be used to tag each activity separately. Hashtags focus the correspondence and facilitate access to information resulting from activity. Examples of use for learning include:

1. Use of films and photographs in lessons discussing visual components such as art, instant photography, and personal experiences, representation of learning materials in a picture, in graphs and in infographics (concise visual representation of information, ideas and trends intended for illustration). The photographs and films can be produced by the students, who can then distribute them to other students and receive feedback.
2. Representation in pictures as a basis for discussion and writing.
3. Production of films from still pictures and excerpts from videos filmed during trips.
4. Use of short video-clips to learn correct pronunciation of language.
5. Presentation of an idea or proposal for a short video-clip for example, presentation of answers to prevalent questions on online course, guidance on activity or process, creation of a personal portfolio and promotion of an event or product.
6. Applications can be adapted to different fields of knowledge. For example, asking students to upload pictures relating to the studied subject and tagging them. Tagging can contribute to the discussion and/or learning process. Instagram can be tested as a tool for marketing and publicity, to learn about trends and to use this for learning, cultures can be investigated and compared with aid

of location data and relying on pictures photographed in different geographical sites, plant growth can be followed and projects and photographs can share different natural phenomenon from all over the network.

Additional features of these four media means described above are: sharing posts on Instagram in real time with different media environments such as Facebook and Twitter to expand their distribution without needing to publish them separately in each of the networks. In Instagram and Twitter an environment may be formed where the lecturer does not see the personal profile of the student and the student does not see the lecturer's profile. Twitter, Instagram and Facebook allow private student-lecturer and student-students communication management.

In the work with pre-service teaching students, after learning about the potential of these different tools for classroom teaching, discussion ensued regarding the use of these tools in different environments.

APPLICATION OF SOCIAL MEDIA TO TEACHING AND LEARNING

Four of the most prevalent social media environments have been reviewed in this chapter. There are many others including information curating environments such as Pearltrees that allows storage, organization, management, sharing and watching of regularly updated dynamic links. Pinterest also permits sharing of visual content such as pictures and video-clips that is categorized according to fields of interest. There is also an environment for collaborative writing in Google.docs, contribution of items for Wikipedia and Cloud environments for the joint management of learning and projects.

Teaching can also be accompanied by a YouTube channel with a focused playlist of lessons that students can listen to and watch. Researchers can also create a personal profile through various tools and channels such as Google Scholar and also a professional-scientific profile in environments such as Research gate and Academia.com. These environments create a foundation for online communication, sharing knowledge, communication between experts and encouraging collaboration within academic communities, and they increase the visibility of scientific work.

But there is a fly in the ointment. The use of social media during lessons has its restrictions, mainly: interference due to distraction during lessons, especially for those with learning disabilities, time may be wasted, communication deviates to a discussion between students, the lecturer becomes involved beyond the time of the lesson and students may write with spelling mistakes that need correcting. Moreover, in order to use social media in the class, the lecturer needs familiarity with the different media environments and applications for the studied knowledge field. Also, when using social media, it is important to consider different possibilities for personal definition of the lecturer and students on the different networks and to be aware that knowledge produced may be unintentionally exposed. Participating in a social network necessitates registration similar to Facebook, this may be problematic for those whose ideology or religion forbids use of social networks. In an open environment with free follow-up such as on Twitter, unwanted users or followers may have to be coped with. Inaccurate writing on the net can harm content composition, text quality and ability to deliver clear messages (Moran, Seaman & Tinti-Kane, 2011). These disadvantages mean that the lecturer should define clear expectations and determine rules of use for social media use in the course.

THE CONTRIBUTION OF THE SOCIAL MEDIA TO THE LEARNING PROCESS

The various social media tools were implemented with two groups of pre-service teaching students (34 students), already licensed to teach various ages and disciplines, who participated over two consecutive years in the course "Social Networks in Educational Contexts" as part of their Master of Education (M.Ed.) in Technology and Education, and with six groups of students (132 students) who participated in two compulsory courses entitled 'Teaching and learning in ICT environments' and 'Teaching and learning in innovative environments' conducted over an academic semester. The courses were taught using the learning management system Moodle. The environment was designed for information presentation and for communication.

The courses deal with the recognition of the complex characteristics of social media and social networks, as well as relevant practices in teaching and learning process. The courses were studied by means of varied experiences in social media and social networks and the students implemented social media and social network-based activities which they developed and applied in peer teaching in the class. The students cited are all pre-service teachers.

Upon completion of the course it became apparent that all the pre-service students had developed attitudes towards this topic. A certain level of reservation was still evident with regard to the implementation of social networks, however the students' suggestions manifested experiential and constructive learning methods which would stimulate and enrich the learning process. One of the students indicated:

I must say, this idea is one of the cutest things I have seen lately. What a delightful way to use creativity and fun as tools for teaching (and learning). Similar to previous assignments, the possibilities with this tool are endless! What I particularly like about it is the sense of 'informality' that this tool affords both to the teacher and the student. It automatically becomes more appealing to work on an assignment because it is not on a boring blank piece of paper, but on fun colorful sticky notes that can be formatted to match the students own personality. What a treat!!! Not only that, but it promotes interaction between students - for the very same reasons. It is fun to add a new sticky note with your own comment or idea. The boards can also be used to organize class activities, plan fundraisers, and other non-academic related topics that are also part of the day-to-day classroom activities…The features of deadlines, and ability to upload pictures, videos and documents are also great for teaching. You can use the same board for conducting research, voicing opinions, presenting counter-arguments, and to promote self-expression, all in the same assignment.

Another student said:

As a result of the collaborative activity, I felt that I could stimulate my future students to express what interests them in a creative, non-routine manner, and even more, that it would be possible to connect and work in cooperation and not necessarily with regular front teaching.

While yet another student talked about the importance of variation in teaching and learning methods:

I learned about different types of participation and how to express them in activities that I bring to the classroom in order to increase motivation to participate. From the administrative process, I learnt how to accept "feedback" from my future students and to trace their learning processes… I can see whether they understood the materials we learned, I can learn about their opinions, their feelings. I can administer knowledge questionnaires on different subjects and in fact on any subject that I wish to … as a student in the activities of others I learned primarily what the students will feel and what will attract them to the activity or be less attractive. I learned that in order for them to want to participate in my activity, I need to market it well and ensure that its appearance and design are attractive, no less than the content of the activity itself. I feel that this course has assisted me to vary the form of my teaching and to attract the students to our shared learning process. I intend preparing inquiry activities which integrate involvement, interest and interaction between the learners.

Yet another student refers to the focus which shifts from the teacher to the pupils:

Also at school the use of a social network as an accompaniment to the lesson shifts the center of gravity from the teacher to the learners, leading learners to become active, collaborative, improves social competences and turns pedagogy into what is should be in my opinion, i.e. constructivist building of learning and collaborative information.

For that purpose, a student deems it important:

To check what the students are writing every day, what the quality of their reactions is. It motivated me to go in again and again to see the students' reactions and to conduct a conversation with them through a collaborative document … I enjoyed writing to the students and reacting and feeling what I and the other students felt in similar exercises in the class and I could imagine what the students would feel during the performance of such assignments.

Furthermore, "there is a reference to pupils who tend less to participate in the course of the lessons", "collaborative work can help students to learn from each other as well as assist more timid pupils to open up". One student noted:

I experienced how the student feels when they take an active part in activities in which each of his classmates can participate. This activity allowed me to think how children really think when they are exposed to new materials. It allowed me to think how I could teach them something new through activity which is fun and creative for them. I think that as a future teacher I should definitely experience the contents from the viewpoint of each and every student.

According to one student: "the social media allows teachers to conduct a discourse with the pupils and introduce a deep approach to learning in class – the pupils are connected to the materials and the learning becomes more relevant". However, first of all, says one of the students: "we should involve teachers and teach them the basics of the social media and social network, showing them its positive sides and what can be derived from the various social media tools. Then teachers should be taught how to change the class management through the social media."

In general, students who have experienced best practices in implementing social media and social networks in learning and teaching processes, have a positive attitude towards technology-assisted learning in the classroom. One student noted:

I can definitely see and appreciate the added value of using and including the different technological tools into education and learning. Not only do they make the teaching/learning process more fun and imaginative, but it allows for the individualization of the material (so that each student can work and understand at their own pace and their own needs). In today's classrooms, we usually find a very heterogeneous student mix, which may pose a challenge when teaching using 'traditional' techniques. The use of technology in the classroom (and outside as well) can help the teacher customize each lesson so that every student gets the information and practice time they need, not to mention, the stimuli to think and reach conclusions in a welcoming and fostering environment, privately, and with confidence...I am convinced of the positive outcomes that technology can bring to a classroom, and all the diversity that it can afford me as a teacher. It's a win-win situation, when the use of technology can help me be a better, more creative and dedicated teacher and it can help my students learn in an environment that challenges them, stimulates them and especially, makes them happy.

Once the limitations have been overcome and the teachers have become friendly with the various aspects of the social media, the students believe that with the help of the social network one can, "set up classes whereby several groups are opened with regard to topics which interest the pupils who chose them. Moreover, pupils can perform inquiry assignments in groups or in a combination of similar age groups from several schools. This can also be done with collaboration of schools abroad (depending on the pupils' age)".

Exposure to varied social media environments and social networks during the course led the students to think about various ways of harnessing the social network to academic teaching, making the students use them and implementing them in teaching and learning processes at school. Consequently, one witnesses a growing importance of personal experience of network-oriented activities, comprehension of security aspects and the policy of using the network. After getting acquainted with the policy of using the network and knowing to adopt the appropriate security measures, one thinks about the options of using the networks and its response to the learning of pupils with different styles of learning, learning outside the boundaries of the classroom and even the continent. As for the lecturers and students, in addition to using the network for learning in the course, they can use the network for establishing relations with colleagues and professionals and being exposed to experts and leaders in the areas relevant to them.

One of the students expressed her opinion:

The learning style of a teacher, pupil, chalk and blackboard is not nurturing or stimulating pupils to think. Hence, I enjoy the M.Ed. studies, aiming to enrich the lessons and stimulate the pupils to adopt an independent, enjoyable and in-depth thinking.

Another student added:

A social network is an inseparable part of learners' life. This is almost their mother tongue. Integrating a social media and social network in a mindful manner which complies with pedagogy can intensify the learning experience, open the classroom walls at the time and place and integrate also the parents in the learning process in class.

As theorized by various scholars (Dede 2008; Greenhow 2011; Siemens, 2005), there is strong pedagogical potential of using social media for learning and to support collaborative knowledge construction. However, there is a need for further evidence of teaching with social media in general, and social networks in particular in classes, as leading new pedagogies (Greenhow & Askari, 2017). Teaching and learning methods which make use of the social network environment, shift the focus of learning from the teacher to the learner and thus break down the boundaries of time and place of teaching and learning processes and facilitate activities that promote involvement, collaboration and engagement (Seifert, 2016). Another contribution is the enhancement of teachers' personal and professional capabilities and the promotion of teaching-learning processes transpiring beyond the classroom boundaries by sharing contents, current communication, active learning and collaborative work. In a study conducted with pre-service teachers licensed to teach in various ages and disciplines (Seifert, 2016), it was found that modeling of best practices using social networks enhances its usage by students, increases students' confidence as to its implementation and creates a paradigm shift to a more personalized, participatory and collaborative learning and a more positive attitude towards its implementation. Moreover, teachers who during their education experience optimal applications and develop from theory to practice SN-guided activities, might also lead an innovative pedagogy and re-shape the learning transpiring in spaces known to them and to their pupils.

CONCLUSION

To summarize: The social media environments open new and varied means for life-long learning and communication and adaptation of teaching to the needs of the 21st century. These environments permit change in the teaching paradigm and redefinition of the roles of the learner, teacher, information, and learning space and the interaction between them and the meanings of a teaching environment, teaching methods and assignment in the global-digital era. The social media environments, that were not initially intended for teaching, do not replace existing teaching methods, rather they vary them and promote learning and teaching processes. Reality requires a change in teaching methods; educators should acquire skills for a variety of teaching methods and should be involved in thinking about and discussing the role of social media in teaching-learning processes and lead pedagogic change. Pre-service teachers need to be familiar with the different environments so that they can make intelligent choices of technological environments including social media for defined teaching goals. In previous research (Seifert, 2016) in addition to the help of pedagogic support centers in different institutions, I suggested that in the transitional period in which we find ourselves, undergoing various changes, lecturers and teachers should also be open to accept technical support from younger generations while making a clear distinction between mastery and control of the field of knowledge and pedagogy and using technological support as a lever for teaching-learning processes. It is also important to support learners who find the social media environments foreign and difficult.

When assimilating these technologies, users should be aware of the need to maintain digital ethical rules and conscious of the implications of learning in a public space. There are issues relating to ownership of knowledge, distinction of private and public, fluency of language, copyright and flattening of relationships and statuses (Friedman, 2007) and security. The lecturer therefore has an important role, among other things, conducting the gentle dance between the area of acquired specialization, the variation of teaching methods and the boundaries of the changing learning space. This delicate balance enables rich learning experiences facilitated by the sophisticated perceptions offered by Web 2.0 environments and the social media.

REFERENCES

Al-Bahrani, A., & Patel, D. (2015). Incorporating Twitter, Instagram, and Facebook in economics classrooms. *The Journal of Economic Education, 46*(1), 56–67. doi:10.1080/00220485.2014.978922

Barr, R. B., & Tagg, J. (1995). From teaching to learning—A new paradigm for undergraduate education. *Change: The Magazine of Higher Learning, 27*(6), 12–26. doi:10.1080/00091383.1995.10544672

Berners-Lee, T. (2000). *Weaving the web: The original design and ultimate destiny of the world wide web*. New York: HarperCollins.

Blankenship, M. (2011). How social media can and should impact higher education. *Education Digest: Essential Readings Condensed for Quick Review, 76*(7), 39–42.

Bruns, A. (2008). *Blogs, Wikipedia, Second Life, and beyond: From production to produsage*. New York: Peter Lang.

Dabbagh, N., & Reo, R. (2011). Back to the future: Tracing the roots and learning affordances of social software. In M. J. W. Lee & C. McLoughlin (Eds.), *Web 2.0 based e-Learning: Applying social informatics for tertiary teaching* (pp. 1–20). Hershey, PA: IGI Global. doi:10.4018/978-1-60566-294-7.ch001

Dede, C. (2008). A seismic shift in epistemology. *EDUCAUSE Review*, May/June, 80–81. Retrieved from http://net.educause.edu

Friedman, T. L. (2007). *The world is flat: A brief history of the twenty-first century* (3rd ed.). New York: Picador.

Greenhow, C. (2011). Online social networks and learning. *On the Horizon, 19*(1), 4–12. doi:10.1108/10748121111107663

Greenhow, C., & Askari, E. (2017). Learning and teaching with social network sites: A decade of research in K-12 related education. *Education and Information Technologies, 22*(2), 623–645. doi:10.1007/s10639-015-9446-9

Johnson, L., Adams Becker, S., Estrada, V., & Freeman, A. (2014). *NMC horizon report: 2014 Higher Education*.

Johnson, L. A., Adams, S. S., & Cummins, M. (2012). *The NMC Horizon report: 2012 Higher Education Edition*. Austin, Texas: The New Media Consortium.

Joosten, T. (2012). *Social media for educators: Strategies and best practices*. John Wiley & Sons.

Kassens, A. L. (2014). Tweeting your way to improved #Writing, #Reflection, and #Community. *The Journal of Economic Education, 45*(2), 101–109. doi:10.1080/00220485.2014.889937

Kennelly, P. J. (2009). An online social networking approach to reinforce learning of rocks and minerals. *Journal of Geoscience Education, 57*(1), 33–40. doi:10.5408/1.3544227

Kent, M., & Leaver, T. (2014). The revolution that's already happening. In *An education in Facebook*.

King, A. (1993). From sage on the stage to guide on the side. *College Teaching*, *41*(1), 30–35. doi:10. 1080/87567555.1993.9926781

Mâţă, L. (2013). Social media tools in initial teacher education. In *E-Learning 2.0 technologies and web applications in higher education.*

Mayer, R. E. (1984). Aids to text comprehension. *Educational Psychologist*, *19*(1), 30–42. doi:10.1080/00461528409529279

Moran, M., Seaman, J., & Tinti-Kane, H. (2011). Teaching, learning, and sharing: How today's higher education faculty use social media. *Babson Survey Research Group*. http://files.eric.ed.gov/fulltext/ ED535130.pdf

Prensky, M. (2001). Digital natives, digital immigrants part 1. *On the horizon*, *9*(5), 1–6. doi:10.1108/10748120110424816

Price, K. (2006). Web 2.0 and education: What it means for us all. *Paper presented at the 2006 Australian Computers in Education Conference*, Cairns, Australia, October 2-4.

Richardson, W. (2006). *Blogs, Wikis, Podcasts, and other powerful tools for classrooms*. Thousand Oaks, CA: Sage.

Rogers, P. C., Liddle, S. W., Peter, C. H. A. N., Doxey, A., & Brady, I. S. O. M. (2007). A Web 2.0 learning platform: Harnessing collective intelligence. *Turkish Online Journal of Distance Education*, *8*(3), 16–33.

Scardamalia, M., & Bereiter, C. (2006). Knowledge building: Theory, pedagogy, and technology. In K. Sawyer (Ed.), *Cambridge Handbook of the Learning Sciences* (pp. 97–118). New York: Cambridge University Press. Retrieved from http://ikit.org/fulltext/2006_KBTheory.pdf

Seifert, T. (2015). Pedagogical applications of smartphone integration in teaching: Lecturers, pre-Service teachers and pupils perspectives. *International Journal of Mobile and Blended Learning*, *7*(2), 1–16. doi:10.4018/ijmbl.2015040101

Seifert, T. (2016). Involvement, Collaboration and Engagement–Social Networks through a Pedagogical Lens. *Journal of Learning Design*, *9*(2), 31–45. doi:10.5204/jld.v9i2.272

Sheely, S. (2006). Persistent technologies: Why can't we stop lecturing online? In L. Markauskaite, P. Goodyear, and P. Reimann (Eds.), *Who's learning? Whose technology? Proceedings of the 23rd ASCI-LITE Conference* (pp. 769-774). Sydney: CoCo, University of Sydney.

Siemens, G. (2005). Connectivism: A learning theory for the digital age. *International Journal of Instructional Technology and Distance Learning*, *2*(1), 3–10.

Wang, A. T., Sandhu, N. P., Wittich, C. M., Mandrekar, J. N., & Beckman, T. J. (2012). Using social media to improve continuing medical education: A survey of course participants. *Mayo Clinic Proceedings*, *87*(12), 1162–1170. doi:10.1016/j.mayocp.2012.07.024 PMID:23141117

Windham, C. (2005). Educating the Net generation. In *Father Google & Mother IM: Confessions of a Net Gen Learner* (pp. 43-58). EDUCASE.

ADDITIONAL READING

Benson, P., & Chik, A. (2014). *Popular culture, pedagogy and teacher education: International perspectives*. New York, NY: Routledge.

Brown, E. L., In Krŭsteva, A., & In Ranieri, M. (2016). *E-learning & social media: Education and citizenship for the digital 21st century*. Charlotte, NC: Information Age Publishing, Inc.

Greenhow, C., Sonnevend, J., & Agur, C. (2016). *Education and Social Media: Toward a Digital Future*. Cambridge, MA: The MIT Press. doi:10.7551/mitpress/9780262034470.001.0001

Niess, M., & In Gillow-Wiles, H. (2015). Handbook of research on teacher education in the digital age. Hershey, PA: IGI Global. doi:10.4018/978-1-4666-8403-4

Wankel, L. A., Blessinger, P., & International Higher Education Teaching and Learning Association. (2012). *Increasing student engagement and retention using social technologies: Facebook, e-portfolios and other social networking services*. Bingley, UK: Emerald.

KEY TERMS AND DEFINITIONS

Google Drive: A file-and-sync service for PC and mobile devices.

Google Scholar: An online search engine that allows users to search the web or libraries for digital or physical copies of articles, technical reports, print reports, theses, books and other documents. The search engine finds the full text of research literature from a wide range of editions and professions, and includes mainly peer-reviewed online journals from Europe and the United States and is the most well-established in the field.

Hashtag #: Marking or tagging a keyword used on social networks, which allows users to search for and find messages with specific content or subject. The indent is marked with # before the tagged word.

Instagram: An application for sharing photos and short video clips. Each contribution is called a "post". The application allows the user to take pictures and even apply a number of graphic filters that enhance their appearance and give them a different look, and then share them with social networks like Facebook, Twitter, Flickr, or e-mail. Instagram enables the user to track other users, view and respond to others' posts. Instagram is built in the style of Twitter: the user can choose the person he follows and see on his home page the photos and videos they share and can share photos he himself took.

Twitter: An online social network, one of the largest in the world, which allows sending and reading short messages of up to 140 characters, a kind of short blog - microblog. The messages on the web, called "tweets", can be obtained via the twitter site, via text messages to a mobile phone and through a wide variety of applications. The service includes receiving and sending updates regularly, searching, adding, deleting and blocking members, all without the need to browse the company's website. Twitter uses a follow-up method. When one of the participants writes a message, it appears in his followers' home page. Unlike other social networks such as Facebook or LinkedIn, the choice of who to follow does not require the approval of the follower, unless he has defined his user profile / account as private. However, Twitter almost does not expose the user to unwanted content, because the user chooses what to see and who to follow, according to his or her interests. In fact, Twitter has created a new reality: every private person can become a news reporter at the same time. As a result, Twitter is an online news' platform that is updated more quickly than any other media.

Web 2.0: A term that defines a second generation of services on the World Wide Web. While the first generation of websites focused on content created by webmasters and allowing limited communication and participation of users, the second generation includes sites and network applications that provide a technological platform for creating and sharing content uploaded to the web by surfers themselves. Web 2.0 can be characterized as having a high level of activity and collaboration among people to create social connections, share human experiences, create new information and disseminate it quickly and to collaborate. These include, among other things, their emergence during the first decade of the 21st century of online social networks, blogs, file-sharing sites, wiki-based sites, and the use of tags.

WhatsApp: An application for instant messaging, pictures, video and voice clips. The application is available for many mobile and desktop operating systems.

Chapter 7
Assessing Multilingual Multicultural Teachers' Communication Styles

Sevinj Iskandarova
James Madison University, USA

Oris T. Griffin
James Madison University, USA

ABSTRACT

As many educational institutions become more globally competitive, and the number of diverse teachers increases, it becomes even more imperative to avoid what some cultures might deem as inappropriate and unprofessional verbal and non-verbal forms of communication. Those behaviors are sometimes interpreted in different ways, depending on the cultural perspective. Any unwanted verbal and non-verbal actions often increase stress, unwelcomed job pressures, and hinder a positive work environment. At the institutional level where teachers are very diverse, understanding verbal and nonverbal behaviors must be addressed. The researchers propose a methodology which will help multilingual, multicultural teachers' communication styles within the workplace and how to improve cross-cultural team collaborations. Additionally, the information provided in this study allows educational leaders to make inferences about their teachers' team performance and expectations based on their motivation, experiences, and skills used when working with a multicultural team.

INTRODUCTION

Mannix and Neale (2005) assert that diversity (e.g. demographic, cognitive, or personality) "reduce[s] discrimination and increase[s] access to career opportunities, and enhance creativity and quality of team performance" (p. 32). At the same time, Mannix and Neale indicate that this diverse environment may also negatively affect people through "social integration, communication, and conflict in groups" (p. 32). Educational institutions must address teacher satisfaction by supporting and encouraging successful team performance to meet positive expectations. Teachers must learn how to address the challenges (e.g.

DOI: 10.4018/978-1-5225-3082-4.ch007

Copyright © 2018, IGI Global. Copying or distributing in print or electronic forms without written permission of IGI Global is prohibited.

deal with coordination and control issues, maintain communication richness, and develop and maintain team cohesiveness) that arise when working with team members from different nationalities and cultural backgrounds (Hong, 2010; Matveev & Nelson, 2004). Some cultural differences, such as verbal and non-verbal mannerisms and gestures should be avoided. Speaking in a neutral tone and being aware of cultural differences when interacting can help to foster effective multilingual teachers' communication styles on multicultural teams.

This study assesses multilingual, multicultural teachers' communication styles, highlights advantages and disadvantages of those communication style differences within the team, and encourages the application of knowledge gained from this study to enhance team performance within an educational setting. The study compared how teachers, from different countries and diverse cultural backgrounds, built and developed strong relationships while working as a team.

MAIN FOCUS OF THE CHAPTER

The lack of knowledge regarding multicultural communication style differences impact on team performance is an essential factor affecting educational settings. As a result, the lack of knowledge will cause an ineffective work environment in multicultural team situations, and the educational workforce may suffer. Educational institutions often fail in this step because they cannot control teachers' motivation. Schools are spending time and resources recruiting broadly talented teachers who will succeed at a diverse educational institution. However, many cultural variables, such as inappropriate team structures, weak team integration, and less confidence and interest are implicated as significant causes of problems in teachers works/projects.

Teaching people to adapt to a new cultural environment is not an easy task. Most diverse workforces are suffering because they continue to receive insufficient training/orientation programming related to different cultures or, in some cases, no training/orientation programs at all. These challenges present a serious problem to educational institutions as they seek to improve their presence in the multicultural arena. Educational administrators are strongly encouraging their teachers to improve their skills in order to be more successful on multicultural teams. In order to become more global, educational institutions must provide training that offers strategies and resources for improving cross-cultural team collaborations.

Research Questions

1. What effect do multicultural communication style differences have on teachers' approaches to multicultural team environments within an educational setting?
2. What multicultural team experiences are educators reporting?
3. What resources or strategies could improve team performance on a multicultural team within an educational setting?

Teaching and Learning in a Multicultural Setting

Educators are simultaneously teachers and students, who are considered lifelong learners. Lifelong learners often share a common space and are encouraged to learn from one another. Learning from one another is easier said than done. As the world becomes more diverse and more complex, the work of performing the task becomes more challenging. In contrast, the workgroup might be in a common space, but the members of the group represent many cultures and nationalities. These situations call for a common understanding of how to work collaboratively while at the same time remaining sensitive to the many cultures within the group. In addition to members of the group offering their cultural backgrounds to the conversation, they also present their personal styles and preferences for working with others (Levin, Walker, Haberler & Jackson-Boothby, 2013).

Exposure to diverse cultural groups benefits more that members of the group. These experiences benefit the whole community. The majority culture gains familiarity with new ways of thinking, and the minority culture receives an education that legitimizes their presence in higher education. Teachers in a diverse environment, using active and collaborative teaching techniques, interacts with students more often (Umbach, 2006; Bernal & Villialpando, 2002). Diverse educational experience, diverse teachers, and various activities benefit all students, not only by sharing diverse backgrounds but also through students gaining familiarity with new ways of thinking and learning about cultures different from their own.

Multicultural Team Performance and Communication Style

As institutions continue to build cross-cultural knowledge, it is essential that they develop a systematic approach for those working in multicultural teams to prevent misunderstandings. By gaining an understanding of cultural knowledge, multicultural communication styles and by sharing values and norms, team members take these shared values and norms into consideration when working in a multicultural team and assisting multicultural team members in meeting team objectives.

Team performance in multicultural environments brings a combination of high interpersonal skills, strong team effectiveness skills, and ability to facilitate cultural blending. In Matveev and Nelson's (2004) study, cross-cultural communication style was considered a vital tool for achieving higher team performance. High task orientation and low socio-emotional behaviors are also important for group success in a team's performance (Gelfand, Erez & Aycan, 2006). If a person is unable to solve problems outside of the institution, this will be a factor inside the institution during team cooperation. Team arrangement or grouping is believed to have a substantial impact on team performance. The effectiveness with which team members are able to communicate and cooperate with one another determines how productive the team will be. Team arrangement requires precise prediction to certain personality traits because team members' personalities have positive or adverse effects on team performance (Bell, 2007).

A challenge for multicultural team members is connecting team-level objectives with cultural values. Stahl, Maznevski, Voigt, & Jonsen (2010) highlighted the importance of having multicultural teams because "diversity brings different contributions to team" (p. 691). In addition, diverse teams can provide members a broad variety of information, tap into a broader range of networks and perspectives, and teach numerous, fruitful problem-solving approaches (Stahl et al., 2010).

Cultural Diversity Matters

Multicultural differences affect teachers working in multi-national institutions. Hong (2010) states in his framework that multicultural difference displays demographic or personality diversity and build specific cultural knowledge. This knowledge includes multicultural communication and behavioral adaptability skills. Hong also defined "multicultural communication skills as the attitude to communicate appropriately and more efficiently in each situation both verbally and non-verbally in a cross-cultural context" (Hong, 2010, p. 101). "Behavioral Adaptability refers to one's ability to appreciate and detect cultural specific aspects of social behavior" (Hong, 2010, p. 101). Hong goes on to explain in his study "significant challenges to multicultural team effectiveness include different communication styles such as direct versus indirect communication and trouble with accents and fluency" (p.101). His findings and recommendations are that if a team with a high level of cross-cultural communication recognizes different communication styles, the team will be patient and demonstrate flexibility and simultaneously focus on the team's goal. Hong suggested adaptation, structural intervention and managerial intervention strategies to solve these problems (2010, p.104). Hong (2010) describes some of the "benefits" and "challenges" of working with multicultural colleagues. According to Hong, benefits of working with multicultural colleagues could be shared understanding, social integration, wide cultural knowledge, communication effectiveness, variety viewpoints; challenges of working with multicultural colleagues are described as communication style, different accent various attitudes.

Indeed, cultural diversity displays context richness, uncertainty prevention, and high-performance orientation. Understanding individuals from culturally different backgrounds often increase productivity while working on a multicultural educational setting. High performance in a multicultural educational institution is essential for group achievements, understanding, rule adherence, and clarity (Matveev & Nelson, 2004).

METHODOLOGY

As a mixed-methods study, this research used both qualitative and quantitative methods to gather data. Qualitative data were collected from the quantitative data to aid in explaining the results obtained. Cultural Intelligence Scale was adopted for survey questions and measured participants' cognition, metacognition, motivation and behavior intelligence factors. Diverse participants and/or diverse populations bring to this study a unique aspect and perspective, such as cultural norms. Because the present research investigated teachers from a variety of cultural norms, communication styles and performance in a diverse environment, mixed-method research was optimal for including the respondents' subjective approach, opinions, feelings, and conceptions about the impact of multicultural communication style difference on team performance. Using both quantitative and qualitative methods provided the foundation for understanding teachers' perceptions and the issues of multicultural team performance. The study participants were teachers at one of the educational institutions (the educational institution is one-hundred and nine years old) at the east cost of Virginia, USA.

Data Analysis

A sequential, explanatory mix-methods design was used to uncover the perceptions of teachers in addition to their practical experiences while participating as members of multicultural teams. The data revealed the benefits and challenges of being part of a multicultural team and speaking in different languages at the educational institution and provided more insight into the teachers' experiences and performances on a multicultural, diverse team. An explanatory sequential design used quantitative data as the initial steps, followed by qualitative data. This design type focused on the two different phases and their step-by-step analysis merging of all the data into a final product. The questionnaire consisted of 27 questions, some which employed a 6 point Likert –type response scale ranging from 1 = strongly disagree to 5 =

strongly agree and with 6 = not applicable. The survey questionnaire was based on five categories: (1) demographic information; (2) teachers' performance: (3) teachers' satisfaction; (4) teachers' experience; and (5) teachers' development.

The research was conducted on teachers at the educational institution and the results obtained outline the impact of multicultural communication style difference on team performance and the critical and/ or challenging aspects of working in a multicultural team.

Next, qualitative face-to-face interview analysis was conducted with eight multicultural teachers (2 female and six male participants). The participants differed concerning cultural background, communication style, and work experience. 35% of the interviewed teachers employed at the U.S institution minimum 1 month and maximum 47 years. The findings provided a deeper understanding of academic institutions and team leaders, as well as for cross-cultural members to achieve higher satisfaction within an educational setting.

Protocol

The research design was submitted to the JMU Institutional Review Board for approval in July of 2015. Once the study protocol was approved, the consent forms were emailed in September to the respective populations using bulk email. On the consent forms, participants confirmed their intent to participate in the survey part of this research study.

Table 1. Teachers demographics in the quantitative part of the study

Table A			Table B		
Variable	**Response**	**Percentage**	**Variable**	**Response**	**Percentage**
Age			Gender		
20-25		1%	Male		45%
26-30		6%	Female		52%
31-35		8%	Other/Choose not to respond		3%
36-40		21%	Total	224	100%
41-45		16%			
46-50		12%	Status		
51-55		9%	National teachers		87%
56-60		13%	International teachers		13%
61-65		9%	Total	224	100%
65+		5%			
Total	224	100%	Years Employed at the U.S. Institution		
			Minimum		1 month
Language Speaking			Maximum		47 years
Minimum	1		Average		10 years
Maximum	7		Standard deviation		8.3
Total	224	100%	Total	224	100%

FINDINGS AND DISCUSSION

To investigate the participants' ages, experience with U.S. culture, and number of years working at the university, we asked teachers to indicate the range of their age, years of experience with U.S. culture, and working at the institution. When displayed as a table, the data showed the teachers varies; the average age is 46 years, the minimum age is 25 years, and the maximum age is 89 years. The sample reported the average age of 46.6 years for teachers. The gender breakdown of the sample was 52.3% female and 44.6% male, compared to 48% female and 52% male, as reported in A Faculty in Transition 2014 Institution Data Source.

Teachers' Perspective

Before measuring the verbal and non-verbal forms of communication, the researchers first evaluated if the study participants have experienced working in a multicultural team in order to gain information regarding teachers' viewpoints, satisfaction level in the diverse institution and main challenges while working with diverse background colleagues (See below Figures 1 & 2).

Around ninety-two percent (92%) of the teacher respondents reported that they have worked with different cultural co-workers on a multicultural team. By contrast, less than 10 percent (8%) reported that they have never worked on a multicultural team. When asked to indicate the benefits and challenges of working in a multicultural team, the vast majority of teachers reported the benefit of working on a multicultural team was "to create a shared understanding" (55%), number-two was "to develop mutual trust" (51%). "To widen cultural knowledge" was number three (44%), "to build interpersonal skills" was number four (44%), and "to socially integrate" was number five (37%). The chart (Figure 1) displays the survey respondents number 1 benefit of working in a multicultural team is "to create a shared understanding" (55%), more than half agree that while they were working in a multicultural team that the team was able to create a shared understanding.

Teachers' challenges while working on a multicultural team were reported as communication style (37%), which was the first obstacle hindering productivity and accent was the second (35%). Various attitudes about the work were third (30%), and management of the work was fourth (25%). Having "challenges" while working on a multicultural team can be an issue when it comes to achieving team and institution success. See the Figure 2 which scales four main "challenges" by the percentage based on responses.

Table 2. Statistical result: participants by age, experience with U.S. culture and number of years working at the institution

	Minimum	Maximum	Average	Standard Deviation
Age	25 years old	89 years old	47 years	13.1
Experience with U.S. culture	4 years	89 years	43 years	15.0
Working at the institution	1 month	47 years	10 years	8.3

Figure 1. Teachers perspective on "benefits" of working on a multicultural team

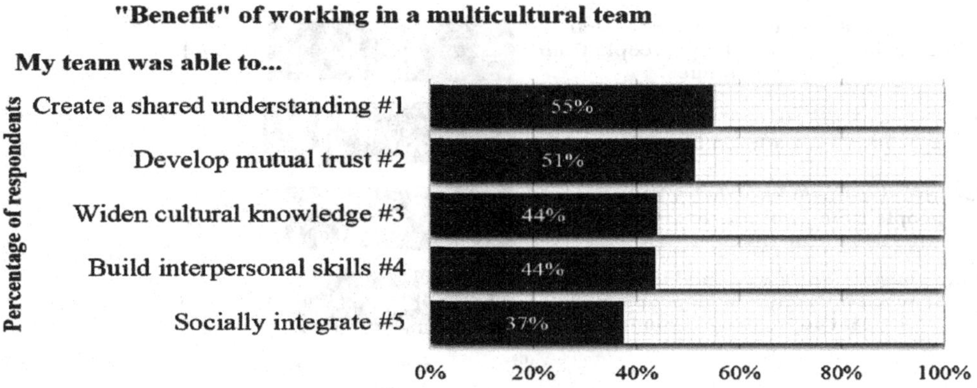

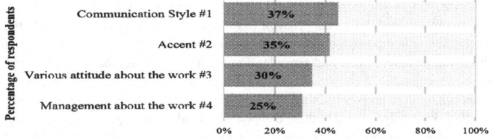

Figure 2. Teachers perspective on "challenges" of working on a multicultural team

Teachers' Experience

Although a significant portion of the participants in this study is confident about their cultural knowledge, skills, and capabilities, less than half of them classified themselves as strongly confident in those mentioned capabilities. As mentioned in the methodology part, the study has adopted "Cultural Intelligence Scale" (CQS) by Van Dyne, Ang & Koh (2008, p. 20) to measure the teachers' experience related to cultural intelligence factors such as motivation, behavior, cognition and metacognition. Verbal and non-verbal communication happens successfully when people are aware of different cultures and have sufficient cultural knowledge. To examine how the awareness and sufficiency regarding diverse culture affect teacher and their verbal and non-verbal communication the survey asked the questions in Figure 3. These categories had multiple questions, with Likert scale responses ranging from 1 = strongly disagree to 5= strongly agree and with 6 = not applicable. The majority of respondents reported that while they interacted with different cultures: 1) teachers checked their accuracy (49% Agree, 34% Strongly Agree); 2) teachers adjust their cultural knowledge (45% Agree, 38% Strongly Agree); and 3) teachers applied their cultural knowledge while interacting with teachers of diverse background (50% Agree, 35% Strongly Agree).

Figure 3. Metacognitive cultural intelligence scale level for teachers

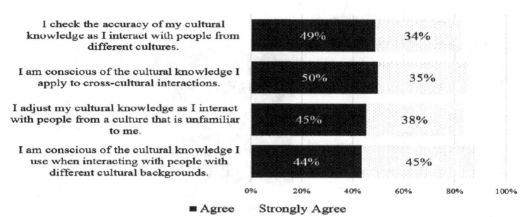

For behavior factor, 33% reported that teachers adjusted facial expressions when multicultural interaction required it; and 39% reported changing their nonverbal behavior in a culturally diverse environment. In addition, 45% indicated that the rate of teachers' speaking varied when the cultural situation required it and 48% reported that verbal behavior (e.g. accent, tone) changed as well when the cultural interaction required it. Regarding the motivational factor, 75% stated that they are confident that they can socialize with culturally diverse background teachers and 92% reported that interacting with diverse cultural teachers is enjoyable. It is always imperative to be aware of various backgrounds, understand the team role and behave in an appropriate way. It is a positive note that the teachers at the institution have enough cognitive knowledge related to these components. In addition, cognitive knowledge also has a huge effect on achieving high team performance and teachers' effective role in an educational setting. Given the responses to these questions, it is reasonable to say that the large teacher population sample was sensitive to cultural differences of co-workers/teammates.

Figure 4. Cognitive cultural intelligence scale level for teachers

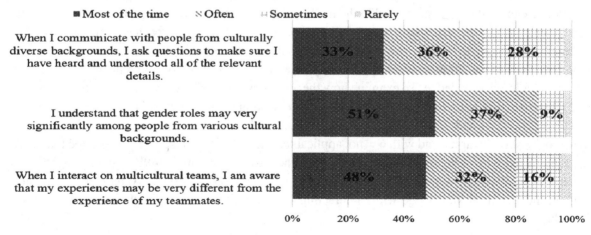

Professional Development

Teachers claim that cross-cultural training is effective in understanding workplace issues regarding multicultural diversity and in increasing confidence, knowledge, and communication skills in diverse work environments. The literature asserts that cross-cultural training is one way to increase the cultural knowledge within an educational setting. The gained knowledge from cross-cultural training fosters strategies and protocols teachers can use to decrease or resolve challenges that appear when working with individuals from culturally diverse backgrounds. Sixty-two percent reported that having cross-cultural training was "Important" and 10% mentioned that cross cultural training was "Not important".

Qualitative Data Analysis

This study involved open-ended questions that were analyzed through coding and emergent themes. The purpose of the qualitative data analysis was to understand, better examine, and present ideas on the teacher's experiences regarding verbal and non-verbal communication, perceptions, satisfaction, and professional development when working with individuals from culturally diverse backgrounds. In order to analyze the data, the audio recordings of the interviewed participants were transcribed. There were eight interviewees (interviewees were selected based on their different cultural background, being senior or junior level teachers, and working with multicultural colleagues) and all audio recording were changed to a monotone voice in order to protect their confidentially and anonymity. No videos were recorded for this study. The components were grouped by themes and subthemes. Themes were considered the main ideas of the study and sub-themes were generalized to support the themes. Through themes and sub-themes, the study's purpose and problem were supported.

After building the thematic framework for the qualitative responses in Table 3, the analysis continued to provide examples from interview responses that support the research ideas and hypotheses.

Table 3. Thematic framework for qualitative responses

Themes and Sub-Themes	Definition	Related Themes (Generated From Results)
Experience working with culturally diverse teachers: • Negative effects: cultural socialization problems, mismatched ideas • Positive effects: creates big picture, brings strength to the group, improve verbal and non-verbal communication	How do teachers experience being in a multicultural team and how do cultural diversity affect verbal and non-verbal communication?	Constraints Problem focused strategies Additional Support
Constraints: • Language constraints • Culture constraints • Time constraints	What are the main effects of constraints on teachers?	Problem focused strategies
Additional support: • Training • Peer support • Handbook	What specific support would be beneficial to improve teachers' verbal and non-verbal communication?	Personal comfort of dealing with cultural diversity

Table 4. Coding of qualitative themes by participants' responses

Themes and Sub-Themes	Responses From Interviewees
Experience Working With Culturally Diverse Teachers	
Negative effects (cultural socialization problems)	"Many of faculty members express themselves most of the time, but not in a verbal sense." "Body language or verbal communication plays an important role, and it especially affects work environment."
Positive effects (shows the big picture)	"Different approaches actually can consider more tools to handle the situation in a better way."
What Are the Main Effects of Constraints on Teachers?	
Constraints	"I had to improve my non-verbal communication - when communicate I was using my body parts a lot and my colleagues were not feeling comfortable with this".
What Specific Support Would Be Beneficial to Improve Teachers' Verbal and Non-Verbal Communication?	
Additional Support Training: Handbook:	"When I came to this institution 20 years ago, we had limited training related to cultural diversity. I think intense cultural training would be a great idea to improve our non-verbal communication and connection with colleagues". "To write a handbook and explain the ways or methods how to deal with various cultural situations would be helpful."

SOLUTIONS AND RECOMMENDATIONS

Teachers reported interest in, supported the idea for, and preferred to participate in culturally diverse training in order to improve communication specifically non-verbal communication, even though some participants may have already attended one before. It was quite evident that the researchers obtained corroboration from the quantitative data that a cultural training for teachers is necessary and preferred the training based on real situation in various case studies. Cultural training may benefit multicultural environments by improving verbal and non-verbal communication style to achieve desired outcomes.

In the interviews with teachers, discussion about problems arose. Dealing with inaccurate assumptions about supporting teachers, knowing how to appreciate work accomplished in an educational environment, and developing strategies that can help to improve communication style in a diverse cultural environment.

In the qualitative data, it was evident that, in many cases, to work in a culturally diverse environment brings strengths to the team and improves verbal and non-verbal communication. For example, many teachers felt that working within a multicultural environment brings benefits, and were not uncomfortable to work with or interact with culturally diverse background colleagues. While several teachers commented to interview questions positively on working in a multicultural environment and with a multilingual colleague (multicultural environment brings strength to the group; shows the big picture).

Concerning additional support that can be provided by educational institutions to teachers, many teachers offered more intensive training (interactive discussion and online training) programs and peer support to all teachers to improve verbal and non-verbal communication style with multilingual teachers.

CONCLUSION

The present research provides a preliminary examination of assessing multilingual, multicultural teachers' verbal and non-verbal communication styles within an educational setting. The results indicate that there is a healthy level of awareness when working in multicultural teams. In particular, teachers have strong working relationships across multicultural lines. Eliminating the cultural constraints and decreasing the cultural challenges will be helpful not only for current teachers but also for future teachers, regardless of cultural background. It is the intent of the researchers to continue with this research in years to come and to explore more beneficial and useful strategies for understanding and promoting more productive teams, team performance and communication styles in multicultural environments within in educational institutions. As researchers, we will continue the research by examining how teachers' communication style in an educational institution may affect to their higher academic level such as promoting higher position, selecting tenure track or switching their job to different directions.

REFERENCES

Bell, S. T., Villado, A. J., Lukasik, M. A., Belau, L., & Briggs, A. L. (2011). Getting specific: A meta-analysis of the demographic diversity variables and team performance. *Journal of Management, 37*(3), 709–743. doi:10.1177/0149206310365001

Bernal, D. D., & Villalpando, O. (2002). An apartheid of knowledge in academia: The struggle over the" legitimate" knowledge of faculty of color. *Equity & Excellence in Education, 35*(2), 169–180. doi:10.1080/713845282

Black, S., & Mendenhall, M. (1990). Cross Cultural Training Effectiveness: A Review and a Theoretical Framework for Future Research. *Academy of Management Review, 15*(1), 113–136.

Broniatowski, D. A., Faith, G. R., & Sabathier, V. G. (2006). The case for managed international cooperation in space exploration. *Center for Strategic and International Studies, 18*(1), 1–7.

Center for Universal Education. (2013). Universal education. Retrieved from http://www.brookings.edu/about/centers/universal-education

Gelfand, M. J., Leslie, L. M., Keller, K., & de Dreu, C. (2012). Conflict cultures in organizations: How leaders shape conflict cultures and their organizational-level consequences. *The Journal of Applied Psychology, 97*(6), 11–31. doi:10.1037/a0029993 PMID:23025807

Hong, H. J. (2010). Bicultural competence and its impact on team effectiveness. *International Journal of Cross Cultural Management, 10*(1), 93–120. doi:10.1177/1470595809359582

Iskandarova, S. (2016). The Effect of Cross-Cultural Differences on Team Performance Within an Educational Setting: A mixed methods study.

Iskandarova, S., & Griffin, O. (2017). *Making the Invisible Visible: Exploring Cultural Differences of Faculty Working on a Multicultural Team*. American Society for Engineering Education.

Iskandarova, S., Griffin, O., El-Tawab, S., & Mousa, F. (2017). Using Mobile Technology as a Tool to Enhance Learning at a Children's Museum in the Shenandoah Valley. In *Proceedings of the Society for Information Technology & Teacher Education International Conference* (pp. 2125-2132). Association for the Advancement of Computing in Education (AACE).

Levin, J. S., Walker, L., Haberler, Z., & Jackson-Boothby, A. (2013). The Divided Self: The Double Consciousness of Faculty of Color in Community Colleges. *Community College Review*, *41*(4), 311–329. doi:10.1177/0091552113504454

Mannix, E., & Neale, M. A. (2005). What differences make a difference? The promise and reality of diverse team in organizations. *Psychological Science in the Public Interest*, *6*(2), 31–55. doi:10.1111/j.1529-1006.2005.00022.x PMID:26158478

Matveev, A. V., & Nelson, P. E. (2004). Cross cultural communication competence and multicultural team performance: Perceptions of American and Russian managers. *International Journal of Cross Cultural Management: CCM*, *4*(2), 253–270. Retrieved from http://search.proquest.com/docview/221216692?accountid=11667 doi:10.1177/1470595804044752

Stahl, G. K., Maznevski, M. L., Voigt, A., & Jonsen, K. (2010). Unraveling the effects of cultural diversity in teams: A meta-analysis of research on multicultural work groups. *Journal of International Business Studies*, *41*(4), 690–709. doi:10.1057/jibs.2009.85

Umbach, P. D. (2006). How effective are they? Exploring the impact of contingent faculty on undergraduate education. *The Review of Higher Education*, *30*(2), 91–123. doi:10.1353/rhe.2006.0080

KEY TERMS AND DEFINITIONS

Cross-Cultural: Relating to different cultures.

Educational Setting: As any setting where one would go in order to have an educational experience.

Multicultural: Constituting several cultural or ethnic groups within a society.

Multicultural Team: "A wide range of cultural differences exist among the employees in the team" Neil Kokemuller (p.1, 2015).

APPENDIX: INTERVIEW QUESTIONS

Introduction

1. Tell me your experience about interacting with people with different cultural backgrounds.

Experience

2. Can you describe an average work day of yours (from the point of view of working in a multicultural environment)?
3. How do you feel about your ability to cope up with multicultural differences in your team?
4. How do you think your experience differs from that of other teachers who are locals?
5. Have you ever considered quitting the project because of stress or pressures caused by multicultural and multilingual differences, and if so, can you describe the context of that situation?
    a. What kept you going? In other words, how did you overcome these obstacles to continue working in your project in a multicultural team?
6. According to your experience how does multicultural differences affect the team performance? (Please mention positive or negative effects)

Resources

7. Are you aware of any training that has helped you to perform better in a current work environment?

Constraints

8. What would you identify as the major barriers to being a teacher who is working in a multicultural environment?

Strategies for Success

9. What strategies or advice might you give to others to help them cope in a similar situation to yours?
10. What resources or supports do you think could be offered-formally or informally- to make your experience as a teacher?

Conclusion

11. Is there anything additional you would like to share about your experiences as a teacher?

Section 3
Global Projects Around the World:
Digital and World Savvy Curriculum

Chapter 8

Learning Content Creation in the Field:
Reflections on Multimedia Literacy in Global Context

Sujatha Sosale
The University of Iowa, USA

ABSTRACT

Media literacy is the raison d'être of journalism and media education in universities. With the advent of digital technologies and generational online developments such as Web 2.0, media literacy has now turned into multimedia literacy, where future media professionals learn to write, produce video and audio, edit, link, curate, and disseminate the content produced as individual communicators rather than members of a production team where each member specializes in one or two of these aspects to media production. Simultaneously there has been an increase in efforts to globalize educational experiences for students. These developments raise questions about new elements to media literacy, pedagogy, assessment, and learning the ethics of responsible communication about foreign cultures in the media. This chapter tackles these questions by reflecting on a Study Abroad course experience where students in a US university traveled to South India, and created content in the field about specific experiences related to development.

INTRODUCTION

Media literacy is the *raison d'être* of journalism and media education in universities. With the advent of digital technologies and generational online developments such as the oft-cited Web 2.0, media literacy has now turned into multimedia literacy. What was until recently exclusively a writing, photo, or video approach to information has transformed from a production team combining these skills into an individual enterprise, with the student having to learn to write, produce video and audio, edit, link, curate, disseminate, and monitor the content produced by her (Carpenter, 2009; Goh & Kale, 2015; Madison, 2014; Sabrina, 2016). This new, multidimensional role for the individual journalist or media profes-

DOI: 10.4018/978-1-5225-3082-4.ch008

Copyright © 2018, IGI Global. Copying or distributing in print or electronic forms without written permission of IGI Global is prohibited.

sional raises some questions from the point of view of media literacy education. What are some new developments in media literacy in this context? How and where do we locate the literacy elements in the pedagogy? How can the content, or output, be assessed (see, for example, Smith, 2017 on assessment rubrics)? If the learning situation occurs outside the home country, how does context become a part of the literacy exercise? These broad questions guide this chapter, and a Study Abroad course experience with multimedia storytelling serves as a case for reflecting upon them. Students in a US university traveled to South India for this course, and created content in the field about specific experiences related to development. The students used local resources for producing multimedia outputs and completed the writing segment of the content also on-site.

Many literacy variables converge in this experience – learning to gather information from linguistically and culturally diverse groups such as tribal populations and farmers, learning media production, and learning to produce information with fewer resources such as erratic and uneven connectivity, to list a few. The goals for the course were to present first-hand accounts of developing communities and the choices they have to make that conveys the dilemmas of emerging economies. This path to media literacy includes a number of learning experiences such as appreciation of unfamiliar cultures and production of information about them that is accessible online to interested audiences, the excitement of discovery and the ethics of responsibly disseminating the information discovered, learning to use multimedia technologies in foreign systems, and learning to compile the expression of this literacy into sense-making packages for print and online audiences.

This chapter is a reflection on the Study Abroad course experience for acquiring multimedia competence in the field, in an emerging economy. Since reflection occurs after the fact, the framework that follows articulates concepts that might not have fully or consciously informed the experience for both the students and the instructor at the time of offering the course. The goals are to offer a framework and points for consideration primarily for Study Abroad instructors of media literacy and education, and to reflect on some lessons learned. Where pertinent, some elements may be useful for coordinators of Study Abroad programs, both in the home and host institutions.

A framework for conceptualizing the Study Abroad multimedia literacy course follows. The framework draws from a few different areas that are important for this reflection – the global citizen, the field, multimedia literacy, and content creation. This is a new course in the institution, offered for the first time for Study Abroad, and a first for both the instructor and the students. Reflections on the decisions taken at each juncture – materials, student composition, assignments, and evaluations are presented following the conceptual framework. Using the conceptual framework as a backdrop, the course details and lessons learned are discussed. E-mail exchanges and notes taken during the process and in the field provided the data. In the final section of the chapter, reflections on lessons learned and some points for consideration in developing such a media literacy course are offered.

CONTEXT AND CONCEPTUAL FRAMEWORK

Four conceptual threads intersect to provide a framework within which to understand this multimedia literacy Study Abroad course. First, the idea of the *global citizen* underpins international education, and this concept is central to Study Abroad courses in general, stimulating more extended and deeper awareness of peoples, cultures, and geographies beyond students' immediate and familiar surroundings within the national context. Secondly, the *field* or the venue outside the country where the course is conducted constitutes the corollary. In the context of journalism education, "global" and "field" become integral parts that provide context for the course. In everyday parlance journalists go out into the field to cover events and people and to generally get their "stories." Thirdly, the term *multimedia literacy* in this specific context refers to the acquisition and effective use of skills across media platforms and technologies, although it entails more, and this discussion follows. Finally, the term *content creation* refers to a variety of content types created within a single message locale, often by a single person or as in this case, a small team. Thus content would include text, images, graphics, video, audio, links, etc., in each sense-making package.

The roots of the idea of global citizenship as used in contemporary contexts can be traced to the concept of cosmopolitanism, which most theorists identified with belonging, place, and identity (Appiah, 2006; Bauman, 2002; Carter, 2001; Papastephanou, 2005; Skrbis, Kendall & Woodward, 2004). The sense that identity definitions occurs within national boundaries both defines and liberates the concept from certain definitional confines. In other words, cosmopolitanism can be recognized in contrast to nationalism, and also as a mix of nationalisms (in the plural). It is this idea of transcending national boundaries in a deeper sense that fostering global citizenship in Study Abroad contexts entails. Cosmopolitanism theorizes individual relations that transcend national boundaries. Tolerance for cultural difference underwrites the notion of cosmopolitanism (Papastephanou, 2005; Skrbis, Kendall & Woodward, 2004). Tolerance for difference translates to global citizenship, but as Carter (2001) points out there is a difference between the two concepts – cosmopolitanism implies tension between tolerance of the "other" on the one hand, and individual (the self's) rights on the other. Global citizenship is based more on an idea of collectivism, with greater emphasis on responsibilities than rights (Carter, 2001; Haigh, 2008). Lewin (2009) raises another dimension to the idea of global citizenship – its much-contested status as a viable concept. In his analysis of the literature, the term citizenship brings the concept too close to the ideas of nation-sate and nationalism to make a meaningful distinction between national and global citizenship. For nations that are relatively new in the postcolonial world, the term global citizenship disregards their national sovereignty and hence continues to represent colonialism. Still others claim that individuals engaging in one or other activity outside the nation-state cannot be called global citizens because that might be a necessary but is not a sufficient condition to warrant this status.

An undercurrent to these interpretations of "global citizenship" is the ethical dimension, whether in terms of embracing the "other" outside one's home culture, or acknowledging responsibilities more than claiming rights that the term cosmopolitanism implies. The United States Institute of Peace describes global citizenship broadly as knowledge and/or experience of the world (http://www.buildingpeace.org/forums/how-do-you-define-global-citizenship). The knowledge and experience could be gained through travel, or learned by other means.

The Institute for Peace sees Study Abroad experiences as a pragmatic way to cultivate the idea of global citizenship, a view that is embraced by institutions offering Study Abroad programs (http://www.buildingpeace.org/studyabroad). Studies support this view. For example, Jurgens and McAuliffe (2004, p. 147) found that a two-week course brought students into "intensive contact" with host country counterparts. With an emphasis on the importance of international education, Medora and Roy (2017) provide guidance for short-term Study Abroad programs. Lewin (2009) has pointed out a fundamental tension apparent in Study Abroad programs -- longer periods that afforded immersive, and more effective, learning experiences but cost the student more, compared with the more affordable programs with shorter periods abroad that provided little opportunity for real learning, beyond minimal exposure. While this may be true, institutions' administrative and students' financial realities become serious considerations in decisions about the duration of the course. Such tensions aside, an important rationale for having Study Abroad courses in a university's course offerings, besides exposure and breadth of experience, is helping students cultivate a stronger ethical sense and the inherent responsibility in being a global citizen, beginning with the development of cross-cultural competencies that Study Abroad courses aim to develop.

The second concept, "field," is used in a few different ways in this chapter – geographical locale, a locale outside one's own home area, a venue where specific and specialized experiences can be gained, and a sense of "being out there" for journalistic purposes. Anthropological references to fieldwork explain the field as a location or locale within which the anthropologist's work takes place. Duration in the field matters for gaining literacy on several levels. The field provides a context for culture. It constitutes part of the host culture. Context provides the opportunity to develop intercultural competencies and build an empathetic viewpoint, something that is especially necessary when students from developed countries visit parts of the world that are not as economically well-endowed. Further, experiential learning takes place in the field, and interactions that cannot be replicated in the home country become vital to the literacy experience abroad. This Study Abroad course was part of the larger mission of the university along similar lines, for broadening horizons, and offering the field experience to cultivate empathy and increased understanding of cultures on host-country terms, as lived in their communities.

The ability to create and produce media content is one among the components of most definitions of *media literacy* (for example, Bergsma & Carney, 2008; Vraga & Tully, 2015; Yildiz, 2002). With traditional mass media technologies, creating media content was confined to print, audio, or audio visual formats, and education in writing, camera work, film, and audio formats were offered as separate tracks of specialization. With the advent and proliferation of digital technologies and the Internet, media literacy entails learning all these skills for individual content production. Having been born into a digital environment, the current generation of college students is typically proficient in the use of these media technologies. This is especially true of advanced and emerging economies, but also to a certain extent in other parts of the world as well. They come to university education as "digital natives" (Prensky, 2001).

A study cited by Barnes, Marateo, and Ferris (2007) showed that the current generation of digital natives places a premium on education, and actively seeks media literacy for producing content. But formal media education is aimed at training students in specialized skillsets, from writing that endures as a basic skill applicable to various media forms and formats, to working with camera and editing software, and learning composite content creation in the digital, networked environment. The first stage of this kind of literacy is for students to function as produsers or prosumers (terms that integrate both user/consumer and producer functions and roles), following which the production aspect is more heavily emphasized. The goal, especially with the undergraduate and the master's professional programs is to prepare future professionals for the journalism, communication, and media labor market.

As Singer (2005), a leading scholar at the forefront of analyzing technology change and its implications for contemporary journalism practice has pointed out, the term "convergence" refers to the confluence of many types of what were formerly discrete media coming together in the creation of content that appears as a single, seamless entity. In response to these developments, Loizzo et al (2016) observe that graduates are expected to be competent in technologies and platforms such as podcasting, social media, and various mobile applications in addition to the bread and butter of journalism training that include traditional media skills in writing, editing, and design. Integral to the literacy for content creation in the current multimedia world are considerations that were important for the practice of traditional mass media and new considerations that have emerged with online media professionalism. For traditional mass media, audience and marketability of content were key considerations. These remain important for contemporary media professionals, but digital and online advances require proficiency in other areas such as search engine optimization, an understanding of various types of metrics, and producing content with these factors in mind. The Study Abroad course did not consciously seek to address all these aspects; the focus was more on the actual content creation, the putting together of elements in meaningful packages, with ethical practices and audiences in mind. To that extent, issues of convergence, quality of writing and visual elements, and a host of other considerations were important for creating outputs that demonstrated both competence and credibility.

The concept of Media Information Literacy (MIL) that is defined more closely around Information Communication Technologies (ICTs) helps address the media production aspect to the course, where the students learned to create audio slide shows, video documentaries, and long form journalism involving publication design of a print magazine that was also produced in digital format. Work with all these formats involved using principles of access, retrieval, understanding, evaluation, and use (UNESCO, 2013; p. 29; Unwin, 2009). Besides collecting data in the field, students were required to complete background research, almost all of which had to be accessed online. Thus access and retrieval were important for documentary research. Understanding the retrieved information and evaluating it for suitability for the projects involves filtering appropriate information for final use.

One other, related concept, transliteracy (Frau-Meigs, 2012) is also useful for assessing the learning experience with considerations of culture and ethics as drivers of responsible communication about disadvantaged communities in a global context. Examining the need for media and information literacy in the digital era, Frau-Meigs suggested that "larger and more complex mediascapes" (2012, p. 18) demand a rethinking of traditional mass media-related literacies, to harness the power of new media for a dynamic literacy that engages with changing media environments. UNESCO's (2013) description of media information literacy as "integrated" and "dynamic," takes into consideration the idea that an individual can have multiple literacies for multiple purposes and contexts. The integrated and dynamic approach to media literacy for traditional media and media information literacy (MIL) in the digital environment provide important nuances to the Study Abroad media production course, where several types of literacy become important at a more macro level: awareness of context and competencies in dealing with the immediate social environment, tempering curiosity with respect for local populations, and achieving mastery over everyday needs such as, for example, independent use of public transport for both professional and personal needs. These learning points find their way into the multimedia products created by the students.

Finally, as Durham (1996) has argued, learning production intricacies like publication design is more than learning tools and applying them to meet requirements, it is a way to consider what these tools communicate at the meta-level. Lee (2011) draws attention to blogging as not merely a space for expression but a platform for critical reflection that contributes to "autonomous learning" (p. 87). In Durham's (1996) analysis and her own classroom practice as an instructor, magazine design education goes beyond training for a clever use of technology tools for eye-catching page design and content, and is treated as an ideologically charged expression. Durham advocates raising awareness of these ideological undercurrents at the learning stage that will help students create messages that communicate in an ethical and responsible fashion. The politics of representation cannot be avoided in the content students produce, and pedagogy in instances of study abroad in developing countries needs to integrate awareness of this aspect into the educational experience. This was done in a few different ways in the course, and is discussed in the section that follows.

CURRICULUM AND PREPARATION

The Study Abroad India program courses are offered in the winter term, for an academic interim term duration (between semesters) of three weeks. Courses were developed and proposed based on considerations of the instructor's subject area expertise and estimations of student interest and enrollment. Hybrid courses were also proposed by instructors, and at times courses were combined by the administrators to form hybrid courses for reaching required enrollments. The multimedia writing course was twinned with a Law and Justice course, but offered as two separate tracks, each with its own instructor. Combining courses in this instance allowed for students to be accommodated in the same facility, and after initial introductions to culture and environment in the early joint class sessions, each course followed its own planned path.

Each individual course was matched with the resources of a specific institution in India. Academic institutions and non-governmental organizations (NGO's) served as host institutions. Long-term grant funding and extraordinary efforts of key individual faculty in the university enabled the institution to work with NGOs for coursework in the field, and for accommodation. The multimedia literacy course was matched with a hosting institution in the southern city of Bengaluru. A well-established organization, the institution specialized in the eradication of gender inequality through girls' education. There were classroom areas on the premises, a library, and common rooms for groups to meet for assignments. Staff members spoke several of the regional languages and dialects, and resourcefully contributed to several classroom presentations in formats such as enactments (role play), short plays (drama), and panel discussions (pertaining to prescribed readings, and also to topical social realities in present-day India). Film and documentary screenings interspersed day-long discussions. Besides projection facilities, the classroom was equipped with wireless connection to access online material when class was in session. Equally importantly, the organization had access to a studio in town with multimedia facilities, professional help, equipment, and (mostly) updated software versions for the local environment and needs.

Seven students were enrolled for the course. The students came to the course with specific skills that allowed them to learn, grasp, and produce content in the field. Others who had expressed interest in the course at some early point in the recruitment process withdrew because of the locale/field – India. Popular destinations for study abroad were more in Europe than any other continent. The course was offered as a Journalism course, but was open to all students who were interested in the subject matter. This was a departure from the regular semester practice where professional courses involving information gathering, reporting and writing, and content creation are typically offered only for Journalism majors. The composition of the students enrolled for this course was interdisciplinary; they were majors in Journalism, Psychology, English, and Cinema Arts. All the students in this class had some basic media skills, but the journalism and film students handled the more technical aspects to assignments involving video editing, publication design on digital media, long-form writing, and aspects to online content.

Preparation common to Study Abroad programs across institutions was similar in this case. Establishing cultural familiarity is a critical component of preparing students for the experience, and it began in the planning phase for the course. Cultural markers were included in publicity materials such as posters and leaflets in the Study Abroad fair, with interpersonal and group communication sessions on the country, the state, and the specific geographical location. Both the novel experience as well as the learning opportunities were emphasized at this early stage. Workshops on the logistics of the university's program, approach, support structure, and other aspects grounded students in the primary reason for the course—developing certain competencies in adapting to unfamiliar cultures and contexts, such as complying with expected norms of behavior, dress codes, etc. Pre-departure workshops were organized for learning useful survival and conversational phrases and sentences in two of the most frequently used languages in the region.

In parallel with student preparation, the curriculum was developed as a joint effort of the instructor and the host organization. The host organization proposed four possible courses based on an advocacy approach that emphasized international development. They could address global citizenship, gender, poverty, or human rights. Following discussion with the instructor and the need to keep the course media-focused, the host organization proposed a course on media and social justice. Meeting departmental requirements for the curriculum and degree, with an emphasis on multimedia skills for professional preparation was important for attracting student interest within the US context. The practical need for creating a portfolio for potential employers was another deciding factor in steering the course focus to media, writing, and presentation more on an informational mode of communication rather than a persuasive mode that advocacy entails. This tension between the advocacy idea from the field, and the needs of the labor market at home finally led to the title of International Development Through Multimedia Storytelling. The content could then be presented in a variety of media forms and formats, from a more features-oriented (rather than news-oriented) approach to content creation for digital media. Readings compiled in the US prior to departure addressed Indian history, society, and culture at a national level. The host organization included some readings on Indian society at large but focused readings on the region where students would travel to collect material for content. Readings constituted a part of the course, albeit an important one. Many other formats were employed, including role playing, drama, panel presentations, documentary screenings, and field visits within the city, prior to leaving for the neighboring state of Kerala for gathering information on rural development. Additionally, a visit to an alternate healthcare facility in the outskirts of the city of Mysuru (between Bengaluru and Wayanad, the Kerala site) was planned to give the students a glimpse of innovative healthcare ideas in practice, for addressing problems resulting from the impact of social inequality on medical and healthcare services. The itinerary was handled by the host organization, with frequent consultations with the instructor by e-mail, phone, and a visit by the instructor to the facilities a few months prior to the course start date.

IN THE FIELD

While the major segments to the course were developed to provide an on-the-ground view of development dilemmas in rural Kerala, coursework started upon arrival in Bengaluru, a densely populated urban area. Visits to various parts of the city showed the contrast that developing countries are known for that might be summed up idiomatically as slums and shopping malls. Exercises were built around observing and to an extent experiencing the difficulties as well as the pleasures of living in a developing country. For example, students were given the wages that a local manual laborer would earn in a day and were asked to manage meals in the city with the given amount. A visit to a mall on the same day drew the contrast in a locale that resembled a city in the west, with no sign of the poverty witnessed earlier.

The core of the course entailed a visit to a specific area in northern Wayanad, a mountainous region in the neighboring southwestern state of Kerala, where historically wealthy landlords and subsequently small farmers displaced the tribal populations native to the region. The main agricultural products grown in the region are coffee, rice paddy, coconut, some cocoa, and the important cash crop of pepper, for which the area is globally renowned. A local non-governmental organization hosted the class, and interpreters for the local language of Malayalam and some of the dialects spoken by tribes were provided by the host organizations in Bengaluru and Wayanad. The hosting organization in Wayanad helped farmers in various ways, such as training them in rain water harvesting, helping them restore soil damaged by chemical fertilizers, teaching planting techniques to use less seed for more yield, initiating local seed exchange programs, and other initiatives. Lessons learned at the stay included using heated water efficiently within a given window of time each day for personal use. During that week students began appreciating the severe water shortages experienced by homesteads on small farms.

The trips to tribal camps and the farmers' cooperative were critical for the students' information gathering activities. Because of the lack of roads and transportation in the hostile terrain and dense forests, it was necessary to walk distances on rough terrain to reach the sparsely populated housing areas. To reach one of the tribal colonies students had to climb steep coffee plantation slopes and upon reaching the colony they discovered precariously constructed houses with television satellite receivers perched on rooftops, signs that even extremely poor communities managed to gain access to broadcast media, especially television. In a neighboring village, a visit to a tribal school that boasted a small library on the premises, and a garden area where food was grown by the tribal school students for their consumption (that also served as part of their curriculum) helped the Study Abroad students see beyond the stark contrasts of the two tribal colonies visited earlier, where in one the members eked out a living in the forest on barely cultivable bits of land, and in the other where the community was fractionally better off in that it could maintain more contact with the outside world. At the tribal school, the students could see that youth in the area were engaged in a new movement, reviving methods of cultivation traditional to their peoples. This immersive learning experience helped the Study Abroad students focus on documenting surroundings and conversations as data for assignments.

Another important stop in Wayanad was the farmers' cooperative. It consisted of owners of small holdings in the area who shared seasonal labor during the harvest season and other resources like tractors since no single farmer could afford to own one. During this visit, students learned of the vagaries of the global market and their effect on cash crops. The pepper crop that season was affected by plant disease, which resulted in a drastic reduction of earnings for the members of the cooperative that year. In this field visit students could explore the tiny holdings that would be considered unprofitable and unsustainable in advanced countries where economies of scale are as important to agriculture as they are to manufacturing. Regardless of the size of the farm, farmers grew other crops like rice, chili peppers, coconut, and cocoa. Students now had information on farmers' survival techniques on a daily and yearly basis.

A visit to the integrated healthcare facility on the return journey from Wayanad allowed the students to learn about innovative measures the hospital board and care providers had taken for making care accessible to all people of all social strata in the region. For example, fees for services were set on a sliding scale based on income. Terminally ill patients, especially those with socially stigmatized illnesses such as AIDS-related illnesses could stay in general wards with other patients, and continued to receive specialized care. Alternate medicine such as Ayurveda, the ancient Indian school of medicine was integrated into the medical services and fee structures.

These two major stops at Wayanad and Mysuru enabled students to learn about measures taken for context-specific change. Farmers and tribal youth in Wayanad had devised a series of self-help measures for resource-sharing and restoration of traditional methods of cultivation aimed more at self-sufficiency than dependence on the global market. Experts at the healthcare facility had calibrated services to cater to the poor in the area as well and integrate patients who are typically segregated in other facilities due to the social stigma attached to certain illnesses.

Such learning experiences contribute toward understanding differences in generating solutions to problems in contexts radically different from the students' own. They expose students to different social realities and context-specific responses and solutions to highly localized problems, and although case studies are available in textbooks, field experience provides opportunities for direct observation.

MULTIMEDIA LITERACY REALIZED: ASSIGNMENTS

Assignments were visualized as informed and evidence-based media outputs that would be of interest to both a general public and to potential employers in the US. Assignments had to demonstrate competence in using media technology to develop content suited to the technology, and intended for production and dissemination of information. One assignment common to all the students in the class involved a social media platform with provision for audience feedback online. The rest involved production of a specific media type, such as an audio slide show, a video documentary, and a print magazine, all of which also had to be made available online. Students were required to bring their own equipment (of their choice), especially video cameras, cameras, digital recorders, and laptop computers. Topics for these assignments were developed using students' self-identified interests on the one hand, and ground realities, travel, and information destinations (such as the farmers' cooperatives, tribal schools, etc.), on the other. Interests were matched to form teams for each of the three assignments. Journalism programs in universities now emphasize individual-level proficiency in several aspects to online media as the future of the industry, and set professional media literacy curricula accordingly. But given the unfamiliar surroundings, radical culture change, relatively scarce resources in the field, and the short duration of the course that did now allow for much more than basic, temporary acculturation, the instructor and host institution coordinators agreed that peer teaching and learning through teamed assignments would enhance the multimedia literacy and content creation experiences. Journalism and film majors had advanced preparation in the technological aspects to content creation, and Journalism majors had also completed writing courses, but team members from the other disciplines contributed different points of view, and as digital natives (Prensky, 2001) they had a modicum of proficiency in the technology as well.

Assignments involved blogging about students' experiences, a feature length multimedia output per group, and two occasions on which students would present their work. The blog served as the exercise across the teams, and allowed for evaluating students' multimedia literacy demonstration against a common set of requirements. The blog served as a publicly visible journal, a place on the Web where students could explore and explain their experiences. A set number of entries/posts was required, with each entry having to respond to a prompt that the instructor provided. Each post was required to have multimedia content, with at least three features denoting the multimedia aspect. All the students in the course were conversant with WordPress, and with features like embedding links, photos, and video. They had come to the course with this knowledge, likely having had to use these technologies in other courses unrelated to the Journalism or Film major, since a hybrid of online and offline course materials and multimedia learning in many disciplines are now the norm in most higher education institutions in the US.

The main assignment for the course consisted of producing a feature-length (longer-form) package. Student teams were formed based on shared interests in certain media and formats. For example, a student from Cinema Arts and another from English teamed to produce a video documentary. A Journalism major was paired with a Psychology major because of shared interests in Web-based information media like audio slides. A third project involved the production of a news magazine and was created by three

Journalism majors interested in long-form writing, photography, and publication design. The instructor and the host team decided on topics for the main assignment after considering the potential for capturing information of certain kinds on certain media technologies (for example, video and still photography), and class work including readings, documentary viewings, guest lectures by local and regional media professionals, etc. The process involved group meetings, research, planning and coordination, and information gathering while on the road. Since the overall schedule was packed into three weeks, occasional breaks for reflection were built into the curriculum.

Experiences in Wayanad gave students an idea of the distances the tribe members would have to traverse for everything, from work for daily wages to hospitals and clinics for medical care, and for supplies and produce that could not be grown on the small patches of land. Meetings with farmers raised awareness of their tenuous existence, especially those dependent on cash crops like pepper. Farmers' self-help groups and cooperatives demonstrated the community-level problem-solving that often does not garner enough attention in international development work. Problems are defined and solutions implemented within local contexts, geared specifically for community needs. Local NGO's run by internally (within India) trained individuals exhibit a level of understanding of local conditions that exogenous help could miss. Tribal youths' orientation toward the future of farming, their own future in relation to it, whether the two are related, and why or why not were questions the students could explore with tribal youth. This exercise broadened their (students') horizons in ways that textbooks and classroom time in the US might not have been able to do so.

Upon return to Bengaluru, students reconvened for writing drafts and final versions, editing, photo and video selection, and designing the magazine. They worked in the studio in town where they could use software, seek professional help with the technology when needed, and work with more steady connectivity rather than the erratic one on campus since the campus was located at the outskirts of the greater metro area. On the day before their return, students presented their assignments to the host institution and the Law and Justice class. A discussion session followed the presentation. Upon return to the home campus, they concluded the projects (finalizing, distribution, posting) and presented them to international studies students. This last assignment brought closure to their multimedia work in global context.

REFLECTIONS AND CONCLUSION

This chapter discussed a multimedia literacy course in global context, as part of a Study Abroad program. The core subject matter, media communication about development and change, served as the platform for learning multimedia literacy to communicate responsibly about unfamiliar cultures. The emphasis here was on literacy for media production, rather than literacy for understanding and critically evaluating media messages. International development is best learned in the field, in a developing country. The Study Abroad opportunity provided students first-hand exposure to some of the issues faced by communities in a developing country, and community members' innovative approaches to solutions. Students witnessed the everyday nature of tough terrains, minimal transport facilities, vagaries of weather, water scarcity, and erratic power supply and connectivity on the one hand, and on the other they saw the leaps in development as a result of locally-based solutions through self-help groups, innovative resource-sharing, in-house low-grade power supply through bio gas, and a series of other measures that have made life sustainable for precarious livelihoods in agriculture in the rural areas. Contrasts of west-inspired built urban areas allowed students to experience more familiar lifestyles. These experiences helped debunk a hazy idea of a distant "other" riddled with problems.

The concept of global citizenship is evoked in this experience in that the course expanded horizons and prompted students to think about and communicate both problems as well as solutions they witnessed on the ground. Related to this concept is the idea of transliteracy (Frau-Meigs, 2012) that comes into play. Cultural and ethical considerations were critical for responsible content creation.

Perhaps the principal lesson learned from this Study Abroad experience from a pedagogical point of view is the need for a more extended period of time to allow students to go beyond the initial shock, wonder, and frustrations to "get under the skin" of needs and solutions. As Lewin (2009) has pointed out, extended time in the field is considered a luxury, yet paradoxically it offers the best learning experience. Literacy is multi-layered, and three weeks in the field enabled students to examine the surface. On a more pragmatic note, preparing students for the idea of global citizenship in conjunction with the specific course, beyond general orientations back home prior to departure, would sensitize students further to their own responses, reflexively, to conditions in the field. Notetaking in an anthropological fieldwork sense, and training students to systematically capture both information and their own responses, thoughts, and opinions against each piece of data will make for rich and plentiful content that could go beyond the course into possible topics for other courses, and even into professional writing in the early career years. This would make the literacy experience in global context more lasting than a fleeting college experience.

REFERENCES

Appiah, K. A. (2006). *Cosmopolitanism: Ethics in a world of strangers*. W.W. Norton and Company.

Barnes, K., Marateo, R. C., & Ferris, S. P. (2007). Teaching and learning with the Net Generation. *Innovate: Journal of Online Education, 3*(1), 1–8.

Bauman, Z. (2002). Space in the globalizing world. In E. Krausz & G. Tulea (Eds.), *Starting the Twenty-First Century, Sociological Reflections and Challenges*. London: Transaction Publishers.

Bergsma, L. J., & Carney, M. E. (2008). Effectiveness of health-promoting media literacy education: A systematic view. *Health Education Research, 23*(3), 522–542. doi:10.1093/her/cym084 PMID:18203680

Carpenter, S. (2009). An application of the theory of expertise: Teaching broad and skill knowledge areas to prepare journalists for change. *Journalism and Mass Communication Educator, 64*(3), 287–304. doi:10.1177/107769580906400305

Carter, A. (2001). *The political theory of global citizenship*. London: Routledge.

Durham, M.G. (1998, Spring). Revolutionizing the Teaching of Magazine Design. *Journalism and Mass Communication Educator*, 23-31.

Frau-Meigs, D. (2012). Transliteracy as the new research horizon for media and information literacy. *Medijske Studue, 3*(6), 14–27.

Goh, G., & Kale, U. (2015). From print to digital platforms: A PBC framework for fostering multimedia competencies and consciousness in traditional journalism education. *Journalism and Mass Communication Educator, 70*(3), 307–323. doi:10.1177/1077695815589473

Haigh, M. (2008). Internationalisation, planetary citizenship and Higher Education Inc. *Compare: A Journal of Comparative Education, 38*(4), 427–440. doi:10.1080/03057920701582731

Jurgens, J., & McAuliffe, G. (2004). Short-term Study-Abroad experience in Ireland: An exercise in cross-cultural counseling. *International Journal for the Advancement of Counseling, 26*(2), 147–161. doi:10.1023/B:ADCO.0000027427.76422.1f

Lee, L. (2011). Blogging: Promoting learner autonomy and intercultural competence through Study Abroad. *Language Learning & Technology, 15*(3), 87–109.

Lewin, R. (Ed.). (2009). *The handbook of practice and research in Study Abroad: Higher education and the quest for global citizenship*. New York: Routledge.

Loizzo, J., Borron, A., Gee, A., & Ertmer, P. (2016). Teaching convergence in 21st century undergraduate agricultural communication: A pilot study of backpack multimedia kits in a blended. Project-based learning course. *Journal of Applied Communications, 100*(2). doi:10.4148/1051-0834.1033

Madison, E. (2014). Training digital age journalists: Blurring the distinction between students and professionals. *Journalism and Mass Communication Educator, 69*(3), 314–324. doi:10.1177/1077695814532926

Medora, N., & Roy, N. (2017). Recruiting, organizing, planning and conducting a 3-week, short-term, Study Abroad program for undergraduate students: Guidelines and suggestions for first-time faculty leaders. *International Journal of Humanities and Social Science Research, 3*, 1–11. doi:10.6000/2371-1655.2017.03.01

Papastephanou, M. (2005). Globalisation, Globalism and Cosmopolitanism as an Educational Ideal. *Educational Philosophy and Theory, 37*(4), 533–551. doi:10.1111/j.1469-5812.2005.00139.x

Prensky, M. (2001). Digital natives, digital immigrants. *On the Horizon, 9*(5), 1–6. doi:10.1108/10748120110424816

Sabrina, D. (2016). *Traditional Journalism is Dying: Why the Publishing Industry Must Adapt to Survive*. Retrieved from http://www.huffingtonpost.com/news/content-creation/

Singer, J. (2005). The political j-blogger: 'Normalizing' a new media form to fit old norms and practices. *Journalism, 6*(2), 173–198. doi:10.1177/1464884905051009

Skrbis, Z., Kendall, G., & Woodward, I. (2004). Locating cosmopolitanism: Between humanist ideal and grounded social category. *Theory, Culture & Society, 21*(6), 115–136. doi:10.1177/0263276404047418

Smith, J. (2017). Assessing creativity: Creating a rubric to effectively evaluate mediated digital portfolios. *Journalism and Mass Communication Educator, 72*(1), 24–36. doi:10.1177/1077695816648866

UNESCO. (2013). *Global Media and Information Literacy (MIL). Assessment framework: Country readiness and competencies*. Paris, France. United States Institute for Peace. Retrieved from http://www.buildingpeace.org/forums/how-do-you-define-global-citizenship

Unwin, T. (2009). *ICT4D Information and Communication Technology for Development*. Cambridge, UK: Cambridge University Press.

Vraga, E., & Tully, M. (2015). Media literacy messages and hostile media perceptions: Processing of nonpartisan versus partisan political information. *Mass Communication & Society*, *18*(4), 422–448. doi:10.1080/15205436.2014.1001910

Yildiz, M. (2002). Analog and digital video production techniques in media literacy education. *National Educational Computing Conference Proceedings*.

Chapter 9
The Shluvim Social–Professional Network:
A Bridge for Educational Challenges and Trailblazers in Education

Smadar Bar-Tal
Levinsky College of Education, Israel

Tami Seifert
Kibbutzim College of Education, Technology, and the Arts, Israel

ABSTRACT

Establishment of the Shluvim network in 2010 responded to the Israeli education profession's need to introduce innovative pedagogical challenges. This social-professional network provides a virtual space for its members, empowering them through discussion on different aspects of education. The article describes a case study, employing both qualitative and quantitative methodology (questionnaires and interviews), to identify the dynamics of quantitative components involved in the evolvement of the network and to elicit members' experiences in the communication process. Findings reveal challenges involved in informed use of social networking in education and show how participation in the professional network can assist members' professional development, although it is necessary to adapt to changes in usage patterns and competition with alternative social networks. The research enhances understanding of the social-professional network's role as an empowering environment for the Israeli education system in general and for teachers' education and professional development in particular.

INTRODUCTION

The last decade has witnessed the introduction and growth of international social networks for a wide range of populations. On these networks millions of people from the farthest reaches of the globe communicate in dozens of languages. This social phenomenon has led to the growth and activity of networks of different scopes and types. The largest of the networks usually focus on social activity and sometimes

DOI: 10.4018/978-1-5225-3082-4.ch009

Copyright © 2018, IGI Global. Copying or distributing in print or electronic forms without written permission of IGI Global is prohibited.

relate to professional issues. Others are more specific and professional in nature and many are entirely devoted to professional matters. This platform has become increasingly widespread among professional communities aiming to promote their members' professional development. In the education field, a small number of social networks operate in different countries.

In 2010, the MOFET Institute decided to construct a professional-social network for teacher-educators and all those working in education named "Shluvim". This network is a pioneer initiative in Israel in the Hebrew language intended to bring different types of educators together on a single platform in a social network to allow them a place where they can expose their innovative work on a national and international level, in the areas of education and teacher-training. It also aims to provide a response for educators who are native Hebrew speakers and/or using Hebrew as a language for interpersonal and group communication. When the present study was conducted, there were 2,200 educators belonging to 152 groups in various areas of education, who had been active in Shluvim at different times: groups that had been active from the moment that they were set up until today, and groups that were opened for limited periods of time for example for supplementary courses or to accompany conferences. The network includes groups which discuss various topics in education, disciplinary issues and pedagogic aspects. The number of groups has grown and today there are more than 200 such groups. One of the main components of the network is a central blog that deals with "hot" issues in education. Additionally, the network permits broad access to various tools. Membership of the network is free of charge, voluntary and open to any educator. There are members who join as individuals or as members of a topic group in order to lead debate on a certain idea or "burning" dilemma in education or as a participant in a course. There are also passive participants who suffice with reading information that is published by others, without publishing anything themselves or contributing materials. These passive participants are known as "lurkers" (Nonnecke & Preece, 2001).

The activity on the Shluvim network has been investigated in research studies relating to the contribution of the network to the promotion of collaborative professional discourse. These studies have examined the types of activity in the different groups and types of activity of the individual learners on the network, using network theory and characteristics of blogs to analyze connections between members (Bar-Tal & Seifert, 2014; Goldstein, 2014; Mor, 2014) and also examining leadership of groups and activity of master's degree courses using the professional network (Lotan, 2012). These studies did not deal with the contribution of the Shluvim network to members' professional development, one of the main purposes of this network. Moreover, the studies in this area have not examined the challenges that the Shluvim network poses for its members and leaders. These aspects of the network are very important for its future design due to changes in its scope and the type of use that users employ in this and other world social networks and in various discussion channels available to educators. The present study aims to fill these gaps in knowledge.

THEORETICAL BACKGROUND

Teachers' Professional Development and Identity

Teachers' empowerment processes are one of the main factors influencing the perception of professional identity and its construction (Beauchamp & Thomas, 2009; Kosminski & Klavier, 2010). There is a strong probability that empowered teachers will encourage the empowerment of others (Somech, 2005).

Continuous professional development is essential in order to maintain professional quality and this is the responsibility of each professional in their field. This need is reinforced by systemic demands for compliance with professional standards (Friedman & Philips, 2004). The relevant professional literature, has gradually consolidated a distinction between professional development and professional learning (Webster-Wright, 2009), such that professional development emphasizes training while professional learning emphasizes the development of an active learner. Moreover, planned professional development does not necessarily lead to professional learning. In the opinion of Webster-Wright (ibid) professional development should be a holistic experience closely adhering to teachers' professional practice.

Professional development is perceived by teachers as a means for continuous improvement of their pedagogic knowledge, and they think it important that this should also include practical components, should be relevant to their teaching context, should be meaningful for them and will help them to become involved in active learning while receiving a suitable reward for the time and effort that they invest in these studies (Birman et al., 2000). Continuous professional training is essential for teachers' professional development over their careers. Professional development should allow teachers to conduct critical reflection on teaching and to shape their knowledge and beliefs on content, pedagogy and learners (Darling-Hammond, 1999) in order to improve their teaching knowledge and practice (Darling-Hammond & Richardson, 2009).

In conclusion, the accelerated development of technology, its increased use in daily life and professional life facilitates the advance of educational communities with an aim to allow educators to construct a professional identity, adopt innovation, and become familiar with and implement novel pedagogy, close communication between educators and a high level of technological literacy among members of the community. The present study aims to understand the professional development processes of educators within an online community on the Shluvim network, investigating their perceptions of the contribution of the network to their professional development and also the challenges that face the network in its future activities.

The Importance of a Social Network

Many educators tend to act in the education field in an almost completely independent manner and they only experience professional participation processes to a very restricted extent (Hindin et al., 2007). This is especially true with regard to school teachers and the teaching staffs of colleges and universities. Educators need frameworks in which they can frequently share knowledge, construct knowledge, continuously become more professional and keep up to date with latest developments, consult with others and receive regular support. Such frameworks can help them to be learn about new teaching methods, learning environments and changing learning contents. Thus, the easy accessibility of the social networks broadens the possibilities for the creation of a variety of general interest groups and more specifically educational communities that facilitate multi-person discourse and professional and educational learning. The variety and quality of contacts that the network offers expands learning opportunities (Cross, 2007).

Social networks reinforce the identification of the user with groups in which they are members (Shilo & Caspi, 2011). These networks also reinforce existing connections with people that already know one another, contributing to the strengthening of a community experience. The possibility of forming new contacts, while maintaining and strengthening existing contacts, creates a dynamic reality of shared learning between the different people who interacting on the network. Support for this picture was given in the Horizon report (Johnson et al., 2014). The authors of the report note that there are 6.3 million accounts (of educators, students, pupils, scientists and the broad public) on the 25 leading platforms in the world of social networks and the influence of the social network is expressed in educational discourse. The network offers informal communication and serves as a professional learning community. According to the authors, understanding the way in which the network can be combined with social learning processes is an essential skill for educators. The Shluvim network aimed to provide a response for the need for broad access to a more intimate network for a professional Hebrew-speaking target audience, using tools that would facilitate communication between educators such as Cloud tags, tools that were only lately added to the Facebook network. In this way the network aimed to construct an online educational community.

Online Professional Communities

Professional learning communities are groups of professionals that correspond one with another to examine their knowledge and practice and discuss them. This helps them to improve their professional work (Birnbaum, 2009). Professional groups that in the past met in face-to-face meetings bridge the restrictions of time and place with the help of sophisticated technology. In recent years, there have been increased initiatives for online learning intended to help professionals who wish to exchange and construct knowledge together. In such communities, the members willingly commit themselves for active participation.

Online knowledge communities operate in an optimal manner, such that structural and cultural components contribute to the creation of a rich texture of trust relations between members, a sense of a common purpose, collaboration and reciprocity (Amin & Roberts, 2008; Hemmasi & Csanda, 2009). Yaniv (2011) notes that a network community provides its members with many opportunities for professional discussion, expressing themselves on common dilemmas and providing professional support from experts and researchers from academic institutions. In fact, they provide members with an opportunity for life-long learning. On-line communities are characterized by computer-mediated communication between the community members without any face-to-face meetings, with a high level of accessibility and availability: seven days a week, twenty-four hours a day. The participants participate by their free choice, according to their similar fields of interest and experiences, a factor that can contribute to the quality of connections created between the network's members. Joining and leaving online communities is usually performed according to the user's free choice, while the main reasons for joining an online community are the desire to discuss a common subject and to access knowledge on it (Horrigan & Rainie, 2001; Ridings & Gefen, 2004).

It is important to note that most members of the community do participate in relevant activities and contribute their knowledge, although many studies have indicated a prevalent phenomenon on online communities, such that a substantial proportion of the members prefer to consume information that is relevant for them without contributing anything in an active manner (Butler et al., 2002; Lev-On & Hardin, 2008). The community may include a significant core of members who also are not widely or regularly active, yet they may still constitute significant potential for participation in shared activities, to help in exposing information and presenting "stars" to the community. Lev-On (2015) described the unique propensities of the size of an online community – online communities can grow unlimitedly, and thus they allow regular interaction and swift consideration by those who know something about a problem or question of one of the community's members, and there is a probability that the community's members can supply different and helpful viewpoints to solve these issues and to help those who join the community to become more professional. This means that a "reservoir of skills" is formed and this leads to the creation of a community of "professional amateurs", enjoying mutual enrichment and growing professionalization on a shared topic that underpins their interaction.

Online communities exist due to the development of technology and the members that join the community. Among the members, there are those who are publicly active and those who take on the role of "lurkers" (Nonnecke & Preece, 2001). The reasons why certain people decide not to publish anything are many but research has indicated the importance of the "listening" of lurkers and their immense contribution to the progress of the discussion on the network and to the fulfilment of the socio-emotional needs of the network's members (Rau, Gao & Ding, 2008). The technology enables members to overcome distance, to enrich their circle of acquaintances in various areas and at different levels and to enrich the participants by recognizing the characteristics of their activities and behavior.

Models from the fields of organization and commerce can be employed to obtain an additional perspective concerning the perception of the network by its members. The SWOT model (Strengths, Weaknesses, Opportunities and Threats) can be used to analyze strategy in the fields of organization and commerce, focusing on internal and external factors that influence the organization (Valentin, 2001). This model examines the strengths and weaknesses of internal factors and the opportunities and threats posed by external factors. At the end of the analytical process a list of insights is drawn up including advantages, weaknesses, opportunities and threats with the aim of reducing the extent of factors which the organization cannot manage and increasing the factors that the organization is able to manage. The organization or community can manage strengths and weaknesses, but they can also identify opportunities in the commercial environment where they can use their strengths and avoid threats that increase their vulnerability to the organization's weaknesses.

The Research Questions

The purpose of the research described here, conducted after four years of the Shluvim network's operation, was to outline a comprehensive picture of the actions on the network, the contribution of the network to its members' professional development and to point out challenges that may face the network in the future. The research questions were therefore:

1. What are the characteristics of use of the Shluvim network?
2. What is the contribution of the Shluvim network to educators' professional development?
3. What challenges face those who direct the Shluvim network?

METHODOLOGY

The research is a case study, focusing on the identification and description of the participants' patterns of activities as individuals and in groups on the Shluvim professional- social network. The study was conducted after the network had operated for four years. The data were collected in 2015, after four years of activity This was a mixed methods study using qualitative and quantitative data collection and analysis (Johnson & Onwuegbuzie, 2004; Keeves, 1998). This combination of approaches allows the identification of dynamics in time of the quantitative components involved in the development of the professional-social network. The implementation of qualitative methods also permits the researchers to conduct a deep investigation of the participants' experiences on the network in their communication with their colleagues. The quantitative analysis was combined with the interpretative analysis reinforcing the qualitative findings and clarifying the different identified themes. The qualitative data were able to supplement the quantitative findings with information that could not be revealed from quantitative statistics alone (Alpert, 2010).

Research Participants

The sample included 2,200 members, who had participated in the Shluvim network at some time during the four years of its operation. Of this sample, 64 members completed the research questionnaire and 15 members participated in interviews.

The Research Tools

The research tools included semi-structured in-depth interviews face to face (Wisker, 2008; Yin, 2008), non-participatory observations of the network materials (Wisker, 2008), analysis of the researcher's journal (Ely et al., 2001) and a questionnaire whose content was tested and validated by two external reviewers. At the first stage, the research was conducted as a pilot study in order to become familiar with the network and to choose the research topic and the type of research, which would be appropriate. The pilot study was conducted with the assistance of a focus group (Wisker, 2008) including four members. The results of the pilot study helped to form the basis for the construction of the face to face informal interviews and research questions.

Data Analysis

Qualitative Methodology

The qualitative data were analyzed through a deeply detailed interpretative description (Geertz, 1973), a "thick" description, aiming to provide a comprehensive picture of the reality as the members of the network and heads of the groups interpreted it from their experiences. This method reflected a "desire to understand and not only to explain" (Sabar Ben-Yehoshua, 1990, p. 16).

The collected data were read several times by two external reviewers, divided into repetitive "units of analysis" that were defined as categories and analyzed with the help of Atlas.ti 7.1 software and through thematic content analysis in order to identify patterns through repeated reading and through a cautious examination of the recorded materials (Neuendorf, 2002).

Quantitative Methodology

The quantitative analysis of the research produced descriptive statistics concerning the groups on the network. Results of the questionnaire were analyzed with the help of SPSS software. There were 64 respondents (constituting 2.9% of all 2,200 members of the network). 42% of the respondents were male and 58% were female. It was clear to the researchers that the sample did not provide full representation for the network participants, nevertheless the statistical data have value since they provided a tentative picture of the activity on the professional-social network over its first four years of operation and added an additional layer to supplement the qualitative data.

FINDINGS

The following description of the Shluvim network relates to four main points: (1) the characteristics of use on the network; (2) the users' motivations for participation; (3) the contribution of the network to the users' professional development and (4) challenges involved in the future leadership of the network. The findings are presented in a holistic manner relating to all the findings obtained through the research tools in accord with the research questions. The data analysis was conducted in consideration of the samples of the groups and their goals.

Characteristics of Use of the Shluvim Network

There are 152 groups on the Shluvim network. 74 focus on technological tools and environments, 52 are groups that accompany courses, workshops, supplementary courses and seminars. Many groups were opened by teachers (53) or by college teaching staff (36); some were opened by senior role-holders in the education system such as superintendents, principals and coordinators (18) instructors (12) and students (11). Many of the members of the network participated in more than one group. Table 1 describes the various subjects with which the groups on the network with the largest number of members and largest number of visits focus on. These include both educational values issues and also practical issues from the educational field. As can be seen, the average number of visits per member ranges between 18.7 to 106.5, and this represents the level of interest in the activities of the groups on the network. It is notable that the " Meaningful learning in education" group was awarded the largest average number of visits (7883). One of the reasons for this, according to the pedagogic manager of the network, relates to this being a closed group, whose members are professionals focusing on particular content. The group manager is very active and supportive. Participation in the group assists members' professional progress and so its scope and the depth of its materials is comprehensive and varied.

Table 1. Network groups with the largest number of members and visits

Name of Group	Open/Closed	Number of Members	Number of Visits	Mean Number of Visits per Member
Absorption of immigrant students	Open	127	6735	53.0
Pedagogic mentors in the computer era	Open	119	2226	18.7
ICT in English – Haifa	Open	105	8448	80.5
Living journal – 6th International Conference on Teacher Training	Open	101	4278	42.4
Work group – social networks in education	Open	77	1042	13.5
Meaningful learning in education	Closed	74	7883	106.5
Assimilation of Moodle – pedagogy and technology	Open	55	1567	28.5
Instructors illustrate	Closed	52	723	13.9
Audio network	Open	48	1378	28.7
Virtual teaching on the Internet – Students group 2012	Open		1428	54.9

Additionally, the groups with the highest average visits were in the main those that were opened to accompany learning in courses. Additional groups operated over the years, sharing professional knowledge and constructing practical knowledge. For example, the group entitled "The Pedagogic Instructor in the Computer Era", was a think-tank of the staff of the MOFET Institute that operated over a decade and set itself the goal of integrating technology in teaching and learning among the college's pedagogic instructors. As part of this group's activities, they conducted theoretical discussion, talking about dilemmas involved in integrating technology in teaching. Moreover, the group identified difficulties in the integration of technology in teaching and various solutions were suggested. A rich variety of models for teaching and learning activities were produced for the use of technology in classroom teaching. Thus too, models of pedagogic instruction assisted by technology were also proposed. Processes of this sort were characteristic of many of the groups and thus the network provided access to professional pedagogic and practical knowledge to a very broad community of educators. Members of the network who answered the questionnaire recognized the network's potential to lead to professional promotion. And indeed, the main motivations that they noted (50%) for participation in the different groups were to meet colleagues and to search for professional information. Additional motivations for choosing to participate in the network were curiosity (21.9%), professional exposure (7.8%), and compulsory participation for a course (6.3%). 14% of the respondents noted that they chose the Shluvim network for other reasons: to express areas of interest and attitudes on educational issues (3), as part of a think-tank (2), to for a social relationship (1), learning activities with students (1), research (1), desire to learn how to use an educational social network (1) and belonging to a system (1).

Forty-four percent (28) of the questionnaire respondents were members of one group, 37.5% (24) were members of between two to five groups, 7.8% (5) were members of more than five groups and 10.9% (7) were not members of a group. The frequency of visits to the network among 42.2% of the respondents was once a month, 17.2% visited the network once in two weeks, 4.7% visited the network once a week, 4.7% visited twice or more times per week and 7.8% visited the network every day or once every two days. It is important to note that 40 of the respondents (64.8%) testified that they were active on other social networks in a more intensive manner than on the Shluvim network, especially on Facebook. Only 22 (35.2%) reported similar use of all the networks.

It also emerged from the questionnaire responses that the respondents felt that what was unique about the Shluvim network was that it stimulated educational discourse and was intended for a community of educators solely in Israel, and "and it does not serve the masses in Israel" (David). Also, the network provides a response for educators from the religious sector who seek activity in a controlled online environment: "it was a win-win situation. On the one hand, we wanted a network that would be comfortable to work in and on the other hand a place where we could work together with religious people, without any advertisements" (Ami). But despite the differentiation and the differences from other networks, the Shluvim network was connected with her "sister" networks, and thus was accessible to and exposed the huge amount of knowledge that was amassed in it even to other platforms, as one questionnaire respondent noted: "I am up-to-date with articles that are published there through Facebook and even react to and share the discussions there, and I don't need to visit the [Facebook] network in order to be informed".

Since the Shluvim network is intended as an educational platform it embodies unique aspects of an educational community, and yet it also challenges that community to act in a relatively new arena in the field of education that is offered as a continuation of the other social networks, and thus contributes to its members' professional development.

Promoting Educators' Professional Development

The Shluvim network is intended primarily to promote educators' professional development. Its unique nature is expressed in the creation and construction of educational, pedagogical and professional discourse, discussing macro-systemic educational dilemmas and issues that relate to a wide range of disciplines and areas of learning. The network's members see the activity on the network as an additional layer of their professional development. Their testimony indicated that the Shluvim network has characteristics that help to form its construction as a robust, unique, challenging and interesting professional community, which is able to facilitate "acquaintance between members of the same area, exchange of opinions, learning materials and reactions to different ideas" (QR [hereafter – Questionnaire Respondant]). An additional example: "[to produce] continuous professional development, up-to-date, innovative and refreshing over the career cycle, necessitates a professional social network for educators, such that will enable critical awareness, multiple voices, new insights and also remarks concerning aspects that are not often discussed" (QR). The network allows participants to focus on educational issues that unite all the different sectors of education "within one network for educators from all the areas. It's a good idea. It really allows more to be done ... bridging between sub-networks, and then that leads ...to the distribution of innovations and new ideas" (Zehava). The network opens up a work environment and activities permitting participants to meet in a professional community. The present study aimed to examine the extent to which participants on the network see it as a factor contributing to their professional development.

The research findings reveal four main components that promote educators' professional development with the assistance of the Shluvim network: sharing knowledge, meeting colleagues, participation in research and professional discourse. These findings emerged from both the interviews and the question-naire responses. Table 2 presents the respondents' perceptions concerning the contribution of activities on the Shluvim network to their professional development as they emerged from the questionnaire.

The findings shown in Table 1 indicate that the questionnaire respondents perceive the activities on the Shluvim network as an important layer in their professional development. Approximately half of the participants (42%) claimed that the network contributed to a reasonable to large extent to their

Table 2. Descriptive statistics (on a scale of 1-4) relating to respondents' perceptions of the Shluvim network as a contribution to their professional development (N=64)

Mean Grade (SD)	Number of Respondents	The Shluvim Network
2.9 (1.3)	48	Contribution of activity on the network to my professional development
3.4 (0.9)	64	There is a place for a professional network in the field of education
2.7 (0.9)	64	The Shluvim network promotes the construction of a professional community between members on educational subjects
3.0 (1.1)	55	Sharing knowledge – I see it as important that a number of members reached my materials
1.8 (0.8)	64	Activity on the network contributed to my acquaintance with colleagues in my discipline
2.0 (1.2)	48	Broadening my circle of friends thanks to my participation on the network
2.5 (1.0)	64	Shluvim network constitutes a platform where ideas can be voiced

professional development (M=2.9, SD=1.3). 56% of the respondents even noted that the network is important to a large extent for the development of a special professional network in the field of education, 28% of the respondents graded this statement as reasonably important. It can also be seen from Table 2 that sharing knowledge is seen by the respondents as an important contribution by the network to professional development. A large proportion (75%) of the respondents graded sharing materials with members of the network as reasonably to very important (M=3.0, SD=1.1). Moreover, the respondents viewed the group of colleagues as meaningful. Approximately one third of them (35%) claimed that the network constituted a platform on which they could meet colleagues from their area of knowledge (M=1.8, SD=0.84) and broadened their circle of friends (M=2.0, SD=1.2). Some (44%) of the network members who responded to the questionnaire noted to a large extent that they thought it was pertinent to publish on the network and they felt it important that members of the network were able to reach the materials that they published and even gave them their consideration and reactions. Some (38%) even testified that they found that the network provided them with a platform on which to present ideas (M=2.5, SD=1.0). This platform formed a fertile bed for the consumption and creation of content, and also for fruitful dialog and discussion on various professional matters.

The respondents' responses to the open questions in the questionnaire confirmed the quantitative findings noted above. Thus, for example, it appeared from these responses that the component of sharing knowledge was seen as assisting professional development. This component reflects the process of professional development since the network empowers and increases access to contents, publication and experts. One of the female members of the network said: "the network exposed me to new contents and ideas and I revealed additional directions of thinking (QR). Another member added: "I found interesting and relevant information on the network" (QR). Members also noted that the network was accessible for them to meet colleagues and to "make contact with those who react" (QR), and allowed them to participate in productive and significant discussion (QR). Some of the members found that Shluvim constituted a platform on which to suggest ideas: "a social professional network should… be a platform on which to suggest ideas, dilemmas, new directions for professionals. And that is what Shluvim does with genuine professionalism (QR).

Another aspect that emerged from the interviews relates to the sharing of professional materials and the exposure of learning materials and academic articles, and this was the expansion of the collection of varied learning materials offered accessibly for every teacher: "one of the teachers told me that she had created a small library from the materials that she experienced in the group for teachers teaching immigrants" (Miki).

One of the main components that emerged from the findings characterizing the work of educators was the need to be continually updated. This need is necessary for professional development throughout their professional careers. Shluvim network has the potential to respond to this need: "when I was a pedagogic instructor I would peek into Shluvim because there were things there that helped and contributed to me. I would explore it …both with regard to the subjects and also the viewpoint of specific writers who, in my opinion, constituted a lighthouse beaming knowledge and leading the way" (Galit). Thus too the members of the network supported the promotion of collaboration between the members on an egalitarian basis, sharing materials, ideals and later even joint initiatives, in order to let in "oxygen" to refresh and energize. "Collaboration, support, innovation … sharing between colleagues (QR). Productive and pleasant participation can occur only in a supportive and favorable environment. It is expected that collaboration between members will create expert professional groups and will lead to a thickening of the existing groups and opening of new professional groups led by professional instructors on a focused issue.

The network also offers a selection of materials for reading and study which are considered front of stage articles including professional discussion on education and teacher-training, sharing educational ideas and dilemmas, either stimulated by personal initiatives or from participation in a learning group such as an academic course, and studies for specialization. "it keeps you up-to-date and is contemporary … relating to what is going on and pointing up burning matters for teacher-educators" (Meirav). One of the members added: "the creation of a good, positive, challenging and professional experience each time that you enter the network. It should be a contribution each time" (QR). The network members are thus able to keep up-to-date with burning educational issues and they are able to express their opinions on these subjects.

Professional development is also expressed in the exposure to experts in the field and construction of a social network in a professional field allows the members to become acquainted with these experts, whom it would be difficult to meet in other ways. Membership of the Shluvim network facilitates contact with those who are most involved and highly professional regarding an educational issue and to engage in dialog with them, permitting professional enrichment and mutually publication one with the other. "if I was not on the Shluvim network, I would not be able to reach the lecturer in the university who has a site on my subject …and I would not reach several other people who have seen my project on Shluvim" (Kalanit). And as one other members noted: "it's a lever for professional development … no it's not a lever its like lightning, its not a lever its … a push to do something" (Galit).

Another issue that emerged from the evidence of the respondents relates to the network's advantage of findings potential partners for research, creating an elite professional group that sees the Shluvim network as a primary home for all their activity and research where they can find colleagues who speak their "language" and also "groups that will facilitate collaboration on academic actions and research" (Ran). Some of the members suggest that the next stage should be to strike for a more academic direction in research, professional discourse led by senior professional and transforming Shluvim into an academic source that is worthy to be quoted: " I think that perhaps for its image, we can define Shluvim as a first generation … but in the second generation it would be worthwhile including expert groups who would elevate the network into something more professional: including opinion papers, publications …I think that the next generation of Shluvim will begin to cite it" (Moshe). It is therefore worth thinking about academic credits and measures of evaluation for articles published on social networks (QR).

The Shluvim network provides a broad foundation for peer learning at various levels of professional knowledge. The network constitutes a large collection of knowledge and a concentration of experts, but these facts are not recognized or known to all. Thus, the research participants claimed that it is very important to take the path of explanation and guidance and to make the network to as wide as possible audience of educators. " As I see it it should develop as a combination of a social network with a knowledge bank, a combination between a network of experts and a social network …convincing experts to serve as significant anchors in the network, like magnets" (Ilan). The respondents recommended that the network should operate in two channels: expanding publication, marketing and enlistment of new members from the community of educators and bringing in "stars" in order to attract more members: "people want to join people who dictate the trends … like they do in restaurants when they give free meals so that they will bring with them all the lurkers. So I think that is the direction that Shluvim should also consider" (Moshe). Social networks are a natural environment in which student teachers act as part of the formal and informal communication, and there is a value for teacher-educators to act and have a presence in those environments. One of the interviewees recommended: "including teachers in the Shluvim network. It's a good opportunity to get to know a professional network for future or practicing teachers" (Ami).

This can be achieved by discussing "hot" issues. The network should provide a platform for different viewpoints, pedagogic theories and various considerations of a particular issue. Such discussion could contribute to all the members – both those who participate actively and those who only visit to read the new information that collects on the network.

The research findings indicate the contribution of the Shluvim network to the professional development of those who participate in it due to a range of different aspects that it contains. The perception of the community as a source aiding professional promotion was evident in several dimensions, especially in the sharing of materials with colleagues and exposure to knowledge and attitudes as well as the construction of a professional social network. Additionally, the respondents suggested recommendations that could contribute to the deepening and broadening of professional development and this constitutes a challenge to those leading the network - the successful groups heads as well as the network pedagogic manager. Quotations from the words of two respondents emphasize the perception of the network as an intimate part of members' professional development. Nili said: "the fact that we engaged in activity there ... and that we later conducted research on it. So yes, it did contribute...to our observation and understanding of what the network is. It is not just a matter of branding, it is also a matter of my development". Another participant noted: empowerment takes place when a member of the Shluvim network knows that he has a voice and that his voice is important and unique, a specific value because of the authenticity that is embodied in this experience, the wisdom of the act and the power that can be found in the knowledge that professional are eager to share with each other, in order to lead moral changes and to feel that they have an influence (QR).

FUTURE CHALLENGES FOR THOSE LEADING THE NETWORK

Those who lead the Shluvim network held a vision of the network as a virtual environment that supports the professional development of educators and contributes to dialog, collaboration, thinking and academic research of professional educators. In the test of reality, at the end of four years of the network's operation, various supportive and challenging entities grew out of the field in the development of the network and a dilemma was set before its leaders and initiators regarding the continuation of its activities. The questions that arise relate to the issue whether to continue with the existing form or to make a change due to the population of members, both those who participate and those who do not participate and whether in parallel to also consider the knowledge that has been collected from the activity on other networks. Analysis of the findings indicates three main dimensions that challenge the participation of the network members: the complex dialog with technology, competing networks and academic development of activities on the network.

One of the challenges faced by the leaders of the network relates to digital gaps in skills for the use and frequency of use of technology among the educator population. "We live in an era of social networks and we must introduce this to education because the students operate there, the teachers are also there and the some of the lecturers are already there ... we need to be familiar with all the possibilities of the network and to recognize the challenges, the difficulties, the risks and the problems" (Nili). But all these plans and suggestions cannot be implemented without focusing on the individual. The network encourages connections between people, encouraging participation, guiding the participants in their first steps and encouraging them to continue to participate. "Dan told me about a very interesting strategy. How he made contact with people, how he encouraged them, how he created interest for them when he wrote" (Zehava). A response is also needed for those who tried by themselves to make contacts and did not succeed: "there are some who search for information, there are some who look for collaboration. Usually they do not receive a response and that's a pity" (Ilan).

Positive reinforcement and evaluation was given by those responsible for the network for the publication of materials on the network and their appearance: "if I received a compliment from my president then it seems that Shluvim from my point of view has done good work beyond expectations" (Moshe).

Today the Facebook network is far more accessible than in the past and the use of it allows the opening of closed groups, responses to questionnaires, uploading pictures and film clips. Moreover there are many designated groups for particular areas of education and a substantial part of the educational community are members of the network. In Facebook there are also professional groups relating to education. The challenge is to motivate people to join the Shluvim network and to prevent the transfer of Shluvim's active members to Facebook. It is important to note that many participants joined Shluvim not because of its unique professional aspects but rather because of the support that they received from the network pedagogic manager. Once they spread their wings and became independent they left the network without hesitation. From the interviews, it was clear that the main uniqueness and the educational challenge that the network can set in the future is not to compete with other existing environments in the Internet space that are often technologically sophisticated and have a larger number of participants and/or members, but rather it should constitute an ensign that attracts people to it and highlights its uniqueness. The respondents emphasized how important it was that such a network would offer its members expanded links and connections to other social network s to interest people active on those other networks to also act there.

Additionally, teachers and many other educators aspire to form discourse with their professional colleagues in order to cope with professional problems and to share insights. As noted the Shluvim network aims to provide a response to this need. One of the challenges is to stimulate many educators to join the network. But the actual affiliation to the community is not enough; the important challenge is to create a positive participation experience for the member, for the other members and for those who lead the network. Since this is a professional managed network, sometimes those who lead the network initiate natural and perhaps even artificial actions in order to empower the user's experience.

Another challenge that faces the network relates to official recognition of the activity that it contains by academic institutions. The teacher-training institutions encourage academic and research writing, as a central component in the promotion of academic staff. However, writing on the Shluvim network is not awarded academic credit that would lead to academic grades granted by the heads of the colleges and so many of the college staffs avoid publishing on the Shluvim network. Moreover, one of the characteristics of the 21st century modern man is a lack of free time. To this is added the personal fear of leaving a personal mark which will be eternally documented. And if this is insufficient, competition, branding, marketing and the presence of colleagues, family and other relatives on the competing networks creates pressure to be active there and not to remain in an environment that is less well known and to "miss out" on what is happening. So that the network can serve as a central platform for professional development one of the network's members suggested: "the challenge is how to operate the network in such a way that it will be active, contributing to the professional development of all educators" (Zehava). Another member noted: "the voice of the teacher-educators needs to be heard through all the means that technology facilitates" (QR). This can be implemented by establishing a professional community in the fields of teaching, learning and consideration of educational issues that are on the public and professional agenda: "to establish intiatives by field of knowledge, interest and friendship. To transform Shluvim into a place for exchange of opinions of communities, to conduct shared projects with Shluvim acting as the meeting place" (QR). A place that will constitute a crossroads of encounters, allowing interpersonal professional relations to form and helping to find partners for creativity and publication of professional research: "bridging between theory and the field and between the school and the teacher-training college, a platform where it is possible to present the viewpoints of students, teachers and lecturers" (QR).

In order to transform the network into an educational-professional platform for teacher education, it is necessary to consider the type of contents, their desirable scope, the character of the network as a place for support and professional development or as a "Hyde Park" forum for the presentation of different ideas and social and pedagogical perceptions that sometimes are not accepted or similar to those of the majority of the public: "a platform for teacher education. I really think that a friendly platform is needed and in my opinion there should be a group of people who beyond having their personal knowledge also pass on that knowledge to others... this can be done by forming meeting and increasing motivation. I think that the meeting should be formed within Shluvim, to constitute a stimulus and challenge for people to visit it" (Meirav).

Additional suggestions focused on giving a broad platform for leading members and to tag them as leaders in the different areas of knowledge, creating dialogs with a wider community within the network: "to tag leading people while broadening the population of participants, in order to provide a broad platform", "more for leading educators and yet with a scope for participants that will convince them to be active in that environment" (Ilan). In order to advance this matter a panel of experts should be established to include leading well known professionals who are not yet members of the network and from that to create a panel of experts which will operate on a particular subject in a regular or temporary manner: "its necessary to convince people to join an experts' panel, to advertise their names, to encourage them ...a large mass is needed and then if they agree to publish through a new posting list that will be a wonderful platform" (Ilan). Others suggested variation in the types of activities that it would be worthwhile creating on the network. For example: "the conference newspaper ...synchronic activities on the network ...publication of initiatives for different subjects" (QR). For these activities to succeed, educators bring their experiences and work styles to the network and so a request was made that the activities would constitute a model for network members to prepare activities in a similar way through modeling used in teacher-training: "its advisable to present models for use of the network, most of the people don't know, it seems, how it can serve their goals" (QR).

An additional challenge noted by network users was to reduce the number of closed groups and to increase the number of open groups in order to make a range of areas of knowledge more accessible. With regard to the visual aspect of the network consideration should be given to the visual appearance of the site, dividing the different active groups from those which are not active in order to use visitors' time more effectively and to increase the probability that they will join the network as members.

The continued extensive activity of the network is not certain. A list of challenges face the leaders of the network, the group heads and their members. The three main problems that must be faced are to harness a population that in part is not technologically literate, to provide a response to competitive networks and to cope with the profitability of professional publication that must compete with publication in other locations where authors may be rewarded with professional-academic credit and promotion in the academic hierarchy.

DISCUSSION

The research presents the professional development of network members, as seen in different perceptions of the network members with regard to their personal and group professional development. The research aimed to examine the contribution of the network to its members professional development and the main challenges that will contribute to the future professional activity of the network.

The contribution of this study is in the creation of a bridge between the activities of the network's members in the past and the challenges set before it if the network wishes to be meaningful and to contribute to the education field and educators in Israel. As noted above these challenges include a variety of subjects such as: coping with the complexity of the dialog between the members and technology, competition between the Shluvim network and other networks while considering the limitation of its members' lack of free time. A further challenge is the need to provide a response to the issues of academic promotion for participants such as academic credits for publication on the network. Coping with these issues can encourage the active participation of its members, while bringing "new oxygen" to revitalize the network with the discussion of "hot" issues.

Educators' Professional Identity and Development

The main purpose of the social-professional network Shluvim in the past, present and future is to provide a place for "meetings" between many educators and different sectors of education in order to allow them opportunities and space for group and personal professional development. The use of the social-professional network in the local language and culture: Hebrew allows various audiences to open a channel for professional development and also to develop a stable and robust professional identity.

One of the foundations of the vision of the Shluvim network was to create a space and anchor for professional development and identity formation for its members. This study indicates that the Shluvim network constitutes a bridge between the training process that continues over the educator's career and professional learning in which the responsibility is on the active learner. It was found that members of the network perceive this community as a source for professional promotion in many dimensions, especially due to their exposure to knowledge and attitudes, discussions with peers, sharing materials and debating dilemmas and "hot" issues, searching for potential partners for research and thus the creation of a professional-social network. The network was found to facilitate discussion on common issues and to expose information (Horrigan & Rainie, 2001; Ridings & Gefen, 2004).

And indeed, many groups were formed relating to a wide range of subjects, some open and some closed. These groups opened up a fertile bed for continuous discussion and dialog. The continuation of this activity depends on the human capital of the members of this online community.

The activity and success of the professional-social network relies on the construction of a professional community/communities that sees itself as the "home" and hothouse for professional development and a platform for professional meeting and the development of professional perceptions by those are leaders in their field of knowledge. In this way, many of the network members have been exposed to and learned about the skills of social network use for teaching purposes (Johnson et al., 2014), something that may help them to consider adopting social networks as a channel for communication with their students (Lev-On, 2015).

Challenges and Innovation

To address the challenges now facing the Shluvim network depends on several factors: the creation of an online knowledge community, understanding the importance and contribution of participants and lurkers; coping with the limitation of members' lack of free time and improvement of the rewards for activity on the network. All these matters are also subject to the test of work in a technology-rich environment.

The findings of this research reinforce previous findings in the relevant literature that the building of a successful network involves the creation and leadership of an online knowledge community with a set of rules for members' behavior and commitment (Amin & Roberts, 2008; Barker, 2006; Shoop, 2009). The success of a professional social network also depends on a process of assimilation and adoption of new technologies by the members. It was found that the Shluvim network enjoys a technological environment that allows its members to be exposed to new, and some unfamiliar technologies. Moreover, an attempt was made not only to adhere to technological innovation but also to pour contemporary contents into the network.

One of the challenges for the network is to harness educational leaders that are already active in the education field to take a leading part in the network and in the opposite direction to brand leading members of the network as educational leaders. The construction of an educational leadership in a sophisticated technological environment is a long path with several stages that only a few manage to complete. One of the difficulties of the Shluvim network is to create an educational leadership that is technologically skilled to employ the possibilities that technology affords to enrich and improve pedagogy and to lead change in teaching and learning methods. It appeared that already at the first stage of change, there were a few participants who did not succeed in adopting the information technology, since they simply registered themselves on the network and did not visit, thus preventing the possibility of their professional development through the network. But there were also those who wanted to maintain the role of "teacher as a participant in learning" and to "embark on the ship", although sometimes they left due to lack of time and/or because they did not receive a response. Those who remained at the first stage, and then went on to the second stage of "the teacher as one who adopts novelty" were characterized by the fact that technology did not constitute an obstacle for them. There were some who chose the role of "lurkers" meaning that they did not contribute their own information with those with whom they shared their learning. The highest stage "the teacher as leader" was attained only by those who managed groups with a large number of members and a large number of viewings.

The researchers chose to analyze the findings according to the SWOT model (Valentin, 2001) from the field of organizational counselling. The findings indicate different directions of strengths, weaknesses, opportunities and threats (SWOT), producing a picture of the development of the Shluvim network over the four years of its existence and the vision for its future existence. The analysis produced the following insights:

1. **Strengths:** Included easy access, a network in Hebrew, focus on educational issues and distinction between social and professional aspects, provision of a response to specific populations, technological and pedagogic support, an active network; provision of a platform on which contacts can be made without distinction between different professional identities, professional knowledge and/ or education background; emotional, professional and social support; empowerment of isolated teachers and groups, provision of a response to different needs through the possibility of choice of level of privacy for individuals and groups (open or closed) and tightening cooperation.

2.   **Weaknesses:** Included the need for mastery of technological skills, ability to express oneself and the fact some of the activities on the network do not contribute to the participants' professional development.

3.   **Opportunities:** The network also offers opportunities that include: exposure to a variety of contents and experts, empowerment of the network based on links to other networks; access to courses and educational activities contributing to professional development, opportunity for all members to publish their works, encouragement of a variety of communities in contact with the MOFET Institute to use the network, promotion of social and educational issues and provision of a platform for self-expression.

4.   **Threats:** Alongside the opportunities there are also several threats: the need to invest time; competition with other networks; and lack of professionalism of some participants.

There are many challenges involved in using the network: the need to create friendly technology-assisted dialog, even for those who do not feel this is their natural environment, to ensure the uniqueness of the network relative to other networks to allow free discussion of educational issues; to promote initiatives and cooperation; to brand educators and assist their academic promotion; to help educators improve their technological literacy and familiarity with this technological environment in which the network necessarily operates.

In conclusion, in the 21st century, when social networks occupy a large area of private and professional life, a social network on the subject of education can contribute significantly to different types of educators if it provides a supportive environment that also assists career-long professional development. Such an environment should encourage revitalization, changes in direction and provision of a response to various challenges that beset such a network as it adapts itself to future needs of its members.

SOLUTIONS AND RECOMMENDATIONS

In an era of technological changes, and powerful competition the continued existence and activity of the Shluvim network for its members' professional development involves much deliberation, challenges and question marks. The Shluvim network provides a basis for professional development and support of its members. However, so that it can continue to hold their attention over time, the leaders of the network need to pay attention to members' needs and recommendations as voiced in the present study. One central question is: how to evaluate the network towards its continued operation and what is needed to enable the network to attain its goals? Based on the research findings the following model, seen in Figure 1, was constructed to answer this question. The model illustrates the components that the Shluvim network should provide in order to continue to assist its members' professional development.

To continue to fulfill its goals the Shluvim network must address each of the components illustrated in Figure 1: a climate that invites participation, use of the local language, participation in and pooling learning resources. Additional components include: high power strength and frequency of activity, a focal point attracting both existing and new members, maintenance of a high level of professionalism in education, academic highlighting and branding for the promotion of members and their research, especially among researchers at the beginning of their careers who can contact and discuss with experienced researchers on the network. Together these components constitute the scaffolding on which leaders of the network can build to continue to provide a platform and environment suitable for educators' profes-

Figure 1. Components needed so that Shluvim network can continue to assist its members' professional development

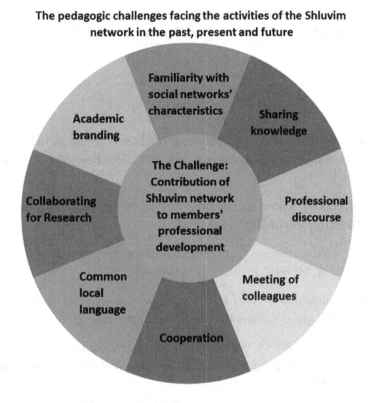

sional development in Israel. If one of the components is missing it may influence the success of the other components and harm the network's ability to cope with the different challenges that it faces. The unique nature of the Shluvim network provides a response for different sectors of Israeli society such as the religious sector, which for ideological, social, philosophical or religious reasons does not participate in other social networks.

Over the years of the Shjluvim network's operation several issues arose: is it enough to suffice with the link in the Shluvim network to other networks such as Facebook or should there be a direct guided entry to the Shluvim network? From the analysis of the findings the visits to Shluvim and their connections it appears that those surfing on other networks are exposed to Shluvim and its groups' activities in an indirect manner. The strength of a social network in general and particularly of a professional-social network such as Shluvim is measured by the number of its members and their commitment and contribution to its professional status. The network needs to find ways that the public of educators can become familiar with the components of the network, its advantages, disadvantages and the opportunities that it offers. This includes its collection of materials, theories and practices and the fact that it unites people involved with academic research with those working in the field, thus improving teaching through interaction with learners, opening doors to new knowledge. Of course, it is necessary to be aware of and cautious when using the social network and to understand their strength and power and its affordances to the particular population. Therefore, one of the main challenges is to push it forwards in order to advance different disciplines that represent innovation and a contribution to members' professional development.

ACKNOWLEDGMENT

This study was conducted to respond to the recommendation of the Inter-Collegiate Research Committee of the MOFET Institute and with the support of the Department for training of teaching staff, Ministry of Education, Jerusalem

REFERENCES

Alpert, B. (2010). Integration of quantitative analyses in qualitative research. In L. Cassan & M. Kromer-Nevo (Eds.), *Data analysis in qualitative research* (pp. 333–356). Beer Sheva: Ben Gurion University of the Negev. (in Hebrew)

Amin, A., & Roberts, J. (2008). Knowing in action: Beyond communities of practice. *Research Policy*, *37*(2), 353–369. doi:10.1016/j.respol.2007.11.003

Bar-Tal, S., & Seifert, T. (2014). *Groups on the social professional network Shluvim – An investigative view. Research report*. Israel: MOFET Institute. (in Hebrew)

Barker, R. (2006). Homo machinus versus Homo sapiens: A knowledge management perspective of virtual communities in cyberspace. *Communication Theory and Research*, *32*, 226–240.

Beauchamp, C., & Thomas, L. (2009). Understanding teacher identity: An overview of issues in the literature and implications for teacher education. *Cambridge Journal of Education*, *39*(2), 175–189. doi:10.1080/03057640902902252

Birman, B. F. et al.. (2000). Designing professional development that works. *Educational Leadership*, *57*(8), 28–33.

Birnbaum, M. (2009). Evaluation for learning and characteristics of a professional school community and the classroom culture that empowers it. In I. Kashti (Ed.), *Evaluation, Jewish education and the history of education: An anthology in memory of Professor Arieh Levy* (pp. 77–100). Tel Aviv: University of Tel Aviv, School of Education and Ramot Publishers. (in Hebrew)

Butler, B., Sproull, L., Kiesler, S., & Kraut, R. (2002). Community effort in online groups: Who does the work and why. In *Leadership at a distance: Research in technologically supported work* (pp. 171-194).

Cross, J. (2007). *Informal learning*. San Francisco, California: Pfeiffer.

Darling-Hammond, L. (1999). *Professional development for teachers: Setting the stage for learning from teaching*. Santa Cruz, CA: Center for the Future of Teaching & Learning.

Darling-Hammond, L., & Richardson, N. (2009). Teachers learning, what matters? *Educational Leadership*, *66*(5), 46–53.

Ely, M., Vinz, R., Downing, M., & Anzul, M. (2001). *On writing qualitative research: Living by words*. London: Falmer Press.

Friedman, A., & Philips, M. (2004). Continuing professional development: Developing a vision. *Journal of Education and Work, 17*(3), 361–376. doi:10.1080/1363908042000267432

Geertz, C. (1973). *The interpretation of cultures*. New York: Basic Books Inc. Publishers.

Goldstein, A. (2014). *Analysis of the Shluvim social-professional network according to network theory. Research report*. Israel: MOFET Institute. (in Hebrew)

Hemmasi, M., & Csanda, C. M. (2009). The effectiveness of communities of practice: An empirical study. *Journal of Managerial Issues, 21*(2), 262–279.

Hindin, A., Morocco, C. C., Mott, E. A., & Aguilar, C. M. (2007). More than just a group: Teacher collaboration and learning in the workplace. *Teachers and Teaching. Theory into Practice, 13*(4), 349–376.

Horrigan, J. B., & Rainie, L. (2001). *Online communities: Networks that nurture long-distance: relationships and local ties*. Pew Internet & American Life Project.

Johnson, B. R., & Onwuegbuzie, A. J. (2004). Mixed methods research: A research paradigm whose time has come. *Educational Researcher, 33*(7), 14–26. doi:10.3102/0013189X033007014

Johnson, L., Adams, S., Estrada, V., & Freeman, A. (2014). *NMC Horizon Report: 2014 higher education edition*. Austin, Texas: The New Media Consortium.

Keeves, J. P. (1988). *Educational inspect methodology, as good as measurement: An international handbook*. Oxford: Pergamon Press.

Kosminski, L., & Klavier, R. (2010). Constructing professional identity of teachers and teacher-educators in a changing reality. *Dafim, 49*, 11–41. (in Hebrew)

Lev-On, A. (2015). Introduction: Online communities – Their functioning and uses. In A. Lev-On (Ed.), *Online communities* (pp. 7–25). Tel Aviv: Rassling. (in Hebrew)

Lev-On, A., & Hardin, R. (2008). Internet-based collaborations and their political significance. *Journal of Information Technology & Politics, 4*(2), 5–27. doi:10.1080/19331680802076074

Lotan, Z. (2012). Learning patterns of student-teachers on a social-professional network. [Hebrew]. *Dafim, 54*, 248–280.

Mor, N. (2014). *The place of the blog on the Shluvim network. Research report*. Israel: MOFET Institute. (in Hebrew)

Neuendorf, K. A. (2002). *The content analysis guidebook*. Thousand Oaks, CA: Sage.

Nonnecke, B., & Preece, J. (2000). Lurker demographics: Counting the silent. In *Proceedings of the SIGCHI Conference on Human Factors in Computing Systems* (pp. 73-80). doi:10.1145/332040.332409

Rau, P. L. P., Gao, Q., & Ding, Y. (2008). Relationship between the level of intimacy and lurking in online social network services. *Computers in Human Behavior, 24*(6), 2757–2770. doi:10.1016/j.chb.2008.04.001

Ridings, C. M., & Gefen, D. (2004). Virtual community attraction: Why people hang out online. *Journal of Computer-Mediated Communication, 10*(1).

Sabar Ben-Yehoshua, N. (1990). *Qualitative research in teaching and learning.* Givataim: Massada. (in Hebrew)

Shilo, R., & Caspi, A. (2011). To climb up the network – Influence of use of social networks in an informal educational framework on identification with a group (electronic version). In I. Eshet-Alkalai, A. Caspi & N. Geri (Eds.), *Book of the Chase Conference for Technological Learning Research, 2011: The learning man in a technological era.* (pp. 239-247). Raanana: The Open University. (in Hebrew) Retrieved from: http://chais.openu.ac.il/chais2011/download/shilo_caspi.pdf

Shoop, M. C. (2009). *Public service employees experience in communities of practice* [Ph.D. dissertation]. Antioch University.

Somech, A. (2005). Teachers personal and team empowerment and their relations to organizational outcomes: Contradictory or compatible constructs? *Educational Administration Quarterly, 41*(2), 237–266. doi:10.1177/0013161X04269592

Valentin, E. K. (2001). SWOT analysis from a resource-based view. *Journal of Marketing Theory and Practice, 9*(2), 54–69. doi:10.1080/10696679.2001.11501891

Webster-Wright, A. (2009). Reframing professional development through understanding authentic professional learning. *Review of Educational Research, 79*(2), 702–739. doi:10.3102/0034654308330970

Wisker, G. (2008). *The postgraduate research handbook* (2nd ed.). Basingstoke: Palgrave. Palgrave Study Guides. doi:10.1007/978-0-230-36494-3

Yaniv, H. (2011). The social network as a learning community – Culture of lifelong learning. *MOFET Institute Journal, 46.* (in Hebrew)

Yin, R. K. (2008). *Case study research: Design and methods* (4th ed.). London: Sage Publications.

KEY TERMS AND DEFINITIONS

Lurker: One of the 'silent majority' in electronic environments. One who posts occasionally or not at all but is known to read the group's postings regularly.

Online Professional Communities: The technological infrastructure provided by the Internet helps employees discuss professional issues and thus contributes to the development of knowledge and dissemination to the wider professional community.

Professional Development: Process of improving and increasing capabilities of staff through access to education and training opportunities in the workplace, through outside organization, or through watching others perform the job.

Professional Learning Communities: Groups of professionals that correspond one with another to examine their knowledge and practice and discuss them. This helps them to improve their professional work.

Shluvim: In 2010, the MOFET Institute decided to construct a professional-social network for teacher-educators and all those working in education named "Shluvim". This network is a pioneer initiative in Israel in the Hebrew language intended to bring different types of educators together on a single platform in a social network to allow them a place where they can expose their innovative work on a national and international level, in the areas of education and teacher-training. It also aims to provide a response for educators who are native Hebrew speakers and/or using Hebrew as a language for interpersonal and group communication.

Social Network: A network of individuals such as acquaintances, coworkers and friends, which connected by interpersonal relationships. The service is an online site, which people create and maintain interpersonal relationships. Millions of people all over the world have become comfortable using to share information about themselves, via the internet.

SWOT: Models from the fields of organization and commerce can be employed to obtain an additional perspective concerning the perception of the network by its members. The SWOT model (Strengths, Weaknesses, Opportunities and Threats) can be used to analyze strategy in the fields of organization and commerce, focusing on internal and external factors that influence the organization.

The MOFET Institute: The MOFET Institute in Israel is a national intercollegiate center for the research and development of curricula and programs in teacher education and teaching in the colleges. It constitutes a unique framework both in Israel and worldwide for supporting teacher educators' professional development.

Chapter 10
Promoting Global Competencies in India:
Media and Information Literacy as Stepping Stone

Aakanksha Rajeev Sharma
Indira Gandhi National Open University (IGNOU), India

ABSTRACT

The Organization for Economic Co-operation and Development (OECD) defines global competence as the capacity to analyze global and intercultural issues critically and to engage in open, appropriate and effective interactions. Since media forms the basis for attaining and sharing information, formulating ideas and opinions about people, events and situations, exploring different cultures, perspectives, rejecting notions as well as accepting truths, media and information literacy (MIL) is an effective and essential way to attain this global competence. As MIL competencies are closely aligned with global competencies, interlinking the two helps in attaining true global citizenship. This chapter explains the problems, prospects and possibilities for MIL training in India. The history and evolution of media and its regulatory structure in India and how this has impacted and continues to influence the spectrum of media and information literacy is the core of this study.

INTRODUCTION

Organization for Economic Co-operation and Development's (OECD) Programme for International Student Assessment (PISA) says that global competence is the capacity to analyse global and intercultural issues critically and from multiple perspectives, to understand how differences affect perceptions, judgments, and ideas of self and others, and to engage in open, appropriate and effective interactions with others from different backgrounds on the basis of a shared respect for human dignity in its proposal on Global Competencies for an Inclusive World (OECD, 2016).

DOI: 10.4018/978-1-5225-3082-4.ch010

Copyright © 2018, IGI Global. Copying or distributing in print or electronic forms without written permission of IGI Global is prohibited.

Since media forms the basis for attaining and sharing information, formulating ideas and opinions about people, events and situations, as well as exploring different cultures, perspectives, rejecting notions and accepting truths, media and information literacy (MIL) is an effective and essential way to attain this global competence.

The United Nations Educational, Scientific and Cultural Organization (UNESCO) defines media and information literacy as essential competencies (knowledge, skills and attitude) that allow citizens to engage with media and other information providers effectively and develop critical thinking and life-long learning skills for socializing and becoming active citizens.

MIL facilitates in communicating across religious, cultural, social, political and economic barriers. This enhances cultural exchange and helps in maintaining plurality. It helps in overcoming disinformation, fighting stereotypes, rejecting biases in physical and virtual spaces. It also becomes an important watchdog that can observe ethical or moral violations by the media. Thus the competencies required to be a global citizen are closely aligned with MIL competencies. MIL can be a stepping stone to attain global competencies. This chapter explains the problems, prospects and possibilities for MIL training in India.

BACKGROUND

Potter (2004, p. 58-59): has said that,

Media literacy is the set of perspectives from which we expose ourselves to the media and interpret the meaning of the messages we encounter. We build our perspectives from knowledge structures. The knowledge structures form the platforms on which we stand to view the multifaceted phenomenon of the media: their business, their content, and their effects on individuals and institutions. The more people use these knowledge structures in mindful exposures, the more they will be able to use media exposures to meet their own goals and the more they will be able to avoid high risks for negative effects.

It constitutes three major elements.

- Having access to media
- Understanding the media
- Creating/expressing oneself using media

The interest in media literacy practices has risen ever since the UNESCO Declaration on Media Education, by representatives of 19 nations at Grunwald in 1982, exaggerated the 'undoubted power of the media' and the role they could play in the process of development, and as 'instruments for the citizen's active participation in society'. It called for 'political and educational systems to recognize their obligations to promote in their citizens a critical understanding of the phenomena of communications' (UNESCO, 1982).

A media and information literate person will be a keen evaluator of content as well as a credible, responsible creator of information or expression. Though the definition and goals of media and information literacy seem to be very simple, they require creation of many competencies. These competencies are a pre-requisite for surviving in the complex, media saturated environment of today.

UNESCO (2013, p.157) defined MIL competencies as ability to

1. Understand the role and functions of media in democratic societies
2. Understand the conditions under which those functions can be fulfilled.
3. Recognize and articulate a need for information.
4. Locate and access relevant information.
5. Critically evaluate information of the content of media and other information providers, including those on the internet in terms of authority, credibility and current purpose.

The arrival of the 21ˢᵗ century has brought along new technologies that have fast become a part of our daily lives. These changes have impacted the creation, collection and dissemination and even retrieval of information. Interpersonal communication is always brushing shoulders with mass communication. Almost anyone having access to new media technologies tries to become a part of the conversation either by critically commenting upon, sharing or exchanging information about themselves, or creating content about everyday issues. Due to the rise in platforms to share personal content, the consumption of information is also at an all time high. This puts a burden on individuals to make sense of information and processes around them quickly and correctly. This highlights the importance of MIL. Especially so, as the Indian media scenario is quite vibrant.

Indian Media and Entertainment Industry

The total size of the Media and Entertainment industry in terms of revenue was estimated to be Indian Rupees (INR) 1262.1 billion in the year 2016. Television reached 475 million consumers in 2016 and continues to be the most preferred form of entertainment. With about 830 channels including 398 news and 432 non-news channels (21 out of which are operated by the public broadcaster Prasar Bharati) the total contribution of the TV industry was INR 588 billion in the year 2016. The number of TV owning households has reached 99 million in rural India while it is 84 million in urban areas with a total penetration of 64%. Out of these Cable and Satellite households are estimated to comprise of 160 million subscribers. Rising income levels, increasing rural electrification, cable TV digitization, higher subscription and advertising revenue and better programming have resulted into TV gaining popularity in rural India.

Even when print businesses are on the decline globally Indian print media reaches 282 million citizens. Despite many international publications shutting shops and several others moving to the 'online only' mode, India still boasts of 16,136 newspapers and more than 94,715 periodicals with a staggering registration of 5423 publications every year (KPMG FICCI, 2017).

There are about 262 radio stations operated by All India Radio (AIR) reaching 92% of the population. About 86 private Frequency Modulation (FM) stations are operational while 188 community radio stations exist. In the third phase of FM spectrum auctions a total of 135 channels were sold in 69 cities. Radio stations encourage call-ins and live programming. Prime Minister Narendra Modi airs a talk show by the name 'Mann ki Baat' (Voice of the heart) that is a forum for addressing general public.

In a total of 15 such addresses, over 60,000 ideas have been discussed and 1.43 lakh listeners have sent in audio clips. The government uses this as a platform to announce schemes, explain benefits and subsidies and encourage responses from public. Internet radio is also doing brisk business and boasts of 331.5 million listeners. The total reach is 110 million.

The film industry has also thrived alongside the Indian television industry. About 1500-2000 films are released every year in India. A majority of these are in Hindi language and popularly referred to as 'Bollywood' films. The footfall of 2.1 billion is second highest in the world. There are 6000 single screen theatres and 2,100 multiplexes against a requirement of 20,000 screens. The total revenue generated is to the tune of USD 2.1 billion.

New vistas have also opened up in the area of digital entertainment. Indian user base of internet is at an all-time high with over 389 million wireless and more than 22 million wireline subscribers adding up to a total of reach of 375 million. Internet penetration in India is currently dismal at 31%.

As of December 2016, there were 432 million Internet users in the country. The divide is clear in terms of urban and rural. 60% (269 million) of the 444 million urban residents log onto Internet as opposed to just 17% (163 million) of the 906 million rural residents. Also, there are over 300 million smartphone users in India. This base is projected to increase to over 700 million by the year 2021. With over one million students, E-learning is worth US $ 3 billion in India. We have one of the highest mobile internet user bases in the world. New app based entertainment formats such as video clips, audios, images and mixed media have gained importance.

As per KPMG-FICCI 2017, the average mobile connected end user in India generates about 251 megabytes mobile traffic every month. Video on demand contributes to about 60% of the mobile data traffic. This has set the stage for video capable devices to proliferate and they are projected to cross 800 million. About 299.7 million users are active on social media in India. (Facebook- 166 million, What-sapp-160 million, Gaming -26.5 million). Mobile gaming is projected to reach USD 790.34 by the year 2020 from USD 413.1 million in 2015.

On-the-go entertainment, video-on-demand (VoD), gaming and digital advertising along with app based entertainment platforms promise to usher in a new era in the Indian media scene. Apart from these, Information and Communication Technologies (ICT's) have been used by the government extensively to bring about Simple, Moral, Accountable, Responsible and Transparent (SMART) governance. Indian government's flagship 'Digital India' programme (launched in 2015) by Department of Electronics and Information Technology (DeitY) is aimed at making Indian society digitally empowered & a knowledge economy. It will attempt to connect 2.5 million Panchayats (local self governments in Indian villages) with broadband by the year 2020. With the increase in usage of new media, there is renewed optimism regarding the possibilities about ICT's in development. Adopting the right approach towards ICTs can help in anticipating cyber attacks (such as the recent ransomware epidemic), handling privacy issues, help in equitable distribution of resources and ensure faster development.

The Global Information Technology Report published by World Economic Forum in partnership with INSEAD and Cornell University issues an annual Network readiness index. This index is directed towards "identification of areas of priority to more fully leverage ICTs for socioeconomic development". India is presently ranked 91 out of 139 nations. (GWITR, 2016). India ranks 138 out of 175 countries listed in the ICT Development Index published by International Telecommunication Union (ITU) in the year 2016.

Despite a promising media landscape, India continues to have low literacy levels with total literacy rate of just 64.8% (Census 2011). The rural literacy rate stood at 58.7% while urban was 79.9%. The digital divide between men and women is stark with about 40% women accessing internet regularly in urban areas and just 25% in rural areas (IAMAI & Kantar IMRB 2016). Only about 10% of the population can speak English. Out of the total number of female population, working women constitute just 25.6%. The overall Gross Enrollment Ratio (GER) improved but 47 million higher secondary students dropped out of school in the year 2016. Clearly, it is difficult to create global competencies when we are still grappling with elementary education.

There is increasing consumption of media in rural areas, vernacular press continues to be leading the pack and television has found a new foothold as cities move to 'on-the-go' and VoD services. A large number of citizens are rapidly coming online and trying to make sense of the huge communication landscape. What this means in essence is that those who are not 'media and information literate' are likely to suffer from long term consequences. On the other hand, those with high exposure to mediated communication have become vulnerable to information saturation. There is also a risk of getting 'lost' or being unable to pick the most appropriate, reliable information from the vast icebergs of knowledge floating around (Ferguson as cited on pg 7. In Kellner & Share, 2007).

Media Regulation and Critical Media Literacy in India: Journey So Far

Such a large and panoramic media industry needs extensive focus on MIL in order to enable full participation in global affairs by its consumers. However, the MIL landscape in India is very confusing in the absence of a specific policy. Ever since India gained independence from the British in the year 1947, media has been viewed as a 'necessary evil'. The government has been expected to protect citizens from 'ills' of media while performing functions of gate keeping and censorship. This has resulted into formation of statutory as well as self-regulatory bodies in media. These bodies discharge their duties under the over-arching rights and laws provided in the Constitution of India.

As a result, consumers of media messages have become dependent on these regulatory mechanisms to 'protect' themselves. Though self-regulation facilitates citizens to critically analyze media messages and raise objections against offensive content, there is no training about how to do this. The popularity of social media has created new complexities. Since social media does not necessarily have the same gate-keeping and editorial flow as print media, lot of fake news and images get circulated online.

In this era of post-truth, the fake quickly becomes accepted. More so, if it is picked up by mainstream media. For instance, ZEE news, a leading news broadcaster consistently rated among top Hindi news channels in India aired a fake news story about nano-GPS enabled chips being embedded in the newly introduced INR 2000 currency notes after the government's massive demonetization drive in India. It was based on unverified messages being circulated on WhatsApp. The Reserve Bank of India had to issue a formal rebuttal to dispel the rumors.

India has a coastline of 7,517 km. Yet, news of salt shortage rumors triggered by WhatsApp messages spread in November 2016 causing four-fold price-rise and panic buying. The ensuing chaos led to the death, looting of grocery shops and the police had to baton-charge crowds to control the situation. Again, the government had to issue a clarification to pacify people (Saldanha, 2016).

In another instance, two men who were wanted in a separate case were attacked by unknown assailants in Bangladesh on April 1, 2017. The next day, video of the incident was put up on Youtube. This video was recently re-circulated on Facebook, albeit with different text by one Ghanshyam Jangid and was shared over 37000 times. It has been circulated twice as the video of a Hindu being killed by Muslims. (Sinha, 2017) The accompanying text is false, misleading and is directed towards inciting violence.

English translation of the accompanying text:

#TheNakedDanceOfSecularism

Hail the unjust media: If a Muslim is killed in Rajasthan, it is "Hindu terrorism", if a Hindu is killed in West Bengal, it is not even covered? No media channel will show this video.. neither will the Congress party in opposition come on the roads to protest this. For the murder of those men who were carrying

40 cows for the purpose of slaughtering, Congress and other opposition MPs went to the town chest beating..Based on this incident, they declared that the National integrity is in danger..In this country where cow slaughter is declared illegal, and even then cows are being cut, then if Hindus get enraged and kill the people who are slaughtering cows then should the Hindus be blamed for this or should those people be blamed who are being unconstitutional and are hurting Hindu sentiments? What is the need to incite our religious feelings?

Continue your silence and keep acting like a Hijra (transgender). (altnews.in)

This clearly explains why we need to become media and information literate. In a country like India where large sections of population are still not educated, any misinformation can become a huge problem even before it is actually identified as fake news. Though the Constitutional mandate restricts using language that can incite violence, the problem is that these types of messages cannot be undone once circulated. Punitive action can be taken but only retrospectively.

The content and statutory regulatory framework is a muddle. The Ministry of Information & Broadcasting, (I&B Ministry) Government of India is the apex body for formulation and administration of the rules and regulations and laws relating to information, broadcasting, the press and films in India. It is the overarching regulatory body in the country. It carries out several media related activities of the government such as publicity of government initiatives, export, promotion and development of films, management and regulation of Press in India etc.

Most importantly, it carries out public service broadcasting through All India Radio (AIR) and Doordarshan (DD) together known as Prasar Bharati (1997). Prasar Bharati has laid down broadcasting codes for content as well as advertisements. The exhaustive guidelines that are adopted by most channels, government or private are 'protectionist' in nature. They prohibit advertisements masquerading as news, ads for alcoholic and slimming products as well as the commercials coercing/threatening/condemning or ridiculing children for not buying products.

The public exhibition of films is done by Central Board of Film Certification (1952), a statutory body under the provisions of the Cinematograph Act 1952. Films can be publicly exhibited in India only after they have been certified by the Central Board of Film Certification. The four categories of certifications are as under:

U: Unrestricted public exhibition
A: Public exhibition restricted to adults only
UA: Unrestricted public exhibition with parental guidance for children below the age of 12
S: Exhibition to restricted audience such as doctors, etc.

Film Certification Appellate Tribunal can be approached in case of a dispute about satellite broadcasting was considered as "wireless cable transmission' another Act, the Telecom Regulatory Authority of India Act was passed in 1997 to regulate telecom services. Till date, TRAI continues to govern the spectrum allocation, tariffs for telecom services as well as cross-media ownership in the country.

Information Technology Act (2000) / IT Act, 2000– The IT Act, 2000 is the primary law in India that deals with cybercrimes and e-commerce. It lays down punishment and penalties for crimes committed using computers/new media e.g.: hacking, phishing, cyber bullying, cyber stalking, publishing obscene, defamatory or derogatory content online, child pornography, piracy, online frauds, identity thefts, breach of privacy etc. As per National Crime Records Bureau (NCRB) 11,592 cybercrimes were committed in India in the year 2015.

The Electronic Media Monitoring Centre (EMMC) has been established as a monitoring mechanism by the government to deal with content violations and non-compliance with the Codes framed under the Cable Television Networks Regulation Act, 1995. It reports the violations to a scrutiny committee where it is then taken up for further action. The channels that commit gross violations may face suspension and revocation of licenses with the approval of Ministry of I & B.

Self-regulation of the broadcast sector continues to be preferred over government regulation in India. The Self-Regulation Guidelines for Broadcasting Sector (2008) necessitate every broadcast service provider (BSP) to categorize programs broadcast as per the following:

U Category: Unrestricted viewing, suitable for all ages
U/A Category: Adults and minors over 12 years of age can view programs of this category under parental guidance. Not suitable for children below 12 years of age.
A Category: Only for mature audience and individuals above 18 years of age.
S Category: Suitable or restricted to members of particular professions (e.g.: doctors, engineers etc.)

In addition to this, a two-tier self-regulatory system was put in place. The first tier is at the BSP level. All BSP(s) are required to have a content auditor in place to check for any ethical violation on their part. The content auditor assists the BSP in adhering to the certification rules and categorization of programs as well as complying with the broadcasting code as stipulated by the government.

The second tier is at the industry level. The channels are mandated to deal strictly with violations brought to their notice by consumers and other complainants. Keeping this in mind, the Indian Broadcasting Federation (IBF) was set up in the year 1999. This is a body of broadcasters that deals with monitoring and self-regulation of content over non-news General Entertainment Channels (GECs). The IBF is responsible for checking violations as well as addressing consumer complaints through the Broadcasting Content Complaints Council (BCCC) set up in 2011. Till August 2015, BCCC had addressed 27,676 complaints.

The news and current affairs channels are regulated by the News Broadcasters Association (NBA) (2008). It is funded entirely by its members. The NBA has presently 23 leading news and current affairs broadcasters (comprising 62 news and current affairs channels) as its members. NBA has issued guidelines through News Broadcasting Standards Regulation (NBSA) that mandate its members to ensure neutrality, objectivity and impartiality in reporting, sensitively handling violence against women and children, not depicting sex and nudity, exercising due diligence in telecast of sting operations and crimes, issuing corrigendum in case of errors in transmission and setting up a feedback mechanism to receive complaints of viewers.

The advertising sector is also self-regulated by the Advertising Standards Council of India (ASCI) (1985), an industry initiative for protecting interest of consumers. The organization seeks to ensure that all advertisements adhere to the Code for Self-Regulation. The fundamental principles of ASCI are:

1.   To ensure the truthfulness and honesty of representations and claims made by advertisements, and to safeguard against misleading advertisements.
2.   To ensure that advertisements are not offensive to generally accepted standards of public decency.

3. To safeguard against the indiscriminate use of advertising for the promotion of products, which are regarded as hazardous to society or to individuals to a degree or of a type and which is unacceptable to society at large.

4. To ensure that advertisements observe fairness in competition so that the consumer's need to be informed of choices in the marketplace and the canons of generally accepted competitive behavior in business is both served.

In spite of the labyrinth of media laws and regulations in India, the broadcast sector is grappling with delivering the 'right content mix'. Violations are frequent, especially so where self-regulation is concerned. The violators, when served with show-cause notices choose to quit the regulatory body rather than taking corrective action.

There are wide discrepancies in regulatory structure where television, print, internet and radio content are not previewed but films are pre-screened to determine violations and suggested edits/cuts before release. Till recently, the right to broadcast news over radio rested exclusively with the government's radio i.e. AIR. The Press Council is expected to deal strictly with ethical violations in the print sector but does not have punitive powers. Therefore, it becomes a toothless body in the face of epidemics such as paid news.

While media is largely handled by Ministry of I & B, the implementation of E-governance and deployment of ICT's is managed by Ministry of Human Resources Development (MHRD) and the 'Digital India' campaign is under the aegis of Ministry of Electronics and Information Technology (MeITY).

The vast regulatory regime is able to govern content to a lot of extent. But except social media, broadcasters are not putting in much effort to allow space for User Generated Content (UGC). Some channels and newspapers give prominence to stories generated on twitter. Newspapers have started giving space to citizen reporters to publish pictures. Blogs and websites of newspapers and channels try to engage readers over important issues.

The viewers cannot be termed passive but there is only a section of population that can identify problems in the depiction. Even fewer take the initiative to complain. The process of registering complaints also favors literate/educated citizens. There is no forum to ensure that there is adequate representation of citizens from North-east India, other remote areas, persons with disabilities, senior citizens etc. on screen. The public broadcaster bears the brunt of offering this opportunity. DD is the only broadcaster (with the exception of ZEE News) that airs news for hearing and speech impaired persons.

This raises pertinent questions about who will take the ownership of sensitizing citizens about MIL and how it can become a part of the discourse. The role of media owners, broadcasters and other stakeholders also comes under review. Where and how can effective MIL training be imparted and by whom?

MIL in India

Schools form the basis of lifelong learning. Placing media and information literacy among school subjects equips students to deal with technological changes and become more knowledgeable about everyday issues. Critical thinking skills of students are developed to the extent that they become not just media and information literate but move to a level of high MIL competency. This competency can then be easily translated into global competencies.

It is believed that an individual with global competence can work in collaboration and contribute towards enhancement of future generations by building sustainable, just and peaceful societies through their holistic decision-making skills. (GCIW, 2016, p. 4) The need for media and information literacy training since a young age has been emphasized in the Grunwald Declaration. It states that:

School and the family share the responsibility of preparing the young person for living in a world of powerful images, words and sounds. Children and adults need to be literate in all three of these symbolic systems, and this will require some reassessment of educational priorities.

The Moscow Declaration also reiterated this aspect by mentioning that for young people, the majority of learning is happening outside of home and thus media networks have gained prominence like never before. Buckingham (2009) observes that the changes in today's day and age, the media environment is not just about technology but also about formation of identities in modern societies. Since young people spend a lot of their time in schools, they should remain central to media education.

Schools will continue to play an important role in helping young people live together. Schools can provide opportunities for young people to learn about global developments of significance to the world and to their lives; equip learners with the means of accessing and analysing a broad range of cultural practices and meanings; let students engage in experiences that facilitate international and intercultural relations, and encourage reflection upon the learning outcomes from such experiences; and foster the value of the diversity of peoples, languages and cultures, encouraging intercultural sensitivity, respect and appreciation. (OECD, 2016, p. 3)

Kumar (1995, p. 75) noted that efforts to include media education in Indian school curriculum started in 1984, where researchers and members of 'Mediaworld' along with others drew up a syllabus for media education under the aegis of the Central Board of Secondary Education (CBSE). There were wide ranging discussions on pedagogy, and whether the subject should be integrated with other subjects or taught separately. Arguing for a non-formal pedagogy with 'openness in curriculum' based in formal school system, he says that including media education in schools allows for 'systematic follow-up' and prevents them from becoming media camps.

These efforts at school level got revived in the form of media clubs introduced in schools by Central Institute of Educational Technology as part of a National Council for Educational Research & Training (NCERT) project launched in 2009-2010. The primary phase of the project focused on the mapping of media literacy initiatives across the world. In the second phase, it was introduced in schools. As part of the project, a total of 100 schools were selected to provide training (out of these 15 schools were in Delhi). These schools were expected to mentor other schools after successfully implementing the programs themselves. (Yadav, 2011) The curriculum developed at this stage dealt with introducing students to different facets of media e.g.: Print media, video etc. but did not include critical cultural discussions about the media.

Yadav reiterates that it was soon realised that most teachers are unfamiliar with the subject as it is not a part of teacher training curriculum. Secondly, introduction of media studies subject increased curriculum load. Keeping these factors in mind it was believed that having media clubs in schools was a better option. These were expected to function as crucibles for fostering creativity, experimentation and knowledge without disturbing the existing school timetable.

The activities conducted in the school included maintaining a Media Diary, making School Newspaper, Expression through Pictures, Documentary, Media Advocacy, Media Literacy Activities, Media Club News Bulletin, Interface with Media, Media Club on Facebook, Media Club Blog and participating in campaigns by writing letters to editor etc.

After this, Media and Information Literacy training got a much-needed fillip when Media Studies was added as a Vocational/ Elective subject in grades 11 and 12 by CBSE in the academic year 2010-11 under the National Vocational Education Qualification Framework (NVEQF). The media studies syllabus of elective and vocational courses varies a lot in its focus and tone.

Since media and information literacy is not explicitly included in the syllabus at senior secondary school level, the only hope for MIL advocates is the inclusion of media studies. At junior school level, i.e (grades 1-5), middle school (grades 5-8) and secondary school (grades 9-10), the media components are included as part of language appreciation skills and social sciences. However, at the secondary school level, there has been an attempt to connect media studies with vocational and after-school learning. However, students now have an option to 'reject' or 'not select' media studies. Though the flexibility to choose what one wants to pursue is considered a very student-friendly move, the problem is that those students who opt out of the course at school level may never get the chance to access MIL training later on in life.

Butler (2010) reinforces Jenkins when he says that as an add-on or elective subject, media studies is in a precarious position because it is likely to be seen as 'superfluous' and 'extracurricular'. He is also against including media studies in high school and argues for the programme to be included in primary school curriculum as by high school most students are already media literate. Training them early allows them more time to practice media and information literacy skills and helps them in entering the public sphere as more critical and engaged participants. Training them at high school level may not give them adequate time to incorporate critical literacy skills.

Though the CBSE media studies curriculum nowhere uses the term 'media and information literacy', it touches upon the essence of the subject by mentioning that media studies is intended to help 'students to express their own voice through media, as well as the ability to see through what mass media offers'. The focus is on making them critical receivers and active producers. One of the objectives of the course clearly spells out that the goal is 'to encourage students to participate in contemporary society as active citizens, through their awareness of the political, social, economic, historical and technological implications of the media." By placing the onus on production as a way of deconstructing media narratives, the curriculum for media studies is essentially constructivist.

How far this curriculum helps in fostering MIL has yet not been assessed. There are no empirical or qualitative studies to substantiate whether this subject has in any way enhanced media and information literacy competency of students. The curriculum incorporates elements of media and information literacy without being explicit. This necessitates a study to understand the impact of introducing this curriculum at secondary school level. There is also a pressing need to understand the changes required in such programs, figure out barriers, enablers in order to develop media literacy competencies.

The issue gets further complicated when we consider that India has a young demographic. Over 50% of the population is aged less than 25. Among these only about 5% are graduate or above. Over 33% population has not completed primary schooling. About 8.4 Crore children have never been to school. MIL trainers need to acknowledge the disparities and problems with these sections of society and push for situating MIL outside of schools.

There is a need to train all types of (school, out-of-school) young persons in dealing with misinformation, propaganda, bias, stereotypes, cultural differences, language and capability barriers, differences in social and economic backgrounds etc. It needs to be done urgently and promptly. The issues faced by teachers and media literacy practitioners are not well understood. Schilder et al. opine that greater understanding about challenges of assessing media literacy can elicit information regarding the teaching practices which in turn will benefit scholars, policy makers and educators. The data gathered via assessment is helpful in finding out the gaps in the system. They help to determine the right approach and means to achieve a desired goal.

An extensive study on Assessment Criteria for Media Literacy Levels in Europe was conducted by European Association for Viewers' Interests (EAVI, 2009). It comprised 27 member countries and concerned itself with clearing the confusion between the overlapping domains of media and information literacy as well as formulating a measurement tool for the same. The study outlined different concepts related to MIL with the objective of highlighting explicitly the media literacy competences "…that should be acquired and measured at national and individual levels…"

Media Literacy was defined as two dimensional where one dimension was about how an individual utilizes media while the other dealt with the impact of contextual and environmental factors. The study established that wherever media literacy had found policy impetus, it had resulted into better media and information literacy results. The individual competence also varied greatly with the degree of environmental support it received. A free, vibrant media with support for acts such as Right to Information and Right to Freedom of Speech and Expression helped foster media and information literacy. The report outlined very clearly that policy cannot alone help in promoting media literacy. The efforts by NGO's, Civil society and other grassroot efforts are equally critical.

Initiatives by Stakeholders

Various stakeholders have contributed towards small, yet significant steps in creating consciousness about MIL competencies. The Ministry of Human Resource Development (MHRD) has created an open access repository for a post-graduate level MIL course as part of the National Mission on Education through ICT (NME-ICT) under the aegis of INFLIBNET Centre (Information and Library Network Centre available via e-PG Pathshala' (e-classrooms). There are a total of 27 modules in the course. The topics include: MIL roles, functions, models, indicators, Media ethics and laws, Right to Information and privacy, Data Literacy, Media Convergence etc.

Indian MIL practitioners have also been able to successfully seek handholding support globally. The Global Alliance for Partnerships on Media and Information Literacy (GAPMIL) formed by UNESCO has been working tirelessly to promote international collaborations in this field. GAPMIL has helped in the formation of Media and Information Literacy University Network for India (MILUNI) in the year 2014.

Elucidating on the role of MILUNI, Singh (2015) has noted that some small yet significant steps have been taken in the form of national consultation meet on a Media and Information Literacy. In the year 2014, the group met with the following objectives:

1. To advise Government of India on MIL policy and strategy
2. To develop a MIL competency framework
3. To develop MIL curriculum as per national aspirations

In its draft policy and strategy paper, they advocated the inclusion of modules such as Fundamentals of MIL, MIL Indicators, Media and Information Ethics and Laws, Media Convergence: Development and Trends, Data Literacy, Information Searching and Browsing, Social Media, Research Metrics, Evaluation of Information, Information Sources and Library Skills and Construction of Media Messages within Media and Information Literacy Curriculum (pp. 54-56).

Charkha Development Communication Network conducts communication skill building sessions with rural groups to sensitize them towards needs of others in the society and become voice of the voiceless.

Gurudev Rabindranath Tagore Foundation, Belgaum Integrated Rural Development Society (Gokak) & South Asia Initiative to End Violence Against Children launched the Peace Gong Media Literacy Programme (PGMILP) along with a manual for program coordinators. The Foundation works towards promoting media and information literacy for the purpose of encouraging peace and sustainable development. The Peace Gong children's newspaper is a quarterly "for children to articulate on community, national or global issues" and "to have open dialogues with their peers and other stakeholders".

A booklet named 'Media Literacy- Keys to Interpreting Media Messages' has been prepared as part of the Digital International Media Literacy e-Book Project (DIMLE).

Despite these efforts, it can be safely said that media education has not gained interest of scholars in India. Das (2009) succinctly puts it,

When the idea of media education as a subfield of education has been recognized as best, it has been dismissed as too elitist a proposition, especially in a society where quite a substantial amount of the population is yet to enjoy the privilege of basic and elementary education. (p.66)

As Appadurai mentions in UNESCO's Media and Information Literacy, Policy and Strategy Guidelines (2013, p. 165):

There continues to be a concern about how to redress the balance between the viral and massive flow of information and disinformation in today's world and the relatively poor development of the institutions of communication, in the sense of community and common humanity, allowing ordinary people to distinguish between information and misinformation, notably when depicting different cultures.

There are encouraging developments in India as far as MIL is concerned. But the journey to being a fully media and information literate society is a long one. Much work still needs to be done on the level of policies, interventions, strategies and approaches. Local perspectives have to be linked with global competencies while preserving the true spirit of inter-cultural dialogue and multi-lingual framework.

REFERENCES

Buckingham, D. (2009). *The Future of Media Literacy in the Digital Age: Some Challenges for Policy and Practice*. Medienimpulse-online. Retrieved from http://medienimpulse.erz.univie.ac.at/articles/view/143

Butler, A. (2010). *Media Education Goes to School: young people make meaning of media & urban education*. New York: Peter Lang.

Das, B. (2009). Media Education as a Development Project: Connecting Emanicipatory Interests and Governance in India. In D. Freu-Meigs & J. Torrent (Eds.), Mapping Media Education Policies in the World: Visions, Programmes and Challenges. New York: UN-Alliance of Civilizations and Grupo Communicar.

European Commission. (2009). *European Association for Viewers Interest (EAVI)*. Brussels: Study on Assessment Criteria for Media Literacy Levels.

Grizzle, A., & Carme Torras Calvo, M. (Eds.). (2013). *Media and Information Literacy, Policy and Strategy Guidelines*. Paris: UNESCO.

IAMAI & Kantar IMRB. (2016). *Internet in India*. New Delhi.

Kellner, D., & Share, J. (2007). Critical media literacy, democracy, and the reconstruction of education. In D. Macedo & S.R. Steinberg (Eds.), Media literacy: A reader (pp. 3-23). New York: Peter Lang Publishing.

KPMG FICCI. (2016). The Future: now streaming, Indian Media and Entertainment Industry Report. New Delhi.

KPMG FICCI. (2017). Media for the masses: The promise unfolds, Indian Media and Entertainment Industry Report. New Delhi.

Kumar, K. J. (1995). *Media Education, Communications and Public Policy: An Indian Perspective*. Bombay: Himalaya Publishing House.

OECD. (2016). *Global competency for an inclusive world*. Paris, France.

Potter, W. J. (2004). Theory of Media Literacy: A Cognitve Approach. *Sage (Atlanta, Ga.)*.

Saldanha, A. (2016, December 27). Top 10 fake news forwards that we (almost) believed in 2016. *hindustantimes.com*. Retrieved from http://www.hindustantimes.com/india-news/top-10-fake-news-forwards-that-we-almost-believed-in-2016/story-hL7pnDYwF51M4cNAwgMtrN.html

Silverblatt, A., & Nagaraj, K. V. Kundu, Vedabhyas & Yadav, Anubhuti (n. d.). *Media Literacy, Keys to Interpreting Media Messages*. Retrieved on December 20, 2016 from www.dimle.org

Singh, J. (2015) From Information Skills for Learning to Media and Information Literacy -A Decade of Transition in South Asia: 2004-2014. In J. Singh, A. Grizzle, S.J. Yess et al. (Eds.), Media and Information Literacy for the Sustainable Development Goals: MILID Yearbook 2015 (pp. 49-58). Gothenburg, Sweden: Nordicom.

Sinha, Pratik (2017, April 15). Killing of one Abu Syed in Bangladesh shared 37000+ times on FB as a Hindu killed by Muslims in West Bengal. *altnews.com*. Retrieved from https://www.altnews.in/killing-one-abu-syed-bangladesh-shared-37000-times-fb-hindu-killed-muslims-west-bengal/

UNESCO. (1982). *Grunwald Declaration on Media Education*. Retrieved from www.unesco.org/education/pdf/MEDIA_E.PDF

UNESCO. (2011) Media and Information Literacy: Curriculum for Teachers. Paris

World Economic Forum. (2016). The Global World Information Technology Report: Innovating in the digital Economy.

Yadav, A. (2011). Media Studies in School Curriculum: Obstacles, Challenges and Possibilities. *Journal of Indian Education*.

ADDITIONAL READING

ASCI- Advertising Standards Council of India. (n. d.). Retrieved from https://ascionline.org/index.php/ascicodes.html

CBFC- Central Board of Film Certification. (n. d.). Retrieved from https://www.cbfcindia.gov.in

EMMC- Electronic Media Monitoring Centre. (n. d.). Retrieved from http://emmc.gov.in/Codesand-Standards1.aspx

Gov. of India. (2011). Census 2011. Retrieved from http://censusindia.gov.in/

Gov. of India. (n. d.). Prasar Bharati. Retrieved from http://prasarbharati.gov.in

Gov. of India. (n. d.). TRAI - About Us: Telecom Regulatory Authority of India. Retrieved from http://www.trai.gov.in

IBF- Indian Broadcasting Foundation. (n. d.). Retrieved from http://www.ibfindia.com/

Meity - Ministry of Electronics and Information Technology. (n. d.). Retrieved from http://meity.gov.in

Gov. of India. (n. d.). Ministry (I & B) –Ministry of Information and Broadcasting. Retrieved from http://mib.nic.in/broadcasting/broadcasting-codes-guidelines-and-policies

NBA- News Broadcasters Association. (n. d.). About NBA. Retrieved from http://www.nbanewdelhi.com/about-nba

KEY TERMS AND DEFINITIONS

Competencies: The ability to meet complex demands by drawing on and mobilizing psychosocial resources (including skills and attitudes) in a particular context.

Curriculum/Syllabus: The various prescribed subjects or topics of study assigned for a particular course to be completed in a particular time period.

Digitization: The process of shifting from analog to digital broadcast by way of installing set-top boxes and connecting the viewer directly to satellites.

Fake News: Fake news is an inaccurate, sometimes sensationalistic report that is created to gain attention, mislead, deceive or damage a reputation. Unlike misinformation, which is inaccurate because a reporter has confused facts, fake news is created with the intent to manipulate someone or something. Fake news can spread quickly when it provides disinformation that is aligned with the audience's point of view because such content is not likely to be questioned or discounted.

Misinformation: False or inaccurate information especially that which is deliberately intended to deceive.

Paid News: Any news or analysis appearing in any media for a price in cash or kind as consideration (Press Council of India).

Panchayat: A body of five elected representatives from the local population who form the local government at village level in India. The term is also in use in Bangladesh and Pakistan. Panchayats as local governance bodies have existed in the subcontinent for over two millennia. Panchayati Raj Institution (PRI) as they are called denotes the local governance structure established under the 73rd Amendment Bill and now prevalent across India in all villages.

Stereotype: A set idea that people have about what someone or something is like, especially an idea that is wrong.

Chapter 11
The Psychological Effects of Violence–Related Information From the Media

Lala Jabbarova
Baku State University, Azerbaijan

ABSTRACT

The media is one of the main resources from which people derive information about events surrounding them. The media tries to mirror realities, transmit various events, including cases of aggression and violence; however, lack of control on quality and quantity of information may result in perilous outcomes. This chapter offers a psychological analysis of the influence of media on crime in society, as well as the relation of crime levels with information about aggression and violence. The results of the research suggest that frequent, overstated, and embellished media disseminations of information of an aggressive character, without considering its possible psychological outcomes, increases viewers' levels of aggression and violence. In order to prevent this increase, it is crucial not to eliminate aggressive information from media completely, but instead to present it while taking into account its psychological effects.

INTRODUCTION

One of the primary sources society receives information from is the media, where aggression, violence, and whatever happens in reality is described in maximum and sensationalized. The quantity and quality of mediated information and its presentation forms should be taken into consideration, because, otherwise it can cause dangerous consequences for society.

Research conducted on this topic in the USA, Canada, and North Africa between 1957-1989 has shown that, always and everywhere, increased exposure to television correlated significantly with increased quantity of murders (Старова, n.d.). Recently a growth has been observed related to the crime of violence and particularly domestic violence crimes in families in Azerbaijan. Naturally, citizens have the right to receive information from media about what happens around the globe, including the crime level of society. While journalists should not hide the facts about crimes committed, they sometimes

DOI: 10.4018/978-1-5225-3082-4.ch011

Copyright © 2018, IGI Global. Copying or distributing in print or electronic forms without written permission of IGI Global is prohibited.

tend to exaggerate details. For example, they often report the details of violence in information on any crime case, offering a comprehensive explanation of how a crime was committed, because they seek to capitalize on the sensation of graphic events which are improper for broadcasting and can pose serious danger for human psychology.

Taking into account that comprehension of violence, victims, criminals and their punishment by members of society depend on how media present them, we can make the conclusion that media has very high impact on people's social attitudes, behavior, and psychology. So, we need to conduct serious investigations in order to define what these impact forms consist of. In this chapter, information related to violence and crime on media, especially TV and Internet information resources and its impact on people has been analyzed. Theories and conceptions on this topic have been studied, and scientific works in this sphere and materials delivered on media have been analyzed and generalized. Surveys and observation methods have been used in this research.

ANALYSIS OF THEORIES AND RESEARCHES

The basic theoretical and methodological source on the subject of this research is A. Bandura's social learning theory (Baron & Richardson, 1977) related to behaviorism. Bandura considered aggression as a specific form of social behavior, as it is based on learning it as one would other social behavior forms. For example, in order to commit any aggression, it is necessary to know how to use weapons, to understand which actions can cause physical pain to victims, and which words or forms of behavior can harm objects of aggression. This kind of knowledge is not inborn, according to Bandura. It is gained in social life, so social life has a great impact on aggression cases. Therefore, we can assume that media scenes with aggressive characters arouse the social learning process, bringing one to learn new behavior types. Such learning processes help potential criminals to use new ways to cover the lack of experience in committing crimes. From the viewpoint of Bandura's social learning theory (Baron & Richardson, 1977), adoption of aggression occurs in one of the following cases:

1. Demonstration of no punishment measures against violence actions;
2. Demonstration of different forms of aggression;
3. Demonstration of absence of consequences occurring as a result of aggression;
4. Quantity of time spent watching TV;
5. Strengthening aggression in real life, demonstration of the possibility of such behaviors by people of authority and prestige.

According to Bandura (Bandura, Ross, & Ross, 1963), aggressive behaviors are learned more easily by the way of observation of actions done by others. That is, no danger is expected to face one as a viewer, but the ideas formed in a viewers' mind on how these behaviors gain shape can become "instructions" for committing real aggressive actions in the future. After the broadcasting of tragic cases of violence on TV, similar events happen in quite different places. For example, four children in the US, Pakistan, India, and Azerbaijan have hung themselves after watching the execution video of former Iraqi president Saddam Hussein on television (В Азербайджане Саддам убивает после смерти, 2007).

However, there is a need to note that social theory does not restrict promotion of violence with scenes of aggression and violence only on TV. According to this conception, in definite circumstances, adopted skills of aggression may pave the way for the realization of aggression. This theory is explained schematically in Figure 1.

According to this scheme, we can assume that hundreds of people watch the same program or report and even if all factors for adopting aggression are present, life conditions, psychological situations, and private qualities which promote aggression are different and so, no assumption can be made decisively that every person will commit an act of aggression. However, we can assume, that these programs pave the way for aggressive actions.

Zillmann and Johnson (Baron & Richardson, 1977) conducted an experiment in which furious and silent subjects of the experiment watched a neutral film, or a film with aggressive scenes. Others were shown no films. After researching their reactions, it was made clear that furious subjects of the experiment became more aggressive in comparison to others after watching a film with a scene featuring aggression. The furious audience that watched neutral scenes without aggressive elements had more silent reactions. Results of the experiment enable us to say that aggressive films and scenes promote and strengthen aggression.

There are other conceptions which try to explain how media influences human psychology and these conceptions are worthy of being noted (Aronson, Wilson, & Akert, 2002; Baron & Richardson, 1977). According to psychophysical theories that try to interpret many psychological phenomena in specific ways, the reason aggression occurred more in the audience after watching aggression TV is hormonal changes in people. So, psychophysical theories assume that aggression and inclination to violence depend on hormonal conditions of a human being, which are in turn, partially dependent upon demonstration of aggressive actions, physical parameters, etc. According to this theory, watching aggressive actions on TV, people increase their aggression in their behavior.

Figure 1. The scheme, which explains the social learning theory

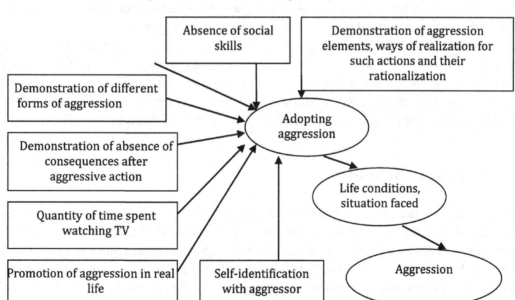

From a psychoanalytic viewpoint, it is worth to note that Freudian theory denies the influence of external stimuli for the formation of aggression and considers aggression as the eternal instinct of human character. However, Fromm (1973) evaluated demonstration of violence scenes on TV as an attempt to compensate for awful tediousness. Passively absorbing scenes full of crimes, disasters, and terror, people generate extreme anxiety inside themselves and relieve their tediousness. But there are only several steps separating between the pleasure of passively watching violent scenes and sadist, destructive actions promoted by these scenes.

From a psychoanalytic viewpoint, for adopting aggression models, evening hours are the most dangerous time. This is also the time during which the most violent scenes are broadcasted. During this time of day, fatigue and exhaustion can cause a lack of self-control and self-criticism, creating better conditions for the easier adoption of negative models. Moreover, models adopted in these late hours may "revive" during the sleeping time in dreams and become adopted by unconsciousness. Unfortunately, analysis of the content of TV programs shows that most violent scenes and information with aggressive character are presented in evening or late hours.

Gerbner (1998) assumes, in his cultivation theory, that watching violent scenes on TV brings one to feel fear and horror, rather than to feel aggression (Dowler, 2003). According to his theory, most people who spent much time watching TV likely become more careful related to criminal events as a result of fear caused by statistics, as they believe in the higher possibility of crimes in comparison to others. Gerbner (1998) argued that criminal elements presented on TV have more violent and dangerous character than criminal events in real life. This supports the idea that depictions of violent scenes create a fearful and dreadful image of aggression and deny internalization of violent characters viewers watch on TV. According to this conception, the formation of dreadful images about reality is characterized by disbelief, doubtfulness, distrustfulness, alienation, and fear of high level of criminal events.

Analyses conducted by Gilbert and Heath (Dowler, 2003) show that the relation between information presented by media and criminal events depend on the character of information and audience. That is, presentation of numerous criminal events by the local level media broadcaster increases fearful feelings in people when the presentation of criminal cases from foreign sources creates an opposite effect – the local audience feels safer in comparison to those living abroad. Local criminal news has much stronger influence on the audience, particularly on victims/survivors of such events.

For many people, TV, radio, and Internet are the only means for receiving information. So, a person who receives information on numerous crime cases can assume that they are surrounded by criminals. Sometimes several crime cases are exaggerated and cause distrustfulness and hopelessness. On the contrary, people are more hopeful and trustful when they receive information of the opposite character. This promotes people to think that there are no criminals around and that they are safe.

SITUATION IN AZERBAIJAN

Media forms imagination and the overall knowledge level of people concerning crime level, violence, and criminal events. According to this investigation, news with legal-criminal content forms 30-40% of all information in Azerbaijan. Before crime cases with the most horrible, cruel and merciless content are presented, the audience is warned to have, "discretion for children and people with weaker nerves or heart diseases". From a psychological viewpoint, it is obvious that people have more interest towards prohibited content and we assume that this warning has an opposite effect and attracts more attention to programs with violent content.

In order to elucidate the reaction of the audience to this precaution, we conducted a survey in which participants were asked "How do you usually react to the call of 'discretion for children and people with weaker nerves or heart diseases' before scenes of aggression, violence and horrible crime cases is presented?". Of all respondents, 87% answered, "I began to expect the content with more interest," while only 13% responded, "I turn off TV or change the channel". As it becomes apparent, though media representatives claim that they take into account content of programs and warn an audience before these programs begin, we face a different reality wherein people have more interest in these programs after receiving the warning.

Though there are separate programs especially dedicated to criminal chronology, the total volume of information with criminal and violent content in evening news continues to increase in Azerbaijan TV broadcasting. Television channels often compete to broadcast programs featuring criminal and violent content. Moreover, this kind of information is presented during the most dangerous time of day – in evening hours, when the number of people watching TV is at its peak. When calculating all broadcasts full of violent scenes that are usually presented at the same time, then we can assume that 60-70% of all information received by people who want to be aware of what happens around them after a workday is full of violence.

According to psychological conformity with natural law, when any emotional irritant stimulus is repeated many times, emotional reaction against it begins to weaken. For example, people become desensitized to seeing blood, dead bodies, and murders on TV. It gives us the basis to say that repeatedly watching programs with violent and aggressive content causes an audience to become insensitive, or detached, towards these events. One illustration of this is found in the media history of the Soviet period.

During the Soviet period, there was strict control over news and programs with violent content and similar events that might shock people. Seeing a dead body might mean a hard-psychological shock not only for children but also for adults. Comparatively, today we can observe ourselves or watch reports on how everyone, including children, ignores and/or cold-bloodedly approaches corpses of people who died in an accident. Scenes with a violent character that people watch every day cause viewers them to perceive such violence as usual. In recent years, we can witness a new change in the character of crimes committed in Azerbaijan.

Family crimes, such as the murder of a wife, a husband, children, parents, and grandparents become more and more usual as we daily hear about this kind of case. Information with such character forms most of the material presented on TV news when special attention is drawn to with how mercilessly a given crime was committed. Naturally, such crimes were committed in past years and before, but they did not attract social attention because the media did not elucidate them. On the contrary, today, the media delivers more attention to these types of cases, especially emphasizing their violence. This can make people with higher aggressive features become more aggressive. As we know, people are different with regard to their psychological characters and may be in various psychological situations depending on many factors. Human psychology is under pressure of daily stressing factors, frustrating elements and all these weaken the human state of mind. People suffering from apathy, despondency, and serious socio-economic needs who are receiving information with extremely violent content, may lose their emotional self-control and become highly affected by the character of such information. In many cases, media "supports" a person who is going to commit a murder, suicide or theft. Through criminal chronology, we can witness that, usually, murders or suicides happen one after another with definite intervals. For example, during first three months of the 2012 year, consecutive news reports featured stories about abandoned infants in Azerbaijan. After that, discussions on the necessity of "infant boxes" spread everywhere (e.g. http://medya.az/; http://www.milli.az/news; http://www.lent.az/news):

- **January 28, 2012:** A 10-day-old infant girl found in the street;
- **February 4, 2012:** A newborn infant girl found in a dump;
- **March 2, 2012:** Two children found in front of an orphanage for infants.

Suicide cases have similar statistics and facts, too. For instance, after the broadcasting of hanging suicide cases on many TV channels, this method of suicide has become a new "fashion". Because of this, in 2000, the World Health Organization (WHO) prepared recommendations and instructions for media experts to prevent the popularization of suicide cases (Geneva, 2000). The instructions contain the results of the research conducted by D. Philips. This research found that during the 10 days after broadcasting information about suicides, the inclination to commit suicide increases.

As it appears, a crime can be an imitation of violence broadcasted on TV. This appearance is called "copycat crime" or imitative crime. There are many examples of such crimes. Usually, imitative crimes are committed a short time after similar violent acts are reported by media and incisively decrease four days after the provocative information. Results of laboratory experiments show that the effect of violence observed continues for about an hour (Geneva, 2000); however, in some cases, this period can be prolonged for several months. According to researchers (Geneva, 2000), information on suicide distributed on media has a significant impact on viewers.

Several places such as bridges, skyscrapers, and castles are traditionally associated with suicides and attract attention as "proper" places for committing suicide. After many reported suicides among the media, the new constructed Koroglu bridge in Azerbaijan has been renamed "the suicide bridge" by the public (http://oxu.az/society/54235). Therefore, government organizations have increased the security system around the bridge in order to prevent future suicidal incidents.

Alternatively, some cases justifying and encouraging the position of Media representatives is observed in Azerbaijan during broadcasting violent acts, particularly, related to the explanation of family crimes. This, in its turn, may promote similar aggressive behaviors in the future.

RESULTS

Investigations conducted in this sphere show that long-term broadcasting of violent scenes on TV may:

1. Increase aggressive behaviors of the audience;
2. Decrease effectiveness of factors for preventing aggression;
3. Decrease sensitivity towards aggression;
4. Promote careless opinion towards torments and difficulties of other people;
5. Form an unreal and inadequate image of real life in the audience;
6. Create groundless fear feelings of surrounding people and events which may form disbelief and doubtfulness towards people.

According to researchers (Anderson, 1997) many people believe that if they act as characters in the movies they watch, then the same changes and events will happen in their life. If a person has seen that any movie character suffers consequences of his aggressive acts, he probably will not be inclined to repeat the behavior. Thus, reminding viewers of tragic consequences of violent acts can prevent an aggressive act. According to investigations (Anderson, 1997; Young, 2010) many criminal cases can be easily observed as repetition of definite movie scenes. However, any criminal case should be considered as a joint result of many factors.

CONCLUSION

The research conducted enables us to conclude that broadcasting information with violence can influence human psychology negatively and may cause crime levels to rise. However, one cannot assume that violence presented by media is the most influential factor of all violent cases in society. The cardinal problem worth attention here is that together with increasing the possibility of violent acts, violent scenes distributed by media increase the possibility of the commitment of these crimes in more merciless ways.

Therefore, we assume that it is necessary to conduct educational activity in this sphere and to prepare proper instructions. The World Health Organization (Geneva, 2000) has prepared special instructions for media representatives in order to prevent suicide cases and has precisely classified which methods are suitable for avoiding the promotion of suicides by media. It appears, however, from this study that Media representatives in Azerbaijan are unaware of these instructions and guidelines of distribution.

The American National Television Violence Study research personnel has prepared several suggestions for media representatives that can be used for defining methods of information presentation in Azerbaijan:

1. Broadcasting more programs with no violent content or decrease of such scenes to minimum;
2. Distributing mostly information and images on negative consequences and punishment of aggressive actions.

Thus, based on the research analyses conducted, this study suggests accounting for the following aspects when elucidating events with criminal and violent character:

1. It is expedient to broadcast and publish violent programs and information on separate channels or media organs;
2. Distributing criminal news to society, a high level of cautiousness for explanation methods is required by taking into account psychological impact effects of these explanation methods;
3. It is highly recommended that attention is paid to presentation of punishment measures against aggressive acts;
4. It is recommended to avoid broadcasting news and scenes with criminal and violent content in late or evening hours;
5. When presenting information with criminal content, the media should avoid exaggeration of such content or making show out of it;
6. Notwithstanding character and reason of crimes committed, it is suggested to avoid using justifying language and explanation methods;

7. It is recommended not to explain or interpret any criminal case as a natural reaction to problems between people, changes in society or worsening situation;

8. It is not suggested to show corpses of victims or to demonstrate methods and means of committing crimes;

9. It is not expedient to replace such information on the first pages of newspapers or to announce it repeatedly on TV channels;

10. It is strongly recommended to propagate spiritual torments and difficulties families and relatives of victims suffer as a result of crimes or aggressions committed;

11. It is expedient to propagate alternative solutions to aggressive acts for solving any problem.

In the end, it is worth to note the call of Federico Mayor—general director of UNESCO—who explained the results of a survey carried out for learning the correlation between violence presented by media and perception of reality by youth (UNESCO, 1998): "Citizens should base on their democratic rights as consumers and citizens and react against violence put on the air". I join this call and hope that my "reaction" as a citizen and an expert will be useful for this purpose.

REFERENCES

АронсонЭ.УилсонТ.ЭйкертР. (2002). *Социальная психология. Психологические законы поведения человека в социуме*. Санкт-Петербург: прайм-ЕВРОЗНАК.

Берон, Р., & Ричардсон, Д. (1998). *Агрессия*. Санкт-Петербург: Питер.

Брайант, Дж., & Томпсон, С. (2004). *Основы воздействия СМИ*. Москва: Вильяме.

Брушлинская, Л. В. (2002). Криминальное насилие в семье и его трансляция средствами массовой информации. In Е. Е. Пронина (Ed.), *Проблемы медиапсихологии* (pp. 72–86). Москва: РИП Холдинг.

СтароваО. (n.d.). *Средства массовой информации как источник агрессии*. Retrieved from http://psyfactor.org/lib/starova.htm

В Азербайджане Саддам убивает после смерти. (2007). Retrieved from http://www.strana.co.il/news/?ID=9787&cat=0

Anderson, C. A. (1997). Effects of violent movies and trait hostility on hostile feelings and aggressive thoughts. *Aggressive Behavior*, *23*(3), 161–178. doi:10.1002/(SICI)1098-2337(1997)23:3<161::AID-AB2>3.0.CO;2-P

Bandura, A., Ross, D., & Ross, S. (1963). Imitation of film-mediated aggressive models. *Journal of Abnormal and Social Psychology*, *66*(1), 3–11. doi:10.1037/h0048687 PMID:13966304

Baron, R. A., & Richardson, D. R. (1977). *Human aggression*. New York: Plenum Press. doi:10.1007/978-1-4615-7195-7

Childs, D. (n.d.). Kids Imitate Saddam's Televised Hanging Death. *ABC News Medical Unit*. Retrieved from http://abcnews.go.com/Health/story?id=2773792&page=1

Dowler, K. (2003). Media consumption and public attitudes toward crime and justice: The relationship between fear of crime, punitive attitudes, and perceived police effectiveness. *The Journal of Criminal Justice and Popular Culture*, *10*(2), 109–126.

Federman, J. (Ed.). (1998). National Television Violence Study (Vol. 3). Santa Barbara, CA: University of California, Center for Communication and Social Policy.

Fromm, E. (1973). *The Anatomy of Human Destructiveness*. London: Penguin Books.

Geneva. (2000). *Preventing suicide: A resource for media professionals*. WHO/MNH/MBD/00.2. Retrieved from http://www.who.int/mental_health/media/en/426.pdf

Gerbner, G. (1998). Cultivation Analysis: An Overview. *Mass Communication & Society*, *3*(4), 175–194. doi:10.1080/15205436.1998.9677855

Report of Federal Communications Commission in the matter of violent television programming and its impact on children. (n.d.). Retrieved from http://www.c-span.org/pdf/fcc_tvviolence.pdf

UNESCO survey highlights correlation between media violence and youth perception of reality. (n.d.). Retrieved from http://www.unesco.org/bpi/eng/unescopress/98-32e.htm

Young, A. (2010). *The Scene of Violence: Cinema, Crime, Affect*. New York, NY: Routledge.

KEY TERMS AND DEFINITIONS

Aggression: Behavior that is intended to harm someone or something. Aggression can emerge in different ways including verbally, emotionally, physically, and mentally.

Copycat Crime: A crime that is committed by imitating or copying a previous crime that has been transmitted and popularized through media.

Cultivation Theory: An approach proposing that media, especially television is responsible for "cultivating" viewers' conceptions of social reality, a reality that is false or unrealistic (Gerbner, 1998).

Media: Communication channels through which information is transmitted. Television, radio, newspaper, journal, internet can be considered media channels.

Social Learning Theory: According to this theory people learn social behavior, including aggression by observing others (Bandura, Ross, & Ross, 1963).

Suicide: The act of intentionally killing oneself.

Violence: An extreme form of aggression that is performed by using physical force to damage, assault, or kill someone or something.

Section 4
Theory to Practice for the Digital Age:
Current Research and Transdisciplinary Approaches

Chapter 12
Learning to Unlearn:
Using Taoism and Critical Pedagogy in Language Education to Foster Global Unity

Matthew E. Lewerenz
Walden University, USA

ABSTRACT

The U.S. and many countries across Europe and around the world are currently experiencing increased cultural tensions and xenophobia, particularly against those whose ethnic, religious, or linguistic orientations make them a minority or an otherwise vulnerable group. This comes despite the fact that we are a more interconnected global society than perhaps ever before in our history. Communication is central to overcoming this obstacle, and language instruction can be an integral locus for directly confronting perceptions and prejudices. Creating practical learning applications and assessments that foster critical thinking and utilize ontological, ethical, and educational practices rooted in the Tao Te Ching, integrated with a critical pedagogical framework, can effect positive social change and help foster global unity through mutual linguistic and ontological identification.

INTRODUCTION

Positive social change is something that is very easy to visualize and discuss, yet often very difficult to enact. The Chinese philosopher Lao Tzu, in discussing his own ideas about the individual and society, said "My words are very easy to understand, and very easy to put into practice, but no one is able to understand them, and no one is able to put them into practice" (Tzu, 1990, p. 45). Educators from Lao Tzu's time to our own often like to think of themselves as philanthropists of a sort, responsible for transmitting vital knowledge that students did not previously have, and bringing about positive social change, one class at a time, through a kind of intellectual alchemy created by their own knowledge of subject matter combined with their ability to transmute and implant this understanding into the minds of students capable of understanding and synthesizing it. Nonetheless, educators from antiquity to now have struggled with how to most effectively accomplish this task, as well as whether or not their efforts are truly in the best interests of their students.

DOI: 10.4018/978-1-5225-3082-4.ch012

Copyright © 2018, IGI Global. Copying or distributing in print or electronic forms without written permission of IGI Global is prohibited.

Within the various Western traditions that have sought to codify this endeavor through formal educational systems, there has been, since at least the time of the Greeks, a dichotomy between teacher and student, one that Brazilian educator Paolo Freire famously termed the "banking concept" of education and which linguist and philosopher David Abram (1997) tied into both the Platonic dichotomy of the natural and human worlds and the concurrent Greek adoption of the Semitic phonetic alphabet (or "aleph-bet"). This system is dependent upon an underlying ontological structure that takes *a priori* the distinct separateness of both the teacher and the student as well as the knowledge to be transmitted. In contrast to this approach, philosophical strains and cultural practices arose in the cultures of Eastern societies that took a unified approach to the practices of self-identity and education. Within a critical pedagogical framework, elements of these can be put to use in the service of transformative education that can educate as well as liberate and unify those engaged in it.

This approach sees, as does the critical pedagogy of Freire, to dissolve the teacher-student dichotomy, but it goes a step further in asserting that, praxis aside, the teacher and the student and every other person on earth are less individuals, ontologically, and more a part of a collective whole. Knowledge is less an objective thing to be possessed by one person and transmitted between discrete individual units than it is a cohesive affirmation about the state of things within a collective consciousness. It is unorthodox in the Western tradition to assert as much, but this approach would say that there is, in fact, nothing to be learned, and no one to learn it. In taking this approach, however, anyone can learn anything.

TAOISM

Depending on the source, Lao Tzu, the founder of Taoism, was either a real or fictitious person who may have lived in China during the Warring States period, before China's unification under the Emperor Qin. The fundamental elements of Taoist philosophy include a rejection of division and labels and equality between masculine and feminine energies. "Tao," which is both a noun and a verb, translates roughly as "way," is conceived of as a unifying force that comprises and runs through all things. Taoism's central text, the *Tao Te Ching*, which translates roughly as "Way integrity book," as its name implies, deals with way of all things, the way to live, and how to cultivate integrity. There are also adages addressed to rulers dispensing advice on governance. This text and its accompanying corpus of work, along with those of Confucianism and Buddhism, laid the foundations for Chinese thought for the next two thousand years. As this essay will go on to discuss, many aspects of Taoism can be integrated with a critical pedagogical context to inform effective pedagogies that offer unique perspectives on the learning process which, interestingly, have their own corollaries within the words of some of modern critical pedagogies prominent thinkers, like Paolo Freire and Henri Giroux.

"If you follow the realized mind you've happened into, making it your teacher, how could you be without a teacher?... When mind turns to itself, you've found your teacher" (p. 21). Here Chuang Tzu (1997), one of Lao Tzu's disciples, articulated ideas about pedagogy in ancient China that might resonate today with Freire and Giroux. Chuang Tzu discussed breaking down the dichotomy between teacher and pupil nearly two thousand years before they were discussed in the West.

In addition to the *Tao Te Ching* and the works of Chuang Tzu, another text, the Hua Hu Ching, plays an important role in the Taoist canon. This text represents a written compendium of two thousand years of oral teachings--similar to the Hadith within Islam--and it elucidates and expands and many of the ideas in the *Tao Te Ching* and the works of Chuang Tzu. The 51st verse of the Hua Hu Ching offers moral imperatives that work well with the goal of mutual humanization that lies at the heart of critical pedagogy: "Those who want to know the truth should practice the four cardinal virtues. The first is reverence for all life...The second is natural sincerity...The third is gentleness...The fourth is supportiveness... [These] are not an external dogma, but part of your original nature" (L. Tzu, 1992). These tenets have informed aspects of Asian culture and thought, especially in China, for over two thousand years, and, as we look for innovations in the 21st century to help us with the problems we as a global society face, these ideas can have a meaningful impact. As Sheng (2015) noted, Taoist thought permeated nearly every aspect of Chinese science, medicine, and philosophy. Taoist contributions to everything from metallurgy, physics, astronomy, aerodynamics--even space travel--have been recorded of the centuries (pp. 219-226).

CRITICAL PEDAGOGY

Critical pedagogy grew out of the efforts of a various thinkers after the Second World War. In the post-modern, atomic era, educational theorists were beginning to look beyond Dewey. Breunig (2011) noted that critical pedagogy resists an easy historical narrative because it is a generalized term that often means different things for the pedagogue utilizing it. Many scholars, though, trace the aims of critical pedagogy to the aims of the Frankfurt School. Thinkers such as Max Horkheimer, Theodor Adorno, and, Herbert Marcuse, argued that the formal education, rather than offering students genuine opportunities for intellectual growth, instead actually stunted their individual abilities and promoted conformism. The members of the Frankfurt School "argued that schools encourage dependency and a hierarchical understanding of authority, and provide a distorted view of history and other 'taken-for-granted truths' that in turn, undermine the kind of social consciousness needed to bring about change and social transformation" (Breunig, 2011, p. 4).

Some of the most influential critical pedagogical thinkers include Paolo Freire, Henry Giroux, Howard Zinn, Noam Chomsky, and Peter McLaren. These scholars and others helped articulate and promote the broad set of principles that fall under the heading of "critical pedagogy." Freire was a Brazilian educator and author who worked with illiterate groups within his native country and, during a period of exile, wrote prolifically about education the critical role it plays in either indoctrinating or liberating individuals and groups. Freire believed that what he called humankind's "ontological vocation" was to become "more human;" Along the way, however, groups become entrenched in various power dynamics that renders one group oppressed by another: "Any situation in which 'A' objectively exploits 'B' or hinders his and her pursuit of self-affirmation as a responsible person is one of oppression. Violence is initiated by those who oppress, who exploit, who fail to recognize others as persons--not by those who are oppressed, exploited, and unrecognized" (Freire, 1993, p. 37).

For Freire, education can either be a tool of oppression or liberation. In the hands of oppressors, education becomes a machine used to dehumanize the oppressed and prepare them for a life of exploitation. For the radical educator, however--Freire's "revolutionary humanist educator--education is a mutual endeavor whereby the teacher/student dichotomy is resolved in the praxis, and teachers empower individuals to see their position in the world and the power they have to act upon the world:

Because it is a distortion of being more fully human, sooner or later being less human leads the oppressed to struggle against those who made them so. In order for this struggle to have meaning, the oppressed must not, in seeking to regain their humanity (which is a way to create it), become in turn oppressors of the oppressors, but rather restorers of the humanity of both. This, then, is the great humanistic and historical task of the oppressed: to liberate themselves and their oppressors as well...Only power that springs from the weakness of the oppressed will be sufficiently strong to free both. (Freire, 1993, p. 26)

For Freire, then, the revolutionary humanist educator seeks to empower individuals and groups change existing oppressive social orders. This requires not simply that a teacher be proficient in a subject and capable of transmitting this information to students, but rather that the teacher and the student must enter into a mutual relationship of solidarity that allows for an exchange of ideas between equal and equally liberated and socially conscious people. Freire believed that "Solidarity requires that one enter into the situation of those with whom one is solidary; it is a radical posture" (Freire, 1993, p. 31).

Although Freire strongly advocated for the overthrow of existing oppressive social orders, he was not an advocate of violence. Rather, his approach is more in keeping with the tactics of passive, non-violent resistance. It is an ethos rooted in the aforementioned notion of solidarity, and one with interesting affiliations with Taoism and the concept of *wu-wei*, or "non-action." For Freire, the oppressive class should not be treated in the same manner that they treated the oppressed. Much like Christ's edict forgive seventy times seven times, Freire believed that oppressors needed to be integrated, not ostracized, from the new order that would emerge after the oppressed liberated themselves: "It is--paradoxical though it may seem--precisely in the response of the oppressed to the violence of their oppressors that a gesture towards love may be found. Consciously or unconsciously, the act of rebellion by the oppressed...can initiate love" (Freire, 1993, p. 38).

Henry Giroux, along with Freire, was one of the leading figures of critical pedagogy during the second half of the twentieth century. An educational theorist, Giroux sought to illuminate the complex ways in which the educational system of the dominant paradigms of Western societies act in collusion with other systems within those societies to program students into accepting the status quo (and, in the cases of minorities and other marginalized groups, their own oppression) and assimilating into it rather than inculcating skills for critical thinking that might empower these same individuals and groups to recognize their situation and challenge the status quo--the latter being a revolutionary process Freire refers to as cognize "*conscientizacao*," or, "consciousness-raising." Giroux declared that:

...traditional educational theory has ignored not only the latent principles that shape the deep grammar of the existing social order, but also those principles that underlie the development and nature of its own view of the world. Schools, in these perspectives, are seen merely as instructional sites. That they are also cultural and political sites is ignored, as is the notion that they represent arenas of contestation and struggle among differentially empowered cultural and economic groups. (Giroux, 1983, p. 3)

To counter this complacency, Giroux advocated for a strident position for critical pedagogy. It should provide the tools that an educator can use to get students to challenge not only overt and explicit injustices in society and the world around them but also force them to question the very nature of our shared constructed reality: "What critical theory provides for educational theorists is a mode of critique and a language of opposition that extends the concept of the political not only into mundane social relations but into the very sensibilities and needs that form the personality and the psyche" (Giroux, 1983, p. 5). Such a method of approach would allow oppressed and disenfranchised groups to develop their own discourse without the negative influences of the oppressive majority. It would also be an organic knowledge base that springs from the groups themselves instead of being derived from or in opposition to the prevailing oppressive structure.

While he strongly advocated for a classroom and a system of knowledge that was grass-roots in its nascence within oppressed groups, Giroux (1983) remained positive about the possibilities for inroads towards this area within even the most authoritative and traditional classrooms. Even here, he argued, there

...are fleeting images of freedom that speak to very different relationships. It is this dialectical aspect of knowledge that needs to be developed as part of a radical pedagogy...critical theory points educators toward a mode of analysis that stresses the breaks, discontinuities, and tensions in history, all of which become valuable in that they highlight the centrality of human agency and struggle while simultaneously revealing the gap between society as it presently exists and society as it might be. (p. 36)

After this pedagogy becomes put into practice, students who have formerly been oppressed can develop the critical thinking skillset needed to further critique the society in which they live and allow them to continue their self-liberation and development. They will be able to recognize and understand the degree to which the society in which they are embedded has molded them, and, in many cases, prevented them from achieving their goals and halted their self-development. For Giroux, it is critical that students become aware of the extent to which they have been affected by their society, because, in doing so, they can not only see that they are part of this same society and thus can affect it but they can also decide which aspects to affirm or reject as they struggle for the "opportunities to lead a self-managed existence" (p. 38).

TAOIST/CRITICAL PEDAGOGICAL INTERSECTIONALITY

There is great potential for incorporating elements of Taoism and Buddhism into a pedagogy that is situated within a critical pedagogical context. In his essay "Socially-Engaged Buddhism as a Provocation for Critical Pedagogy in Unsettling Times" (Eppert & Wang, 2008), Robert Hattam of the University of South Australia, discusses the continuing relevance for integral Eastern ideas, in this case Buddhism. He describes both critical theory and Tibetan Buddhism as "dynamic, rejuvenating traditions--very much alive and involved in translation in an increasingly East-West globalizing culture" (p. 111). He seeks to promote a pedagogy that uses principles of Taoism, including being adaptive and water-like, receptive and fluid to the varied needs of diverse learners and dynamic situations.

This ethos is being explored in a number of ways in pedagogy. Buckingham (2014), in "Communicating Not-Knowing: Education, Daoism and Epistemological Chaos," described how:

...teaching and learning are at their richest and most fruitful when they are not just concerned with communicating knowing, but when they communicate not-knowing. Thus, a rich educational context is one in which knowing and not-knowing, assurance and non-assurance swirl around each other chaotically; and teaching is as much about communicating not-knowing, tentativeness, uncertainty... hypotheses...as it is about communicating knowing, assurance, certainty, wellmapped paths, proofs, solutions, clarifications, illuminations and clarities. (p. 10)

Buckingham noted that the same "banking" system of education that Freire railed against remains essentially unchanged in modern Western schools and universities. He argues that what he terms "epistemological chaos," the quality of not-knowing, has a valuable role to play in the pedagogical process. "The further one goes, the less one knows…" (Lao Tzu, 1990). Buckingham echoed this sentiment, saying "There is a process of lessening assurance that goes with a deeper engagement with questions of knowledge and its value. The deeper one knows, the more one is open to qualifications, hesitations, exceptions and uncertainties" (p. 17).

This deeper level engagement is not one to which we should aspire to teach individuals once they have crossed a particular threshold--only after, say, twelve years of "banking" education--but rather that should be integrated with the best existing practices in education to offer an experience that seeks to do more than fill a student with epistemological certainties and also with the confidence to question this knowledge and the process of knowing in general: "the skilful educator would be one who understands that not-knowing always accompanies knowing, and who is skilled not only in navigating this epistemological chaos, but also in leading students through it" (Buckingham, 2014, p. 15).

Eppert and Wang (2008) echoed the idea of finding ways to integrate Taoist-oriented practices into pre-existing educational environments: when "thoughtful teachers" are presented with a static, banking-system-style curriculum, because they are "…attuned to the ebb and flow of a lived curriculum, dwell in the interstices of two curricula and reconstitute new pedagogies…" (p. 330). They also noted that such flexibility--emulating, true to Taoist form, the adaptive nature of water--in important not only in pedagogical situations, "they are also an essential part of language. Bringing fluidity into language itself is an educational task that holds the potential for transforming our intellectual landscape at large. When language is treated only as a rigid structure, the medium of our life becomes hardened" (p. 330). Here we can see great potential for the combination of Taoist principles, critical pedagogy, and language.

CONCLUSION

There is more connectivity than ever before in the world today, and thus more of an opportunity for we humans to connect as a global society, yet we paradoxically live in a time where this interconnectivity is, like tectonic plates whose shifting creates earthquakes, creating tensions and backlashes in many of these societies, the U. S. being no exception. We stand at a fork in the road of our development as a nation; down one path lies greater pluralism and integration--the continuation of our "melting pot" tradition--and down the other path lies xenophobia and isolation, a rejection of pluralism and the upsurge of an oppressive impulse rooted in nostalgia for a hegemonic past that was never as great as it is portrayed.

A critical nexus of this struggle in American society is language. Many who advocate an "English only" position are using language to mask deeper-seated prejudices. In this climate, language becomes a tool, one which can be used to oppress but one which can also be used to liberate. Linguistics, the study of language, can be harnessed in this struggle and used to help break oppression, empower the oppressed, and bring unity through mutual understanding. By utilizing aspects of linguistic areas of study, such as morphology and etymology, within a critical pedagogical framework, language pedagogies can be created that can accomplish these ends.

For example, one common argument for English as a national language in the United States goes that English was the language spoken by the Founding Fathers. By utilizing history and etymology, however, this argument can be refuted on number of levels. Firstly, of course, there is the historical fact that linguistic pluralism was plentiful among the native peoples of North America before the arrival of Europeans. Then there is the fact that the oldest city in the United States, St. Augustine, FL, was founded by Spanish conquistador Ponce de Leon, thus making Spanish the first European language spoken in the U.S. Then, too, there is the fact that the Founding Fathers, while obviously speaking English, were, on the whole, a well-educated group of landed gentry who often spoke other languages--Thomas Jefferson, for example, spoke English, French, Italian, and Latin. Finally, there is the etymological history of English itself, which is a history of absorption and amalgamation--of synthesis and heterogeneity, rather than exclusion and homogeneity. This is just one example, but it illustrates the potential for utilizing linguistics within a critical pedagogical theoretical framework.

The critical pedagogical framework provides a broad template for enacting positive social change through linguistic pedagogy, but it also needs focus and a specific tactic for implementation. To this end I seek to integrate elements of Taoism and Buddhism into this framework, creating a specific context of reunification with the self as Other and a pedagogical approach rooted in mutual understanding, edification, and empowerment. For some this will be a radical shift, as it assumes that there is no distinction between instructor and student, and, through integration of concepts like *wu-wei* ("non-action"), that the process of learning is not necessarily a process of "acquisition," as it is understood in the West, but can instead be a process more akin to discovering what one already knows.

REFERENCES

Abram, D. (1997). *The Spell of the Sensuous: Perception and Language in a More-Than-Human World*. New York: Vintage Books.

Bender, J. (2016). Justice as the practice of non-coercive action: A study of John Dewey and classical Daoism. *Asian Philosophy*, *26*(1), 20–37. doi:10.1080/09552367.2015.1136200

Buckingham, W. (2014). Communicating not-knowing: Education, Daoism and epistemological chaos. *China Media Research*, *10*(4), 10–19.

Chia, M., & Huang, T. (2005). *Secret teachings of the Tao Te Ching*. Rochester, Vermont: Destiny Books.

Eppert, C., & Wang, H. (Eds.). (2008). *Cross-cultural studies in curriculum: Eastern thought, educational insights*. New York: Lawrence Earlbaum.

Hoyt, M. (2016). Teaching with mindfulness: The pedagogy of being-with/for and without being-with/for. *JCT: Journal Of Curriculum Theorizing*, *31*(1), 126–142.

Mcdonough, R. (2016). Plato's cosmic animal vs. the Daoist cosmic plant: Religious and ideological implications. *Journal For The Study Of Religions And Ideologies*, *15*(45), 3.

Moon, S. (2015). Wuwei (non-action) Philosophy and Actions: Rethinking actions in school reform. *Educational Philosophy and Theory*, *47*(5), 455–473. doi:10.1080/00131857.2013.879692

Piller, I. (2016). *Linguistic diversity and social justice*. Oxford: Oxford University Press. doi:10.1093/acprof:oso/9780199937240.001.0001

Reagan, T. G., & Osborn, T. A. (2001). *The foreign language educator in society: Toward a critical pedagogy*. Routledge.

Roberts, P. (2012). Bridging east and west—or, a bridge too far? Paulo Freire and the *Tao Te Ching*. *Educational Philosophy and Theory*, *44*(9), 942–958. doi:10.1111/j.1469-5812.2011.00797.x

Roberts, P. (2013). Acceptance, resistance and educational transformation: A Taoist reading of The First Man. *Educational Philosophy and Theory*, *45*(11), 1175–1189. doi:10.1080/00131857.2013.772700

Tzu, C. (1996). *The book of Chuang Tzu* (M. Palmer & E. Breuilly, Trans.). London: Arkana.

Tzu, C. (1997). *The inner chapters* (D. Hinton, Trans.). Washington, D. C.: Counterpoint.

Tzu, L. (1990). *Tao te ching*. New York: Bantam.

Tzu, L. (1992). *Hua hu ching: The unknown teachings of Lao Tzu* (B. Walker, Trans.). New York: Harper-Collins.

Yutang, L. (1948). *The wisdom of Laotse*. New York: Random House.

KEY TERMS AND DEFINITIONS

Buddhism: Philosophical and religious belief system based on the teachings of Siddhartha Gautama. Basic tenets include the impermanence of all things, suffering as a fundamental aspect of life, and enlightenment through detachment from material and psychic phenomena.

Critical Pedagogy: A collection of educational theories and praxes that came into being in the 1960s. Proponents include Paolo Freire, Henry Giroux, Peter McLaren, and many others. Basic tenets include a rejection of traditional educational systems and bureaucracies, an emphasis on education as a means to individual and community self-awareness, and solidarity with oppressed groups.

Cultural Studies: Term for a discipline or collection of disciplines that examines facets of culture, both intra- and inter-culturally.

Global Studies: Term for a discipline or collection of disciplines that examines facets of global culture.

Ontology: The branch of philosophy dealing with existence and the nature of being.

Language: The term for the abstract vocal and orthographic systems of communication utilized by humans.

Linguistics: A discipline of education and research that is concerned with the nature of language.

Taoism: A philosophical and religious belief system developed in ancient China and attributed to Lao Tzu. Its central tenets include following the Tao, or "Way," a conceptualized force that runs throughout the universe, non-attachment to material or psychic phenomena, and a concern with living mindfully and harmoniously.

Chapter 13
Teaching Undergraduate Finance via a Digital Literacy Platform

Flory A. Dieck-Assad
Tecnologico de Monterrey, Mexico

ABSTRACT

Teachers and professors are searching for the best academic strategy to support an educational process that could provide an effective digital learning experience. After the evaluation of Learning Management Systems (LMS's), this chapter proposes the hypotheses that through the use of Microsoft OneNote Class Notebook (MONCN) as a teaching innovation in undergraduate Finance courses, the student's learning process is enhanced, and the students themselves perceive this LMS as a tool that enriches their education and improves their academic experience. The smart way to implement intelligent technology such as the use of MONCN will be to create an evolution through innovation, not a revolution; but the impact of this digital notebook could prove to be revolutionary if applied wisely. MONCN will enable faculty and students to survive the current challenges of media literacy and to thrive in the years to come; it could be replicated with great success in any university.

This is an institution of learning... Discipline is not the enemy of enthusiasm. – Principal Joe Clark (Morgan Freeman) in the motion picture "Lean on Me", 1989

INTRODUCTION

The world has experienced constant and challenging changes since the beginning of the 20th century as a result of technological advancements and innovations. The use of the Internet was not greatly accepted from the start, similar to the reaction to the use of airplanes for human transportation in the 20th century. Yet, just as airplanes became an indispensable tool for everyone around the world, the advancements in the use of the Internet for educational purposes is becoming an everyday challenge for educators.

DOI: 10.4018/978-1-5225-3082-4.ch013

Copyright © 2018, IGI Global. Copying or distributing in print or electronic forms without written permission of IGI Global is prohibited.

According to "NC State Industry Expansion Solutions" (2015) an online method of education can be a highly effective alternative for the students who are mature, self-disciplined and motivated, well organized and have a high degree of time management skills. This is especially applicable for students at the university level. Even though classes might not be completely online, the use of a Learning Management System (LMS) requires the students to organize themselves and perform collaborative activities with their classmates in a more efficient manner, regardless if they work inside or outside the physical classroom.

The Partnership for 21st Century Learning—P21 (2016) states that learning and innovation skills are what separate students who are prepared for increasingly complex life and work environments in today's world and those who are not. Furthermore, in a technology and media-driven environment, they emphasize on finding the adequate technological tool to increase the professor's ability to develop critical thinking skills, such as media literacy.

There is a vast selection of LMS's to choose from: Adobe Captivate Prime, DoCeBo, TalentLMS, Google Classroom, Microsoft OneNote Class Notebook (MONCN), among others. The first three LMS's of the list are sophisticated, provide no education discounts, are designed towards a more business-oriented learning environment, and need institutional approval for their use.

MONCN and Google Classroom are two types of LMS's that are similar in their simplicity and are more suitable for university applications. Their purpose is not to increase learning, but to manage the learning experience more effective and efficiently. Professors can take advantage of these LMS's to assess students' acquisition of knowledge, and to provide students with feedback on their progress using both formative and summative assessment. Both LMS's were tested before launching an innovation strategy in class with the following results: Using MONCN as a learning platform in class is more effective than Google Classroom because it provides a more effective way to manage the course content and organize students' work. Google Classroom is more of a file repository, while MONCN is more like a digital notebook, classroom, discussion, and collaboration space all in one. Preparing and organizing all the material required for a specific class is easier with MONCN. Through the use of the MONCN Creator, the professor can easily create all the sections needed for all the students enrolled in a particular course simultaneously, while Google Classroom does not provide this capability. Google Classroom required the download of additional applications to complete certain tasks that MONCN includes without the use of any other applications. Thus, MONCN was the LMS chosen for testing an innovation strategy.

The use of MONCN could transform a traditional classroom into a paperless learning digital environment from which the students are encouraged to be creative, to feel free to navigate among all the available media sources and share this media with their classmates, and to submit their activities in a more effective manner. Similarly, students will be able to keep all their notes and activities in one same place to improve their learning and feedback experience in the classroom.

As John Adams wrote to his colleague Benjamin Rush in a letter dated November 11, 1806: "If we take a survey of the greatest actions which have been performed in the world … we shall find the authors of them all to have been persons whose brains had been shaken out of their natural position" (Adams, 1806). That is the objective of this chapter – to show how the application of MONCN, as a teaching innovation in some undergraduate Finance courses at Tecnologico de Monterrey in Monterrey, Mexico, has been successful in the transmission of knowledge, in the promotion of values through the observation and guidance of the students in a controlled digital environment where the uploaded media can be analyzed and discussed for suitability, and in the encouragement of learning in digital environments.

This was accomplished by implementing the use of MONCN as a new tool for students, where they could get acquainted with a new digital environment for learning: a new way of taking notes, submitting activities and homework, getting timely feedback from the professor, working collaboratively with their classmates, working together in the classroom through the use of each students' mobile devices, etc. (Microsoft, 2015).

It was a discovery to demonstrate that undergraduate students managed to make the classroom time more effective and efficient for learning new topics and that they perceived freedom and contact with reality through the analysis of any available media source when using MONCN as a classroom tool. Furthermore, the way MONCN was applied in some courses at Tecnologico de Monterrey, in Mexico, could be replicated with great success in any other university around the world.

The proposed hypothesis of this chapter is to demonstrate that through the use of a Learning Management System, MONCN in this case, the student's learning process is enhanced, and the students themselves perceive this LMS as a tool that enriches their education and improves their academic experience. MONCN will enable faculty and students to survive the current challenges of media literacy and to thrive in the years to come.

Having a digital classroom could be seen as an important challenge not only for professors, but also for students. Although having a digital classroom may not be an absolute solution to improve pedagogy, there are numerous practical advantages that outweigh the disadvantages (Microsoft, 2016a). Thus, the use of MONCN could enhance the learning experience in the coming years.

It is important to emphasize that the objective of this chapter is not to propose a technological invention, but the new administration of the existing ones, with the purpose to transform them in an academic innovation that could help professors improve their efficiency in class. Invention develops new ideas, concepts, and processes, while innovation combines the existing elements and applies them in new ways. Nowadays, professors need innovation to take advantage of the technological inventions already in existence. Using MONCN as a digital notebook and combining the mix of human potential, processes, and faculty ingenuity could become an innovation in the academic environment to promote a better learning experience. The smart way to implement intelligent technology such as the use of MONCN will be to create an evolution through innovation, not a revolution; but the impact of this digital notebook could prove to be revolutionary if applied wisely. This will enable faculty and students to survive the current challenges of media literacy and to thrive in the years to come.

In order to achieve the objective of testing the hypothesis, this chapter is structured as follows: a literature review is offered in order to get a fruitful insight of this digital teaching technique; a brief definition of Microsoft OneNote Class Notebook is presented to familiarize the reader with this digital technological platform; the methodology used to test the hypothesis in finance courses at Tecnologico de Monterrey, Mexico, is described, and the results are explained in order to arrive at the conclusions and recommendations presented at the end of the chapter.

LITERATURE REVIEW

The existence of digital media is not new. In the academic arena, digital media has changed throughout generations. Several decades ago, all knowledge was learned through talking in person and writing on paper, but nowadays that is regarded as tedious. Hernandez (2016) states that there are many research approaches that support personalized digital education; however, there are many others who still discredit its benefits. Today's generations are easily capable of adapting to technological changes; children immediately learn to handle digital devices, even though they have just recently launched. These new generations are ready to learn with technology, whereas professors sometimes tend to resist technological change and find it difficult to teach using digital devices. As a result, just as generations rapidly change, professors should also change their teaching methods using technological learning platforms to develop enthusiasm in the students' learning experience.

"Once Noticias" (2013) explains how technology has become an important aspect in education since preschool. Technology can positively and negatively influence the behavior and learning outcomes in children. That is why it needs to be appropriately controlled by the professor. The role the professor plays in this activity becomes more important as an observer and a source of guidance for the students in a controlled digital environment where the uploaded media can be analyzed and discussed for suitability. Heins & Cho (2003) state that "Media literacy has become as essential a skill as the ability to read the printed word" (p. 1).

According to Katherine (2012), some of the advantages for using digital media for learning are:

- **Enhanced Search of Information:** Nowadays, few people visit physical libraries to consult information; individuals prefer to use digital libraries or web articles, due to its timely availability versus paper references, which takes hours or even days to retrieve.
- **Personalization:** Each professor can adopt their own particular teaching style using the Internet and the students submit their activities adding their personal touch.
- **Commitment and Interactivity:** Since students sometimes lack commitment for learning in the classroom, having a database or digital application where they can participate and interact to improve their grades, enables their course commitment and facilitates their academic endeavors.
- **Participation:** Student involvement in class using digital media, helps them participate inside and outside the classroom. In case the students fail to participate, the professor can easily identify it and take the necessary measures to motivate, support, and inspire the students to partake in order to get better grades.
- **Collaboration:** Students and professors can create virtual conferences within digital media where all participants can collaborate in forums and generate digital contributions without being present in the classroom; thus, learning can be upgraded. For example, if a professor cannot teach a class in person, this method could be used to film a video about the lecture's topic and avoid the students to fall behind on the course topics. Another example is the usage of this digital space for media literacy: ask the students to access and analyze any type of media and propose it for discussion by all the students, guided by the professor's ethical compass.
- **Digital Files:** Nowadays, many professors require students to print out their homework and projects to submit in class; however, submitting files digitally to the Internet or any academic technological platform has its advantages. Environmentally speaking, paper is saved and students can access digital documents where the professor grades and provides feedback directly through the learning platform. Additionally, timetables for digital activity submissions are established to foster student commitment with the course assignment submission policies. There are no more student excuses for late submissions because the homework activities can be uploaded anywhere a wireless connection is available. The student freely decides which documents to print and which ones to keep digitally and which media to share and propose for discussion in class.

The use of technological learning platforms started several years ago. Hoise and Schibeci (2005) analyzed how to improve teaching techniques for online learning in higher education. Similarly, Veiga (2009) explained how the Universidad Nacional Experimental de los Llanos Occidentales Ezequiel Zamora (UNELLEZ) in Venezuela, performed academic innovations to their own learning platform "EduDigital," to promote interactive chats between graduate students.

In 2010, Palomo and Montalvo (2010) shared the educational innovations they apply in the transition towards technological platform usage. This was discussed in the "Primeras Jornadas de Innovación Educativa" at King Juan Carlos University in the Mostoles Campus in Madrid, Spain. They started with experimental work using the iCollege learning platform to enrich teaching activity through information technology. Later, they created the iWiki College to promote collaboration among students to facilitate online work and make it available for all users. Additionally, it helps professors grade the material which is chronologically organized in digital format. This academic platform seeks to support the collaborative learning teaching strategy and improve teaching practices.

March (2012) presents ideas about the advantages of using Internet platforms to publish digital media:

- **Global Publications That Transcend Borders:** When submitting digital manuscripts, the public is collaborating in the Internet and anyone can have access to them; thus, any type of information can be collected to aid students and faculty in fulfilling their work.
- **Online Learning Communities:** The creation of online spaces exclusively dedicated to make learning groups is an interesting method of class interaction. For example, a team of classmates who cannot get together in person can share their thoughts virtually or online to interact and exchange ideas to timely accomplish their final task or project at hand.
- **"Serving the Net":** Originally, young people use the Internet just for surfing and taking up unused time; many students even abuse its use and forget that the Internet should be regarded as an ideal aid to learn, research, and transmit knowledge, mainly related with education. Al Rogers, one of the pioneer professors in global classroom learning stated: "I didn't want students to just 'Surf the Net', but to 'Serve the Net'." Students need to be aware that the Internet can be used as an effective tool for improved learning in higher education.

While evaluating the advantages in using digital media, the following ideas can be analyzed:

1. Classes become practical and attractive.
2. Sending homework via email or another digital method becomes a reality.
3. Students and faculty can be updated on information of any nature.
4. Time is considerably saved.
5. Students' attention span is improved when providing dynamic digital content.
6. Evaluating and providing feedback becomes easier: students create tangible products as evidence of their learning.
7. Collaborative learning is enhanced. For example, students are allowed to freely navigate among all the available media sources and encouraged to share this media with the group.
8. The professor is allowed to design alternative and eye-catching didactic material instead of the traditional one.
9. Users are allowed to access a large flow of information, where the search results are infinite.

Even though the use of technology for learning has its noteworthy advantages, some of its disadvantages are that they require:

1. Previous learning to avoid students to be frustrated when venturing into something new.
2. Positive attitude and disposition from the professors towards new technology updates.
3. Professor commitment as guide towards learning instead of using technology as the students' "nanny", leaving them unattended in the classroom for extended periods of time.
4. Professors to be a mentor within the technological platform to advise the students what information is better to use for academic, research, or learning purposes.
5. Time investment on behalf of the professor to plan the use of these technological resources.
6. Additional financial investment from the academic institution to purchase equipment and technological applications.
7. Preventive and corrective maintenance of equipment.
8. Awareness on behalf of the faculty member on the role to play when using the technological platform.
9. Knowledge of eye health implications of excessively using digital media for everyday activities. The American Academy of Ophthalmology (2011) recommends taking regular breaks from these activities.

Acknowledging the need of an academic-friendly technological platform to help universities homogenize their teaching processes, Microsoft Corporation, as a company specializing in digital technology and communication, launched a new LMS for academic application to promote interactive learning; this digital learning platform is known as Microsoft OneNote Class Notebook (MONCN).

MICROSOFT ONENOTE CLASS NOTEBOOK (MONCN)

According to Microsoft (2016b), OneNote is an application bundled up in any Microsoft Office package and is designed to help people to organize and find the data they need in a way that better adapts to their personal style. Gonzalez (2016) states that OneNote is similar to a customizable digital notebook that can integrate different types of files. OneNote is a digital data organization tool that saves the use of tangible material such as paper, pencils, pens, etc.

The academic institutions that have Microsoft Office 365 provide professors with the possibility of creating their own digital notebook through OneNote. Moreover, within the traditional OneNote and the Office 365 access, professors can create their own customizable teaching digital notebook using the MONCN Creator. It is important that professors know how to use OneNote so that each one can design their own MONCN according to their course interests, objectives and mission (OneNote, 2013).

Through the use of the teaching digital notebook (MONCN) and everyday technology as an innovative teaching method fosters a dynamic learning space for the student. This is just one of the benefits derived from applying this digital tool along with taking notes, saving information in an organized manner, sharing media, and submitting digital tasks. Regardless of all the innovations and technological advancements, professors face a daily challenge to motivate their students to submit digital activities, trying to overcome their resistance to change because some students still feel comfortable and accustomed to traditional learning with the use of paper and pencil to submit their tasks. According to Walter (2015), the resistance to change can also be generated within the faculty because they need to learn how to use the OneNote application as well as dedicate time to design their own teaching digital notebook for each of their courses; however, once the professor does so, the results are so friendly and positive, that the hours invested in designing the notebook for the first time are transformed into significant time savings for their educational work. This results in more effective teaching practices wherein the professor can follow the evolution of each student, control the digital environment, and guide them with ethical counseling.

Using MONCN offers a range of benefits to the faculty: having a tool to help organize information creatively and orderly, reducing efforts, taking advantage of time efficiency, creating a free digital environment to chat and share media, and decreasing the university's expense budget in office writing supplies that would be required to organize information in the absence of this digital tool. The students also benefit economically from MONCN usage by eliminating the use of paper and other writing materials.

To understand how MONCN works, it is important to start with the basic understanding of OneNote as a notebook (Rosales, 2013). OneNote is an application designed to help users to make their time more efficient without the use of paper for note-taking. The notebook is made up of sections and pages as can be seen in Figure 1.

OneNote is designed to make note-taking easy, gather information, and foster multi-user collaboration. OneNote can be divided into many different notebooks (for example "Work", "Personal", and "Classes"). Within each notebook, several sections can be created. For example, the "Classes" notebook can be transformed into a 3-subject notebook by adding the "Math", "Bio", and "Histo" sections. Each section within the notebook can have as many pages as the user decides; thus, the students can use them for adding the course calendar, taking notes for each class session, etc. Anyone could have their personal OneNote for future references of their note-taking. MONCN is considered an extension of OneNote for use in education through the university's sharepoint (central cloud storage within an institution), when the university has a Microsoft Office 365 education package. Once the course is over, the student can transfer a notebook from the professor's MONCN to a personal OneNote and keep it for future reference.

Having Microsoft Office 365 enables the professor to adapt OneNote into Microsoft OneNote Class Notebook (MONCN), an instrument that allows faculty to increase teaching effectiveness: grading work easily, reducing paper use, effective counseling and guidance, and supporting the students' learning process through improved and innovative teaching practices.

Figure 1. Digital notebook in OneNote

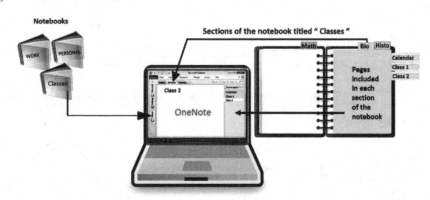

MONCN is user-friendly and does not require any specific skill. Five activities enabled through this technological teaching platform are:

1. **Organize Course Content:** The professor can gather all the content needed to share with the students organizing it in sections; each section can be further divided into pages to satisfy personal course styles. It is a process similar to creating folders (sections) and pages inside each folder.
2. **Create and Offer Interactive Lessons:** Existing lessons can be gathered and inserted in the specific sections to create the personalized teaching style. Audio and video lessons can also be included, which was not possible in the traditional teaching process. The students can express their comments and doubts about the course material in real time, and propose any material from the media for debate, increasing the class-professor interaction anytime, anywhere.

Students can take advantage of all the available tools in MONCN to create their activities, such as: homework, class notes, drawings, annotations in slides, diagrams, etc. (OneNote, 2013). The note-taking process in MONCN can even be performed using the finger or a digital pen, as shown in Figure 2. This improves the professor-student interaction.

Making personal annotations with the use of MONCN is especially helpful in courses that require high numerical content because the student can comfortably take notes digitally, as if they were on paper. This concept is also known as electronic ink (Sanchez, 2014), which is the pioneering idea of what is known today as tablets or any other digital devices to make digital reading easier.

3. **Make Personal Comments:** The professor provides special and personal feedback by writing private notes with the objective of giving a faster and timely response to the student without the need to see him personally in the classroom. The professor writes these private notes and feedback in the section (folder) where the student needed a response.

Figure 3 shows an example of these types of private annotations written by a professor to suggest a correction to the student in the particular section where the student prepared his work. The student can see the feedback anytime and anywhere, without the need to see the professor in person in the classroom or office. The professor could also provide private counseling and guidance about the media accessed by the student to be debated in class.

Figure 2. Interactive lessons with annotations in Microsoft OneNote Class Notebook (MONCN)

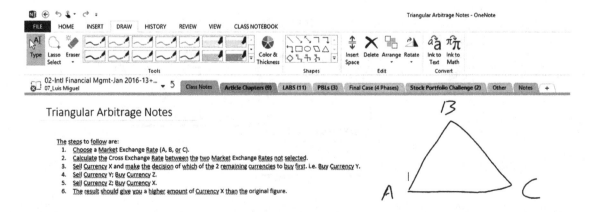

Figure 3. Personal comments in Microsoft OneNote Class Notebook (MONCN)

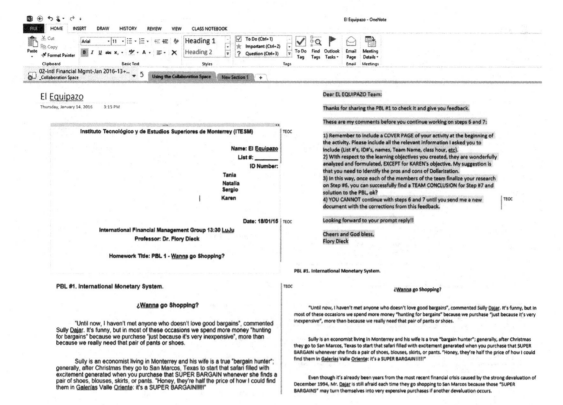

4. **Apply the Collaborative Learning Teaching Strategy:** MONCN encourages students to decide to work together and allow the professor to observe their progress and at the same time provide feedback and guidance in real time (Babcock, 2016). Additionally, students can prepare teamwork with their classmates in and out of the physical classroom without any difficulty in real time. Figure 4 shows an example of collaborative interaction in a course, where each of the student's input is registered with their initials to indicate what part of the work is contributed by each student. The initials of each student are marked with an arrow to visualize this process better.

5. **Gather All Students' Work in One Place:** Since each student has a personal section in MONCN, the professor gathers all their work (homework, projects, exams, media analysis, discussions, etc.) in one place and professors can see the digital notebook of each student. This helps the professor trace the students' progress during the school period.

Creation of the Microsoft OneNote Class Notebook (MONCN)

As the process for creating MONCN starts, the steps to follow are described in such a friendly way that technological expertise is not needed. This is one advantage of MONCN compared to other similar LMS's used as teaching technological platforms. Additionally, MONCN has the advantage of coming from the Microsoft Office family, whereas the majority of the users are already acquainted with the use of its applications (Word, Excel, Power Point, etc.), making the MONCN creation easier.

Figure 4. Collaborative interaction in a course using Microsoft OneNote Class Notebook (MONCN)

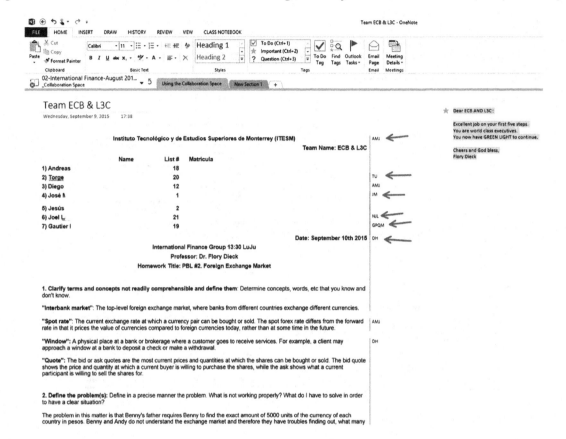

MONCN is composed of three fixed general sections that automatically appear when the digital teaching notebook is created: "Collaboration Space," "Content Library," and "Student Notebooks" (OneNote Team, 2014b). Figure 5 shows the sections and how MONCN can digitally connect the professor with the students.

According to OneNote Team (2014a), the basic meaning of each general section, is briefly described as follows:

1. **Collaboration Space:** This space is designed to encourage students to upload files, media, videos, notes, etc., that they would like to share with the entire classroom and to work in smaller teams to interact. Students can also feel free to upload any type of media they find. This makes the collaborative learning teaching strategy more attractive, efficient, and successful.

2. **Content Library:** In this space professors can place all the course material needed for the students to perform their activities and foster their learning experience. Students have access to the general information of the course and the activity submission calendar created by the professor, without the need to have paper printouts distributed in the classroom. Additionally, the student can have access to the course program at any moment without the hassle of printing and carrying physical documents.

Figure 5. Fixed general sections in Microsoft OneNote Class Notebook (MONCN)

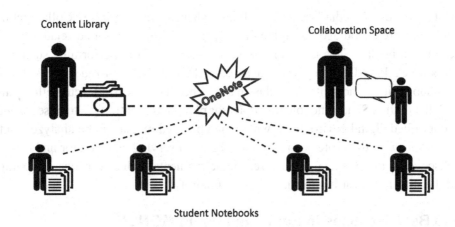

3. **Student Notebooks:** This is the personal space designed for each student, where they can take their own private class notes; students can decide to share their material with their classmates and submit their tasks where the professor can grade them. It should be emphasized that the professor always has access to the student notebooks to check their academic progress, grade homework, provide feedback and even motivate them in a personalized manner. It is similar to a 24/7 academic guidance that extends the professor-student contact beyond the physical classroom.

Figure 6 shows the three general sections of MONCN in a course. This figure is shown from the professor's point of view, where the Student Notebooks already have the name of each student.

Figure 6. General sections in Microsoft OneNote Class Notebook (MONCN) Course

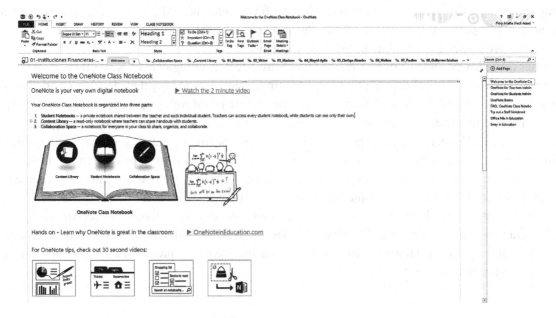

Teachable Moment Using Collaboration Space in Class to Promote Media Literacy

One of the best practices of media literacy was found when interacting in the Collaboration Space in MONCN. Students were encouraged to upload any type of media they found related to the financial topic being discussed in class. The interesting aspect discovered from performing such activities was that the students were allowed to freely navigate among all the available media sources and to share this media in the Collaboration Space with their classmates. Since the professor teaching the course also has access to the Collaboration Space, the role the professor plays in this activity is to observe and guide the students in a controlled digital environment where the uploaded media can be analyzed and discussed for suitability. In this way, the professor plays a vital role in serving as mediator and counsel to what the students discover in the financial media. Teachable moments such as this one, encourage both the professor and the students towards a media literacy suitability.

Migration to Best Practices in Education Using MONCN

Adapting to the use of MONCN on behalf of the students can be tedious during the first sessions because regardless of all the possible benefits provided by the new technological platforms, the way to habituate students to take notes and submit activities digitally and avoid tangible submissions could be overwhelming. This is especially true when dealing with courses that require a high degree of written homework and activity submissions. However, with the adequate motivation and inspiration on behalf of the professor, the student could be guided to understand the learning advantages of using this smart tool: the students could be able to perceive that they are also developing a new technological skill that will be useful in their future curricular profile.

It is important to point out the advantages of MONCN as a friendly platform: less expensive than other LMS's, the professors could adapt it according to their needs (great flexibility and adaptation to the needs of any course), the storage capacity is the one offered from the professor's cloud on the OneDrive from their university's sharepoint, and once the course is over, the student can transfer a digital notebook from the course's MONCN to a personal OneNote for future reference. MONCN also has disadvantages: it is not a robust platform standardized for all the university and each professor must invest time to adapt it and improve its design according to the course content.

After using MONCN in a course, the students learn new technological skills and they are trained to replicate their technological experience in any other institution or company they decide to work for, even in their own homes. MONCN was designed with the objective to develop specific skills in the students besides the traditional teaching process of giving information and knowledge in class. Among those skills are: facing a challenge, engaging in professor-student debates, and connecting with the world through media literacy, among others. The student needs to be transformed from a passive to an active actor, from an indifferent person to a digitally connected person with the world. At the end of the course they feel prepared to use an LMS to become efficient mentors of team work activities in the future.

There is well known literature which concludes that a good lecture could transfer knowledge with verbal and non-verbal expressions. However, the development of the ability to listen to others digitally will exponentially increase the effectiveness in the teaching-learning process in a classroom. This can be achieved through MONCN.

The teaching and learning processes are related. A professor who knows how to teach is one who is also eager to learn from students. MONCN could be an effective LMS for giving this type of vitality to a classroom which could be transformed into a social academic network, from which inspiration surges towards excellence. The personal education becomes a team work looking for synergies and intellectual collaboration among the professor and the students with better results in education and a higher degree of personal satisfaction in their own educational process.

The objective of this chapter is to present the evaluation of the educational process where finance students at Tecnologico de Monterrey in the state of Nuevo Leon, Mexico, face the challenge of using MONCN as a digital LMS platform. Moreover, it will evaluate its role in the effective transference of knowledge and supporting the transformation of the students into digitally connected persons with the world.

EVALUATION OF THE USE OF MICROSOFT ONENOTE CLASS NOTEBOOK (MONCN) AS AN EFFECTIVE LEARNING MANAGEMENT SYSTEM (LMS)

With the objective to evaluate MONCN as an effective LMS which enhances the application of any didactic technique for the strengthening of education, an experiment was applied at Tecnologico de Monterrey. The procedure undertaken aimed to identify the strength of MONCN as a digital LMS platform that could become an effective tool for the transference of knowledge. This was done through the application of a survey at the end of the courses.

Hypothesis Definition

The definition of the hypothesis consists in testing if the students perceive improvement in the quality of their learning experience through the use of MONCN for the first time, as an innovation in the teaching practices in class. This was done in undergraduate finance courses on campus at Tecnologico de Monterrey. These courses were taken in a physical classroom, not online.

To better understand the students' perception of their learning experience, researchers used the tool to test this hypothesis through a written survey delivered to the students; it was used to evaluate their opinions about: the migration process of submitting activities in paper to a digital environment, the improvement in their technological skills, and their perception about group interaction enhancement with the freedom of being connected with digital media during the course.

Methodology

The experiment was applied to eight undergraduate Finance classes. Because there is no numerical evaluation of the effectiveness of the hypothesis so far, the objective of this research is to test it through a written survey applied to the students at the end of the course's semester with questions that were transformed into quantitative results. Additionally, a brief free format essay was prepared by each student to express their personal learning experience and provide qualitative results to support or reject the hypothesis.

Four groups of undergraduate courses were considered each semester during the period from August 2015 to May 2016: two groups of the course "Financial Institutions" and two groups of the course "International Finance" for each semester. During each semester, one group of a course, considered the Core

Sample, used the traditional classroom method of submitting activities without sharing digital media through a LMS. The other group was considered the Experimental Sample and was taught with the use of MONCN as a digital classroom with the possibility to share digital media:

Semester 1 (August-December 2015)

Group 1, Semester 1: Financial Institutions taught in Spanish as a Core Sample.
Group 2, Semester 1: Financial Institutions taught in Spanish as an Experimental Sample.
Group 3, Semester 1: International Finance taught in English as a Core Sample.
Group 4, Semester 1: International Finance taught in English as an Experimental Sample.

Semester 2 (January-May 2016)

Group 1, Semester 2: Financial Institutions taught in Spanish as a Core Sample.
Group 2, Semester 2: Financial Institutions taught in Spanish as an Experimental Sample.
Group 3, Semester 2: International Finance taught in English as a Core Sample.
Group 4, Semester 2: International Finance taught in English as an Experimental Sample.

Two academic periods (semesters) were considered to make the research more robust rendering the total data of each sample as follows:

1. **Core Sample**: 87 surveyed students.
2. **Experimental Sample:** 92 surveyed students.

Quantitative Research Results

The applied survey was identical for both the Core Sample and the Experimental Sample; each sample was composed of four Groups in total. To verify that the student sample was suitable for the research, the first part of the survey was structured with questions to show the student profile on digital knowledge for both the Core and the Experimental Samples. The behavior of these numerical indicators individually per group is similar; thus, only the global results are presented. The numerical results of the first part of the survey can be seen in Table 1. Since the majority of the students had not used MONCN before, it was an ideal sample to test the students' perception of the usefulness of MONCN.

The interpretation of the numerical findings, after analyzing the students' responses to the first part of the survey, show that the samples are not skewed and have similar characteristics as follows:

1. Since more than 60% of the students in both samples used Apple-brand computers, the research results of this experiment are not skewed because both samples show similar computer skill knowledge.
2. The results show that 83% of the students in the Core Sample as well as 71% of the students in the Experimental Sample did not know of the existence of MONCN. Thus, the students had an innovative educational experience by encountering something totally new to them.
3. Students from both sets of samples (Core: 89% and Experimental: 87%) had never used the OneNote application before this experiment.

Table 1. Quantitative survey global results August 2015-May 2016

	Core Sample * 87 Students Percentage of the Sample	Experimental Sample** 92 Students Percentage of the Sample
Computer type used for class: Apple	62%	65%
Computer type used for class: Other	38%	35%
Unknown previous knowledge of MONCN***	83%	71%
Never used OneNote before	89%	87%
Never used OneNote individually before	93%	88%
Never used OneNote as a group before	97%	99%
Have used another digital tool for other activities and to submit homework in class	78%	54%
Have used another digital tool for other activities and to submit homework in class: Blackboard	80%	70%
Preferred method to submit homework: Digital	82%	91%
Preferred method to submit homework: Paper	18%	9%
First time to be able to share media for discussion in class**		97%
Not knowing MONCN, would prefer BlackBoard *	70%	
Knowing MONCN, would prefer to use MONCN **		87%

Source: elaborated with the survey results
* Groups without MONCN.
** Groups with MONCN.
*** Microsoft OneNote Class Notebook.

4. On an individual basis, 93% of the students in the Core Sample had not used OneNote in other courses for personal use. This percentage can similarly be confirmed with the students from the Experimental Sample which reached 88%.

5. It was noteworthy to check the results of not using OneNote for team-related activities before this experiment: 97% of the students in the Core Sample and 99% of the students in the Experimental Sample confirmed that they had not used OneNote for coordinating teams and collaborative learning.

6. It is important to acknowledge the existence of other technological academic platforms for task submissions in class. In the Core Sample, 78% of the students had used another tool for submitting activities where 80% of these students recognized the Blackboard teaching platform as the one they mostly used. With respect to the Experimental Sample, only 54% had used another digital tool for delivering their homework where 70% of them also confirmed the use of the Blackboard academic platform. This reveals that, in the absence of other innovative technologies, students used the technological platform officially offered by their academic institution; in this case, Tecnologico de Monterrey.

7. One of the key questions of this research is related to the students' preferred method for submitting activities, paper or digital: 82% of the students in the Core Sample and 91% of the students in the Experimental Sample coincided in their choice of submitting their work through digital means. It is important to emphasize that 70% of the students who answered 'digital' in the Core Sample, were acquainted and preferred performing such activities through Blackboard. On the other hand,

87% of the students who answered 'digital' in the Experimental Sample preferred using MONCN again in future courses, once they learned its advantages during this course.

8. Another key question was about the opportunity that MONCN offered the students to share media to be discussed in the digital platform. Of the students in the Experimental Sample, 97% revealed that this was the first time they were able to share media for discussion in class.

There were some questions in the survey directed towards the objective of evaluating the specific experience that the students from the Experimental Sample had with the use of MONCN in order to identify the strengths and weaknesses of this LMS as a digital teaching platform. The results are presented in Table 2; it is important to emphasize that in the survey, the evaluation was made on a Likert scale from 1 to 5, where the number 5 is considered a Totally Agree response and the number 1 is considered a Totally Disagree response.

The results on Table 2 show that there is a significant improvement in the students' perception of their own educational process when using MONCN. The students in the Experimental Sample perceived the following benefits of using MONCN: they sensed a more dynamic class, they experienced easier collaborative teamwork, and while getting acquainted with MONCN, they considered it an easy user-friendly tool to also help them organize their time better. Even though the students from the Experimental Sample had a harder semester with a higher work burden due to the development of extra technological skills to learn to use MONCN and becoming accustomed to a digital classroom with no more paper consumption, they considered this no additional complication to the course. They admitted that they had no problem understanding and operating this digital learning platform because once they got into the habit of working on a digital environment, the process involving the upload of projects, homework, and notes in MONCN was easy. Moreover, the application of this LMS as an academic innovation increased the students' sensation of freedom with the possibility to be connected with the world through the access and share of financial media.

Table 2. Strengths and weaknesses of Microsoft OneNote Class Notebook (MONCN) quantitative results for the experimental sample August 2015-May 2016

Concept	Average Result on a Scale of 1 to 5	Standard Deviation *	Independentt-Test *
MONCN makes the class more dynamic	4.15	0.8507	9.558263
MONCN makes collaborative work easier	4.27	0.9504	7.349342
MONCN is an easy digital tool to use	4.36	0.8462	7.269058
MONCN helps organize time better	4.21	0.9237	8.126106
MONCN gave me freedom to access and share financial media	4.82	0.5121	3.461405
MONCN is an additional complication to the course	2.03	0.9994	9.909763
Had problems understanding MONCN	2.09	1.0125	10.296173
Difficulty submitting activities, homework, and notes in MONCN	1.83	1.0441	7.588335

Source: elaborated with the survey results

* $p \leq 0.05$ with a 95% confidence interval and a normal distribution assumption.

It is also important to point out in Table 2 that the standard deviations and the independent t-test of the survey results of the Experimental Sample show that the personal perception of the students' education is significantly improved in all concepts. The disadvantages for using MONCN were statistically insignificant, because the students perceived the strengths for using MONCN to greatly exceed its possible weaknesses. The standard deviations and the independent t-test were calculated with a 95% confidence interval, concluding that the students feel more satisfied with their process of education when MONCN is used. Furthermore, those students who indicate having some problems with MONCN in the beginning of the semester report that once they understood its dynamics, the learning process in class positively increase.

Figure 7 presents the graphic results according to the applied survey where the students highly accept their pathway towards a digital teaching environment. The results show an improvement in the perception of the students of their own educational process in the courses where MONCN was applied. The behavior of these numerical indicators individually per group is similar; thus, only the global results are presented.

In all the groups where MONCN was used, there is a significant improvement in the perceived personal learning on behalf of the student, even though it became a tougher semester due to the need to dedicate extra time to learn and incorporate a new and unknown LMS as a technological learning tool in the course workload. These results show that the personal insight of the student who used MONCN considerably improves in all the surveyed features.

Due to the improvement in the perception of the students' personal learning process with this experiment, there is a strong tendency to incorporate the use of MONCN permanently in Finance courses as an adequate and innovative teaching technique for transmitting knowledge in the classroom. This LMS was kept in the syllabus of these financial courses at Tecnologico de Monterrey.

Figure 7. Strengths and weaknesses of Microsoft OneNote Class Notebook (MONCN) August 2015-May 2016

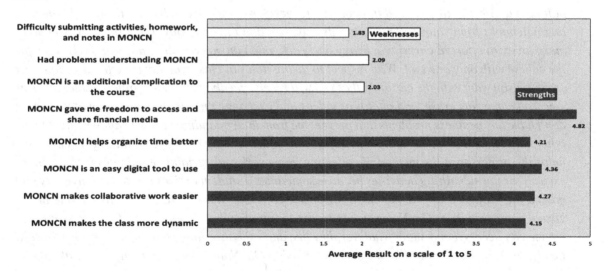

Qualitative Research Results (Feedback From the Students)

The quantitative research results were complemented with a qualitative evaluation. The surveyed students were required to hand in a free format essay, explaining their perception of MONCN in their own process of education during the course. Five of these essays are presented as examples of teachable moments. The students expressed their experience with MONCN as an effective LMS for submitting activities, interacting in the classroom, transferring knowledge, and feeling connected with the world.

Student 1: *OneNote is a very useful program where you can develop homework and activities in a very simple way. It is a program designed to easily take notes and is focused on enabling tools to make diagrams, organize assignments, and insert voice and videos, among other key activities used when taking notes. This program is an excellent working tool where ideas can be written to be transformed into different work strategies. In the Financial Institutions course, we have used this software to upload all the homework and assignments of the course. Many of the students in our classroom, had never used this software before and, as the semester was ending, the majority of us realized that OneNote is a very useful tool for us as students, as well as for all the professors.*

Student 2: *In my experience as a OneNote user, I can say that I am satisfied except for the last weeks of the course. The reason for this is that I don't know why I lost access to MONCN from my computer. From any other computer I can access OneNote, but curiously I can't in mine. I considered the fault to be my own computer, but fortunately, the problem was solved later. However, everything else in OneNote was positive. Without question, technological advances in the digital area have boosted educative development. OneNote makes learning easier in class and it is also free to use. Of course, there are still social sectors in our world without access to this tool.*

Student 3: *In my case, I was part of the traditional school where all my work was made by hand and was collected by the professor in person. I never complained of this method, but now that I use OneNote to manage my notes and assignments in class, I consider this the best method from my own point of view. First, all you need is a computer; therefore, you are eliminating the use of notepads and notebooks from your backpack. In this way, you don't need to buy office supplies, you don't make an extra effort in carrying a heavy backpack, and you can organize all your study work for the course with only one tool. With respect to taking notes in class, you have the freedom to insert anything you want with the certainty that you will receive feedback from the professor that inspires you. You can write, erase, add photos or videos and exchange them with some classmates. Then, I don't have any neatness problems that prevent me from understanding my own handwriting. On the other hand, I can upload my assignments from any place as long as I have an Internet access. This helps the professor in the method of collecting homework and certainly eliminates extraordinary excuses for not submitting activities because sometimes a student arrives late to the university and missed the professor to give her the assignment. OneNote literally transforms the course into a virtual classroom. With OneNote you can create a platform where students and the professor of the course can access it and share whatever they like and exchange information publicly or privately. Lastly, the advantage that I like the most when using OneNote is that I can only worry about one thing in class: my computer. I only have to remember to bring one tool to class to take notes and this avoids me to forget things. It is easier than carrying many notebooks as I did in high school.*

Student 4: *In my personal experience using OneNote, it is an organized tool and contains all the practical characteristics for its use. The system is fast, simple, and easy to use; it is efficient to see how we can shift from document to document easily, download and upload files regardless if they are PDFs or any other file type I wish to upload. You can edit and change documents, personalize them as you please, save changes in the documents without the need to use a 'save' button because they automatically save themselves through the use of the network (file syncing). The professor's opinions and comments are easily received without a need of a personal appointment with her. These are just a few of the advantages that OneNote offers, making it very good and effective. However, OneNote could have other characteristics that could make it more original and authentic. In my opinion, it would be an important and original breakthrough if it could provide notifications or an 'alarm system' to remind you of pending assignments or any other errand or activity that needs to be prepared for in class. For example, if you had a homework to hand in, you could program the software to remind you the time and day you require to submit the work and send you a notification. Another thing is that OneNote should provide all the editing features like 'Word' provides and avoid the difficulty of sometimes starting to prepare the work in 'Word' and then pass them onto OneNote. Another idea to improve OneNote could be that, there could be a system that allows the professor to 'lock' certain sections in order for students to know where to upload certain specific assignments. This could avoid the confusion when assignments are required to be submitted in specific sections; this happened to me several times in the semester and could be of great help for everyone.*

Student 5: *According to my experience, I can say that using OneNote is an effective and easy to use platform to submit activities and projects. However, it is the first time I use this method and honestly, I was not accustomed to work this way; that is why, I didn't get a very high grade for the first assignments I submitted in class. I could not identify the exact number of pages of an assignment when writing directly in OneNote, so I had to use Microsoft Word to prepare my task before uploading it into OneNote. Since I never used any type of digital methods for submitting my work when I was in elementary and high school, my education method was more traditional. Thus, I was not familiarized with using this methodology to improve my learning and my academic life. At first, I struggled to get accustomed to OneNote, but I honestly noticed that it is much better to use not only OneNote, but any other digital media because it is practical and simple to use. I noticed it is a very advantageous method for the professor to grade my work because she can check the last date in which I submitted my work and even the previous versions of the assignments I submit in order to guide me in my work. Unfortunately, when dealing with assignments with a due date and time, I had some trouble because if I typed something on the assignment page after the due date, it would be registered as the 'last modification' in the platform and this would affect my grade. Nevertheless, I spoke with the professor and explained to her and she helped me out; however, I think this is a problem in OneNote. I imagine I wasn't the only one who has experienced this, and it was up to the student to tell the truth about submitting assignments on time. The world is changing and we have been a generation who have experienced many of these drastic changes having to be flexible in order to better adapt ourselves to whatever situation that comes in our way; this helps us become more practical and have a different vision than other individuals. Therefore, I agree that OneNote should be used in class and am satisfied to have done so; the good thing is that I have learned from my mistakes and will surely not repeat them again. This is one of the many new things I will learn in my undergraduate classes with respect to introducing technology in my life and I am very happy to have adapted and understood it rapidly.*

As can be observed through the opinions of students regarding the use of MONCN, even though there are occasionally small problems related with new and unknown technological tools, there is a successful transference of knowledge, a transformation of the student who seriously takes on the leadership of their own learning plan and the possibility of adopting technological improvements in the classroom to enhance education. The professor must be prepared for the arrival of different types of student attitudes towards media literacy, and the advice is to inspire students to lead a successful academic experience based on a daily learning to learn experience. This means that the learning process will not end when they graduate; their success requires an open state of mind prone to continue learning in a dynamic and evolving environment.

With the statistical and qualitative results obtained from this research, the hypotheses cannot be rejected. It was observed that a significant improvement was registered in the education process perceived by the students themselves precisely in the groups in which MONCN was applied.

CONCLUSION

The use of digital media in the classroom has been highly debated due to the belief that it could become a disruptive agent of learning, and students tend to get distracted in the classroom. Instead of causing the professors to take special measures to maintain student attention in the classroom, digital media could become a technological ally to improve teaching practices. This is the great benefit of using MONCN as a digital LMS in the classroom.

There are many advantages that support the use of MONCN; however, it is important for the professor to adopt the serious commitment of guiding the students and balancing technology use with the encouragement to develop their analytical skills and critical thinking. This is especially so when analyzing and guiding the class discussion on the media uploaded in the Collaboration Space to promote media literacy.

The aim of this research is to motivate professors to accept the challenge of testing this digital teaching method in their classes with which they are going to experience benefits for them as well as for the students. Among the lessons learned in this chapter, the one that stands out is that the resistance to change makes the endeavor of educating persons to be professionals with the skills necessary for this competitive and challenging society increasingly difficult. It is important for students to be enriched by all the aspects of what is known as "interactive learning": transferring knowledge that includes, not only the course content, but also the promotion and development of ethics, honesty, justice, liberty, peace, and other fundamental values to be successful in an aggressive, global, and competitive world. This could be done by letting students feel the connection to the world through the sharing and discussing of digital media. This should be the result of the "educational curiosity" of the modern educator.

MONCN is one of many resources available to help strengthen a new change in life, always visualizing the benefits and great results of incorporating technology in our daily lives, but at the same time being cautious of the possible negative aspects to be ready to guide the students towards the best actions to take, specifically in the debate of the media uploaded in class.

Entrepreneurs always search for the best way to make people's lives easier. In most cases, they succeed, in other cases, they fail; but with MONCN the digital programmers hit the bullseye. The simplicity of MONCN allows the student to use tools to develop a variety of abilities in order to excel in their curricular profile and to improve their daily activities. It can be viewed as a LMS that offers discipline and order of doing things, modelling their lives for the future.

The results of this research support the hypothesis that MONCN is a digital LMS didactic strategy that enhances the transference of knowledge. The success of MONCN can be visualized as an interactive learning process, because the students could communicate with other students in the classroom digitally as well as in person.

The Finance students were positively satisfied with the use of MONCN. This confirms that the academic arena is not only involved in teaching and learning concepts, but also is the place where technology plays an important role to enhance the process of education. MONCN also supports media literacy as a committed response to the challenging mission of education in the 21st century, characterized by abundant digital sources of information that must be included and analyzed in class, where the professor can become the ethical compass that guides the students simultaneously in the process of teaching.

It has been a real discovery to find the effectiveness of MONCN in undergraduate education. This digital LMS empowers the professor to be able to motivate the students to participate in their own educational process.

This research could be replicated in the future in order to find new elements for successfully applying MONCN: different levels of education (pre-school, elementary, high school, graduate, professional, etc.), different types of schools (private vs. public), different types of disciplines (social sciences vs. medicine vs. engineering, etc.). Media literacy is here to stay, but it is everyone's responsibility to know how to model it, guide it, and control it for the welfare of our academic environment. MONCN is revealed as an effective LMS to assess it.

People must continue learning all their lives through the process of learning to learn; that is, learning doing, learning interacting, and learning using. The use of MONCN in the classroom can be summarized in C.S. Lewis's (n. d.) quote: "The task of the modern educator is not to cut down jungles, but to irrigate deserts."

REFERENCES

Adams, J. (1806). From John Adams to Benjamin Rush, 11 November 1806. *Founders Online, National Archives*. Retrieved from http://founders.archives.gov/documents/Adams/99-02-02-5152

American Academy of Ophtalmology. (2011). Uso de la computadora y la fatiga visual. Retrieved from http://www.aao.org/salud-ocular/consejos/uso-de-la-computadora-y-la-fatiga-visual

Babcock, A. (2016). Office 365 in the Classroom: Brainstorming and Delegating in OneNote Collaboration Space. Retrieved from http://blog.adambabcock.com/2016/04/20/office-365-in-the-classroom-brainstorming-and-delegating-in-onenote-collaboration-space/

Clark, J. (1989). Quote from Principal Joe Clark (Morgan Freeman) in the motion picture "Lean on Me", 1989. Retrieved from http://www.imdb.com/title/tt0097722/quotes

Gonzalez, I. (2016). Disponible en consumer preview el complemento Class Notebook para OneNote. Retrieved from http://www.microsoftinsider.es/100020/disponible-cosumer-preview-complemento-class-notebook-onenote/

Heins, M., & Cho, C. (2003). *Media Literacy: An Alternative to Censorship*. New York: Free Expression Policy Project.

Hernandez, A. (2016). Stop Trying to Define Personalized Learning. *EdSurge*. Retrieved from https://www.edsurge.com/news/2016-05-11-stop-trying-to-define-personalized-learning

Hoise, P., & Schibeci, R. (2005). Checklist and context-bound evaluations of online learning in higher education. *British Journal of Educational Technology*, *36*(5), 881–895.

Katherine. (2012). Ventajas y Desventajas de la Tecnología en el ámbito educativo. Retrieved from https://katherineiliana.wordpress.com/2012/06/01/ventajas-y-desventajas-de-la-tecnologia-en-el-ambito-educativo/

Lewis, C. S. (n.d.). *Brainyquote.com*. Retrieved from http://www.brainyquote.com/search_results.html?q=C.+S.+Lewis

March, T. (2012). *13 Reasons Why Digital Learning is Better*. Retrieved from http://tommarch.com/2012/01/digital-learning/

Microsoft. (2015). Creación de lecciones interactivas. Retrieved from http://onenoteforteachers.com/es-MX/Guides/Creaci%C3%B3n%20de%20lecciones%20interactivas%20con%20OneNote

Microsoft. (2016a). Frequently Asked Questions about the OneNote Class Notebook app. Retrieved from https://support.office.com/en-us/article/Frequently-Asked-Questions-about-the-OneNote-Class-Notebook-app-9183c502-9374-42a7-8d59-3a17c377077d?ui=en-US&rs=en-US&ad=US

Microsoft. (2016b). One Note. Retrieved from https://www.onenote.com/

NC State Industry Expansion Solutions. (2015). Pros and Cons of Online Education. *NC State White Papers*. Retrieved from https://www.ies.ncsu.edu/resources/white-papers/pros-and-cons-of-online-education/

Once Noticias. (2013). Ventajas y desventajas del uso de la tecnología en niños. Retrieved from www.oncenoticias.tv, https://youtu.be/gXDgyY1RVqY

OneNote. (2013). Bloc de notas de clase de OneNote. Retrieved March 10, 2016 from https://www.onenote.com/classnotebook

OneNote Team. (2014a). Introducing OneNote Class Notebooks—a flexible digital framework for teaching and learning. Retrieved from https://blogs.office.com/2014/10/07/introducing-onenote-class-notebooks-flexible-digital-framework-teaching-learning/

OneNote Team. (2014b). OneNote Class Notebook Creator updated with top educator requests and new language support. Retrieved from https://blogs.office.com/2014/12/09/onenote-class-notebook-creator-updated-top-educator-requests-new-language-support/

Palomo, J., & Montalvo, S. (2010). *Plataforma para el apoyo a la docencia basada en la Web 2.0 y la actualidad relevante. E-learning en la enseñanza universitaria. I Jornadas de Innovación y TIC (Tecnologías de Información y Comunicación) Educativas* (pp. 43–46). Madrid, España: JITICE.

Partnership for 21st Century Learning—P21 (2016). Framework for 21st Century Learning. Retrieved from http://www.p21.org/our-work/p21-framework

Rosales, J. (2013). ¿Qué es OneNote y para qué sirve? *Apuntes de Office*. Apuntesdeoffice.blogspot.mx. Retrieved from http://apuntesdeoffice.blogspot.mx/2013/10/que-es-onenote-y-para-que-sirve.html

Sanchez, G. (2014). Qué es la tinta electrónica. Retrieved from http://www.gusgsm.com/que_es_la_tinta_electronica

Veiga, A. (2009). *El Chat como herramienta didáctica en la administración de un curso de postgrado. Revista Científica: Teorías, Enfoques y Aplicaciones en las Ciencias Sociales (TEACS), 2(1), Junio, Universidad Experimental de los Llanos Occidentales Ezequiel Zamora.* UNELLEZ.

Walter, D. (2015). Microsoft OneNote for beginners: Everything you need to know. *PCWorld*. Retrieved from http://www.pcworld.com/article/2686026/microsoft-onenote-for-beginners-everything-you-need-to-know.html

KEY TERMS AND DEFINITIONS

Digital Learning: The use of digital media in the process of learning.

Digital Learning Platform: A virtual learning space created to facilitate education in companies and academic institutions.

Digital Media: Encoded (digitally compressed) audio, video, and image content.

Educator: A professor who is convinced inside his mind and his heart that he is transforming persons and not only transferring knowledge.

Electronic Ink: A liquid digital material that is inserted into a flat electronic device simulating a notepad, considered the pioneer of current digital tablets and electronic books. This liquid has a technology that connects to electrical impulses to facilitate digital text writing and image uploads.

Ethics in Finance: Finance Theory in service of human kind. The Financial Analysis of any project could be approached from a profitable point of view without forgetting the importance of values: responsibility, freedom, unity, creativity, respect to others, caring for the less privileged, and caring for our planet.

Leadership: The ability to guide others with an inspired vision to the right decision in a dynamic and efficient way.

Learning Management System: An application installed in a cloud server that manages, distributes, and controls the activities of any group within an institution or organization.

Media Literacy: The process in which the professor becomes an ethical compass to guide students towards critical thinking in evaluating digital media.

Microsoft OneNote Class Notebook (MONCN): An academic digital tool designed to help professors to save time and make course activities more efficient through a paperless environment.

Teaching Innovation: Practical conversion of ideas into new systems and social interactions with the objective of promoting continuous improvements in the teaching processes to trigger quality in education. It is the combination of existing elements which are applied in new ways.

Technology: Scientific knowledge and skills applied to obtain practical outcomes.

Chapter 14
A Trans*+ Media Literacy Framework for Navigating the Dynamically Shifting Terrain of Gender in Media:
Considering Assessment of Key Competencies

Steven S. Funk
Montana State University – Billings, USA

ABSTRACT

Of the many identity markers that students claim and encounter throughout their educational journeys, none might be more salient than gender. While much of the European Union seems to be sloughing off the gender binary as a vestige of the 20th century, many educators and students in the U.S. continue to reinforce the binary through explicit and implicit strategies that normalize the cisgender condition while othering those who are trans*+. The purpose of this chapter is to explore the entrenchment of the gender binary in the American post-secondary system, to analyze the media frenzy currently addressing trans*+ identities, and to offer a theoretical framework of Trans*+ Media Literacy, borne of Critical Media Literacy, to address specifically how post-secondary educators and students can create gender expansive and inclusive spaces that might foster the growth of students prepared to think of gender representation and media production that challenge the binary and encourage gender expansiveness to flourish.

INTRODUCTION

Critical Media Literacy, as defined by Funk, Kellner, and Share (2016), "provides a theoretical framework and transformative pedagogy to empower students to question media, challenge hegemony, and participate in society as justice-oriented global citizens" (23). As media increasingly connect individuals globally, so too do they allow students to access an increased variety of entertainment and communicative

DOI: 10.4018/978-1-5225-3082-4.ch014

Copyright © 2018, IGI Global. Copying or distributing in print or electronic forms without written permission of IGI Global is prohibited.

tools, and differing ideological frameworks, which could enhance their capacity to engage in a global citizenship that acknowledges and appreciates, not merely tolerates, differences. Of the many identity markers that students claim and encounter throughout their educational journeys, none might be more salient than gender. While much of the European Union seems to be sloughing off the gender binary as a vestige of the 20th century, many educators and students in the U.S. continue to reinforce the binary through explicit and implicit strategies that normalize the cisgender[1] condition while othering or exoticizing those who are trans*+[2]. This chapter aims to explore the entrenchment of the gender binary in the American post-secondary system, to analyze the media frenzy currently addressing trans*+ identities, and to offer a theoretical framework for Trans*+ Media Literacy. Borne of Critical Media Literacy, the Trans*+ Media Literacy Framework seeks to address specifically how post-secondary educators and students can create gender expansive and inclusive spaces that might foster the growth of students prepared to think of gender representation and media production that challenge the binary and encourage gender expansiveness to flourish.

THE GENDER BINARY IN POST-SECONDARY EDUCATION IN THE U.S.

Gender identity is, arguably, one of the most salient identity markers of college students today. While completing scholarship applications, on-campus housing forms, and myriad requisite forms, university students declare their gender and/or sex assigned at birth repeatedly. With most colleges in the U.S. using sex assigned at birth to assign dormitory living arrangements, the gender binary has become one of the most normalized ideological state apparatuses[3] on campus. Only recently have a handful of progressive universities offered students mixed-gender living arrangements[4] and the common[5] application offered more than two options for sex and gender identity. With only 23 colleges in the U.S. offering gender neutral housing arrangements and non-discrimination clauses protecting trans*+ students, higher education in the U.S. is known for its gender rigidity (collegeequalityindex.com).

The gender binary, reinforced on college campuses through housing arrangements, is also deeply embedded into college athletics. The National Collegiate Athletic Association (NCAA) requires that trans*+ students, to compete with the team in accordance with their gender identity, must be treated with hormone suppression and/or hormone supplementation of their identified gender for no less than one year (Transathlete.com, 2017) prior to the competition season. This stance regarding trans*+ students reinforces the gender binary, allows for no gender fluidity, and is imposed regardless of the lack of empirical evidence demonstrating the safety and efficacy of hormone treatment[6]. Moreover, it allows no inclusion for intersex students or trans*+ students who may be unable to undergo hormone therapy for a variety of reasons. In fact, recent media coverage of trans*+ NCAA athletes Schuyler Bailar, Kye Allums, and Chris Mosier, rather than taking the opportunity to challenge the gender binary, merely reinscribe it, by referring to these athletes' abilities to compete as males with other cisgender male athletes.

With the growing media attention surrounding trans*+ issues in the U.S., particularly their inclusion and/or exclusion in dorm life, sports, and various facets of the college experience, now is the time to harness the power of the trans*+ media discourse in the college classroom. To this aim, this chapter now turns its attention to trans*+ identities and how they are typically narrativized in American media.

THE TRANS*+ NARRATIVE ARC IN MEDIA

The media sensation created by the attention to contemporary trans*+ individuals is unlike any seen in the before the 21st century. While the medical gender transitions of Christine Jorgensen and Roberta Cowell were publicized throughout the U.S. and U.K. during the early 1950s, popular media simply did not have the technology and reach to spread messages as ubiquitously as they can today. Newspapers of the 1950s published articles about these trans*+ women, and they were offered guest spots on popular television and radio shows, but since a full 40% of citizens in the U.S. and U.K. owned no television during this era (UNSECO, 1963, p. 81-82), the public simply did not have the level of media saturation that it does today. The Jorgensen and Cowell stories likely reached urban areas with dense populations and audiences interested in learning about the developing conversation about the emerging distinction between biological and psychological sex; however, the average individual who was disinterested in the topic would have been able to avoid it with ease.

Sixty years later, media are omnipresent and pervasive, particularly for traditional college students, 96% of whom use cell phones and 88% of whom own lap top computers (Smith, Rainee, & Zickuhr, 2011). Research indicates that 69% of these students read/watch/hear news daily from social media feeds and 70% say that the news they receive regularly features viewpoints contrary to their own (American Press Institute, 2015). Thus, today's college students receive and interact with current events in a way previously unimagined. While this opens exciting new potential for the student interested in gaining global awareness, it also highlights the need for educators to consider ways to incorporate digital and global citizenship learning objectives throughout their curricula. For as much as media coverage of trans*+ individuals has increased in the past 10 years, so too has the violence committed against trans*+ people (Steinmetz, 2015). This suggests that media coverage alone does nothing to reduce trans*+ discrimination and stigmatization, and that educational interventions may be needed.

With *Glee*, *Orange is the New Black*, *I am Cait*, and *Transparent* seemingly heralding a new era of trans*+ media inclusion, many contest the idea the media visibility will inevitably lead to inclusivity for trans*+ individuals. For example, in Transparent and Glee, the role of the trans*+ character is played by a cisgender actor. Moreover; in *I am Cait* and *Orange is the New Black*, the characters are not fully developed, rounded characters critical to the narrative arc who merely happen to be trans*+. It is precisely their identity marker of trans*+ around which their characters are predicated. It is as if there is nothing more to these characters than their gender transition, or their inability to live a cisgender lifestyle. Importantly, these characters' trans*+ identities are honored only after they acquiesce to the medical community's idea of conforming to the gender binary through hormone use and/or surgical procedures to affirm their genders[7].

The recent trans*+ media spectacle underscores the need to problematize trans*+ media narratives, ironically, some of which are created and disseminated by trans*+ individuals. For example, as Caitlyn Jenner, on *I am Cait*, discusses genital surgery with Dr. Marci Bowers, she tells her viewers that she is pre-operative, but plans to have a penectomy and orchiectomy, with a vaginal construction (Bonner 2016). As Hilton-Morrows and Battles (2015) explain:

All of these questions [about trans*+ genitalia] focus on areas of the body generally considered private, but associated with deep-seated cultural assumptions of what it means to be a man or a woman. By the mere adoption of the identity of trans[gender], people find themselves under the powerful and disciplining cisgender gaze. (p.240)

It is precisely the cisgender gaze that has framed the trans*+ narrative of popular American media. Mainstream media frame genital surgery as the final step a character must complete to be considered "transitioned," as if one's identity is ever static, ever not in flux, or transitional.

The exposition of a trans*+ media narrative plot inevitably begins with a trans*+ person realizing "ever since I was four" (Soloway 2014), "I've always had the soul of a woman," (TMZ, 2015), and "my body was betraying me" (Oprah.com, 2011). It is important to note that this realization early on, coupled with an extreme level of discomfort in one's body has been normalized as part and parcel of the trans*+ experience. Thus, the cisgender condition is normalized among media as healthy, while the trans*+ condition is abnormalized as diseased by physical abnormality and mental anguish.

Next comes the rising action of the trans*+ media narrative plot. This will typically offer the cisgender audience a litany of experiences that prove a dysphoric development during puberty for the trans*+ individual. Laverne Cox (2016) claims, "[male puberty] is horrible. It's awful". According to Janet Mock (2011), "I felt my body did not match who I was." And, in the words of Balien Buschbaum, "When you feel uncomfortable in your own body, you feel rage" (Sunrayne, 2013). To date, there is no trans*+ media narrative suggesting that an individual who transitioned did not suffer immensely during puberty. It is as though the same "nature/nurture" argument that often propelled the gay rights movement has been extended into the trans*+ media narrative. Thus, a trans*+ individual enjoying a well-adjusted childhood and typical puberty might be deemed an imposter.

Once the exposition and rising action have both firmly established that the trans*+ media character was experiencing great physical and emotional distress, the climax is revealed in the trans*+ media narrative. Often characterized as a result of seeing another trans*+ person, the climax is the pivotal "coming out" to oneself and the perfunctory "coming out" to all of their cisgender family and friends. Of great significance in this "coming out" climax is the revelation of whether the trans*+ individual will go through with the "final step in an arduous odyssey" (Grundahl, 2011) of transitioning from one gender to another.

The next step in the trans*+ media narrative is the falling action. While this step is most often the shortest portion of a plot in any fictional narrative, the trans*+ media narrative instead emphasizes this step. The prominence of this element undoubtedly relates to Hiltion-Morrow and Battles' theory of the cisgender gaze dominating media portrayals of trans*+ individuals. Inevitably, readers, viewers, listeners, and online subscribers are told the story of how the cisgender relatives and friends of the trans*+ individual all "cope with," "deal with," or "handle" the news of transition.

Following Chaz Bono's transition, myriad headlines advertised that they could explain to readers and viewers how Cher "came to terms with" (Parker, 2013) Chaz's transition. Kim Kardashian has revealed that the Kardashians "attend group therapy to help deal with Caitlyn Jenner's transition" (Hind, 2015). Thus, rather than attending to the complexities involved in gender transition from the perspective of a trans*+ individual, media tend to use the trans*+ narrative to normalize the cisgender condition by explaining to cisgender people how trans*+ people go about making their gender presentation conform with cisgender constructs of normalcy (Michael, 2016). The "falling action" often focuses on what *falls apart* for the cisgender friends and family of the trans*+ individual.

For mainstream media, the resolution of the trans*+ narrative plot attends to how the trans*+ individual will "pass" as cisgender, or become virtually "stealth." Articles such as "42 Celebs We Bet You Didn't Know are Transgender" (Milham, 2015) and "20 Beautiful Transgender Women Who Make Your Girlfriend Look Like a Dude" (Scribol, 2015) tell readers and viewers how amazing it is to imagine these people having been born the "opposite" sex. By emphasizing the post-transition gender conformity that these individuals display, they work to allay any fears in the cisgender audience that trans*+ people may seek to undo the gender binary. These websites explain how before these individuals transitioned, they were labeled as gay. By popularizing how these trans*+ individuals were once considered gay, and how they can now be considered heterosexual post-transition, these sites simultaneously reinforce cisgender bias and heteronormativity.

The narrative arc of the transgender media plot is marked by the exposition of the transgender individual having a realization of difference at a very young age. The rising action, characterized by dysphoric development and discomfort in one's skin, sets in during puberty. Next is the climax - the "coming out" to one's self, but seemingly more important, the "coming out" to cisgender friends and family. According to the dominant media's narrative arc, this act is pivotal, for without the validation or rejection (of cisgender individuals) of one's gender performance, one has no place in the media trans*+ narrative arc. In no other contemporary trans*+ media narrative is this illustrated more clearly than in *Transparent* (Soloway, 2014).

Indeed, the entire narrative arc in *Transparent* is bent toward tasking the dominant cisgender audience to accept protagonist Maura as a woman, predicated upon her moving through this routine trans*+ media narrative plot. Maura explains to her family that she felt different since she was very young, that her adolescent development was particularly trying, and that she began to find herself only after seeing cross-dressers. Next, her family nearly unravels as they all begin to question not only who their parent is, but also their own gender and sexual identities. Finally, Maura begins to "pass" in public as a woman, and conform to gender binary norms, evidenced by her growing her hair long, her wearing makeup, and her accepting lessons from other trans*+ women on walking and sitting in a more "feminine manner." All of this deems the trans*+ person who wishes not to disclose their gender transition as dubious and deceitful:

According to the popular trans* coming out narrative as depicted on Transparent and among popular American televised programs since the 1990s, trans* people who do not "come out," or fully disclose their birth and medical history are deceptive and dishonest. Therefore, "coming out" has become a euphemism for honesty. (Funk & Funk, 2016a, p. 901)

The popularity of *Transparent* proves that this narrative arc is one the cisgender gaze has come to expect, one that is highly profitable. In the year it released *Transparent*, Amazon Prime recorded a 53% growth in subscribers (Kashdan, 2015). While not all this growth can be attributed to the release of *Transparent*, the show was profitable for Amazon Prime (season four premiers in the fall, 2017). This profit, however, may come at the price of favoring the cisgender audience, rather than by truly advocating for more gender freedom and equity.

While the show has many advocates and adversaries battling online and in scholarly circles (Funk & Funk, 2016a), it is important to note the cisgender-centrism of the show and its leading actors. Jeffrey Tambor, who plays protagonist Maura, reveals this perspective when he recalls, "[People] stop and tell me a story, either about the transgender community or more important, their own family and how they relate to this family, because down and dirty, this family is about 'Will you still love me? Will you still be there if I change?'" (Kashdan, 2015). This anecdote reveals two fundamental flaws in the dominant media characterization of trans*+ narratives.

Firstly, Tambor's use of the term "the transgender community" implies that there exists a space where trans*+ individuals "commune," or share common values, interests, and ideological perspectives. Contemporary research suggests this is far from true. In fact, according to the preliminary findings of a current study, many trans*+ individuals report feeling no sense of community, as they describe their gender transition to be "purely medical" in nature, or the "LGBT community" as hostile towards them (Funk & Funk, in press). Vitriolic campaigns such as "Drop the T," (Yiannopoulos, 2015) authored by gay "activists," best illustrate the isolation many trans*+ individuals experience.

Yiannopoulos (2015) contends that it is time to question, "whether many of the people who currently describe themselves as 'trans' are anything other than confused and a bit gay". He also calls hormone replacement therapy and gender affirmation surgery "gruesome bodily mutilation" and considers asking for recognition as another gender the equivalent of asking to be declared Napoleon Bonaparte (Yiannopoulos, 2015). Yiannopoulos is a gay man who has over 2.2 million Facebook followers, and despite his blatantly anti-trans*+ sentiments and outright trans*+ harassment, he was voted the LGBTQ Nation's "Person of the Year" (Hasson, 2017). Thus, the anti-trans*+ sentiment brewing among LGB people is palpable and the use of the term "transgender community" by a cisgender actor reflects a fundamental misunderstanding about what it means to be trans*+ by romanticizing the fantasy of a "community" devoted solely to the interests of trans*+ people. While Tambor likely intended no offense to trans*+ individuals, his comment reflects the dominant cisgender perspective through which mainstream media are produced; therefore, his assumption that trans*+ individuals are primarily concerned with maintaining relationships with their cisgender friends and family aligns with and reinforces this cisgender dominance at the expense of trans*+ autonomy.

Tambor's question, "Will you still love me" implies that there was a static "me" to be loved by the cisgender individual in the first place. This is contrary to contemporary understandings of gender identity. As Butler explains, the trans*+ body, when considered within the cisgender binary ideological framework, "is the marked corporeality—at once all too represented and radically unrepresentable'' (Buter & Anathasiou, 2013, p. 132). Simply put, asking a cisgender person to imagine being trans*+ is as futile as asking a person to imagine being another ethnicity. While the exercise may offer intellectual stimulation, or even promote a modicum of awareness, it is simply impossible. To ask a cisgender individual to imagine loving a trans*+ "me" is to ask that person to imagine the impossible. They simply will not know until they have interacted with the inquirer as a trans*+ individual while validating that person's gender transition. Moreover, "Will you still be there if I change" suggests that a cisgender person has always been there for the trans*+ individual. The adverb "still" implies that the cisgender acquaintance has "been there," yet to "be there" for one carries the semantic weight that implies being positioned in one's life as a safe harbor. This calls into question the authenticity of the relationship to begin with by assuming gender roles were *a priori* paramount to the foundation of the relationship. Lastly, "Will you still be there if I change" connotes that the trans*+ individual is undergoing a fundamental change of personhood, which is not what a gender transition prompts.

While cisgender individuals may see a gender transition as a change fundamentally affecting the core identity of an individual, trans*+ people know otherwise. Current research explains that gender identity is innate, yet one's gender performance may vary depending upon circumstances such as trans*+ hatred, homophobia, class, racism, sexism, etc. Thus, the "change" a cisgender person sees in their trans*+ loved one is merely performative. It is the cisgender individual's rigidity in the gender binary that makes this "change" appear monumental. "Will you still be there if I change" suggests that the cisgender individual's presence in or exodus from the life of the trans*+ person may have some influence over the trans*+ individual's expression of gender. *Transparent* and other mainstream trans*+ media representations aptly highlight how a loved one's gender transition should call into question the binary gender system so rigidly adhered to in the U.S., anecdotally, medically, and legally. Unfortunately, these shows typically stop just shy of doing so, thereby implicitly calling attention to the importance of the cisgender individual's reaction to a trans*+ identity. This only reifies the gender binary and reinforces cisgender privilege. Much of this binary reification results from the difficulty of language, as there are few words a trans*+ person can use to describe their experience; yet as increasingly more people begin to identify as gender fluid and create new terminology, myriad possibilities are being created.

Contemporary trans*+ research suggests that the future of gender expression will expand and evolve as rapidly as has the terminology that describes it. Ehrensaft (2011) calls transitioning the discovery of one's "True Gender Self," which need not conform to the extremes of the gender binary, but indeed may fall somewhere along a spectrum of masculine and feminine, or may be defined by an individual as authentically unique. Ehrensaft (2011) urges professionals working with trans*+ youth to "train [them] selves to live with ambiguity for extended periods of time" while youth discover their "True Gender Self," which ultimately may be genderfluid and may cause a fundamental shift in the way cisgender and transgender are currently perceived as oppositional binary, like male and female (p. 354).

The future of gender identity and gender identity terminology is pregnant with potential; however, in order to seize this "trans media moment" (GLAAD, 2014), students must have the means necessary to further the conversation in a critical manner. To these aims, this chapter now turns its attention to Trans*+ Media Literacy, a framework borne of the Critical Media Literacy framework (Funk, Kellner, & Share, 2016).

THEORETICAL FRAMEWORKS FOR ADDRESSING MEDIA STUDIES IN THE CLASSROOM

The frameworks discussed in this chapter are the products of many organizations and scholars. One of the most influential frameworks in Critical Media Literacy was created by the National Association for Media Literacy Education (NAMLE). According to NAMLE's Core Principles of Media Literacy Education in the United States (2007), media literacy education "help[s] individuals of all ages develop the habits of inquiry and skills of expression that they need to be critical thinkers, effective communicators and active citizens in today's world" (p. 1). Building upon NAMLE's core principles and the Media Literacy National Leadership Conference's (Aufderheide, 1993) core concepts, Kellner and Share (2005) published *Toward Critical Media Literacy: Core Concepts, Debates, Organizations, and Policy*, which outlines five core concepts that are unique to Critical Media Literacy.

CRITICAL MEDIA LITERACY'S FIVE CORE CONCEPTS

As Keller and Share (2005) define it, Critical Media Literacy is predicated upon five core principles: Non-Transparency: All media messages are constructed'; Codes and Conventions: Media messages are constructed using a creative language with its own rules; Audience Decoding: Different people experience the same media message differently; Content and Message: Media have embedded values and points of view; and Motivation: Media are organized to gain profit and/or power. While some media scholars conduct analyses of media in the classroom, most merely focus on the rhetorical devices, persuasive techniques, or language used in media. Critical Media Literacy, however, emphasizes the examination of power relations and the politics of representation inherent in media.

Building upon the five core principles of Critical Media Literacy (Kellner and Share, 2007), Funk, Kellner, and Share (2016) published the Critical Media Literacy Framework. This framework introduces a sixth core concept that underscores the need to interrogate the social and environmental justice impact of mediated spaces and texts.

SIX CONCEPTUAL UNDERSTANDINGS OF CRITICAL MEDIA LITERACY

The six conceptual understandings in the Critical Media Literacy Framework highlight for educators the historical origins of Critical Media Literacy and offer more specific learning objectives. The first conceptual understanding states that "all information is co-constructed by individuals and/or groups of people who make choices within social contexts." This conceptual understanding is based on the theory of social constructivism initiated by Lev Vygotsky and popularized in the early 1980s as educators increasingly rejected Piaget's theory that learning is an action performed by a child in concrete stages with the child being the agent of action. Vygotsky theorized that learners do not necessarily pass through four concrete stages in even development, and more importantly, that learners acquire knowledge vis à vis the cultural milieu in which they develop. According to Vygotsky (1978):

Every function in the child's cultural development appears twice: first, on the social level and, later on, on the individual level; first, between people (interpsychological) and then inside the child (intrapsychological). This applies equally to voluntary attention, to logical memory, and to the formation of concepts. All the higher functions originate as actual relationships between individuals. (p. 57)

Extrapolating from this theory, social constructivism postulates that learning is phenomenologically social and that learners create meaning for themselves within their social contexts. It is thus vital to show students how mediated messages that may even appear "neutral" are always the products of complex processes occurring in relation with a dynamic cultural backdrop.

The second conceptual understanding, "each medium has its own language with grammar and semantics," is based upon the field of semiotics, or the study of signs, specifically, words as signs. Popularized by Roland Barthes, semiotics posits that the sign or symbol should never be mistaken as an element of the natural world. In *Mythologies*, Barthes uses the example of the symbol of wine to illustrate his point. Analyzing print media advertisements, Barthes (1972) demonstrates how media can use wine to be a symbol of sustenance, virility, relaxation, intoxication, and ultimately France (pp. 58-61). Wine itself has no intrinsic properties that are French. The land on which the wine grapes are grown has been signified by humans as French, and people all over the world imbibe wine without becoming French; yet wine has become a symbol of all things French because of our desire to attribute elements of the natural world to that which is purely symbolic. He sums up his analysis with, "to believe in wine is a coercive collective act" (Barthes, 1972, p. 59).

The ways in which language is used in a commercial differs greatly from how it is used in a film. The very medium through which one accesses a text affects one's reading of or interaction with it. Students may feel as though the flow and sequence of a prime-time television show is "natural," but it only appears this way because they have been acculturated into the sign system of television, so they may feel that the break to commercial comes "naturally" in the entertaining narrative, when its sole function is to sell products, not to entertain. Once students have a heightened sense of awareness to the symbols used in media, they can begin to disrupt some patterns that have historically disenfranchised minority groups.

Positionality, the third conceptual understanding, underscores the need to assess one's position as a reader, listener, audience member, message receiver, etc. "Individuals and groups understand media messages similarly and/or differently depending upon multiple contextual factors." This conceptual understanding reminds educators to highlight how students actively negotiate meanings, rather than passively accept them. Developed by qualitative researchers to describe how researchers affect their own research subjects (Mullings, 1999), positionality explains that readers, listeners, and those who otherwise engage with media do so not from a neutral position, but rather from the perspectives they have developed as a result of their ability, class, ethnicity, gender, sexuality, and other identity markers. By considering their own positionality, students can begin to question what kind of audience members they are and how their interpretation of media might change if their identity markers were different.

The fourth conceptual understanding, the politics of representation, calls attention to how, "media messages and the medium through which they travel always have bias and support and/or challenge dominant hierarchies of power, privilege, and profit." As articulated by Kellner and Hammer (2009), "Representations can serve pernicious interests of cultural oppression by positioning certain groups as inferior, thus asserting the superiority of dominant social groups and reinforcing their hegemonic position" (xxxi). The politics of representation reminds educators to task students to consider what is typically represented and, often, more importantly, what is omitted. For what is most frequently depicted will likely be interpreted as "normal." For example, if television viewers were to base their ideas about the relationship between ethnicity and crime by what they see depicted on primetime news, then they would likely assume that Blacks commit the most crime in the U.S. This assumption, however, would be false. Even though Blacks are portrayed as criminals on televised news twice as often as Whites, Whites continue to outnumber Blacks in prison (Chiricos & Eschholz, 2002). Conversely, the average American student may not realize how common mental and physical disabilities are, as people with mental and physical disabilities are rarely cast in prominent roles on primetime television or in films created by major labels. Moreover, when disabled people are cast or portrayed in media, they are frequently used to symbolize evil, or stereotyped (Sauder, 2017). As whiteness and ableism have been dominant identity markers of television and film historically, media tend to represent characters in a way that supports the hegemony of whiteness and ableism. It is important for students to challenge this dominance to increase social justice.

Production/Institutions is the fifth conceptual understanding the framework delineates. "All media texts have a purpose (commercial or governmental) that is shaped by the creators and/or systems within which they operate." This concept pushes educators to remind students why media, especially "entertainment media," are distributed. Many students will defend media as being constructed purely for entertainment. All too often, they forget about the capital produced by media, capital that funds the parent companies of production companies, record labels, technology development, etc. Good examples of this are found in Time Warner and Viacom, two record labels producing "gangsta rap" and hip-hop albums - both record labels with parent companies that heavily invest in the Corrections Corporation of America (CCA), or the private prison system in the U.S. (Davey, 2013). While these connections should not be interpreted to mean that Time Warner and Viacom encourage illegal activities to fill private prisons, critical citizens would benefit from a deep exploration of these relationships and understand that record labels are in business not to entertain, but to profit.

The sixth conceptual understanding of the Critical Media Literacy framework focuses on social and environmental justice, reminding students that "media culture is a terrain of struggle that perpetuates or challenges positive and/or negative ideas about people, groups, and issues; it is never neutral." This key concept differentiates Critical Media Literacy from other schools of Media Studies, which focus more on the utility of digital and media literacies and discrete competencies as a means of furthering learning, as explained by Hobbs and Coiro (2016):

We believe that books, movies, music, television, video games, websites, apps, and social media can serve a variety of learning purposes both in school and in the world outside the classroom. Although the saturation and ubiquity of these forms of communication and expression are integral to our daily life experiences, no one yet has a complete understanding of the full scope of competencies required for participating in digital culture. (p. 628)

For Critical Media Literacy scholars, media do not merely offer learning purposes; rather they embed hierarchical power relations:

that ultimately benefit dominant social groups at the expense of subordinate ones. Hence, [C]ritical [M]edia [L]iteracy provides a theoretical framework and transformative pedagogy to empower students to question media, challenge hegemony, and participate in society as justice-oriented global citizens. (Funk, Kellner, & Share, 2016, p. 23).

While Media Studies researchers have examined rhetorical devices of argumentation and persuasion and the technical skills needed to engage with digital media, those aligned with the tenets of Critical Media Literacy focus on fostering social justice by challenging the myth of objectivity and the neutrality of education engendered among most media. Consequently, Trans*+ Media Literacy is rooted within this framework.

TRANS*+ MEDIA LITERACY

Developing from Critical Media Literacy, Trans*+ Media Literacy challenges the cisgender privilege resulting from the reification of the gender binary. As such, its framework reviews four core considerations that are rooted in Critical Media Literacy while specifically challenging students to identify and disrupt binary and hegemonic representations of gender. Each concept relates to a conceptual understanding of Critical Media Literacy and is defined on the outer side of the circle. Each core consideration is featured in the inner core of the circle. The cycle was utilized, as no one consideration is more important than another and all continually cycle back and are inter-related.

Four Core Considerations of Trans*+ Media Literacy

As Trans*+ Media Literacy is borne of Critical Media Literacy, its theory is undergirded by those conceptual understandings. The proposed Trans*+ Media Literacy Framework builds upon the Critical Media Literacy Framework and specifically focuses on gender representations among media. (See Figure 1)

Pulling from social constructivism, the first core consideration states, "All media are made by individuals and institutions influenced by a matrix of gender roles and expectations that influence various contexts." This consideration reminds educators and students that the knowledge created within a culture can never be parsed out from the gender roles within that culture. For example, the recent push for STEM (Science, Technology, Engineering, and Mathematics) education in the U.S. is a result of the past masculinization of math and science. Because, historically, only men were encouraged and funded for learning math and science until second-wave feminism highlighted many gender inequalities, the U.S. now suffers from a gender imbalance in these fields. This imbalance is reinforced through much mainstream media, as mathematicians, physicians, scientists, and people working outside the home, in general, are continually depicted as male (Lauzen, Dozier & Horan, 2008). Moreover, gender imbalance in media can sometimes be attributed to the way which women and underrepresented people themselves have often internalized and reproduced sexism and genderism within media. Therefore, increasing representation alone will not undo the damaging stereotyping that cyclically reproduces sexism and genderism. Students must begin to acknowledge the way in which gender binarism functions as an ideological state apparatus (Althusser, 1971) in media.

Figure 1. Trans*+ Media Literacy Framework

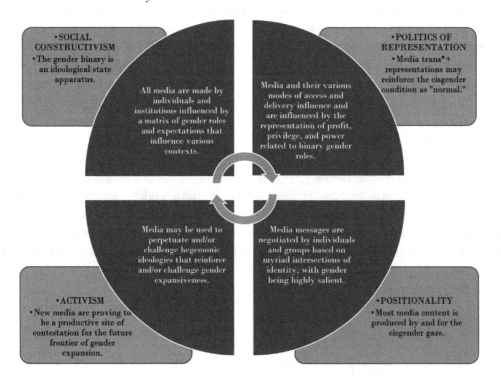

According to Althusser (1971) every ideological state apparatus "'accommodates', in its fashion, some, or all of these themes, their component parts and their resonances" (pp. 138-139): nationalism, liberalism, economism, and humanism. The paradox of ideological state apparatuses, and the reason they become so powerful, is that they can both symbolize a nation's values and the rebellion against these values. With gender, for example, the U.S. has a deeply embedded binary system. That is, people are labeled as male or female on their birth certificates and legal forms of identification. Moreover, schools, religious institutions, and media generally reinforce this binary so that it is seen as "normal." The ideological state apparatus becomes evident when examining forms of "non-binary" or "transgender" identity markers. The very language itself does not accommodate these identities, for they merely become oppositionally binary to "binary" and "cisgender" identity markers. Cisgender binary privilege is weaved into the very fabric of the U.S. culturally and linguistically, serving to benefit the dominant class, which is comprised of cisgender individuals. Returning to Vygotsky's theory of social constructivism, this means that knowledge, especially in the in the U.S., is socially constructed within a strict gender binary. This can have grave implications for trans*+ students, who through their gender presentation, can be interpreted as bucking U.S. patriotism and undermining American cultural norms that undergird capitalism and the stereotypical heteronormative family structure.

The second core consideration of Trans*+ Media Literacy returns to the politics of representation and reminds students that "Media and their various modes of access and delivery influence and are influenced by the representation of profit, privilege, and power related to binary gender roles." As stories about trans*+ individuals gain popularity among media and trans*+ characters are now more frequently depicted in TV and film, it is important to note the often "desexualizing and hypersexualizing mechanisms of media" (Espineira, 2016, p. 326) that cannot be "appreciated as a rupture with biological determinism" (326) but may, in fact, ironically reinforce the gender binary by portraying trans*+ people.

Trans*+ participants in a recent study conducted by McInroy and Craig (2015) explained how trans*+ representation among media may do little to advance the social justice movement for trans*+ individuals:

[That] stupid phrase, like 'sex is between the legs and gender is between the ears,' which is like really transphobic, they [TV media] use it in the shows because that's like the heteronormative way of looking at things so they're just like 'oh because everyone's going to understand that,' but really they don't understand that that actually affects a lot of people who have transitioned. (McInroy & Craig, 2015, p. 610)

This rhetoric, which is designed to portray trans*+ individuals as having a disconnect between their bodies and their minds, merely reinforces the stereotype of trans*+ individuals as physically or mentally ailing, or as needing correction. Positive media trans*+ representation, instead, would feature trans*+ characters whose roles do not focus on the fact they are trans*+. One participant described watching a cupcake show that featured a trans*+ character:

So she just mentioned it [being trans*+] and then the show went on about cupcakes, you know. So it was things like that, where I was just like, 'that's awesome,' . . . So yeah, things like that would be cool to not have the story line focus on the queer character. But some people would argue, 'Well then how do they get visible?' And I'm like, 'That's how they get visible, by being considered like a person ... not like a checkpoint.' (McInroy & Craig, 2015, p. 612)

As indicated by this participant, students need to think critically about whether a trans*+ character in media is being depicted as one who happens to be trans*+ and portrays a rounded development, or whether that character is being flattened, fetishized, or used for shock value merely to increase ratings.

Trans*+ Media Literacy's third consideration returns to the conceptual understanding of positionality to examine how one's gender may affect one's response/reading/participation with a media text. "Media messages are negotiated by individuals and groups based on myriad intersections of identity, with gender being highly salient." It is important for students to understand that although they may have spent many years feeling as though their gender was a "natural" part of who they are, this element of their identity has had a profound impact on the ways in which they interpret media.

Because cisgender and heterosexual identity markers are the dominant ideologies in the U.S., most media content is produced for this audience. It is important to note, however, that just because these identity markers appear hegemonic, that does not make them "natural." It is equally important for educators to try to help students to position themselves differently in order to imagine reading a text differently. A good example of this is the "Cisgender Questionnaire (Funk & Funk, in press b)." Adopted from Rochlin's 1972 "Heterosexual Questionnaire," the "Cisgender" positions participants to feel as though their cisgender identities are under suspect.

The "Cisgender Questionnaire" was used in a recent workshop to understand how it may change a cisgender person's positionality and make them more amenable to using the Trans*+ Media Literacy Framework. The cisgender respondents in the workshop all noted how it highlighted that they assumed superiority without even being cognizant of it because of their cisgender condition. This superiority was often displayed by the invasive questions they felt they could ask trans*+ individuals and the personal and intimate information they felt was typical for trans*+ people in media to reveal. One respondent wrote, "The assumption of inferiority is built into the questions people ask the 'other'" (Funk & Funk, under review, b). Likewise, the assumption of superiority is often built into one's cisgender positionality. It is critical that educators teach students to challenge any assumptions they may unwittingly bring to their interactions with media.

The fourth core consideration of the Trans*+ Media Literacy Framework, activism, reminds educators and students not to insulate themselves from the mediated world, but to harness its power to further social justice for gender expression. "Media may be used to perpetuate and/or challenge hegemonic ideologies that reinforce and/or challenge gender expansiveness." By using the term "gender expansiveness," this core concept disrupts the gender binary by while challenging students to engage productively with media.

New media are proving to be a productive site of contestation for the future frontier of gender expansion. As McInroy and Craig (2015) explain, "Transgender populations are increasingly active producers of online knowledge about transgender identity and issues through active blogging and resources sharing." Thus, new media offer myriad points of connectivity for trans*+ individuals. "The internet also offers the opportunity to develop communities and support networks while remaining geographically dispersed (Heinz, 2012). The importance of developing networks of support for trans*+ individuals cannot be understated, as research indicates a significant positive correlation between social support and mental health (Birkett, Newcomb, & Mustanski, 2015; Mustanski, Newcomb, & Garofalo, 2011; Ryan, Huebner, Diaz, & Sanchez, 2009).

Clark (1969) argues that mediated representations of ethnic minorities develop through four stages: non-representation (no media visibility), ridicule (used among media as mere fodder for comedy), regulation (depicted in hegemonically acceptable roles), and respect (depicted in a variety of roles with depth of character). Raley and Lucas (2010) apply Clark's model to gay, lesbian, and bisexuals individuals, arguing that they have progressed into the stage of ridicule in dominant media, with a few media outlets casting them into roles symbolizing the regulation phase. The initiation of LGB characters into the regulation stage is evident in shows such as "Modern Family" and The "L" Word, shows that depict LGB characters who are monogamist, consumerist, and generally mimic dominant heterosexual coupling. LGB romantic interest on these shows are typically portrayed as couples in which one partner is "butch" - resembling a stereotype of a masculine, heterosexual, cisgender man - and one is "fem" - resembling a stereotype of a feminine, heterosexual, cisgender woman. Rather than celebrating LGB identity markers as diverse and authentic, they mimic the hegemonic standard of romantic coupling in the regulation phase. While LGB characters are climbing Clark's Ladder of media representation, trans*+ characters are frequently struggling to pass the first two rungs of non-representation and ridicule.

Despite much media *coverage* of trans*+ folks, the *representation* is minimal. That is, media erase trans*+ at a rate of approximately 66% (Funk & Funk, 2016b). Research indicates that when trans*+ individuals play roles, or are depicted in television and film, they are most commonly vilified and mocked (Jobe, 2013). When they do achieve representation, they often reinforce "wrong body rhetoric", reinforcing the gender binary in the cisgender imaginative. Yet, the media landscape can be utilized as a catalyst for transformation. As Lovelock (2016) reminds us, "Far from simply a platform for the representation of discourses and debates generated in other domains, media texts are dynamic sites at which cultural identities are produced through the internal logics and conventions of these particular media forms" (4). The Trans*+ Media Literacy Framework is designed to help educators bring the potential of this domain to the foreground while teaching critical thinking skills that can prepare students as global citizens in a highly mediated society. While recent research (Funk & Funk, in press b) suggests that the Trans*+ Media Literacy Framework is a powerful tool for challenging cisgender privilege and developing students' critical thinking skills, the assessment of Critical Media Literacy and Trans*+ Media Literacy remains ripe with potential; therefore, the subsequent section address the literature on Critical Media Literacy assessment, offering recommendations for assessment practices in Trans*+ Media Literacy.

ASSESSING TRANS*+ MEDIA LITERACY

To date, little published research has addressed assessing Critical Media Literacy, so the field remains relatively unchartered for educators wishing to incorporate Trans*+ Media Literacy and assess its outcomes. This offers educators an opportunity to articulate learning outcomes and criteria that are altogether unique. Now is the time to trans*+form assessment.

CRITICAL MEDIA LITERACY ASSESSMENT

Very little research has been published on the assessment of Critical Media Literacy, but extant evidence suggests it is a highly effective framework for teaching critical thinking skills and encouraging global citizenship (Funk, 2013). Recent research has noted assessment as a struggle for Critical Media Literacy instructors who attribute this to their use of "authentic assessment" (Janesick, 2006) and the "creat[ion] of counter-narratives and offering creative multi-media analyses to their [student] colleagues for discussion" (Funk, 2013, p. 93). In one study (Funk, 2013), Critical Media Literacy instructors believed uniformity among assignments (both produced by students and created by instructors) to be "antithetical to the course"

(95). As instructors pushed students to create projects that demonstrated engagement with the material and high levels of criticality, they also encouraged them to use media that the students found "relevant and engaging" (Funk, 2013, p. 95). This, in turn, increased the workload for the instructors who needed to assess the projects, give feedback, and assess edited projects during an iterative, creative process.

Students in this study created counter-narratives to popular texts, analyzed marketing trends in social media, and presented on how popular media construct and reconstruct the hegemony of heteronormativity, white privilege, and monogamy. For example, one student rewrote the Goldilocks and the Three Bears from a feminist perspective that positioned Goldilocks as an architect performing renovations on the bears' cabin, rather than as a weary traveler infantilized through fitting with the "baby" bear's belongings. Another student produced a mock "People" magazine that showed a diversity of gender expression, ethnicity, and adult coupling to challenge gender and sexuality stereotyping. Interested in the science behind advertisements on Facebook, one Critical Media Literacy student presented to the class his experiment with creating different Facebook profiles and recording the advertisements offered to him. This underscored for the class the assumptions that are made by advertisers, while it reminded his colleagues how those assumptions may begin to inform their own self-expectations. The Critical Media Literacy instructors in the study described the assessment process as labor intensive, as they often provided students with feedback and the chance to edit their projects (Funk, 2013, p. 93).

More recently, researchers (Kesler, Tinio, & Nolan, 2016) assessed eighth-grade special education students' critical engagement with popular websites over the course of an eight-week Critical Media Literacy learning module developed by the researchers. The researchers used authentic assessment, measuring their students' learning through the students' production of glogs (graphical blogs that allowed interaction between the students and educators). They found that, "The opportunity to produce counternarratives in the form of glogs had strong outcomes for the student' C[ritical] M[edia] L[iteracy] understandings" (Kesler, Tinio, & Nolan, 2016, p. 21).

Rather than introducing Critical Media Literacy with pre- and post-tests to assess students' learning, Keser, Tinion, and Nolan (2016) argue "these interventions [Critical Media Literacy] are best provided in the context of authentic activity, in which students are asked to locate, navigate, negotiate, and respond to online information with specific purposes in mind" (p. 22). As the researchers scaffolded their students' learning with worksheets and handouts based on the Critical Media Literacy Framework, they reiterated the importance of using Critical Media Literacy to help students "engage in 21st century literacies, establish voices as authors, and construct identities" (Kesler, Tinio, & Nolan, 2016, p. 23). Similarly, the assessment of Trans*+ Media Literacy will likely require formative and authentic assessment methods.

According to Hinrichsen and Coombs (2013) the "critical" dimension of literacy inevitably refers to the "discourses of power around technology" (4). This is underscored in their discussion of "persona" as they address how individuals construct their digital identities (Hinrichsen & Coombs, 2013, p. 12). "Reputation, image projection and interpersonal relations are both mediated by and become repositories in the digital. This has lasting impact on professional profile, both positively and negatively" (Hinrichsen & Coombs, 2013, p. 12). While Hinrichsen and Coombs (2013) underscore the need to integrate critical digital literacies into "syllabus content" and in "assessment design and grading criteria," they ultimately conclude with, "How would it [criticality] be recognised" (p. 13)?

As Critical Media Literacy is a pedagogy focused on social justice, the means of assessment used to measure learning outcomes should also promote social justice. Because each student brings to Trans*+ Media Literacy a different set of challenges, biases, and ideological frameworks, offering students the chance to demonstrate their learning authentically seems appropriate. Assessment is one field that highlights the differences between Critical Media Literacy and Media Literacy; however, as those who seek to teach Trans*+ Media Literacy will invariably be called upon to be accountable for their students' learning, much can be learned from examining assessment in Media Literacy.

MEDIA LITERACY ASSESSMENT

To date, the most oft cited Media Literacy assessment was conducted by Hobbs and Frost (2003). In this study, the researchers compared a control group of 11th graders to a group taking a year-long course on Media Literacy. Conducting a pre- and post-test, the researchers demonstrated a significant positive correlation between the Media Literacy course and the students' development of critical thinking skills (Hobbs & Frost, 2003, p. 352). The media literacy course in this study used the Media Literacy five framing questions, which focus on discerning the author's purpose, techniques used to hold attention, points of view represented, different interpretations, and omissions. While these framing questions share much in common with the Critical Media Literacy framework, they focus more on analysis than production, techniques of rhetorical persuasion than social justice, and do not challenge the construct of normalcy created by media, but instead inadvertently trestle it by failing to address the politics of representation and social constructivism.

The pre- and post-test administered by the researchers consisted of open-ended and multiple-choice questions about a *Times* article reporting on mosquitoes spreading encephalitis; about a three-minute National Public Radio news story about Richard Brinkley; and about a five-minute Channel One news story that reported on Hurricane Andrew (Hobbs & Frost, 2003, p. 342). Concerning each text, students were asked to "describe the most memorable detail," "identify the 'who, what when, where, why,'" and to "put the main idea of th[ese] broadcast[s] into sentences" (Hobbs & Frost, 2003, pp. 341-342). Thus, the emphasis in this assessment was on textual comprehension, not critical analysis. One student's "most memorable detail" may be another's least, depending upon their positionalities (Takacs, 2002; 2003). When asked about a text's target audience, students were offered a list from which they could choose all applicable identity markers from "age-range categories (from age 2 to over 60), two genders, five different racial categories, and five different social class categories (from poor to wealthy)" (Hobbs & Frost, 2003, p. 343). Thus, the assessment questions and answer options themselves reified the gender binary, while they may have also reinforced ageist, racist, and classist ideologies.

A study by McLean, Paxton, and Wertheim (2016), aimed at reducing eating disorders, delineated six measures of media literacy that identify two major components of assessment: media processing and critical thinking. Media processing, according to the authors, involves the processes "by which individuals interpret and internalise media messages and images, and ultimately, whether media messages and portrayals are accepted or rejected" (McLean, Paxton, & Wertheim, 2016, p. 2). Critical thinking entails the process that "inform[s] interpretation of media and facilitate[s] independent and informed judgements about media (McLean, Paxton, & Wertheim, 2016, p. 2). Using various quantitative measures (Likert-scale answers), the researchers measured participants' media processing and critical thinking to decipher whether the participants' level of media literacy inversely correlated with their body dissatisfaction and internalization of the thin ideal (McLean, Paxton, & Wertheim, 2016, p. 4). Indeed, the study found that participants who demonstrated a higher level of criticality were more aware of potentially damaging body messages in media and therefore less likely than their non-critical peers to internalize unhealthy body image stereotypes.

As indicated by the research on Critical Media Literacy, assessing the skills gained by students' use of the Trans*+ Media Literacy framework will likely not be done through multiple-choice tests, pre- and post-tests, or any derivation of any of these means of assessment that can be standardized. Instead, this will require a wholly trans*+formative epistemology of assessment itself.

TRANS*+ MEDIA LITERACY FRAMEWORK: RECOMMENDATIONS

Educators seeking to utilize the Trans*+ Media Literacy Framework to disrupt the gender binary and create more equitable and safe classrooms can take small steps to do so. By using subjective/objective plural pronouns "they/them" when referring to students, instructors will avoid inadvertently misgendering students while teaching how liberating gender expansiveness can be. Moreover, instructors should be mindful of eliminating cisgender privilege by naming the pronouns that are appropriate for themselves in the beginning of the course. Workshops conducted by the Gender Spectrum (2017) have indicated that these small steps can have monumental impact on the classroom and set the tone of the course to be gender expansive and inclusive.

As gender performance is a publicly expressed and regulated identity characteristic, students should respond well to using the Trans*+ Media Literacy Framework in group projects, peer-, and self-assessment. By its trans*+formative nature, the Trans*+ Media Literacy Framework seeks to confront notions of gender normalcy and encourage educators and students to look at the classroom and pedagogy utilized therein as a safe space to explore myriad gender expressions and analyses of mediated gender representations. As the framework is aligned with Critical Media Literacy, and not merely Media Studies, it should push students to consider social justice and the ways in which mediated spaces and communicative acts can expand gender and create more gender equity. Future research addressing the assessment of Trans*+ Media Literacy might offer multiple means and myriad modes of gender expression in the classroom, and more gender equity for everyone.

REFERENCES

Althusser, L. (2014). On the reproduction of capitalism: Ideology and ideological state apparatuses. Brooklyn, NY: Verso.

American Press Institute. (2015). How millennials get news: Inside the habits of America's first digital generation. Retrieved from https://www.americanpressinstitute.org/publications/reports/survey-research/millennials-news/single-page/

Aufderheide, P. (1993). *Media literacy. A report of the National Leadership Conference on Media Literacy*. Aspen Institute: Queenstown, MD.

Barthes, R. (1972). *Mythologies: Roland Barthes*. New York: Hill and Wang.

Birkett, M., Newcomb, M. E., & Mustanski, B. (2015). Does it get better? A longitudinal analysis of psychological distress and victimization in lesbian, gay, bisexual, transgender, and questioning youth. *The Journal of Adolescent Health*, *56*(3), 280–285. doi:10.1016/j.jadohealth.2014.10.275 PMID:25586226

Bonner, M. (2016). *'I Am Cait' Recap: Caitlyn Jenner Considers Gender Confirmation Surgery, Meets with Surgeon.* Retrieved from http://www.usmagazine.com/entertainment/news/i-am-cait-recap-caitlyn-jenner-considers-gender-confirmation-surgery-w203059

Brydum, S. (2015). The true meaning of the word cisgender. *The Advocate.* Retrieved from http://www.advocate.com/transgender/2015/07/31/true-meaning-word-cisgender

Butler, J., & Athanasiou, A. (2013). *Dispossession: The performative in the political.* Cambridge: Polity Press.

Chiricos, T., & Eschholz, S. (2002). The racial and ethnic typification of crime and the criminal typification of race and ethnicity in local television news. *Journal of Research in Crime and Delinquency, 39*(4), 400–420. doi:10.1177/002242702237286

Clark, C. (1969). Television and social controls: Some observations on the portrayal of ethnic minorities. *Television Quarterly, 9*(2), 18–22.

College Equality Index. (2017). List of colleges with gender neutral housing. Retrieved from http://www.collegeequalityindex.org/list-colleges-gender-neutral-housing

Commonapp.org. (2016). The common application expands gender identity options. *The Common Application.* Retrieved from http://www.commonapp.org/whats-appening/news/common-application-expands-gender-identity-options

Cox, L. (2016). Transgender star Laverne Cox backs puberty blocking treatment. *Belfast Telegraph.* Retrieved from http://www.belfasttelegraph.co.uk/entertainment/news/transgender-star-laverne-cox-backs-pubertyblocking-treatment-35159084.html

Davey, D. (2013). Jailhouse ROC: The facts about hip hop and prison for profit. *Hip Hop and Politics.* Retrieved from http://hiphopandpolitics.com/2013/04/24/jailhouse-roc-the-facts-about-hip-hop-and-prison-for-profit/

Domonoske, C. (2017). 17-year-old transgender boy wins Texas Girls' Wrestling Championship. Northcourtrypublicradio. Retrieved from https://www.northcountrypublicradio.org/news/npr/517491492/17-year-old-transgender-boy-wins-texas-girls-wrestling-championship

Eherensaft, D. (2010). Look mom, I'm, a boy: Don't tell anyone I was a girl. *Journal of LGBT Youth, 10*(1-2), 9–28. doi:10.1080/19361653.2012.717474

Ehrensaft, D. (2011). From gender identity disorder to gender identity creativity: True gender self child therapy. *Journal of Homosexuality, 59*(3), 337–356. doi:10.1080/00918369.2012.653303 PMID:22455324

Espineira, K. (2016, July 02). Transgender and transsexual people's sexuality in the media. *Parallax, 22*(3), 323–329. doi:10.1080/13534645.2016.1201922

Funk, J., Vanderhorst, S., & Funk, S. S. (in press a). Trans*+ and intersex representation and pathologization: An argument for increased medical privacy. *The Journal of Law, Medicine & Ethics.*

Funk, S. S. (2013). Critical Media Literacy in pedagogy and in practice: A descriptive study of teacher education instructors and their students [Doctoral Dissertation].

Funk, S. S., & Funk, J. (2016a). Transgender dispossession in Transparent: Coming out as a euphemism for honesty. *Sexuality & Culture, 20*(4), 879–905. doi:10.1007/s12119-016-9363-0

Funk, S. S., & Funk, J. (2016b). *Engaging Gender Expansive Youth through Critical Media Literacy.* Oakland, CA: Gender Spectrum Professionals' Symposium.

Funk, S.S. & Funk, J. (in press). *Healthcare, sex, and gender survey: Findings from a mixed methods study.*

Funk, S.S. & Funk, J. (in press b). Trans*+ Media Literacy Framework: Findings from and reflections on a gender inclusive workshop addressing cisgender privilege".

Funk, S. S., Kellner, D., & Share, J. (2016). Critical media literacy as transformative pedagogy. In M. N. Yildiz & J. Keengwe (Eds.), *Handbook of Research on Media Literacy in the Digital Age.* Hershey, PA: IGI Global. doi:10.4018/978-1-4666-9667-9.ch001

GLAAD. (2014). Network responsibility index. Retrieved from http://www.glaad.org/nri2014

Grundahl, P. (2011). The long, difficult journey of how a man became a woman. *Times Union.* Retrieved from http://www.timesunion.com/local/article/The-long-difficult-journey-of-how-a-man-became-a-2341891.php

Hasson, P. (2017). Milo's 'Legions Of Followers' Force Liberal Website To Name Him 'Person Of The Year'. *Daily Caller.* Retrieved from http://dailycaller.com/2017/01/09/milos-legion-of-followers-force-liberal-website-to-name-him-person-of-the-year/

Heinz, M. (2012). Transmen on the web: Inscribing multiple discourses. In K. Ross (Ed.), *The handbook of gender, sex, and media* (pp. 326–343). Chichester, UK: John Wiley & Sons. doi:10.1002/9781118114254.ch20

Henrichsen, J. & Coombs. (2013). The five resources of critical digital literacy: A framework for curriculum integration. *Research in Learning Technology, 21*(1), 1–16.

Hilton-Morrow, W., & Battles, K. (2015). *Sexual identities & the media: An introduction.* New York, NY: Routledge.

Hind, K. (2015). Kim Kardashian reveals family attend group therapy to help deal with Caitlyn Jenner's transition. *Mirror.* Retrieved from http://www.mirror.co.uk/3am/celebrity-news/kim-kardashian-reveals-family-attend-5979298

Hobbs, R., & Frost, R. (2003). Measuring the acquisition of media literacy skills. *Reading Research Quarterly, 38*(3), 330–355. doi:10.1598/RRQ.38.3.2

Janesick, V. J. (2006). *Authentic Assessment.* New York, NY: Peter Lang.

Jobe, J. N. (2013). *Transgender Representation in the Media. Honors Theses. Paper 132.* Eastern Kentucky University.

Kashdan, J. (2015). Jeff Bezos on 'Transparent' and Amazon's 'insurmountable opportunity'. *CBS News.* Retrieved from http://www.cbsnews.com/news/amazon-ceo-jeff-bezos-transparent-director-jill-soloway-jeffery-tambor-on-disrupting-industries/

Kellner, D., & Hammer, R. (Eds.). (2009). *Media/Cultural Studies: Critical Approaches*. New York, NY: Peter Lang.

Kellner, D., & Share, J. (2005). Toward Critical Media Literacy: Core concepts, debates, organizations, and policy. *Discourse (Abingdon)*, *26*(3), 369–386. doi:10.1080/01596300500200169

Kellner, D., & Share, J. (2007). Toward Critical Media Literacy: Core concepts, debates, organizations, and policy. *Discourse (Berkeley, Calif.)*, *26*, 369–386.

Kesler, T., Tinio, P. P. L., & Nolan, B. T. (2016). What's our position? A Critical Media Literacy study of popular culture websites with eighth-grade special education students. *Reading & Writing Quarterly*, *32*(1), 1–26. doi:10.1080/10573569.2013.857976

Lauzen, M., Dozier, D. M., & Horan, N. (2008). Constructing Gender Stereotypes through Social Roles in Prime-Time Television. *Journal of Broadcasting & Electronic Media*, *52*(2), 200–214. doi:10.1080/08838150801991971

Lovelock, M. Call me Caitlyn: Making and making over the 'authentic' transgender body in Anglo-American popular culture. *Journal of Gender Studies*. doi:10.1080/09589236.2016.1155978

McInroy, L. B., & Craig, S. (2015). Transgender representation in offline and online media: LGBTQ youth perspectives. *Journal of Human Behavior in the Social Environment*, *25*(6), 606–617. doi:10.1080/10911359.2014.995392

McLean, S. A., Paxton, S. J., & Wertheim, E. H. (2016). The measurement of media literacy in eating disorder risk factor research: Psychometric properties of six measures. *Journal of Eating Disorders*, *4*(30), 1–12. doi:10.1186/s40337-016-0116-0 PMID:27895912

Michael, L. (2016). Call me Caitlyn: Making and making over the 'authentic' transgender body in Anglo-American popular culture. *Journal of Gender Studies*. doi:10.1080/09589236.2016.1155978

Milham, E. (2015). 42 celebs we bet you didn't know are transgender. *Likesharetweet*. Retrieved from http://www.likesharetweet.com/inspiring/21-celebs-transgender/

Miller, S. (2016). Trans*+ing classrooms: The pedagogy of refusal as mediator for learning. *Social Sciences*, *5*(3), 1–17. doi:10.3390/socsci5030034

Mock, J. (2011). More than a pretty face: Sharing my journey to womanhood. *JanetMock.com*. Retrieved from http://janetmock.com/2011/05/17/janet-mock-comes-out-transgender-marie-claire/

Mullings, B. (1999). Insider or outsider, both or neither: Some dilemmas of interviewing in a crosscultural setting. *Geoforum*, *30*(4), 337–350. doi:10.1016/S0016-7185(99)00025-1

Mustanski, B., Newcomb, M. E., & Garofalo, R. (2011). Mental health of gay, lesbian and bisexual youths: A developmental resiliency perspective. *Journal of Gay & Lesbian Social Services*, *23*(2), 204–225. doi:10.1080/10538720.2011.561474 PMID:21731405

National Association for Media Literacy Education. (2007). *Core principles of MLE*. Retrieved from https://namle.net/publications/core-principles/

Oprah.com. (2011). *Chaz Bono on when he knew he was transgender*. Retrieved from http://www.oprah.com/own-oprahshow/chaz-bonos-on-when-he knew-he-was-transgender-video

Parker, H. (2013). 'It's a strange thing for a mother to go through': Cher on how she came to terms with Chaz undergoing sex change. *Daily Mail*. Retrieved from http://www.dailymail.co.uk/tvshowbiz/article-2430741/Cher-came-terms-Chaz-undergoing-sex-change.html

Raley, A. B., & Lucas, J. L. (2006, October). Stereotype or success? *Journal of Homosexuality, 51*(2), 19–38. doi:10.1300/J082v51n02_02 PMID:16901865

Rochlin, M. (1972). Heterosexual Questionnaire. *Gender and Sexuality Center*. Retrieved from https://www.uwgb.edu/pride-center/files/pdfs/Heterosexual_Questionnaire.pdf

Ryan, C., Huebner, D., Diaz, R. M., & Sanchez, J. (2009). Family rejection as a predictor of negative health outcomes in white and Latino lesbian, gay, and bisexual young adults. *Pediatrics, 123*(1), 346–352. doi:10.1542/peds.2007-3524 PMID:19117902

Sauder, K. (2017). If you're disabled in an M. Night Shyamalan film, you are either a villain or a super-crip (mostly a villain though). *Crippled Scholar*. Retrieved from https://crippledscholar.com/category/media-representation-of-disability/

Scribol. (2015). 20 Beautiful transgender women who make your girlfriend look like a dude. Retrieved from http://scribol.com/pop-culture/celebrities/beautiful-transgender-women/

Smith, A., Rainee, L., & Zickuhr, K. (2011, July 19). College students and technology. *Pew Research Center*. Retrieved from http://www.pewinternet.org/2011/07/19/college-students-and-technology/

SolowayJ. (2014). Pilot. *Transparent*. Retrieved from http://www.amazon.com/gp/product/B00I3M-PRUK/ref=dv_dp_ep1

Spectrum, G. (2017). *Gender Spectrum*. Retrieved from https://www.genderspectrum.org/quick-links/trainings/

Steinmetz, K. (2015). Why transgender people are being murdered at a historic rate. *Time.com*. Retrieved from http://time.com/3999348/transgender-murders-2015/

Sunrayne, S. (2013). *Profile of a man: Balien Buschbaum*. Retrieved from https://samanthasunrayne.com/2013/07/15/profile-of-a-man-balian-buschbaum/

Takacs, D. (2002). Positionality, epistemology, and social justice in the classroom. *Social Justice (San Francisco, Calif.), 29*(4), 168–181.

Takacs, D. (2003). How does your positionality bias your epistemology? *Thought & Action: The NEA Higher. Education Journal*, 27–28.

TMZ. (2015, April 24). I've always had the soul of a woman. Retrieved from http://www.tmz.com/2015/04/24/bruce-jenner-diane-sawyer-interview-woman-transgender/

Transathlete.com. (2017). Retrieved from https://www.transathlete.com/policies-college

UNESCO. (1963). Statistics on radio and television: 1950 - 1960. Paris: France. Retrieved from http://unesdoc.unesco.org/images/0003/000337/033739eo.pdf

Vygotsky, L. (1978). *Mind in Society*. London: Harvard University Press.

Yiannopoulos, M. (2015). I Am So Done With The Trans Outrage Brigade: Why I'm Supporting 'Drop The T'. *Breitbart*. Retrieved from http://www.breitbart.com/big-government/2015/11/10/i-am-so-done-with-the-trans-outrage-brigade-why-im-supporting-drop-the-t/

ADDITIONAL READING

Grant, J. M., Mottett, L. A., Tanis, J. T., Harrison, J., Herman, J. L., & Kiesling, M. (2011). *Injustice at every turn: A report of the national transgender discrimination survey*. Washington: National Center for Transgender Equality and National Gay and Lesbian Task Force.

Haas, A. P., Rodgers, P. L., & Herman, J. L. (2015). *Williams suicide report: Findings of the national transgender discrimination survey*. American Foundation for Suicide Prevention & The Williams Institute, UCLA. Retrieved from http://williamsinstitute.law.ucla.edu/wp-content/uploads/AFSP-Williams-Suicide-Report-Final.pdf

Holland, L., Matthews, T. L., & Schott, M. R. (2013, April). That's so gay: Exploring college students attitudes toward the LGBT population. *Journal of Homosexuality*, *60*(4), 575–595. doi:10.1080/00918369.2013.760321 PMID:23469818

Ingrey, J. (2012). The public school washroom as analytic space for troubling gender: Investigating the spatiality of gender through students self-knowledge. *Gender and Education*, *24*(7), 799–817. doi:10.1080/09540253.2012.721537

Miller, J. (2017). Why (a)gender identity matters now, more than ever: Perspectives during a Trump era. New York: Metropolitan Center for Research on Equity and the Transformation of Schools: New York University.

Rankin, S., Weber, G., Blumenfeld, W., & Frazer, S. (2010). Campus pride 2010 national college climate Survey. Q Research Institute for Higher Education. Retrieved from https://www.campuspride.org/wp-content/uploads/campuspride2010lgbtreportssummary.pdf

Schull, D. (2015). Communicative acts of identity: Non-binary individuals, identity, and the internet [Master's Thesis]. California State University.

Vanderhorst, B. (2015). Whither lies the self: Intersex and transgender individuals and a proposal for brain-based legal sex. *Harvard Law & Policy Review*, *9*(1), 241–275.

KEY TERMS AND DEFINITIONS

Cisgender: The identification with one's sex marker at birth.

Gender Binary: The idea that only two genders, male and female, exist.

Gender Identity: The association one feels with the cultural traits assigned to a gender in that culture.

Politics of Representation: The idea that representation, and the lack thereof, is political in nature, and often reinforces hegemonic ideologies.

Positionality: The concept that an individual's position, or viewpoint, in society is never static, but constantly mediated by various identity markers, with some being more salient than others, depending upon the circumstance.

Social Constructivism: The understanding of learning as a collaborative endeavor relying upon interpersonal interactions.

Trans*+: A term published by SJ Miller (2016) that refers to gender identities outside of cisgender. Among others, these identities may include agender, gender fluid, gender queer, transgender, transsexual, and many others.

ENDNOTES

[1] The term "cisgender" denotes the condition wherein one's gender identity is congruent, or synonymous with one's natal birth marker. For more, see Brydum (2015).

[2] Miller created the term "trans*+" to be inclusive of non-binary and/or non-cisgender identities. According to Miller (2016): "While some activists draw on the use of trans (without the asterisk and/or the plus sign), which is most often applied to trans men/women, the asterisk with the plus sign more broadly references ever-evolving non-cisgender gender identities, which are identified as, but certainly not limited to, (a)gender, cross-dresser, bigender, genderfluid, genderf**k, genderless, genderqueer, non-binary, non-gender, third gender, trans man, trans woman, transgender, transsexual, and two-spirit. How the term trans*+ continues to take form will evolve as identities and theories morph in indeterminate ways" (2).

[3] For more on ideological state apparatuses, see Althusser (1971).

[4] Currently only 38 universities in the U.S. offer gender-neutral housing (college equality index). Of those 38, 15 have no gender identity non-discrimination clauses, leaving 23 universities (at the time of publication) capable of offering non-discriminatory housing to trans*+ students.

[5] According to commonapp.org (2016), the common application will allow 2016-2017 applicants the option to name their "sex assigned at birth" as different from their current gender identity, which will offer applicants a "free response text field" that should facilitate among potential students and universities utilizing the common application the opportunity for students to present themselves authentically and for universities to honor their commitment to campus diversity.

[6]   Further, it would require a trans*+ student to either stop competing for one year, or undergo hormone treatment with all of the accompanying morphological changes while competing alongside cisgender individuals whose endocrine systems use different hormones. For an example of this conundrum, see the media coverage over the controversial title held by Mack Beggs. As a trans*+ man in Texas, he is barred from competing on his school's male wrestling team. Beggs won the 2017 Texas Girls' Wrestling Championship although living as male and undergoing hormone therapy for over a year (Domonoske, 2017).

[7]   For more on the struggle for contemporary gender autonomy in medicine and trans*+ legal rights to privacy, see Funk, Vanderhorst, & Funk (under review).

Chapter 15
Teaching Digital and Media Literacy as Cross-Cultural Communication

Mary Catherine Boehmer
English Language Fellow Program, USA

ABSTRACT

As technology increasingly becomes a part of our day-to-day lives in the United States and throughout the globe, there is a greater push for students to develop the digital and media literacy skills necessary for the twenty-first century. In the United States, students learning these skills often come from a wide range of linguistic and cultural backgrounds. The diversity of the U.S. is one of its greatest strengths, but with this diversity come cultural differences in access to technology and how it is used across different cultural contexts. This chapter analyzes the constructs of digital and media literacy, the ways in which culture can be defined and how that can affect the intersectional identities performed in the social and participatory world of Web 2.0. It also examines access to technology and how technology is used for communication and accessing information in Russia, Germany, and Azerbaijan, and how approaching digital and media literacy through the lens of cross-cultural communication can help teachers to better meet the needs of learners from diverse backgrounds.

INTRODUCTION

Digital literacy and media literacy, and digital literacy in particular, have recently become a major area of focus in education. Much emphasis is placed on working with students to become both digitally and media literate, and many teaching positions list as a requirement that instructors have a background in technology. Yet, in educational settings, there is a tendency to focus on the development of discrete skills, providing physical access to technology in a given educational institution (e.g. SMART Boards, Wi-Fi networks, computer labs, laptop carts, and 1:1 iPad programs) and using learning management systems (e.g. Blackboard, Moodle) in the classroom. Emphasis is often placed on the use of technology in the classroom rather than on teaching students the various ways to access information, communicate,

DOI: 10.4018/978-1-5225-3082-4.ch015

Copyright © 2018, IGI Global. Copying or distributing in print or electronic forms without written permission of IGI Global is prohibited.

and produce content, and in what contexts a given format or medium is appropriate. Developing digital literacies can often take the form of learning to use given programs or devices rather than focusing on conceptual dimension of use (Lankshear & Knobel, 2008).

Compounding this is a lack of consensus on what digital literacy is. Since Gilster's (1997) seminal *Digital Literacy*, there has been a seemingly endless revision to the definition due to constantly evolving technology which often outpaces any discussion of what digital literacy actually entails. In it, Gilster described digital literacy as the mastery of a set of core competencies necessary to access, understand, and use information from a variety of formats using a network of computers. Gilster noted that shifting in technology meant that digital literacy was ultimately the ability to remain aware of these shifts and to find ways to access information and communicate about issues and seek help from the network of people also connected to these computer networks.

Later, Bawden (2001) expanded on this broad definition of digital literacy and attempted to define literacy in terms of specific skills. Of these, he included the ability to accumulate information from diverse and reliable sources; analyze and evaluate the validity of retrieved information; understand content in with non-sequential and incomplete information; interact with both digital tools and more traditional tools; use networks of people to share ideas and access missing information; and publishing, communicating, and accessing information.

More recently, Warschauer and Matuchniak (2010) viewed digital literacy through the lens of 21st century skills, and listed three areas of skills: information, media, and technology; learning and innovation skills; and life and career skills. As a precursor to these skills, information literacy, media literacy, and information communicative technologies must first be achieved. Additional skills within these skill sets include the what was termed the "Four Cs of 21st century learning: creativity and innovation, critical thinking and problem solving, and communication and collaboration skills as part of learning and innovation skills, and the ability to adapt, lead, be proactive, and communicate effectively fall under the umbrella of career skills. Aviram & Eshet-Alkalai (2010) approached digital literacy as focused on discrete and practical skills. They included photo-visual literacy, the ability to analyze visual representations of information; reproduction literacy, the ability to use technology to create a piece of work using information accessed digitally; branching literacy, the ability to search for and access information in a non-linear way; information literacy, the ability to access, evaluate, and assess both digital and traditional information; and socio-emotional literacy, or connecting with others online and navigating those interactions.

In today's world, Digital literacy and media literacy are inevitably linked. Whereas in the past television and newspapers were the primary source of media consumption, today media is accessed primarily through the Internet in some form or fashion – watching YouTube videos on a smartphone, opening up a news app, or reading an article (or maybe just the headline) a Facebook friend has posted. Media does not exist in a vacuum, and we employ a variety of tools to access it. In many cultures, social media is increasingly the way media is accessed.

Media literacy is intrinsically tied to digital literacy in today's increasingly digital world since media is increasingly accessed through digital means. With digital tools that allow for content to be more quickly and easily produced, the ability to analyze and evaluate media has become increasingly important as media moves away from its traditional print and audiovisual formats. Just as digital literacy evolves as new digital tools and competencies appear, how media literacy is defined is changing (Livingstone, 2010).

Following Livingstone (2003), media literacy can be defined as ability to access, analyze, evaluate, and produce media in and across different networks, platforms, and mediums). Media literacy is cultural, critical, and creative – that is, understanding, evaluating, and analyzing media involves cultural and contextual knowledge, the ability to pass judgment, and engaging with and transforming information in a given text from words on a page (or screen) to our own perceptions (Burn and Durren, 2007). The process of making meaning from media is both tied to one's cultural background, personal preferences, and ability to transform meaning.

However digital and media literacy are defined, there is some element of personal decision-making and transformation of meaning, particularly in the Web 2.0 world. Web 2.0 tools are social, participatory, and interactive, meaning that content accessed in the Web 2.0 world comes with a series of choices and as well as a variety of social relationships to be formed, developed, and maintained. With one post, a huge audience can be reached, and with one email, information can be sent via attachment and shared with multiple parties as direct or indirect recipients. Previous technology did not allow for this. A phone call or a letter would generally be a one-to-one interaction. Even when taking into account the use of the Internet, Web 1.0 technology was generally static and not intended to be interactive or social. Web 2.0 tools, conversely, are mutable, social, and interactive. Anyone can be a creator of content, and many end up being consumers of content without any real intentionality behind it. One glance at a Facebook news feed shares information that a given user was not searching for, but ends up with all the same - YouTube videos that friends have shared, pictures of life events like weddings and children being born, news articles, and general status updates. That content is available, even without searching for it. This content can be avoided, but it would take unfollowing or unfriending someone to truly avoid it. Web 2.0 encourage users to create content without the deliberateness that Web 1.0 tools required, and content is shared with users even if they are not looking for it. What's more, no two users will experience that information in the same way. Users have a choice – even a series of choices – with any content they consume via Web 2.0. Like it, upvote or downvote it, comment on it, share it, all of the above – in the world of Web 2.0, everything is possible, and we interact with the content in various ways.

Because Web 2.0 tools come with a variety of decisions to be made, culture is a necessary factor to consider when working with students on developing digital and media literacy skills. Our patterns of behavior identify us as members of a particular cultural group, both online and offline, and we perform our identities by behaving in ways that are culturally acceptable, both cognitively and affectively, within a given context. Culture is also intersectional. In each context, we perform the identity – or intersecting identities - that match a given context. None of these identities is mutually exclusive. Within countries, regions, cities, age groups, institutions, people perform the identities that correspond to their interactions within a given setting.

Any place that people can be found, there is culture – an implicit set of rules and behavior that is expected to be used based on the people with whom we are interacting and where these interactions take place. There are ways that we interact with our boss in face-to-face interactions as well as over email, and ways we interact with a close friend in person and online. Cultures exist within digital spaces as well, and within various countries. Although Facebook is available in nearly every country, Facebook behavior varies from place to place. The digital tools may be available—or they may not. Even so, approaches to online interactions vary because people vary, both as members of their culture and as members of smaller subcultures.

Culture is organized, and even the most complex and perplexing systems have a rationale behind them, although it might not be clear at first glance. In high-context cultures, connections to people are crucial, while in low-context cultures, these connections become less important. Culture is organized, but the reason why something is done in a given way is far more understood and accepted to someone coming from that cultural background.

Finally, culture is stable yet mutable. This is important to note in light of the increasingly digital world we know live in. Technology, and particularly the Internet, has made it easier than ever for people to connect with each other. Web 2.0 tools by their nature focus on making the Internet a collaborative, participatory, and social experience in which no two users interact with content in the same way. Where there are people, there is culture, though, meaning that in addition to the cultures and subcultures in which we exist, there is the added layer of culture in how we use technology to communicate and access information. How can we interact with people in a culturally acceptable way using technology? How do we know how and where to access information, understand and evaluate it? How can we be a creator of content in this new, participatory world of technology – and should we? These are all questions we face when using technology to communicate and to access information, but somehow within our own culture we often know the rules – or at least many of them – without having to consider these questions too carefully. For those coming from different cultural backgrounds, these questions become a bit more difficult to answer – if we even realize these are questions we need to answer. How can we know something if we aren't even sure what questions to ask?

A LOOK AT TECHNOLOGY USE IN OTHER CULTURES

Russia

In 2007, I was a Fulbright English Teaching Assistant in Russia, teaching English and American Studies at Irkutsk State Linguistic University (IGLU). Technology at IGLU was limited. There was no Wi-Fi in the university, and perhaps two to three computers in the lone university building could access the Internet. Teachers were allowed to print only about 10 pages a week for all of their classes. Many of the classrooms did not have chalkboards. As for Internet in the dorm where I was living, there were a few options. An Internet card, similar to a calling card, could be bought from a kiosk that would allow dial-up using the landline. Other options included getting a cell phone plan with Internet (if one had access to a high-end cell phone) or going to an overpriced Internet café.

It was certainly possible to use technology as part of the classroom with a little resourcefulness. I used Internet to come up with creative lessons for my classes and to research information. I had a laptop and could play YouTube videos with Internet, then replay them without Internet. My classes varied. One day I might be asked to explain the American health care system; another day I might be asked to discuss cheerleading as a sport. I was an English Teaching Assistant, so I didn't have classes of my own. Instead, every few days, a teacher would tell me what they wanted me to teach, and I would develop something. Sometimes I would get a topic and feel completely stumped about what to do in the classroom, or I just would be given no topic at all and need to come up with something. What to do? Luckily, the 13 Fulbright ETAs scattered all over Russia had a Google group. We emailed regularly, shared lesson plans and offered advice in the classroom, complained about culture shock and offered solutions for adjusting. We lived in a country spanning eleven time zones, but even so, we had a community. The Internet gave me access to information, ideas, solutions, and people who experienced similar situations.

It was easy to be judgmental of the Russian teachers and students I worked with. I could find materials and ideas for classes online and research information about the topics we were covering on the Internet. Why couldn't they? It was not until years later when I realized how fortunate I had been to have had access a computer and Internet, and when I went off to college, I had a laptop and Wi-Fi spanning the whole college campus. Even going to a country with limited access to technology, I still had digital literacy skills that came with living in a world where technology was nearly always immediately available. If I could just find a way to access technology, I was fine. Coming from a middle-class background, I also had money that many of my Russian colleagues and students did not. I had a laptop and could spend my money on Internet cards from the local kiosks and at Internet cafes. Many Russians were not so fortunate.

Few Russians I knew had Facebook. Instead, many used VKontakte, Odnoklassniki, and Odnogrupniki. VKontakte, or VK, is the most popular social networking site in Russia, with 55.7 million users ("Number of monthly VKontakte users," 2017). It is essentially an exact replica of Facebook, with a few small exceptions. First – nearly everyone on the site speaks Russian. Facebook is a far more globalized and multilingual space. In a country where the concept of *svoi* (one of the clan, related by marriage, one of us) and *chuzhoj* (stranger, foreigner, alien, outsider, someone else, other) Russian social groups of any kind existed in silos – small, tight-knit clans.

Svoj and *chuzhoj* is a key cultural concept. One can exist in multiple silos, but there is always a clear understanding of who is *svoj* and who is *chuzhoj* in any given setting. Being and maintaining one's status as *svoj* in Russian society is crucial, and becoming or even becoming acquainted with someone who is *chuzhoj* is strongly avoided (Galie, 2007). One's perception of another's status as *svoj* or *chuzhoj* even affects how Russians approach conversation (Yokoyama, 1995).

In the social and participatory world of Web 2.0, a site like VK helps eliminate the risk of encountering someone who is *chuzhoj* by providing a space primarily only for Russian speakers – a group of *svoj*. An added bonus is the ability to share media, especially music and films, in a way that is not possible on Facebook due to copyright laws (Kozlov, 2011). Such laws are considerably more flexible in Russia. Odnoklassniki and Odnogrupniki allow Russians to reconnect with former classmates and members of their cohort at university. (The Russian university system follows a cohort model – students are placed in groups have every single class with that group until graduation). These social media sites allow Russians to access people easily determine those who are *svoj* and avoid those who are *chuzhoj*.

This use of VK – or of other Russian-language social networks – demonstrates how digital tools can influence access to information. In a Russian-language social network, any media shared is also likely to be in Russian, meaning it can portray information with a degree of bias – Russian journalists who are critical of the government or of policies, for instance, can easily find themselves to be a target, and so who volunteer as a source. A VK user will not have access to media in the same way as a Facebook user, simply because the language limits access to a wide range of sources. A Fulbright ETA in my cohort shared an English-language article on the revocation of the European University in St. Petersburg. A few of his Russian Facebook friends, in relatively faraway Novosibirsk, commented on it with surprise and dismay. They had heard nothing about it until his Facebook post.

Germany

In 2013, I moved to Essen, Germany. I was an English instructor at a few universities, including the Universität Duisburg-Essen. I had expected that technology use and access would be quite similar to that of the U.S., but it was not. It was significantly less digitized than an American higher education setting – or workplace setting, for that matter. Onboarding documents, bank account information, and others had to be signed on paper rather than scanned and sent back. Class lists and room assignments were not available through a faculty portal – instead, they were emailed to the instructor shortly prior to the first day of class. Instructors were expected to keep track of attendance on their own, then email the attendance list back to the main office at the end of the semester. When applying for a full-time instructor position at another university, I was surprised to find that a paper application was required. A colleague explained that paper was more official and emphasized the importance of such formality in German culture.

Wi-Fi was available, but much less readily available than in the United States. This was due to potential legal issues – if an illegal activity, such as downloading a pirated movie, took place over a Wi-Fi network, the owner of the Wi-Fi network would be held legally responsible. To avoid this, many coffee shops and cafes did not have Wi-Fi available. The university had Wi-Fi available with a username and password, but in contrast to many universities and community colleges in the U.S., no guest login option was available.

Adding to the lack of digitalization was a concern for privacy. There were a number of Germans I knew who did not have Facebook out of digital data privacy concerns, and many of those who did added only those they would count as actual friends rather than acquaintances. This was not all like in the United States, where a friend request will often appear after meeting someone. A number of German Facebook users used shortened versions of their names so that they would be more difficult to find. There were far fewer posts from German friends on Facebook compared to those from American friends, who seemed to be constant creators of Facebook content. This is due primarily to privacy concerns, rather than over a desire to avoid connecting with others (Kowalewski et al, 2015).

Germans generally preferred consumption over creation in social media. Many German friends only posted once every few months. A person who posted on Facebook constantly was considered to be narcissistic, a friend once told me. Party invitations were done as a group message through the messaging service WhatsApp or Facebook messenger rather than through a Facebook event – or at least until many abandoned WhatsApp over privacy concerns for sharing data with Facebook. Emails and landline phone calls are a common way to keep in touch with friends and family. Social media is simply used differently than it is in the U.S.

In Germany, the most valuable use of the Internet seemed to be in accessing, assessing, and verifying information, especially news. In 2013, more than 48.03 million Germans aged 14 years and older read newspapers several times a week in their spare time – more than half of the country ("Number of persons reading newspapers," 2017). In 2014, roughly 12.84 million Germans aged 14 years and older used the internet at least once a day to get access to the latest news and information, and 19.39 million did so at least once a week ("How frequently do you use Internet," 2017).

In 2016, shortly after Donald Trump was elected president, I met up with a German friend, V. V told me she joined Twitter solely to follow Donald Trump. She had read about Donald Trump's tweets in the reputable German news source *Der Spiegel*. Suspicious that *Der Spiegel* had published an elaboration of the actual tweets, she decided to join Twitter to follow the primary source to ensure the information from news sources was accurate. She has yet to publish a single tweet herself. Instead, like many Germans, she prefers to be consumer rather than producer of digital content.

Azerbaijan

In 2016, I moved to Baku, Azerbaijan for an English Language Fellowship with the Office of English Language Programs at the U.S. Department of State. Through this grant, I have taught English and developed English language projects and programs in conjunction with the U.S. Embassy in Baku. Many of the issues I faced with technology in Russia 2007 have been similar here, at least in educational institutions. There is no outright lack of access to technology, but it is limited nonetheless. The university where I teach has three Wi-Fi networks. None of them will actually connect. There is likely access to a projector if I ask the right person, but it seems like more trouble than it is worth. Few students or teachers have the money to pay for data on their phones, making it a challenge to use phones as a point of access to Internet in class.

A few Ministry of Education-favored primary and secondary institutions do have access to technology. At one school where a colleague works, there are SMART Boards in several classrooms, but unfortunately, no one was ever shown how to use them, and as a result they are not used. At another university, I saw a computer science class held in the computer lab. Each student has access to a computer, but the students had pushed the keyboards away and were instead writing on notebooks. When the digital tools are available, there seems to be no clear idea of how they could be integrated meaningfully into the learning process.

This is compounded by a mutual-face culture, meaning that there is a high level of concern for both self-face and other-face (Hofstede, 1991). There is a heavy focus on theory over practical application in educational contexts in general, but especially in terms of using digital tools. Practical application of technology presents a face-threat, and as a result, there is not a wide variation in using technology in innovative and participatory ways. Facebook, Instagram, and the messaging service WhatsApp are the primary digital tools used by Azerbaijanis, because these allow Azerbaijanis to communicate the most quickly and easily. Azerbaijani culture has a strong focus on social relationships and their connection with status, and social maintenance and displays of status can be easily done through these tools – sending voice or text messages to individuals or groups, posting selfies and tagging prestigious Facebook acquaintances to gain likes and therefore raise their status, and liking and commenting on other posts as a form of social maintenance. Other tools, even sending email and attaching documents, present a challenge to many Azerbaijanis, or are simply not used because Facebook, Instagram, and WhatsApp are all the digital tools they feel they need to communicate.

This is not to say that all educational institutions are devoid of technology or and that all educators are uncomfortable with technology. There are institutions working with technology in innovative ways, but they are few and far between. However, in such a face-oriented culture, there is tendency to use technology-related buzzwords with confidence, even when a given educator does not know what a given educational technology tool is or does not know how to actually use it. For instance, a select group of schools participated in ICT-based school collaboration in eTwinning, in which classes participate in online collaborations with students in Europe. While an excellent initiative, its funding for technology seems to be concentrated in a handful of institutions. Many teachers that I know claimed to use eTwinning in their classes, but I have been to many of their schools, and there seems to be a lack of technology to make eTwinning possible in their classrooms, yet eTwinning is now all over Facebook. Once the first eTwinning status updates appeared, suddenly far more educators were posting that they, too, had begun eTwinning with their students. It had become a technology buzzword, it seemed that every teacher started to do it, or at least create the illusion that they have through Facebook posts.

Young and old Azerbaijanis alike are very active on Facebook, and actively create, develop, and maintain friendships. This is especially true for women. Gender roles are strong in Azerbaijan, and women generally do not have the same mobility as men. It is frowned upon for women to go out after dark, and their primary duty is to care for their families at home. Facebook offers a tool to promote one's own status through posts, perform social maintenance through liking and commenting on others' posts, and the ability to message social connections without stepping foot outside the door. Often Facebook users will attempt to establish a potential social connection through Facebook prior to meeting. Friend requests are often sent without having met the recipient, or only meeting the recipient in passing. A relationship can be established through likes and comments on social media before resulting in a face to face meeting. This, too, is a way to increase status. Pearce (2015) tells a story of a young Azerbaijani photographer who was able to build a friendship with socialites through commenting and liking posts on social media and gaining access to their outer circle. In terms of maintaining relationships, it provides young women – who often have low mobility in the evenings and are not permitted to venture outside – the opportunity to connect with others without leaving their home. Birthday and holiday greetings can be shared via social media easily and at no cost and further solidify and maintain both new and existing relationships.

Instagram is also incredibly popular among young Azerbaijanis, and much of the content includes selfies and carefully posed pictures. On social media, there is a tendency to be producers over consumers of content in social media, primarily with photos. Facebook is also a very popular source for the creation of content, but it mostly consists of similar content to Instagram. For Azerbaijani women in particular, the Internet, and particularly social media, allow users to show a wider audience - beyond those who were invited to a given event or gathering, such as a wedding – how lavish, prestigious, or exclusive it was (Kama, Chu, & Pedram, 2013).

The result of this cultural focus on the social aspect of technology is a tendency to access media incidentally. When a Facebook contact shares media, the result will often be numerous likes, comments, and (if the headline is interesting enough) shares. Often media that is shared is by Azerbaijani news sources such as AzerNews or fake news. News is spread through word of mouth or virtual word of mouth – meaning Facebook.

CONCLUSION

There remains a debate about the constructs of areas of literacy, particularly in light of the mutable nature of the digital tools used to consume and produce content and the numerous ways in which we can interact with media using digital tools. Cultural backgrounds play a part, as users of technology make a series of decisions with every click and opportunity for interaction, whether that decision is to engage or not to engage with the content or with other people in these digital spaces. As Lankshear & Knobel (2008) noted, it is easy to focus on discrete skills and programs for students to master rather than to focus on how and why digital and media literacy skills should be developed. In working with diverse students, it is important to meet them where they are and consider how and why they are used to accessing technology in the past and their goals in using technology both in and out of the classroom. What may seem to be an intuitive use of educational technology may come across as technology for the sake of technology to a student from a different cultural background. Being aware of these possible differences can help educators to make informed choices about incorporating technology in a way that is accessible, culturally relevant, and meaningful to students. Similarly, media can be quite different outside of the U.S., and even within the U.S. As an example, my parents, both Mississippians, come to the Boston area relatively often and are always stunned by the way television news in the Northeast portrays current events in contrast to Mississippi – not only how these events are covered, but which events are considered worth covering at all. Even seemingly simple tasks such as finding information about a current event may be approached in an altogether different manner. When working with diverse groups of students, make no assumptions about how they use technology or access media. A needs analysis focusing on digital literacy or media literacy skills, a simple class-based discussion, or activating schemata in are excellent ways to gauge students' pre-existing knowledge comfort levels. From there, educators can make informed decisions about the best way to approach using – and improving – these skills.

REFERENCES

Bawden, D. (2008). Origins and concepts of digital literacies. In L. Co & K. Mi (Eds.), *Digital Literacies: Concepts, Policies and Practices* (pp. 17–32). New York, NY: Peter Lang.

Burn, A., & Durran, J. (2007). *Media Literacy in Schools: Practice, Production and Progression*. London, NY: SAGE Publications.

Eshet-Alkalai, Y., & Chajut, E. (2010). You can teach old dogs new tricks: The factors that affect changes over time in digital literacy. *Journal of Information Technology Education*, *9*, 173–181.

Galie, J. (2007). *The clan, the clique, and the alien in Russian literature and society*. New York, NY: ProQuest Dissertations Publishing.

Gilster, P. (1997). *Digital Literacy*. New York, NY: Wiley Press.

Hofstede, G. (1991). *Cultures and Organizations: Software of the Mind*. London, UK: McGraw- Hill.

Kamal, S., Chu, S.-C., & Pedram, M. (2013). Materialism, attitudes, and social media usage and their impact on purchase intention of luxury fashion goods among American and Arab young generations. *Journal of Interactive Advertising*, *13*(1), 27–40. doi:10.1080/15252019.2013.768052

Kowalewskia, S., Zieflea, M., Ziegeldorfb, H., & Wehleb, K. (2015). Like Us On Facebook! – Analyzing user preferences regarding privacy settings in Germany. *Paper presented at the meeting of the 6th International Conference on Applied Human Factors and Ergonomics*, Aachen, Germany. doi:10.1016/j.promfg.2015.07.336

Kozlov, V. (2011). In the cross hairs: Russian social network VKontakt sparks piracy worries. *Billboard*, *123*(5).

Lankshear, C., & Knobel, M. (2008). *Digital Literacies: concepts, policies, and practices*. New York, NY: Peter Lang.

Livingstone, S. (2003). The changing nature of audiences: From the mass audience to the interactive media user. In A. Valdivia (Ed.), The Blackwell Companion to Media Research (pp. 337-359). Oxford: Blackwell.

Livingstone, S. (2003) The changing nature and uses of media literacy. *Media@LSE Electronic* Working Papers, No. 4

Livingstone, S. (2010). Giving people a voice: On the critical role of the interview in the history of audience research. *Communication, Culture & Critique*, *3*(4), 566–571. doi:10.1111/j.1753-9137.2010.01086.x

Pearce, K., Barta, K., & Fesenmaier, M. (2015). The Affordances of Social Networking Sites for Relational Maintenance in a Distrustful Society: The Case of Azerbaijan. *Social Media+ Society*, 1(2).

Statista. (n. d.). How frequently do you use the internet to consume or access online press or news content? Retrieved March 8, 2017 from https://www.statista.com/statistics/661910/online-news-usage-frequency-germany/

Statista. (n. d.). Number of monthly active VKontakte users via desktop connections in Russia from December 2012 to December 2014 (in millions). Retrieved March 8, 2017 from https://www.statista.com/statistics/425423/number-of-monthly-active-vkontakte-users/

Statista. (n. d.). Number of persons reading newspapers during their free time in Germany from 2010 to 2015, by frequency (in millions). Retrieved March 8, 2017 from https://www.statista.com/statistics/383150/leisure-newspaper-reading-frequency-germany/

Warschaeur, M., & Matuchniak, T. (2010). New technology and digital worlds: Analyzing evidence of access, equity, and outcomes. *Review of Research in Education*, *34*(1), 179–225. doi:10.3102/0091732X09349791

Yokoyama, O. (1995). Slavic Discourse Grammar and the literary text. in O.T. Yokoyama (ed.), *Harvard Studies in Slavic Linguistics*, *3*, 187-212.

Zong, J., & Batalova, J. (2017). *Frequently Requested Statistics on Immigrants and Immigration in the United States*. Retrieved March 9, 2017, from http://www.migrationpolicy.org/article/frequently-requested-statistics-immigrants-and-immigration-united-states

KEY TERMS AND DEFINITIONS

Buzzword: A word or phrase that is very popular at a given time.

eTwinning: A platform for educators and students to collaborate on projects and participate in cultural exchange with European students.

Face: The avoidance of embarrassment for those in a given interaction at all costs.

Mutual-Face Culture: A culture in which there is concern for how one is perceived in a given interaction as well as concern for how other participants are perceived.

Selfie: A picture, often flattering, taken of oneself by oneself.

SMART Board: An interactive whiteboard. A projector displays the computer screen (or a plain white screen), and users can write on the board using SMART Board markers. Notes can then be saved as a file.

Social Maintenance: Maintaining meaningful social relationships through regular contact.

Social Network: A digital network used to connect others.

VKontakte: A Russian social networking site, far more popular in Russia than Facebook. Its interface is nearly identical to Facebook. The major differences are language (Russian vs. multilingual).

WhatsApp: A messaging application that allows users to send messages over data rather than using text messaging. Users can send photos, videos, voice recordings, and share locations. Individuals can be messaged, and groups can be created, managed, and messaged. Voice calls and video calls are also possible. Facebook bought WhatsApp in 2014, leading to privacy concerns for some.

Chapter 16

A Counterpoint on American Education and Media:
One Fulbright Scholar's Quest to Prepare Students for Travel to America

Shahla Naghiyeva
Azerbaijan University of Languages, Azerbaijan

ABSTRACT

Coming from Azerbaijan to America as a Fulbright Scholar, I packed as many assumptions as I did suitcases. After conducting my research, I realized that everything I learned while visiting the United States should be shared with my students, to prevent them from some culture shock and to prepare them to be globally-minded, thinking of mediated messages about foreign countries in a critical manner. This chapter is a result of this endeavor, a sort of auto-ethnographical tour through the America that I saw through my positionality as an Azerbaijani woman.

INTRODUCTION

Emerson once wrote, "Life is a succession of lessons which must be lived to be understood" (Brainyquote. com). I have had several lessons in my life, three of which are closely connected with the Fulbright Visiting Scholar Program that has fantastically been playing the role of a life teacher for the great number of world scholars such as myself for seventy years by establishing their network and enabling them to visit abroad and to share their experience. Upon my return from the United States, my answer to questions about my international exchange was: "I consider America to be Heaven and the people living there angels." One can find my expression exaggerated, but this is view of an Azerbaijani woman making a trip to a foreign country by herself, having never had other trips to foreign countries except Moscow. In the U.S., I found myself alone among Americans, apart from my three children, experiencing cultural shock, feeling desperate and lonely, yet I was surrounded by love, concern, and smiling faces. What follows are few specific lessons regarding American education and media that I share with my own students to increase their global awareness and media criticality.

DOI: 10.4018/978-1-5225-3082-4.ch016

Copyright © 2018, IGI Global. Copying or distributing in print or electronic forms without written permission of IGI Global is prohibited.

Coming from Azerbaijan to America as a Fulbright Scholar, I packed as many assumptions as I did suitcases. After conducting my research, I realized that everything I learned while visiting the United States should be shared with my students, to prevent them from some culture shock and to prepare them to be globally-minded, thinking of mediated messages about foreign countries in a critical manner. This chapter is a result of this endeavor, a sort of autoethnographical tour through the America that I saw through my positionality as an Azerbaijani woman.

After receiving my first Fulbright award in 2003, I conducted a research study on poetry translation from Azerbaijani into English and vice versa at East Carolina University, NC in collaboration with American poets Julie Fay, Peter Mackuk. Based on my collaborations, I published a textbook entitled *Literary Translation: Theory and Practice* for my students at the Azerbaijan University of Languages. In addition, I published another textbook called *Usual and Unusual America*, sponsored by the US Embassy to Azerbaijan with my husband, Musallim Hasanov, a screenwriter at Public TV visited the U.S. as well. The goal of the book was to prevent Azerbaijani students travelling to the U.S. for the first time from having cultural shock. For the purposes of this chapter, I focus on American education and media, and trying to incorporate these lessons into a curriculum to develop students' global citizenship and media criticality.

AMERICAN EDUCATION THROUGH AN AZERBAIJANI PERSPECTIVE

The American education system of America is vastly different from the Azerbaijani education system. This chapter will first explore the primary school grades. I had the opportunity of getting acquainted with work system of one of the elementary schools of Greenville city. The school principal, Isabella Weaker, informed me that there were 485 pupils at the school. She also mentioned that majority of the pupils were African American and 25% of the students were representatives of other ethnicities. With a high population of this school's student being from economically disadvantaged families, many of the school children walk directly from the bus that takes them to school to the cafeteria for a free breakfast.

As I discussed the school with Weaker, I noticed there is a TV set in all the rooms and in the room of the principal. The principal can watch what is happening in the classrooms. As the classes begin in the morning, the principal greets all the schoolchildren and the teachers. Then two pupils give a talk on the most important events taking place in the history of America this day. They also memorize the names of the celebrities born this day. After all this, the principal urges the schoolchildren and teachers to take a loyalty oath to the state flag of the country. The text of the oath consisting of is as following:" "I pledge allegiance to the Flag of the United States of America, and to the Republic for which it stands, one Nation under God, indivisible, with liberty and justice for all." During taking this oath the pupils and the teachers stand in a queue turning their faces to the state flag hung in the classroom putting their hands on their hearts.

Following the Pledge, I attended a music class at the school. The teacher does not make the pupils recite the text of the poem comprising the song. A copy of the text is given to each pupil and they sing the text of the music from the paper. Students seldom recite the texts; rather they approach the texts analytically and learn to analyze the texts in America. A fellow Azerbaijani, Rana Mammadli (personal interview), a music teacher in America, characterizes the pupil-teacher attitude this way: "They don't get the pupils tired like in our country. That is why the Americans look for an entertainment in every-thing." It was surprising to me when I heard parents ask their school-aged children, "Have you had fun today?" Azerbaijani parents typically ask, "How did you answer the teacher's question? What mark, or grade, did you get?" There is freedom in learning in America. There is an implicit understanding that learning should be fun.

The majority of the pupils finishing the secondary schools where I was situated preferred to continue their study at the universities or colleges. Though East Carolina University is financed by the American government, education there is not free of charge. The students living in North Carolina pay for their annual education about $7000 per academic year, while for the ones coming from other states pay much more. The annual tuition for foreign students is about $20,000 to $22,000. The American students are free to decide their clothing and every building on campus is modern technological conveniences. In Azerbaijan, when we say "library," we mean shelves with dusty books on them. But one may envy the tidiness of the libraries in the US. Any person may come to the library freely, and may use a book, or any document there. Use of internet and computer in the libraries is free of charge in the libraries. All the libraries there are open to public. One can easily find where any book has been placed on the shelves using a computer and take it without causing any trouble for anyone. This level of technology makes knowledge easily accessible to students. Also, accessible to students is a deluge of media.

Journalism and journalists are quite different in America from those in Azerbaijan. In America, jour-nalism is considered to be an influential profession, and journalists belong to the category of the best living people like advocates and medical doctors. There is no practice (that I witnessed) of encouraging the reporters to write article for the newspaper by offering fee or bribe. And there is no need for the journalists to come to the office and sit there till the evening. They can write the article at home having gathered the material by going to the places of the accidents and send them online to the editorial office. The main task for all working for the newspaper is to accomplish the task given by editorial on a high level.

I had the opportunity to speak with officials at the editorial office of "The Daily Reflector" published in Greenville city. At the end of my talk with the head of the news department of the newspaper, I wanted to know about their salary our interlocutor answered our question diplomatically: "Salary of our editors give them the chance of buying the most expensive car." Then she added: "About $60 000-$70 000." A big part of the income of the newspaper in America comes from advertising, and benefit taken from it promises the journalists to get high salary. Thus, one should question the amount of influence these companies have on the publications they publish.

Along with having privileges, the journalists in America have some restrictions too. All these restric-tions are connected with deep respect to human rights. For example, an American telejournalist must get permission to take the image of any person except at public events. And this permission is officially confirmed in written form. There are special contract forms for it. The reporter should have the person whom he/she will shoot with camera take sign the contract. That person may ask money for it, too. The reporter should be ready to pay at least a symbolic amount. The short content of this permission con-tract is, "I understand my voice, name and image to be shot and recorded by different mechanical and electronic devices and have no restrictions on the producers and other employees." Even the reporters cannot shoot the private houses with the camera without permission of the owners. Privacy seemed to be a deep American cultural value.

WHAT DO AMERICAN STUDENTS AND TEACHERS KNOW ABOUT AZERBAIJAN?

The imaginations of majority of Americans about former Soviet Union are conflicting. Nowadays, Russia is considered to be a source of "danger" for some Americans. The countries that gained independence after the collapse of the Soviet Union are regarded as miserable developing countries. For example, my landlady wanted "to teach" me how to use the electrical modern house conveniences. When she discovered that the majority of those conveniences were familiar to me, she apologized and confessed that she had little information about my country. And she was an educated woman – a professor at East Carolina University. Later, I got to know that her 22-year-old son had heard of my country and he had made a citizen of "Small Azerbaijan" situated on the foot of Caucasus Mountains the main hero of his short story that he had written some months before.

Within the last years, much has been done in the direction of presenting Azerbaijan to the world. Today, Azerbaijan has become a partner of the USA strategically. Our country is one of the closest allies of the U.S. in antiterrorism coalition. The leading oil companies of the USA play a crucial role in exploring the oil fields of the Caspian Sea. However, the majority of Americans did not seem to know a country by the name Azerbaijan. It is not because of discrimination, or information blockade.

It seems that in America, not having certain kinds of knowledge, even that considered rudimentary by many, is culturally acceptable. For example, a university professor in America might know a simple fact that one learns in secondary school textbooks, yet it is not considered to be mistake for them. They are usually busy with their own work and do not think it necessary to "waste time" reciting facts and figures. When they need any information, they look it up the internet. From this point of view, there are hundreds of small countries like Azerbaijan in the world and it is unbelievable and impossible for Americans to know all of them.

ADDRESSING MY ASSUMPTIONS

I had supposed that the Americans' attitude towards Muslims would have changed for the worse after 9/11, but after my talks with Muslims living there, and reading statistics on the newspapers, I realized that I had been mistaken. According to statistics cited (Yee, David, & Patel, 2017), about 7 million Muslims live in the U.S. Islam is considered to be a religion developing in a high speed and spreading widely. The experts explain it with ration increase, high birth rate in Muslim families, and the strengthening of interest to Islam in the last years.

CONCLUSION

These are the visions of the American that I have seen. I should also mention that a five-month trip is not enough to see the whole America, or to know it well. One needs years to live there and understand the things deeply. Every state in the U.S. is considered to be a separate governing body; every state has its own characteristic features, differing values, and traditions. So, my observations may be different from the impressions of one who visits another state.

My aim is not to idealize Americans or America, or discover "a new America." Undoubtedly, there are also disadvantages of America as the other societies. Like many other nations Americans are not "white spoons taken out from the milk." Notwithstanding the facts that there are many wrongs in the policy of the U.S. Government, all can confess that USA is a country of the free people. And the way leading to the development and progress within our educational institutions begins from freedom.

America is a country of rich traditions. A country rooting from the respect to the superiority of laws. America is a country guaranteeing equal development of different cultures and free development of religions. America is a country of equal opportunities for all. America is a country of high development and very modern technologies.

My Fulbright research period enabled me to learn more about America and different aspects of American life. Senator William Fulbright said: "The Fulbright Program aims to bring a little more knowledge, a little more reason, and a little more compassion into world affairs, and thereby to increase the chance that nations will learn at last to live in peace and friendship" (Fulbright, p.5).

In the field of Media Literacy, the path from criticality to cynicism can seem a slippery slope, yet my travels in America assured me that educators can continue to infuse curricula with technology, choice, and freedom of speech while fostering deep intellectualism and global democracy. The more I learned about America, the more I was sure that the ways leading to peace and democracy for all nations passes through the U.S.

ACKNOWLEDGMENT

Special thanks to Dr. Steven S. Funk for copy-editing my work.

REFERENCES

Brainyquote.com (n. d.). Ralph Waldo Emerson. Retrieved from https://www.brainyquote.com/quotes/quotes/r/ralphwaldo103524.html

Guide for Fulbright visiting scholars. (n. d.). Privileges and Obligations Under the Fulbright Scholar Program. Retrieved from https://docs.google.com/viewer?url=http%3A%2F%2Fwww.cies.org%2Fsites%2Fdefault%2Ffiles%2Fdocuments%2FVisiting-Scholar-Guide.pdf

Yee, V., David, K., & Patel, J. K. (2017). Here's the Reality About Illegal Immigrants in the United States. *Migrationpolicy.org*. Retrieved from http://www.migrationpolicy.org/article/frequently-requested-statistics-immigrants-and-immigration-united-states

ADDITIONAL READING

Core Fulbright US Scholar Program. (n. d.). Retrieved from http://www.cies.org/program/core-fulbright-us-scholar-program

Fulbright. (n. d.). Retrieved from https://eca.state.gov/fulbright

Fulbright Scholar Visiting (Non-U.S.) Program. (n. d.). Retrieved from http://www.cies.org/fulbright-program-and-general-requirements

Fulbright US Student Program. (n. d.). Retrieved from https://us.fulbrightonline.org/about/fulbright-us-student-program

World Fact Book. (n. d.). Azerbaijan. Retrieved from https://www.cia.gov/library/publications/the-world-factbook/geos/aj.html

KEY TERMS AND DEFINITIONS

Azerbaijan: A nation with a majority-Turkic and majority-Shia Muslim population - was briefly independent (from 1918 to 1920) following the collapse of the Russian Empire; it was subsequently incorporated into the Soviet Union for seven decades. Azerbaijan attained independence from the Soviet Union in 1991. Capital city is Baku. It is located in the Caucasus region surrendered by Caspian Sea to the east, Iran to the south, Russia and Georgia to the North, Armenia to the west of the country.

Cultural Shock: A sense of confusion and uncertainty sometimes with feelings of anxiety that may affect people exposed to an alien culture or environment without adequate preparation.

Fulbright Visiting Scholar Program: The Fulbright Program is the flagship international educational exchange program sponsored by the U.S. government and is designed to increase mutual understanding between the people of the United States and the people of other countries. The Fulbright Visiting Scholar Program provides grants to approximately 850 foreign scholars from over 100 countries to conduct post-doctoral research at U.S. institutions from an academic semester to a full academic year (https://exchanges.state.gov/non-us/program/fulbright-visiting-scholar-program).

Appendix

GLOBAL EDUCATION RESOURCES AND ORGANIZATIONS

- AFS-USA (formerly the American Field Service) http://www.afsusa.org/
- Asia Society http://asiasociety.org/education/global-cte-toolkit
- Belouga https://belouga.org/
- Bright https://brightreads.com/
- ByKIDS Their world their films http://bykids.org/2016/films/see-the-world-through-my-eyes/
- The Centre for Global Education (CGE) https://www.centreforglobaleducation.com/
- The Centre for Global Education: an international education http://globaled.us/
- Connections based learning http://www.connectionsbasedlearning.com/clp.html
- Edutopia A comprehensive website and online community that increases knowledge, sharing, and adoption of what works in K-12 education. https://www.edutopia.org/
- ePals: Create real world, culturally-enriching learning experiences with worldwide ePals classroom matching. http://www.epals.com
- Erasmus+ EU's programme http://ec.europa.eu/
- Generation Station: Play an energy game to create a working power plant. http://education.nationalgeographic.com/education/media/plan-it-green-generation-station/?ar_a=4
- GEO Awesomeness http://geoawesomeness.com/
- Give Something Back International http://gsbi.org/
- Global Classrooms http://www.global-classrooms.org/
- Global Dimension: Find classroom ideas for demonstrating how our daily decisions have a global impact. (Grades K-12) http://globaldimension.org.uk/classroom/
- Global Issues Network (GIN) http://globalissuesnetwork.org/
- Global Media Literacy Education Resources http://galeri.wikispaces.com/GML
- Global Learning Resources https://awesome-table.com/-Kp0VFXrsMGun8MlqmsO/view
- Global Lives Project http://globallives.org/
- Global Math Project https://www.theglobalmathproject.org/
- Global Oneness Project https://www.globalonenessproject.org/
- Global Partnership for Education http://www.globalpartnership.org/
- Global SchoolNet: Link your class or school to students from around the world.
- http://www.globalschoolnet.org/gsntour/
- Global Virtual Classroom http://www.virtualclassroom.org/
- Google for Education https://edu.google.com/case-studies/brooklyn-prospect/

- Globe Trottin' Kids https://www.globetrottinkids.com/about/
- Fear Inc. Explore the $57 million network fueling Islamophobia in the United States. https://islamophobianetwork.com/
- Five Clue Challenge http://5cluechallenge.weebly.com/
- Free Rice: For each correct answer, they donate 10 grains of rice to "Help End Hunger." http://freerice.com/#/english-vocabulary/1515
- Fulbright. https://eca.state.gov/fulbright
- Fulbright US Scholar Program. http://www.cies.org/program/core-fulbright-us-scholar-program
- Fulbright Scholar Visiting (Non-U.S.) Program. http://www.cies.org/fulbright-program-and-general-requirements
- Fulbright US Student Program. https://us.fulbrightonline.org/about/fulbright-us student-program
- Hello Elephant https://www.helloinelephant.com
- Iearn Learning with the world https://iearn.org/
- ISTE Global Collaboration Network https://sites.google.com/view/isteglobalpln/home
- Kids Go Global: Explore global issues, take action, and inspire others to do the same. http://www.kidsgoglobal.net/site-tour-schools/
- Migrant Integration Policy Index http://www.mipex.eu/
- Mission US- Interactive way to learn history http://www.mission-us.org/
- NASA Quest Challenges: http://quest.nasa.gov/
- National Center for Education Statistics (NCES) https://nces.ed.gov/nationsreportcard/
- National Education Association http://www.nea.org//home/37409.htm
- National Geographic: Explorer Classrooms https://www.nationalgeographic.org/education/programs/explorer-classroom/
- PBS: Engineering games can help young learners to think critically and solve problems. http://pbskids.org/games/engineering/
- PBS: Young learners can play teamwork games in groups.
- http://pbskids.org/games/teamwork/
- Peace Corps https://www.peacecorps.gov/
- Peace Crane Project https://peacecraneproject.org/
- Peace Village http://www.peacevillageinc.org
- Plan it Green: As Mayor, students use critical thinking skills to plan and build a city. http://education.nationalgeographic.com/education/media/plan-it-green-big-switch/?ar_a=4
- TakingITGlobal For Educators TIGed http://www.tigweb.org/tiged/
- Teaching Travelling https://www.teachingtraveling.com/
- Time For Kids: Stay on top of current world events and global issues. http://www.timeforkids.com/
- Travel Beyond Excuse http://travelbeyondexcuse.com/grants/
- Travelling Teddy http://travelingteddybear.com/
- UNESCO IBE - Global Citizenship Education http://en.unesco.org/gced
- UNESCO- Global Citizenship Education (GCED)- http://www.unesco.org/new/fileadmin/MULTIMEDIA/HQ/ED/pdf/GCED4-infographic.pdf
- US Census serve as the leading source of quality data about the nation's people and economy https://www.census.gov/

- Your Challenge: Create a wearable or transportable way to generate 1 watt of electricity. http://education.nationalgeographic.com/education/media/engineering-exploration-challenge-3/?ar_a=4
- World Community Grid What if you could support causes you care about while reading this post? Your device's unused computing power can help scientists tackle cancer, HIV/AIDS, Zika, clean energy and other humanitarian issues. https://www.worldcommunitygrid.org/
- World Oceans Day http://www.unesco.org/new/en/oceans-day
- WorldSavy http://www.worldsavvy.org/resources
  70+ Stupendous Sites to Promote Global Education | PODLS http://www.podls.com/strategies/view/?ID=1332769913

Compilation of References

Abram, D. (1997). *The Spell of the Sensuous: Perception and Language in a More-Than-Human World.* New York: Vintage Books.

Adams, J. (1806). From John Adams to Benjamin Rush, 11 November 1806. *Founders Online, National Archives.* Retrieved from http://founders.archives.gov/documents/Adams/99-02-02-5152

Akkoyunlu, B. (1996). The influence of computer literacy competencies and existing curriculum programs on student achievement and attitudes. *Hacettepe University Education Faculty Journal, 12*(12), 127–134.

Al-Bahrani, A., & Patel, D. (2015). Incorporating Twitter, Instagram, and Facebook in economics classrooms. *The Journal of Economic Education, 46*(1), 56–67. doi:10.1080/00220485.2014.978922

Alper, M., & Herr-Stephenson, R. (2013). Transmedia Play: Literacy Across Media. *Journal of Media Literacy Education, 5*(2), 366–369.

Alpert, B. (2010). Integration of quantitative analyses in qualitative research. In L. Cassan & M. Kromer-Nevo (Eds.), *Data analysis in qualitative research* (pp. 333–356). Beer Sheva: Ben Gurion University of the Negev. (in Hebrew)

Althusser, L. (2014). On the reproduction of capitalism: Ideology and ideological state apparatuses. Brooklyn, NY: Verso.

American Academy of Ophtalmology. (2011). Uso de la computadora y la fatiga visual. Retrieved from http://www.aao.org/salud-ocular/consejos/uso-de-la-computadora-y-la-fatiga-visual

American Press Institute. (2015). How millennials get news: Inside the habits of America's first digital generation. Retrieved from https://www.americanpressinstitute.org/publications/reports/survey-research/millennials-news/single-page/

Amin, A., & Roberts, J. (2008). Knowing in action: Beyond communities of practice. *Research Policy, 37*(2), 353–369. doi:10.1016/j.respol.2007.11.003

Amore, D. (2002). *Internet future strategies: How pervasive computing services will change the World. Amerika.* Prentice Hall.

Anderson, J., Franklin, T., Yinger, N., Sun, Y., & Geist, G. (2013, September). Going mobile, lessons learned from introducing tablet pcs into the business classroom. In *Proceedings of the Clute Institute International Academic Conference*, Las Vegas, NV.

Anderson, M., & Perrin, A. (2015). 15% of Americans don't use the Internet. Who are they? *Pew Research Center.* Retrieved from http://www.pewresearch.org/fact-tank/2015/07/28/15-of-americans-dont-use-the-Internet-who-are-they/

Anderson, C. A. (1997). Effects of violent movies and trait hostility on hostile feelings and aggressive thoughts. *Aggressive Behavior, 23*(3), 161–178. doi:10.1002/(SICI)1098-2337(1997)23:3<161::AID-AB2>3.0.CO;2-P

Anderson, L. W., & Krathwohl, D. R. (Eds.). (2001). *A taxonomy for learning, teaching, and assessing: A revision of Bloom's taxonomy of educational objectives*. New York, NY: Longman.

Appiah, K. A. (2006). *Cosmopolitanism: Ethics in a world of strangers*. W.W. Norton and Company.

Atav, E., Akkoyunlu, B., & Sağlam, N. (2006). Prospective teachers' internet access facilities and their internet usage. *Hacettepe University Education Faculty Journal, 30*, 37–44.

Aufderheide, P. (1993). *Media literacy. A report of the National Leadership Conference on Media Literacy*. Aspen Institute: Queenstown, MD.

Ayala, N. A. R., Mendívil, E. G., Salinas, P., & Rios, H. (2013). Kinesthetic learning applied to mathematics using kinect. *Procedia Computer Science, 25*, 131–135. doi:10.1016/j.procs.2013.11.016

Babcock, A. (2016). Office 365 in the Classroom: Brainstorming and Delegating in OneNote Collaboration Space. Retrieved from http://blog.adambabcock.com/2016/04/20/office-365-in-the-classroom-brainstorming-and-delegating-in-onenote-collaboration-space/

Bandura, A., Ross, D., & Ross, S. (1963). Imitation of film-mediated aggressive models. *Journal of Abnormal and Social Psychology, 66*(1), 3–11. doi:10.1037/h0048687 PMID:13966304

Barker, R. (2006). Homo machinus versus Homo sapiens: A knowledge management perspective of virtual communities in cyberspace. *Communication Theory and Research, 32*, 226–240.

Barnes, K., Marateo, R., & Pixy Ferris, S. (2007). Teaching and learning with the Net Generation. *Innovate, 3*(4). Retrieved from http://csdtechpd.org/pluginfile.php/1622/mod_glossary/attachment/25/Teaching_and_Learning_with_the_Net_Generation.pdf

Barnes, K., Marateo, R. C., & Ferris, S. P. (2007). Teaching and learning with the Net Generation. *Innovate: Journal of Online Education, 3*(1), 1–8.

Baron, R. A., & Richardson, D. R. (1977). *Human aggression*. New York: Plenum Press. doi:10.1007/978-1-4615-7195-7

Barr, R. B., & Tagg, J. (1995). From teaching to learning—A new paradigm for undergraduate education. *Change: The Magazine of Higher Learning, 27*(6), 12–26. doi:10.1080/00091383.1995.10544672

Bar-Tal, S., & Seifert, T. (2014). *Groups on the social professional network Shluvim – An investigative view. Research report*. Israel: MOFET Institute. (in Hebrew)

Barthes, R. (1972). *Mythologies: Roland Barthes*. New York: Hill and Wang.

Bates, A. (1995). *Technology, open learning and distance education*. London: Routledge.

Bauman, Z. (2002). Space in the globalizing world. In E. Krausz & G. Tulea (Eds.), *Starting the Twenty-First Century, Sociological Reflections and Challenges*. London: Transaction Publishers.

Bawden, D. (2008). Origins and concepts of digital literacies. In L. Co & K. Mi (Eds.), *Digital Literacies: Concepts, Policies and Practices* (pp. 17–32). New York, NY: Peter Lang.

Beauchamp, C., & Thomas, L. (2009). Understanding teacher identity: An overview of issues in the literature and implications for teacher education. *Cambridge Journal of Education, 39*(2), 175–189. doi:10.1080/03057640902902252

Beavis, C. (2002a). *RTS and RPGs: New Literacies and Multiplayer Computer Games*, Paper presented at the Annual Conference of the Australian Association For Research in Education, University of Queensland, December 1-5. Retrieved from http://www.aare.edu.au/02pap/bea02658.htm

Beavis, C. (2002b). Reading, writing and role-playing computer games. In L. Snyder (Ed.), Silicon literacies: Communication, innovation and education in the electronic age (pp. 47-61). London: Routledge.

Behrens, S. J. (1994). A conceptual analysis and historical overview of information literacy. *College & Research Libraries, 55*(4), 309–322. doi:10.5860/crl_55_04_309

Bell, S. T., Villado, A. J., Lukasik, M. A., Belau, L., & Briggs, A. L. (2011). Getting specific: A meta-analysis of the demographic diversity variables and team performance. *Journal of Management, 37*(3), 709–743. doi:10.1177/0149206310365001

Bender, J. (2016). Justice as the practice of non-coercive action: A study of John Dewey and classical Daoism. *Asian Philosophy, 26*(1), 20–37. doi:10.1080/09552367.2015.1136200

Bergsma, L. J., & Carney, M. E. (2008). Effectiveness of health-promoting media literacy education: A systematic view. *Health Education Research, 23*(3), 522–542. doi:10.1093/her/cym084 PMID:18203680

Bernal, D. D., & Villalpando, O. (2002). An apartheid of knowledge in academia: The struggle over the" legitimate" knowledge of faculty of color. *Equity & Excellence in Education, 35*(2), 169–180. doi:10.1080/713845282

Berners-Lee, T. (2000). *Weaving the web: The original design and ultimate destiny of the world wide web.* New York: HarperCollins.

Best, R. A. (2016). An online statistics course from faculty and students' perspectives: A case study, Unpublished doctoral dissertation, University of Walden, United States of America.

Birbaumer, N., Ruiz, S., & Sitaram, R. (2013). Learned regulation of brain metabolism. *Trends in Cognitive Sciences, 17*(6), 295–302. doi:10.1016/j.tics.2013.04.009 PMID:23664452

Birkett, M., Newcomb, M. E., & Mustanski, B. (2015). Does it get better? A longitudinal analysis of psychological distress and victimization in lesbian, gay, bisexual, transgender, and questioning youth. *The Journal of Adolescent Health, 56*(3), 280–285. doi:10.1016/j.jadohealth.2014.10.275 PMID:25586226

Birman, B. F. et al.. (2000). Designing professional development that works. *Educational Leadership, 57*(8), 28–33.

Birnbaum, M. (2009). Evaluation for learning and characteristics of a professional school community and the classroom culture that empowers it. In I. Kashti (Ed.), *Evaluation, Jewish education and the history of education: An anthology in memory of Professor Arieh Levy* (pp. 77–100). Tel Aviv: University of Tel Aviv, School of Education and Ramot Publishers. (in Hebrew)

Blackboard. (2017). *Bb student.* Retrieved from http://www.blackboard.com/mobile-learning/bbstudent.aspx

Black, S., & Mendenhall, M. (1990). Cross Cultural Training Effectiveness: A Review and a Theoretical Framework for Future Research. *Academy of Management Review, 15*(1), 113–136.

Blankenship, M. (2011). How social media can and should impact higher education. *Education Digest: Essential Readings Condensed for Quick Review, 76*(7), 39–42.

Blaschke, L. M. (2012). *Heutagogy and lifelong learning: A review of heutagogical practice and self-determined learning.* Retrieved from http://www.irrodl.org/index.php/irrodl/article/view/1076/2087

Bloom, B. S. (1956). *Taxonomy of educational objectives, handbook I: The cognitive domain.* New York: David McKay Co Inc.

Bonner, M. (2016). *'I Am Cait' Recap: Caitlyn Jenner Considers Gender Confirmation Surgery, Meets with Surgeon.* Retrieved from http://www.usmagazine.com/entertainment/news/i-am-cait-recap-caitlyn-jenner-considers-gender-confirmation-surgery-w203059

Boxer, P., Groves, C. L., & Docherty, M. (2015). Video games do indeed influence children and adolescents aggression, prosocial behavior, and academic performance: A clearer reading of Ferguson (2015). *Perspectives on Psychological Science*, *10*(5), 671–673. doi:10.1177/1745691615592239 PMID:26386004

Brainyquote.com (n. d.). Ralph Waldo Emerson. Retrieved from https://www.brainyquote.com/quotes/quotes/r/ralph-waldo103524.html

Brancati, N., Caggianese, G., Frucci, M., Gallo, L., & Neroni, P. (2015). In Intelligent Interactive Multimedia Systems and Services. In E. Damiani, R. Howlett, C. Jain et al. (Eds.), Touchless target selection techniques for wearable augmented reality systems (pp. 1-9). Switzerland: Springer International Publishing.

Broadband Florida Initiative. (2016). *Broadband Florida initiative*. Retrieved from http://broadbandfla.com/

Broadband, U. S. A. (2010). *Connecting America's communities*. Retrieved from http://www2.ntia.doc.gov/files/grantees/ALL_USCAID.pdf

BroadBandNow. (2016). *Broadband service in Florida*. Retrieved from http://broadbandnow.com/Florida

Broadfoot, P. (1991). *Assessment: a celebration of learning*. Australian Curriculum Studies Association.

Broniatowski, D. A., Faith, G. R., & Sabathier, V. G. (2006). The case for managed international cooperation in space exploration. *Center for Strategic and International Studies*, *18*(1), 1–7.

Brown, J. D. (2006). Media Literacy has Potential to Improve Adolescents Health. *The Journal of Adolescent Health*, *39*(4), 459–460. doi:10.1016/j.jadohealth.2006.07.014 PMID:16982377

Brown, J. S. (2000). Growing up digital: How the Web changes work, education, and the ways people learn. *Change*, *32*(2), 10–20. doi:10.1080/00091380009601719

Bruce, C. S. (1999). Workplace experiences in information literacy. *International Journal of Information Management*, *19*(1), 33–47. doi:10.1016/S0268-4012(98)00045-0

Bruns, A. (2008). *Blogs, Wikipedia, Second Life, and beyond: From production to produsage*. New York: Peter Lang.

Brush, T., Glazewski, K., Rutowski, K., Berg, K., Stromfors, C., & Van-Nest, M. et al.. (2003). Integrating technology in a field-based teacher training program: The PT3@ASU Project. *Educational Technology Research and Development*, *51*(2), 57–72. doi:10.1007/BF02504518

Brydum, S. (2015). The true meaning of the word cisgender. *The Advocate*. Retrieved from http://www.advocate.com/transgender/2015/07/31/true-meaning-word-cisgender

Buckingham, D. (2009). *The Future of Media Literacy in the Digital Age: Some Challenges for Policy and Practice*. Medienimpulse-online. Retrieved from http://medienimpulse.erz.univie.ac.at/articles/view/143

Buckingham, D. (2003). Digital literacies: Media education and new media Technologies. In K. Tyner & B. Duncan (Eds.), *Visions/Revisions: Moving forward with media education* (pp. 3–11). Madison, Wisconsin: National Telemedia Council.

Buckingham, D. (2003). *Media Education: Literacy, Learning and Contemporary Culture*. Cambridge: Polity Press and Blackwell Publishing.

Buckingham, D. (2009). Media Education Policy: The future of Media Literacy in the Digital Age: some challenges for policy and practice. In *Euromeduc – Media Literacy in Europe*. Brussels: Euromeduc.

Buckingham, W. (2014). Communicating not-knowing: Education, Daoism and epistemological chaos. *China Media Research*, *10*(4), 10–19.

Bulunmaz, B. (2011). Otomotiv sektöründe sosyal medyanın kullanımı ve Fiat örneği. *Yeditepe Üniversitesi Global Media Journal, 2*(3), 19–50.

Burn, A., & Durran, J. (2007). *Media Literacy in Schools: Practice, Production and Progression.* London, NY: SAGE Publications.

Butler, B., Sproull, L., Kiesler, S., & Kraut, R. (2002). Community effort in online groups: Who does the work and why. In *Leadership at a distance: Research in technologically supported work* (pp. 171-194).

Butler, A. (2010). *Media Education Goes to School: young people make meaning of media & urban education.* New York: Peter Lang.

Butler, J., & Athanasiou, A. (2013). *Dispossession: The performative in the political.* Cambridge: Polity Press.

Çakır, H., & Koçer, M. ve Aydın, H. (2012). Medya okuryazarlığı dersini alan ve almayan ilköğretim öğrencilerinin medya izleme davranışlarındaki farklılıkların belirlenmesi. *Selçuk İletişim Dergisi, 7*(3), 42–54.

Canbaz, N. (2010). Analysing the technology literacy education needs of female trainees who attend the adult education courses. Unpublished Master Thesis, Çanakkale Onsekiz Mart University, Çanakkale.

Canvas by Instructure. (2016). *Canvas by Instructure mobile features.* Retrieved from https://s3.amazonaws.com/tr-learncanvas/docs/Mobile_CanvasbyInstructure.pdf

Caon, M., Tagliabue, M., Angelini, L., Perego, P., Mugellini, E., & Andreoni, G. (2014, September). Wearable technologies for automotive user interfaces: Danger or opportunity. *Paper presented at 6th International Conference on Automotive User Interfaces and Interactive Vehicular Applications*, Seattle, WA, USA. doi:10.1145/2667239.2667314

Carbonara, D. D. (Ed.). (2005). *Technology literacy applications in learning environments.* Hersey, NJ: IGI Global. doi:10.4018/978-1-59140-479-8

Carpenter, S. (2009). An application of the theory of expertise: Teaching broad and skill knowledge areas to prepare journalists for change. *Journalism and Mass Communication Educator, 64*(3), 287–304. doi:10.1177/107769580906400305

Carter, A. (2001). *The political theory of global citizenship.* London: Routledge.

Caumont, A. A. (2013). Who's not online? 5 factors tied to the digital divide. *Pew Research Center,* retrieved from http://www.pewresearch.org/fact-tank/2013/11/08/whos-not-online-5-factors-tied-to-the-digital-divide/

Çelik, A. (2012) The effect of QR code assisted mobile learning environment on productive vocabulary learning in foreign language studies and student reviews: The example of Mobile Dictionary. Unpublished Master Thesis, Gazi University, Institute of Educational Sciences, Ankara.

Celot, P., & Pérez Tornero, J. M. (2009). *Study on assessment criteria for media literacy levels.* Retrieved from http://ec.europa.eu/culture/media/literacy/studies/index_en.htm

Center for Universal Education. (2013). Universal education. Retrieved from http://www.brookings.edu/about/centers/universal-education

Cesarini, P. (2004). Computers, technology, and literacies. *The Journal of Literacy and Technology, 4*(1). http://www.literacyandtechnology.org/v4/cesarini.htm Retrieved June 10, 2007

Chapman, L., Masters, J., & Pedulla, J. (2010). Do digital divisions still persist in schools? Access to technology and technical skills of teachers in high needs schools in the United States of America. *Journal of Education for Teaching, 36*(2), 239–249. doi:10.1080/02607471003651870

Chaudron, S. (2016). Young Children, Parents and Digital Technology in the Home Context Across Europe: The Findings of the Extension of the Young Children (0-8) and Digital Technology Pilot Study to 17 European Countries (oral presentation). *Presented at DigiLitEY Project Meeting 3*, Larnaca, Cyprus, May 17-18.

Chaudron, S. (2015). *Young Children & Digital Technology: A qualitative exploratory study across seven countries.* Luxembourg: Publications Office of the European Union.

CheapInternet.com. (n. d.). *Inexpensive Internet service for Florida: Low-income qualifications, DSL, cable, mobile Internet.* Retrieved from http://www.cheapInternet.com/states/florida-Internet-service

Chia, M., & Huang, T. (2005). *Secret teachings of the Tao Te Ching.* Rochester, Vermont: Destiny Books.

Childers, S. (2003). Computer literacy: Necessity or buzzword? *Information Technology and Libraries, 22*(3), 100–105.

Childs, D. (n.d.). Kids Imitate Saddam's Televised Hanging Death. *ABC News Medical Unit.* Retrieved from http://abcnews.go.com/Health/story?id=2773792&page=1

Chiricos, T., & Eschholz, S. (2002). The racial and ethnic typification of crime and the criminal typification of race and ethnicity in local television news. *Journal of Research in Crime and Delinquency, 39*(4), 400–420. doi:10.1177/002242702237286

Christ, W. G. (2004). Assessment, media literacy standards, and higher education. *The American Behavioral Scientist, 48*(1), 92–96. doi:10.1177/0002764204267254

Clapman, L. (2016). Wi-Fi-enabled school buses leave no child offline. *PBS NewsHour.* Retrieved from http://www.pbs.org/newshour/bb/wi-fi-enabled-school-buses-leave-no-child-offline/

Clark, J. (1989). Quote from Principal Joe Clark (Morgan Freeman) in the motion picture "Lean on Me", 1989. Retrieved from http://www.imdb.com/title/tt0097722/quotes

Clark, C. (1969). Television and social controls: Some observations on the portrayal of ethnic minorities. *Television Quarterly, 9*(2), 18–22.

Coffman, T., & Klinger, M. B. (2015, March). Google Glass: Using wearable technologies to enhance teaching and learning. *Paper presented at the Society for Information Technology & Teacher Education International Conference,* Las Vegas, NV.

Coiro, J., Knobel, M., Lankshear, C., & Leu, D. J. (Eds.). (2014). *Handbook of research on new literacies.* Routledge.

College Equality Index. (2017). List of colleges with gender neutral housing. Retrieved from http://www.collegeequalityindex.org/list-colleges-gender-neutral-housing

Commission of the European Communities. (2001). Comunicação da Comissão ao Conselho e ao Parlamento Europeu Plano de acção eLearning -Pensar o futuro da educação. Retrieved from http://eur-lex.europa.eu/LexUriServ/LexUriServ.do?uri=CELEX:52001DC0172:PT:HTML

Commission of the European Communities. (2007). Comunicação da Comissão ao Parlamento Europeu, ao Conselho, ao Comité Económico e Social Europeu e ao Comité das Regiões - Uma abordagem europeia da literacia mediática no ambiente digital. Retrieved from http://ec.europa.eu/avpolicy/media_literacy/ec_com/index_en.htm

Commission of the European Communities. (2009). Commission Recommendation on media literacy in the digital environment for a more competitive audiovisual and content industry and an inclusive knowledge society. Retrieved from http://eur-lex.europa.eu/LexUriServ/LexUriServ.do?uri=OJ:L:2009:227:0009:0012:EN:PDF

Commonapp.org. (2016). The common application expands gender identity options. *The Common Application.* Retrieved from http://www.commonapp.org/whats-appening/news/common-application-expands-gender-identity-options

Complete Florida. (2015). *Finish your degree: Let's get started.* Retrieved from https://www.completeflorida.org/

Conheady, S. (2014). Social engineering in IT security: Tools, tactics, and techniques. Toronto: McGraw-Hill Education.

Considine, M., Horton, J., & Moorman, G. (2009, March). Teaching and Reading the Millennial Generation Through Media Literacy. *Journal of Adolescent & Adult Literacy*, *52*(6), 471–481. doi:10.1598/JAAL.52.6.2

Council of the European Union. (2012, 19 December). Council conclusions of 26 November 2012 on literacy. Official Journal of the European Union. Retrieved from http://eur-lex.europa.eu/legal-content/EN/TXT/PDF/?uri=OJ:C:2012: 393:FULL&from=EN

Cox, L. (2016). Transgender star Laverne Cox backs puberty blocking treatment. *Belfast Telegraph.* Retrieved from http://www.belfasttelegraph.co.uk/entertainment/news/transgender-star-laverne-cox-backs-pubertyblocking-treat-ment-35159084.html

Craig, A. B., Brown, E. R., Upright, J., & DeRosier, M. E. (2016). Enhancing children's social emotional functioning through virtual game-based delivery of social skills training. *Journal of Child and Family Studies*, *25*(3), 959–968. doi:10.1007/s10826-015-0274-8

Cross, J. (2007). *Informal learning.* San Francisco, California: Pfeiffer.

Csikszentmihalyi, M. (1985). Emergent motivation and the evolution of the self. In D. A. Kleiber & M. Maehr (Eds.), *Advances in motivation and achievement* (Vol. 4, pp. 93–119). Greenwich, CT: JAI Press.

Csikszentmihalyi, M. (1998). *Finding flow: The psychology of engagement with everyday life.* New York: Basic.

Cunningham, S., Dezzuani, M., Goldsmith, B., Burns, M., Miles, P., Henkel, C., & Murphy, K. et al. (2016). *Screen Content in Australian Education: Digital Promise and Pitfalls.* Brisbane: Digital Media Research Centre.

Dabbagh, N., & Reo, R. (2011). Back to the future: Tracing the roots and learning affordances of social software. In M. J. W. Lee & C. McLoughlin (Eds.), *Web 2.0 based e-Learning: Applying social informatics for tertiary teaching* (pp. 1–20). Hershey, PA: IGI Global. doi:10.4018/978-1-60566-294-7.ch001

Dahlberg, N. (2015). Comcast expands low-income Internet program. *Miami Herald.* Retrieved from http://www.mi-amiherald.com/news/business/article29973996.html

Danesi, M. (2016). Technology, Society, and Education. In Learning and Teaching Mathematics in The Global Village (pp. 37-73). Springer International Publishing. doi:10.1007/978-3-319-32280-3_2

Darling-Hammond, L. (1999). *Professional development for teachers: Setting the stage for learning from teaching.* Santa Cruz, CA: Center for the Future of Teaching & Learning.

Darling-Hammond, L., & Richardson, N. (2009). Teachers learning, what matters? *Educational Leadership*, *66*(5), 46–53.

Das, B. (2009). Media Education as a Development Project: Connecting Emancipatory Interests and Governance in India. In D. Freu-Meigs & J. Torrent (Eds.), Mapping Media Education Policies in the World: Visions, Programmes and Challenges. New York: UN-Alliance of Civilizations and Grupo Communicar.

Davey, D. (2013). Jailhouse ROC: The facts about hip hop and prison for profit. *Hip Hop and Politics.* Retrieved from http://hiphopandpolitics.com/2013/04/24/jailhouse-roc-the-facts-about-hip-hop-and-prison-for-profit/

de Abreu & Tomé. V. 2017. Mobile Learning through Digital Media Literacy. New York: Peter Lang.

de Abreu, B. (2011). *Media Literacy, Social Networking and the Web 2.0 Environment for the K-12 Educator.* New York: Peter Lang Publishing.

Dede, C. (2008). A seismic shift in epistemology. *EDUCAUSE Review*, May/June, 80–81. Retrieved from http://net.educause.edu

Dogan, B. (2015). Educational Uses of Digital Storytelling in K-12: Research Results of Digital Storytelling Contest (DISTCO) 2014. In D. Slykhuis & G. Marks (Eds.), *Society for Information Technology & Teacher Education International Conference 2015,* Las Vegas, NV (pp. 595–604). AACE. Retrieved from http://www.editlib.org/p/150056

Dogan, B. (2010). Educational Use of Digital Storytelling: Research Results of an Online Digital Storytelling Contest. In D. Gibson & B. Dodge (Eds.), *Proceedings of Society for Information Technology & Teacher Education International Conference 2010* (pp. 1061–1066). San Diego, CA: AACE. Retrieved from http://www.editlib.org/p/33494

Dogan, B. (2011). Educational Uses of Digital Storytelling: Results of DISTCO 2010, an Online Digital Storytelling Contest. In M. Koehler & P. Mishra (Eds.), *Proceedings of Society for Information Technology & Teacher Education International Conference 2011* (pp. 1104–1111). Nashville, Tennessee: AACE. Retrieved from http://www.editlib.org/p/36434

Dogan, B. (2012). Educational Uses of Digital Storytelling in K-12: Research Results of Digital Storytelling Contest (DISTCO) 2012. In P. Resta (Ed.), *Proceedings of Society for Information Technology & Teacher Education International Conference 2012* (pp. 1353–1362). Austin, Texas: AACE. Retrieved from http://www.editlib.org/p/39770

Dogan, B. (2014). Educational Uses of Digital Storytelling in K-12: Research Results of a Digital Storytelling Contest (DISTCO) 2013. In M. Searson & M. N. Ochoa (Eds.), *Society for Information Technology & Teacher Education International Conference 2014* (pp. 520–529). Jacksonville, FL: AACE. Retrieved from http://www.editlib.org/p/13080

Dogan, B., & Robin, B. (2008). Implementation of Digital Storytelling in the Classroom by Teachers Trained in a Digital Storytelling Workshop. In K. McFerrin, R. Weber, R. Carlsen, & D. A. Willis (Eds.), *Society for Information Technology & Teacher Education International Conference 2008* (pp. 902–907). Las Vegas, NV: AACE. Retrieved from http://www.editlib.org/p/27287

Domonell, K. (2014). Bridging the digital divide: How institutions are making iPads and laptops accessible to all students. *University Business*. Retrieved from https://www.universitybusiness.com/article/bridging-digital-divide

Domonoske, C. (2017). 17-year-old transgender boy wins Texas Girls' Wrestling Championship. Northcourtrypublicradio. Retrieved from https://www.northcountrypublicradio.org/news/npr/517491492/17-year-old-transgender-boy-wins-texas-girls-wrestling-championship

Donald, B. (2016). Stanford researchers find students have trouble judging the credibility of information on-line. *Stanford Graduate School of Education News*. Retrieved from https://ed.stanford.edu/news/stanford-researchers-find-students-have-trouble-judging-credibility-information-online

Dowler, K. (2003). Media consumption and public attitudes toward crime and justice: The relationship between fear of crime, punitive attitudes, and perceived police effectiveness. *The Journal of Criminal Justice and Popular Culture*, *10*(2), 109–126.

Doyle, C. S. (1994). *Information literacy in an information society: A concept for the information age*. New York: Diane Publishing.

Dubey, P. (2011). Overcoming the digital divide through machine translation. *Translation Journal*, 15(1). Retrieved from http://translationjournal.net/journal/55mt_india.htm

Durham, M.G. (1998, Spring). Revolutionizing the Teaching of Magazine Design. *Journalism and Mass Communication Educator*, 23-31.

Eherensaft, D. (2010). Look mom, I'm, a boy: Don't tell anyone I was a girl. *Journal of LGBT Youth, 10*(1-2), 9–28. do i:10.1080/19361653.2012.717474

Ehrensaft, D. (2011). From gender identity disorder to gender identity creativity: True gender self child therapy. *Journal of Homosexuality, 59*(3), 337–356. doi:10.1080/00918369.2012.653303 PMID:22455324

Elder, S., & Vakaloudis, A. (2015). A technical evaluation of devices for smart glasses applications. Internet Technologies and Applications, 5, 98-103. doi:10.1109/ITechA.2015.7317377

Ellsworth, J. H. (1994). *Education on the internet*. Indianapolis: Sams Publishing.

Ely, M., Vinz, R., Downing, M., & Anzul, M. (2001). *On writing qualitative research: Living by words*. London: Falmer Press.

Eppert, C., & Wang, H. (Eds.). (2008). *Cross-cultural studies in curriculum: Eastern thought, educational insights*. New York: Lawrence Earlbaum.

Eppler, M. J., & Mengis, J. (2004). The concept of information overload: A review of literature from organization science, accounting, marketing, MIS, and related disciplines. *The Information Society, 20*(5), 325–344. doi:10.1080/01972240490507974

Erbaş, Ç., & Demirer, V. (2014). Augmented reality practices in education: Google Glass example. *Journal of Instructional Technologies & Teacher Education, 3*(2), 8–16.

Eshet-Alkalai, Y., & Chajut, E. (2010). You can teach old dogs new tricks: The factors that affect changes over time in digital literacy. *Journal of Information Technology Education, 9*, 173–181.

Espineira, K. (2016, July 02). Transgender and transsexual people's sexuality in the media. *Parallax, 22*(3), 323–329. doi:10.1080/13534645.2016.1201922

European Commission. (2007). Report on the results of the public consultation on Media Literacy. Retrieved from http://ec.europa.eu/avpolicy/media_literacy/docs/report_on_ml_2007.pdf

European Commission. (2008). B-Brussels: study on criteria to assess media literacy levels - SMART 2008/0005. Retrieved from http://ted.europa.eu/Exec?DataFlow=ShowPage.dfl&Template=TED/N_one_result_detail_curr. htm&docnumber=89657-2008&docId=89657-2008&StatLang=EN

European Commission. (2009). *European Association for Viewers Interest (EAVI)*. Brussels: Study on Assessment Criteria for Media Literacy Levels.

Evans, C. (2008). The effectiveness of m-learning in the form of podcast revision lectures in higher education. *Computers & Education, 50*(2), 491–498. doi:10.1016/j.compedu.2007.09.016

EveryoneOn. (2016). *About us*. Retrieved from http://everyoneon.org/about/

Facer, K. (2003). Computer games and learning: Why do we think it's worth talking about computer games and learning in the same breath? Retrieved June 12, 2007, from http://www.futurelab.org.uk/resources/publications_reports_articles/ discussion_papers/Discussion_Paper261/

Falowo, R. O. (2007). Factors impeding implementation of web-based distance learning. *AACE Journal, 15*(3), 315–338.

Fantin, M. (2012). Mídia-educação no currículo e na formação inicial de professores. In *Mónica Fantin e Pier Cesare Rivoltella, orgs, Cultura Digital e Escola: pesquisa e formação de professores*. Campinas, SP: Papirus Editora.

Farkas, M. (2016). The new digital divide. *American Libraries Magazines*. Retrieved from https://americanlibraries-magazine.org/2016/01/04/new-digital-divide-mobile-first-design/

Fastrez, P. (2009). *Evaluating media literacy as competences: What can we agree on?* Retrieved from http://www.slide-share.net/pfastrez/evaluating-medialiteracy-as-competences-what-can-we-agree-on

Federal Communications Commission. (2016). *2016 Broadband progress report.* Retrieved from https://www.fcc.gov/reports-research/reports/broadband-progress-reports/2016-broadband-progress-report

Federal Communications Commission. (n. d.). Connecting America: The national broadband plan. *Federal Communication Commission.* Retrieved from http://download.broadband.gov /plan/national-broadband-plan.pdf

Federman, J. (Ed.). (1998). National Television Violence Study (Vol. 3). Santa Barbara, CA: University of California, Center for Communication and Social Policy.

Ferguson, C. J. (2015). Do angry birds make for angry children? A meta-analysis of video game influences on children's and adolescent's aggression, mental health, prosocial behavior, and academic performance. *Perspectives on Psychological Science, 10*(5), 646–666. doi:10.1177/1745691615592234 PMID:26386002

Ferreira, J. (2014). *The digital divide and America's achievement gap* [The Knewton Blog.] Retrieved from https://www.knewton.com/resources/blog/ceo-jose-ferreira/the-digital-divide/

Fleming, N. (2012). Digital divide strikes college-admissions process. *Education Week, 32*(13), 14–15.

Fleming, N. (2012). Digital divide strikes college-admissions process: Some students lack hardware, savvy. *Education Week, 32*(13), 14.

Florida Department of Education. (2016). *English language learners.* Retrieved from http://www.fldoe.org/academics/eng-language-learners/

Florida LambdaRail. (n. d.) *About us.* Retrieved from http://www.flrnet.org/?page_id=491

Follett, J. (2014). Fashion with function: Designing for wearables. Designing for emerging technologies. Retrieved from http://www.safaribooksonline.com/library/view/designing-for-emerging/9781449370626/ ch01.html

Foreman, J. (2003). Next-generation: Educational technology versus the lecture. *EDUCAUSE,* (July/August), 13-22, Retrieved May 25, 2007 from http://www.educause.edu/ir/library/pdf/erm0340.pdf

Frau-Meigs, D. (2012). Transliteracy as the new research horizon for media and information literacy. *Medijske Studue, 3*(6), 14–27.

Frau-Meigs, D., & Torrent, J. (2009). *Mapping Media Education Policies in the World – Visions, Programmes and Challenges.* New York: UN – Alliance of Civilizations.

Friedman, A., & Philips, M. (2004). Continuing professional development: Developing a vision. *Journal of Education and Work, 17*(3), 361–376. doi:10.1080/1363908042000267432

Friedman, T. L. (2007). *The world is flat: A brief history of the twenty-first century* (3rd ed.). New York: Picador.

Fromm, E. (1973). *The Anatomy of Human Destructiveness.* London: Penguin Books.

Funk, S. S. (2013). Critical Media Literacy in pedagogy and in practice: A descriptive study of teacher education instructors and their students [Doctoral Dissertation].

Funk, S. S., & Funk, J. (2016b). *Engaging Gender Expansive Youth through Critical Media Literacy.* Oakland, CA: Gender Spectrum Professionals' Symposium.

Funk, S.S. & Funk, J. (in press b). Trans*+ Media Literacy Framework: Findings from and reflections on a gender inclusive workshop addressing cisgender privilege".

Funk, S.S. & Funk, J. (in press). *Healthcare, sex, and gender survey: Findings from a mixed methods study.*

Funk, J., Vanderhorst, S., & Funk, S. S. (in press a). Trans*+ and intersex representation and pathologization: An argument for increased medical privacy. *The Journal of Law, Medicine & Ethics.*

Funk, S. S., & Funk, J. (2016a). Transgender dispossession in Transparent: Coming out as a euphemism for honesty. *Sexuality & Culture, 20*(4), 879–905. doi:10.1007/s12119-016-9363-0

Funk, S. S., Kellner, D., & Share, J. (2016). Critical media literacy as transformative pedagogy. In M. N. Yildiz & J. Keengwe (Eds.), *Handbook of Research on Media Literacy in the Digital Age*. Hershey, PA: IGI Global. doi:10.4018/978-1-4666-9667-9.ch001

Galie, J. (2007). *The clan, the clique, and the alien in Russian literature and society.* New York, NY: ProQuest Dissertations Publishing.

Galusha, J. M. (1997). Barriers to learning in distance education. *Interpersonel Computing and Technology: An Electronic Journal of the 21st Century, 5*(3-4), 6-14.

Gandyer, V. S., Krishnamurthy, M., & Venkatesan, S. (2015, July). *Brain painter: a novel p300-based brain computer interface application for locked-in-syndrome victims.* In *Proceedings of the International Conference on Information Technology and Computer Science* (pp. 88-93).

Garris, R., Ahlers, R., & Driskell, J. E. (2002). Games, motivation, and learning: A research and practice model. *Simulation & Gaming, 33*(4), 441–467. doi:10.1177/1046878102238607

Gee, J. P. (2003). Learning about learning from a video game: Rise of Nations. Retrieved from http://simworkshop.stanford.edu/05_0125/reading_docs/Rise%20of%20Nations.pdf

Geertz, C. (1973). *The interpretation of cultures.* New York: Basic Books Inc. Publishers.

Gelfand, M. J., Leslie, L. M., Keller, K., & de Dreu, C. (2012). Conflict cultures in organizations: How leaders shape conflict cultures and their organizational-level consequences. *The Journal of Applied Psychology, 97*(6), 11–31. doi:10.1037/a0029993 PMID:23025807

Geneva. (2000). *Preventing suicide: A resource for media professionals.* WHO/MNH/MBD/00.2. Retrieved from http://www.who.int/mental_health/media/en/426.pdf

Gentile, D. A., & Anderson, C. A. (2003). Violent video games: The newest media violence hazard. In D. A. Gentile (Ed.), *Media violence and children.* Westport, CT: Praeger Publishing.

Gentile, D. A., Lynch, P. J., Linder, J. R., & Walsh, D. A. (2004). The effects of violent video game habits on adolescent aggressive attitudes and behaviors. *Journal of Adolescence, 27*, 5–22. doi:10.1016/j.adolescence.2003.10.002 PMID:15013257

Georgieva, E., Smrikarov, A., & Georgiev, T. (2005). A general classification of mobile learning systems. *Paper presented at the International Conference on Computer Systems and Technologies*, Varna, Bulgaristan.

GEPE – Gabinete de Estatísticas e Planeamento da Educação & Direção de Serviços de Estatística. (2011). *Educação em Números – Portugal 2011*. Lisboa: GEPE.

Gerbner, G. (1998). Cultivation Analysis: An Overview. *Mass Communication & Society, 3*(4), 175–194. doi:10.1080/15205436.1998.9677855

Giang, W. C., Hoekstra-Atwood, L., & Donmez, B. (2014). Driver engagement in notifications a comparison of visual-manual interaction between smartwatches and smartphones. *Proceedings of the Human Factors and Ergonomics Society Annual Meeting*, *58*(1), 2161-2165.

Gilster, P. (1997). *Digital Literacy*. New York, NY: Wiley Press.

GLAAD. (2014). Network responsibility index. Retrieved from http://www.glaad.org/nri2014

Goh, G., & Kale, U. (2015). From print to digital platforms: A PBC framework for fostering multimedia competencies and consciousness in traditional journalism education. *Journalism and Mass Communication Educator*, *70*(3), 307–323. doi:10.1177/1077695815589473

Goldstein, A. (2014). *Analysis of the Shluvim social-professional network according to network theory. Research report.* Israel: MOFET Institute. (in Hebrew)

Gonnet, J. (1999). *Éducation et Médias*. Paris: PUF.

Gonzalez, I. (2016). Disponible en consumer preview el complemento Class Notebook para OneNote. Retrieved from http://www.microsoftinsider.es/100020/disponible-cosumer-preview-complemento-class-notebook-onenote/

Goundar, S. (2014). The distraction of technology in the classroom. *Journal of Education & Human Development*, *3*(1), 211–229.

Gredler, M. E. (2004). Games and simulations and their relationships to learning. In D. H. Jonassen (Ed.), *Handbook of research for educational communications and Technology* (pp. 571–581). New York: Simon & Schuster Macmillan.

Greenhow, C. (2011). Online social networks and learning. *On the Horizon*, *19*(1), 4–12. doi:10.1108/10748121111107663

Greenhow, C., & Askari, E. (2017). Learning and teaching with social network sites: A decade of research in K-12 related education. *Education and Information Technologies*, *22*(2), 623–645. doi:10.1007/s10639-015-9446-9

Grizzle, A., & Carme Torras Calvo, M. (Eds.). (2013). *Media and Information Literacy, Policy and Strategy Guidelines*. Paris: UNESCO.

Grundahl, P. (2011). The long, difficult journey of how a man became a woman. *Times Union*. Retrieved from http://www.timesunion.com/local/article/The-long-difficult-journey-of-how-a-man-became-a-2341891.php

Guide for Fulbright visiting scholars. (n. d.). Privileges and Obligations Under the Fulbright Scholar Program. Retrieved from https://docs.google.com/viewer?url=http%3A%2F%2Fwww.cies.org%2Fsites%2Fdefault%2Ffiles%2Fdocuments%2FVisiting-Scholar-Guide.pdf

Haigh, M. (2008). Internationalisation, planetary citizenship and Higher Education Inc. *Compare: A Journal of Comparative Education*, *38*(4), 427–440. doi:10.1080/03057920701582731

Hamlen, K. R. (2015). Understanding Children's Choices and Cognition in Video Game Play. *Zeitschrift fur Psychologie mit Zeitschrift fur Angewandte Psychologie*.

Hartmann, T., & Klimmt, C. (2006). Gender and computer games: Exploring female's dislikes. *Journal of Computer-Mediated Communication*, *11*(4), 910–931. Retrieved from http://jcmc.indiana.edu/vol11/issue4/hartmann.html doi:10.1111/j.1083-6101.2006.00301.x

Hase, S., & Kenyon, C. (2000). *From andragogy to heutagogy*. Ultibase, RMIT. Retrieved from http://ultibase.rmit.edu.au/Articles/dec00/hase2.htm

Haslaman, T., Kuskaya-Mumcu, F., & Kocak-Usluel, Y. (2008). *Integration of ICT Into The Teaching-Learning Process: Toward A Unified Model*. In J. Luca & E. Weippl (Eds.), *Proceedings of World Conference on Educational Multimedia, Hypermedia and Telecommunications 2008* (pp. 2384-2389). Chesapeake, VA: AACE.

Hasson, P. (2017). Milo's 'Legions Of Followers' Force Liberal Website To Name Him 'Person Of The Year'. *Daily Caller*. Retrieved from http://dailycaller.com/2017/01/09/milos-legion-of-followers-force-liberal-website-to-name-him-person-of-the-year/

Heath, P. (1990). Teaching about Science, Technology, and Society in Social Studies: Education for Citizenship in the 21st Century. *Social Education, 54*(4), 189–193.

Heins, M., & Cho, C. (2003). *Media Literacy: An Alternative to Censorship*. New York: Free Expression Policy Project.

Heinz, M. (2012). Transmen on the web: Inscribing multiple discourses. In K. Ross (Ed.), *The handbook of gender, sex, and media* (pp. 326–343). Chichester, UK: John Wiley & Sons. doi:10.1002/9781118114254.ch20

Hemmasi, M., & Csanda, C. M. (2009). The effectiveness of communities of practice: An empirical study. *Journal of Managerial Issues, 21*(2), 262–279.

Henrichsen, J. & Coombs. (2013). The five resources of critical digital literacy: A framework for curriculum integration. *Research in Learning Technology, 21*(1), 1–16.

Hernandez, A. (2016). Stop Trying to Define Personalized Learning. *EdSurge*. Retrieved from https://www.edsurge.com/news/2016-05-11-stop-trying-to-define-personalized-learning

Hew, K. F., & Brush, T. (2007). Integrating technology into K-12 teaching and learning: Current knowledge gaps and recommendations for future research. *Educational Technology Research and Development, 55*(3), 223–252. doi:10.1007/s11423-006-9022-5

Hicks, K. (2013). How Google glass can help students make better music. Retrieved from http://edcetera.rafter.com/how-google-glass-can-help-students-make-better-music/

Hilton-Morrow, W., & Battles, K. (2015). *Sexual identities & the media: An introduction*. New York, NY: Routledge.

Hind, K. (2015). Kim Kardashian reveals family attend group therapy to help deal with Caitlyn Jenner's transition. *Mirror*. Retrieved from http://www.mirror.co.uk/3am/celebrity-news/kim-kardashian-reveals-family-attend-5979298

Hindin, A., Morocco, C. C., Mott, E. A., & Aguilar, C. M. (2007). More than just a group: Teacher collaboration and learning in the workplace. *Teachers and Teaching. Theory into Practice, 13*(4), 349–376.

Hixson, C. (2016). Personal interview.

Ho, A., Chuang, H. A., Reich, J., Coleman, C., Whitehill, J., Northcutt, C., . . . Petersen, R. (2015). *HarvardX and MITx: Two years of open online courses* (HarvardX Working Paper No. 10). doi:10.2139/ssrn.2586847

Hobbs, R. (1998). Teaching with and about film and television: Integrating media literacy concepts into management education. *Journal of Management Development, 17*(4), 259–272. doi:10.1108/02621719810210136

Hobbs, R. (2010). *Digital Media Literacy – A Plan of Action*. Washington: The Aspen Institute.

Hobbs, R., & Frost, R. (2003). Measuring the acquisition of media literacy skills. *Reading Research Quarterly, 38*(3), 330–355. doi:10.1598/RRQ.38.3.2

Hofstede, G. (1991). *Cultures and Organizations: Software of the Mind*. London, UK: McGraw- Hill.

Hoise, P., & Schibeci, R. (2005). Checklist and context-bound evaluations of online learning in higher education. *British Journal of Educational Technology*, *36*(5), 881–895.

Holloway, D., Green, L., & Livingstone, S. (2013). *Zero to eight. Young children and their internet use. LSE.* London: EU Kids Online.

Holt, D., Smissen, I., & Segrave, S. (2006, January). New students, new learning, new environments in higher education: Literacies in the digital age. In Who's learning? Whose technology?: *In Proceedings of the 23rd annual conference of the Australasian Society for Computers in Learning in Tertiary Education*, University of Sydney, Sydney, Australia (pp. 327-337). Sydney University Press.

Hong, J., & Tan, X. (1989, May). Calibrating a VPL DataGlove for teleoperating the Utah/MIT hand. In Robotics and Automation. In *Proceedings of 1989 IEEE International Conference* (pp. 1752-1757). IEEE.

Hong, H. J. (2010). Bicultural competence and its impact on team effectiveness. *International Journal of Cross Cultural Management*, *10*(1), 93–120. doi:10.1177/1470595809359582

Horrigan, J. B. (2015). The numbers behind the broadband 'homework gap'. *Pew Research Center.* Retrieved from http://www.pewresearch.org/fact-tank/2015/04/20/the-numbers-behind-the-broadband-homework-gap/

Horrigan, J. B., & Rainie, L. (2001). *Online communities: Networks that nurture long-distance: relationships and local ties.* Pew Internet & American Life Project.

Hoyt, M. (2016). Teaching with mindfulness: The pedagogy of being-with/for and without being-with/for. *JCT: Journal Of Curriculum Theorizing*, *31*(1), 126–142.

Hsu, H.-Y., & Wang, S.-K. (2010). Using gaming literacies to cultivate new literacies. *Simulation & Gaming*, *41*(3), 400–417. doi:10.1177/1046878109355361

Hsu, H.-Y., Wang, S.-K., & Runco, L. (2013). Middle school science teachers confidence and pedagogical practice of new literacies. *Journal of Science Education and Technology*, *22*(3), 314–324. doi:10.1007/s10956-012-9395-7

Huang, A. (2006), Remembering Blizzard North and Diablo II. Retrieved from http://www.diabloii.net/columnists/a-memories-blizzard.shtml

Hui-mei, J. H. (2011, July). The Potential of Kinect as Interactive Educational Technology. In *Paper presented at 2nd International Conference on Education and Management Technology*, Singapur.

IAMAI & Kantar IMRB. (2016). *Internet in India.* New Delhi.

İnceoğlu, Y. (2006). *Reading the media correctly. I. International Media Literacy.* İstanbul: Marmara University Faculty of Communication Conference Texts.

International Information and Communication Technologies (ICT) Literacy Panel. (2002). *Digital transformation: A framework for ICT Literacy.* Princeton, NJ: Educational Testing Services (ETS). Retrieved from http://www.ets.org/Media/Research/pdf/ICTREPORT.pdf

International Reading Association. (2012). *Standards for English Language Arts.* Retrieved from http://www.reading.org/downloads/publications/books/bk889.pdf

International Society for Technology in Education. (2016). Retrieved from http://www.iste.org/standards

Iskandarova, S. (2016). The Effect of Cross-Cultural Differences on Team Performance Within an Educational Setting: A mixed methods study.

Iskandarova, S., Griffin, O., El-Tawab, S., & Mousa, F. (2017). Using Mobile Technology as a Tool to Enhance Learning at a Children's Museum in the Shenandoah Valley. In *Proceedings of the Society for Information Technology & Teacher Education International Conference* (pp. 2125-2132). Association for the Advancement of Computing in Education (AACE).

Iskandarova, S., & Griffin, O. (2017). *Making the Invisible Visible: Exploring Cultural Differences of Faculty Working on a Multicultural Team*. American Society for Engineering Education.

Istance, D., & Kools, M. (2013). OECD Work on Technology and Education: Innovative learning environments as an integrating framework. *European Journal of Education*, *48*(1), 43–57. doi:10.1111/ejed.12017

Jackson, L. A., Zhao, Y., Kolenic, A. III, Fitzgerald, H. E., Harold, R., & Von Eye, A. (2008). Race, gender, and information technology use: The new digital divide. *Cyberpsychology & Behavior*, *11*(4), 437–442. doi:10.1089/cpb.2007.0157 PMID:18721092

Jakes, D. (2006, March). Standards-Proof Your digital storytelling Efforts. *TechLearning*. Retrieved from http://www.techlearning.com/story/showArticle.jhtml?articleID=180204072

Jakes, D. S., & Brennan, J. (2005). Capturing stories, capturing lives: An Introduction to digital storytelling. Retrieved from http://bookstoread.com/etp/earle.pdf

Janesick, V. J. (2006). *Authentic Assessment*. New York, NY: Peter Lang.

Jan, M., Tan, E. M., & Chen, V. (2015). Issues and Challenges of Enacting Game-Based Learning in Schools. In T. Lin, V. Chen, & C. Chai (Eds.), *New Media and Learning in the 21st Century* (pp. 67–76). Singapore: Springer. doi:10.1007/978-981-287-326-2_5

Jobe, J. N. (2013). *Transgender Representation in the Media. Honors Theses. Paper 132*. Eastern Kentucky University.

Johannesen, M., Øgrim, L., & Giæver, T. H. (2014). Notion in motion: Teachers' digital competence. *Nordic Journal of Digital Literacy*, *4*, 300–312.

Johnson, K. M. (2014). An investigation into the smart watch interface and the user driven data requirements for its applications. Retrieved from http://www.cs.ru.ac.za/research/g10j6110/Final%20Proposal%20%20K.%20M.%20Johnson.pdf

Johnson, L., Adams Becker, S., Estrada, V., & Freeman, A. (2014). *NMC horizon report: 2014 Higher Education*.

Johnson, B. R., & Onwuegbuzie, A. J. (2004). Mixed methods research: A research paradigm whose time has come. *Educational Researcher*, *33*(7), 14–26. doi:10.3102/0013189X033007014

Johnson, L. A., Adams, S. S., & Cummins, M. (2012). *The NMC Horizon report: 2012 Higher Education Edition*. Austin, Texas: The New Media Consortium.

Johnson, L., Adams, S., Estrada, V., & Freeman, A. (2014). *NMC Horizon Report: 2014 higher education edition*. Austin, Texas: The New Media Consortium.

Johnson, L., Smith, R., Willis, H., Levine, A., & Haywood, K. (2011). *The 2011 Horizon Report, Texas*. Austin: The New Media Consortium.

Joosten, T. (2012). *Social media for educators: Strategies and best practices*. John Wiley & Sons.

Jung, Y., & Cha, B. (2010). Gesture recognition based on motion inertial sensors for ubiquitous interactive game Contents. *IETE Technical Review*, *27*(2), 158–166. doi:10.4103/0256-4602.60168

Jurgens, J., & McAuliffe, G. (2004). Short-term Study-Abroad experience in Ireland: An exercise in cross-cultural counseling. *International Journal for the Advancement of Counseling*, *26*(2), 147–161. doi:10.1023/B:ADCO.0000027427.76422.1f

Kadous, M. W. (1996, October). Machine recognition of Auslan signs using PowerGloves: Towards large-lexicon recognition of sign language. In *Proceedings of the Workshop on the Integration of Gesture in Language and Speech* (pp. 165-174).

Kafai, Y. B., & Burke, Q. (2015). Constructionist gaming: Understanding the benefits of making games for learning. *Educational Psychologist, 50*(4), 313–334. doi:10.1080/00461520.2015.1124022 PMID:27019536

Kamal, S., Chu, S.-C., & Pedram, M. (2013). Materialism, attitudes, and social media usage and their impact on purchase intention of luxury fashion goods among American and Arab young generations. *Journal of Interactive Advertising, 13*(1), 27–40. doi:10.1080/15252019.2013.768052

Karataş, A. (2008). Media literacy levels of the candidate teachers. Unpublished Master Thesis, Afyon Kocatepe University, Social Sciences Institute, Afyon.

Kashdan, J. (2015). Jeff Bezos on 'Transparent' and Amazon's 'insurmountable opportunity'. *CBS News*. Retrieved from http://www.cbsnews.com/news/amazon-ceo-jeff-bezos-transparent-director-jill-soloway-jeffery-tambor-on-disrupting-industries/

Kasperkevic, J. (2014). Connection failed: Internet still a luxury for many Americans. *The Guardian*. Retrieved from http://www.theguardian.com/money/us-money-log/2014/jan/26/Internet-luxury-low-income-americans

Kassens, A. L. (2014). Tweeting your way to improved #Writing, #Reflection, and #Community. *The Journal of Economic Education, 45*(2), 101–109. doi:10.1080/00220485.2014.889937

Katherine. (2012). Ventajas y Desventajas de la Tecnología en el ámbito educativo. Retrieved from https://katherineiliana.wordpress.com/2012/06/01/ventajas-y-desventajas-de-la-tecnologia-en-el-ambito-educativo/

Keeves, J. P. (1988). *Educational inspect methodology, as good as measurement: An international handbook*. Oxford: Pergamon Press.

Ke, F., & Grabowski, B. (2007). Gameplaying for maths learning: Cooperative or not? *British Journal of Educational Technology, 38*(2), 249–259. doi:10.1111/j.1467-8535.2006.00593.x

Kellner, D., & Share, J. (2007). Critical media literacy, democracy, and the reconstruction of education. In D. Macedo & S.R. Steinberg (Eds.), Media literacy: A reader (pp. 3-23). New York: Peter Lang Publishing.

Kellner, D., & Hammer, R. (Eds.). (2009). *Media/Cultural Studies: Critical Approaches*. New York, NY: Peter Lang.

Kellner, D., & Share, J. (2005). Toward Critical Media Literacy: Core Concepts, Debates, Organizations, And Policy. *Discourse (Abingdon), 26*(3), 369–386. doi:10.1080/01596300500200169

Kellner, D., & Share, J. (2007). Toward Critical Media Literacy: Core concepts, debates, organizations, and policy. *Discourse (Berkeley, Calif.), 26*, 369–386.

Kennelly, P. J. (2009). An online social networking approach to reinforce learning of rocks and minerals. *Journal of Geoscience Education, 57*(1), 33–40. doi:10.5408/1.3544227

Kent, M., & Leaver, T. (2014). The revolution that's already happening. In *An education in Facebook.*

Kesler, T., Tinio, P. P. L., & Nolan, B. T. (2016). What's our position? A Critical Media Literacy study of popular culture websites with eighth-grade special education students. *Reading & Writing Quarterly, 32*(1), 1–26. doi:10.1080/10573569.2013.857976

Khoshelham, K. (2011). Accuracy Analysis Of Kinect Depth Data. In *ITC Faculty of Geo-information Science and Earth Observation*. Netherlands: University of Twente.

King, A. (1993). From sage on the stage to guide on the side. *College Teaching, 41*(1), 30–35. doi:10.1080/87567555. 1993.9926781

Knight, G. (2016). Could a tweet or a text increase college enrollment or student achievement? *The Conversations*. Retrieved from http://theconversation.com/could-a-tweet-or-a-text-increase-college-enrollment-or-student-achievement-57939

Knight, D. K., & Kim, E. Y. (2007). Japanese Consumers need for Uniqueness – Effects on Brand Perceptions and Intention. *Journal of Fashion Marketing and Management, 11*(2), 270–280. doi:10.1108/13612020710751428

Koc, M., & Barut, E. (2016). Development and validation of New Media Literacy Scale (NMLS) for university students. *Computers in Human Behavior, 63*, 834–843. doi:10.1016/j.chb.2016.06.035

Köse, U., Koç, D., & Yücesoy, S. A. (2013). An augmented reality based mobile software to support learning experiences in computer science courses. *Procedia Computer Science, 25*, 370–374. doi:10.1016/j.procs.2013.11.045

Kosminski, L., & Klavier, R. (2010). Constructing professional identity of teachers and teacher-educators in a changing reality. *Dafim, 49*, 11–41. (in Hebrew)

Kowalewskia, S., Zieflea, M., Ziegeldorfb, H., & Wehleb, K. (2015). Like Us On Facebook! – Analyzing user preferences regarding privacy settings in Germany. *Paper presented at the meeting of the 6th International Conference on Applied Human Factors and Ergonomics*, Aachen, Germany. doi:10.1016/j.promfg.2015.07.336

Kozlov, V. (2011). In the cross hairs: Russian social network VKontakt sparks piracy worries. *Billboard, 123*(5).

KPMG FICCI. (2016). The Future: now streaming, Indian Media and Entertainment Industry Report. New Delhi.

KPMG FICCI. (2017). Media for the masses: The promise unfolds, Indian Media and Entertainment Industry Report. New Delhi.

Kruth, J. P., Leu, M. C., & Nakagawa, T. (1998). Progress in additive manufacturing and rapid prototyping. *Annals of the CIRP, 47*(2), 525–540. doi:10.1016/S0007-8506(07)63240-5

Küçükyıldz, G., Ocak, H., Şayli, Ö., & Karakaya, S. (2015). Real Time Control of a WheelChair based on EMG and Kinect for the Disabled People. *Paper presented at National Congress of Medical Technologies*, Türkiye, Bodrum. doi:10.1109/TIPTEKNO.2015.7374606

Kumar, K. J. (1995). *Media Education, Communications and Public Policy: An Indian Perspective*. Bombay: Himalaya Publishing House.

Kuzu, B. Elif., & Demir, K. (2015). Education technology readings 2015. In B. Akkoyunlu, A. İşman ve F. Odabaşı (Eds.), Wearable technology and its use in education (pp. 252-253), Ankara: Pegem Academy.

Lambdin, D. V., Duffy, T. M., & Moore, J. A. (1997). Using an interactive information system to expand preservice teachers' visions of effective mathematics teaching. *Journal of Technology and Teacher Education, 5*(2), 171–202.

Lambert, J. (2003). *Digital storytelling cookbook and traveling companion*. Berkeley, CA: Digital Diner Press. Retrieved from http://www.storycenter.org/cookbook.pdf

Lankshear, C., & Knobel, M. (2008). *Digital Literacies: concepts, policies, and practices*. New York, NY: Peter Lang.

Lauzen, M., Dozier, D. M., & Horan, N. (2008). Constructing Gender Stereotypes through Social Roles in Prime-Time Television. *Journal of Broadcasting & Electronic Media, 52*(2), 200–214. doi:10.1080/08838150801991971

Ledford, D. M. (2016). Development of a Professional Learning Framework to Improve Teacher Practice in Technology Integration [Doctoral dissertation]. Boise State University.

Lee, L. (2011). Blogging: Promoting learner autonomy and intercultural competence through Study Abroad. *Language Learning & Technology, 15*(3), 87–109.

Leu, D. J., Kinzer, C. K., Coiro, J. L., & Cammack, D. W. (2004). Toward a theory of new literacies emerging from the Internet and other information and communication technologies. *Theoretical models and processes of reading, 5*(1), 1570-1613.

Leu, D. J., Kinzer, C. K., Coiro, J. L., & Cammack, D. W. (2004a). *Toward a theory of new literacies emerging from the internet and other information and communication technologies.* Retrieved from http://www.readingonline.org/newliteracies/leu/

Leu, D. J., Zawilinski, L., Forzani, E., & Timbrell, N. (2014). Best practices in teaching the new literacies of online research and comprehension. Retrieved from http://www.orca.uconn.edu/orca/assets/File/Best%20Practices%20in%20new%20literacies.pdf

Leu, D. J., Kinzer, C. K., Coiro, J. L., & Cammack, D. W. (2004b). Toward a theory of new literacies emerging from the internet and other information and communication technologies. In R. B. Ruddell & N. J. Unrau (Eds.), *Theoretical models and processes of reading* (5th ed., pp. 1570–1613). Newark, DE: International Reading Association. (Original work published 2000)

Levin, J. S., Walker, L., Haberler, Z., & Jackson-Boothby, A. (2013). The Divided Self: The Double Consciousness of Faculty of Color in Community Colleges. *Community College Review, 41*(4), 311–329. doi:10.1177/0091552113504454

Lev-On, A. (2015). Introduction: Online communities – Their functioning and uses. In A. Lev-On (Ed.), *Online communities* (pp. 7–25). Tel Aviv: Rassling. (in Hebrew)

Lev-On, A., & Hardin, R. (2008). Internet-based collaborations and their political significance. *Journal of Information Technology & Politics, 4*(2), 5–27. doi:10.1080/19331680802076074

Lewin, R. (Ed.). (2009). *The handbook of practice and research in Study Abroad: Higher education and the quest for global citizenship.* New York: Routledge.

Lewis, C. S. (n.d.). *Brainyquote.com.* Retrieved from http://www.brainyquote.com/search_results.html?q=C.+S.+Lewis

Lim, C. P., Teo, Y. H., Wong, P., Khine, M. S., Chai, C. S., & Divaharan, S. (2003). Creating a conducive learning environment for the effective integration of ICT: Classroom management issues. *Journal of Interactive Learning Research, 14*(4), 405–423.

Liu, Y. (2014). Tangram race mathematical game: Combining wearable technology and traditional games for enhancing mathematics learning. Unpublished doctoral dissertation, Worcester Polytechnic Institute, Worcester, MA, USA.

Liu, G. Z., Kuo, F. R., Shi, Y. R., & Chen, Y. W. (2015). Dedicated design and usability of a context-aware ubiquitous learning environment for developing receptive language skills: A case study. *International Journal of Mobile Learning and Organisation, 9*(1), 49–65. doi:10.1504/IJMLO.2015.069717

Livingstone, S. (2003) The changing nature and uses of media literacy. *Media@LSE Electronic* Working Papers, No. 4

Livingstone, S. (2003). The changing nature of audiences: From the mass audience to the interactive media user. In A. Valdivia (Ed.), The Blackwell Companion to Media Research (pp. 337-359). Oxford: Blackwell.

Livingstone, S. (2007). *Internet Literacy: Young People's Negotiation of New Online Opportunities.* The John D. and Catherine T. MacArthur Foundation Series on Digital Media and Learning.

Livingstone, S. (2004). Media literacy and the challenge of new Information and communication technologies. *Communication Review*, 7(1), 3–14. doi:10.1080/10714420490280152

Livingstone, S. (2010). Giving people a voice: On the critical role of the interview in the history of audience research. *Communication, Culture & Critique*, 3(4), 566–571. doi:10.1111/j.1753-9137.2010.01086.x

Li, X. (2009). Review of distance education used in higher education in China. *Asian Journal of Distance Education*, 7(2), 22–27.

Loizzo, J., Borron, A., Gee, A., & Ertmer, P. (2016). Teaching convergence in 21st century undergraduate agricultural communication: A pilot study of backpack multimedia kits in a blended. Project-based learning course. *Journal of Applied Communications*, 100(2). doi:10.4148/1051-0834.1033

Lotan, Z. (2012). Learning patterns of student-teachers on a social-professional network. [Hebrew]. *Dafim*, 54, 248–280.

Loton, D., Borkoles, E., Lubman, D., & Polman, R. (2016). Video game addiction, engagement and symptoms of stress, depression and anxiety: The mediating role of coping. *International Journal of Mental Health and Addiction*, 14(4), 565–578. doi:10.1007/s11469-015-9578-6

Lovelock, M. Call me Caitlyn: Making and making over the 'authentic' transgender body in Anglo-American popular culture. *Journal of Gender Studies*. doi:10.1080/09589236.2016.1155978

Lv, Z., Feng, S., Feng, L., & Li, H. (2015, March). Extending touch-less interaction on vision based wearable device. In *Proceedings of the 2015 IEEE Virtual Reality (VR) conference* (pp. 231-232). IEEE.

Mack, S. (2013, June). What we mean when we talk about Florida's digital divide. *State Impact Florida*. Retrieved from https://stateimpact.npr.org/florida/2013/06/10/what-we-mean-when-we-talk-about-floridas-digital-divide/

Madison, E. (2014). Training digital age journalists: Blurring the distinction between students and professionals. *Journalism and Mass Communication Educator*, 69(3), 314–324. doi:10.1177/1077695814532926

Maloney, E. J. (2007). What Web 2.0 can teach us about learning. *The Chronicle of Higher Education*, 53(18), B26.

Mannix, E., & Neale, M. A. (2005). What differences make a difference? The promise and reality of diverse team in organizations. *Psychological Science in the Public Interest*, 6(2), 31–55. doi:10.1111/j.1529-1006.2005.00022.x PMID:26158478

Mann, S. (1997). Wearable computing: A first step toward personal imaging. *Computer*, 30(2), 25–32. doi:10.1109/2.566147

March, T. (2012). *13 Reasons Why Digital Learning is Better*. Retrieved from http://tommarch.com/2012/01/digital-learning/

Markey, P. M., Markey, C. N., & French, J. E. (2014). Violent video games and real-world violence: Rhetoric versus data. *Psychology of Popular Media Culture*, 4(4), 277–295. doi:10.1037/ppm0000030

Markus, M. L., & Robey, D. (1988). Information technology and organizational change: Causal structure in theory and research. *Management Science*, 34(5), 583–598. doi:10.1287/mnsc.34.5.583

Marquez, B. Y., Alanis, A., Lopez, M. A., & Magdaleno-Palencia, J. S. (2012). Sport education based technology: Stress measurement in competence. In *Proceedings of the 2012 International Conference one-Learning and e-Technologies in Education (ICEEE)* (pp. 247–52). IEEE.

Marsh, J. (2014). Young Children's Online Practices: Past, Present and Future. *Paper presented at the Literacy Research Association Conference*, Marco Island, December 3-6. Retrieved from https://www.academia.edu/9799081/Young_Childrens_Online_Practices_Past_Present_and_Future

Martens, H. (2010). Evaluating Media Literacy Education: Concepts, Theories and Future Directions. *Journal of Media Literacy Education, 2*(1), 1–22.

Martin, F., & Ertzberger, J. (2013). Here and now mobile learning: An experimental study on the use of mobile technology. *Computers & Education, 68*, 76–85. doi:10.1016/j.compedu.2013.04.021

Mâţă, L. (2013). Social media tools in initial teacher education. In *E-Learning 2.0 technologies and web applications in higher education.*

Matveev, A. V., & Nelson, P. E. (2004). Cross cultural communication competence and multicultural team performance: Perceptions of American and Russian managers. *International Journal of Cross Cultural Management: CCM, 4*(2), 253–270. Retrieved from http://search.proquest.com/docview/221216692?accountid=11667 doi:10.1177/1470595804044752

Ma, Y., Williams, D., Prejean, L., & Richard, C. (2007). A research agenda for developing and implementing educational computer games. *British Journal of Educational Technology, 38*(3), 513–518. doi:10.1111/j.1467-8535.2007.00714.x

Mayer, R. E. (1984). Aids to text comprehension. *Educational Psychologist, 19*(1), 30–42. doi:10.1080/00461528409529279

Mcdonough, R. (2016). Plato's cosmic animal vs. the Daoist cosmic plant: Religious and ideological implications. *Journal For The Study Of Religions And Ideologies, 15*(45), 3.

McInroy, L. B., & Craig, S. (2015). Transgender representation in offline and online media: LGBTQ youth perspectives. *Journal of Human Behavior in the Social Environment, 25*(6), 606–617. doi:10.1080/10911359.2014.995392

McLean, S. A., Paxton, S. J., & Wertheim, E. H. (2016). The measurement of media literacy in eating disorder risk factor research: Psychometric properties of six measures. *Journal of Eating Disorders, 4*(30), 1–12. doi:10.1186/s40337-016-0116-0 PMID:27895912

Mead, S. (2012, May). *Sara Mead's policy notebook: Teddy Rice, President and Co-Founder, Ellevation.* Retrieved from http://blogs.edweek.org/edweek/sarameads_policy_notebook /2012/05/ teddy_rice_president_and_co-founder_ellevation.html

MediaSmarts. (n. d.). *The intersection of digital and media literacy.* Retrieved from http://mediasmarts.ca/digital-media-literacy/general-information/digital-media-literacy-fundamentals/intersection-digital-media-literacy/

Medora, N., & Roy, N. (2017). Recruiting, organizing, planning and conducting a 3-week, short-term, Study Abroad program for undergraduate students: Guidelines and suggestions for first-time faculty leaders. *International Journal of Humanities and Social Science Research, 3*, 1–11. doi:10.6000/2371-1655.2017.03.01

Mehdi, M., & Alharby, A. (2016). Purpose, Scope, and Technical Considerations of Wearable Technologies. In J. Holland (Ed.), Wearable Technology and Mobile Innovations for Next-Generation Education. doi:10.4018/978-1-5225-0069-8.ch001

Mehlman, B. P. (2003). Technology administration ICT literacy: Preparing the digital generation for the age of innovation. Retrieved from http://www.technology.gov/Speeches/p_BPM_030124-DigGen.htm

Members Council on Library Services Executive Board Members (2016, September 22). Phone conference call.

Members Council on Library Services. (2016, November 30). Web conference focus interview at regular meeting at University of Central Florida.

Meyer, L. (2015). White House announces ConnectHome initiative to address the homework gap. *THE Journal.* Retrieved from https://thejournal.com/articles/2015/07/15/white-house-announces-connecthome-initiative-to-address-the-homework-gap.aspx

Meyers, E., Erickson, I., & Small, R. (2013). Digital literacy and informal learning environments: An introduction. *Learning, Media and Technology, 38*(4), 355–367. doi:10.1080/17439884.2013.783597

Microsoft. (2015). Creación de lecciones interactivas. Retrieved from http://onenoteforteachers.com/es-MX/Guides/Creaci%C3%B3n%20de%20lecciones%20interactivas%20con%20OneNote

Microsoft. (2016a). Frequently Asked Questions about the OneNote Class Notebook app. Retrieved from https://support.office.com/en-us/article/Frequently-Asked-Questions-about-the-OneNote-Class-Notebook-app-9183c502-9374-42a7-8d59-3a17c377077d?ui=en-US&rs=en-US&ad=US

Microsoft. (2016b). One Note. Retrieved from https://www.onenote.com/

Miejan, T. (2010). Just how connected are we? *Edge Magazine*. Retrieved from http://www.edgemagazine.net/2010/04/just-how-connected-are-we/

Milham, E. (2015). 42 celebs we bet you didn't know are transgender. *Likesharetweet*. Retrieved from http://www.likesharetweet.com/inspiring/21-celebs-transgender/

Miller, S. (2016). Trans*+ing classrooms: The pedagogy of refusal as mediator for learning. *Social Sciences, 5*(3), 1–17. doi:10.3390/socsci5030034

Ministério da Educação e Ciência. (2011). Recomendação no 6/2011 sobre Educação para a Literacia Mediática. Retrieved from http://dre.pt/pdf2s/2011/12/250000000/5094250947.pdf

Mock, J. (2011). More than a pretty face: Sharing my journey to womanhood. *JanetMock.com*. Retrieved from http://janetmock.com/2011/05/17/janet-mock-comes-out-transgender-marie-claire/

Monahan, R. (2014). What happens when kids don't have Internet at home? *The Atlantic*. Retrieved from http://www.theatlantic.com/education/archive/2014/12/what-happens-when-kids-dont-have-Internet-at-home/383680/

Moon, S. (2015). Wuwei (non-action) Philosophy and Actions: Rethinking actions in school reform. *Educational Philosophy and Theory, 47*(5), 455–473. doi:10.1080/00131857.2013.879692

Moran, M., Seaman, J., & Tinti-Kane, H. (2011). Teaching, learning, and sharing: How today's higher education faculty use social media. *Babson Survey Research Group*. http://files.eric.ed.gov/fulltext/ED535130.pdf

Mor, N. (2014). *The place of the blog on the Shluvim network. Research report*. Israel: MOFET Institute. (in Hebrew)

Morris, J. B. (2015). *Language and citizenship may contribute to low Internet use among Hispanics*. U.S. Department of Commerce, National Telecommunications and Information Administration. Retrieved from https://www.ntia.doc.gov/blog/2015/language-and-citizenship-may-contribute-low-Internet-use-among-hispanics

Mullings, B. (1999). Insider or outsider, both or neither: Some dilemmas of interviewing in a crosscultural setting. *Geoforum, 30*(4), 337–350. doi:10.1016/S0016-7185(99)00025-1

Mumtaz, S. (2000). Factors affecting teachers' use of information and communications technology: a review of the literature. *Journal of information technology for teacher education, 9*(3), 319-342.

Murphy, D., Walker, R., & Webb, G. (2013). *Online learning and teaching with technology: case studies, experience and practice*. Routledge.

Murray, J. (2003). Contemporary literacy: Essential skills for the 21st century. *MultiMedia Schools, 10*(2), 14–18.

Murray, J. (2008). Looking at ICT literacy standards through the Big6™ lens. *Library Media Connection, 26*(7), 38–43.

Mustanski, B., Newcomb, M. E., & Garofalo, R. (2011). Mental health of gay, lesbian and bisexual youths: A developmental resiliency perspective. *Journal of Gay & Lesbian Social Services, 23*(2), 204–225. doi:10.1080/10538720.2011.561474 PMID:21731405

Nantz, K., & Kemmerer, B. (2005).Technology literacy applications in learning environments. In B. Akkoyunlu, & D. D. Carbonara (Eds.), Understanding the Role of Type Preferences in Fostering Technological Literacy (s.107-108), United States of America: Idea Group.

National Association for Media Literacy Education. (2007). *Core principles of MLE.* Retrieved from https://namle.net/publications/core-principles/

National Center for Education Statistics. (n. d.). *IPEDs Data Center.* Retrieved from https://nces.ed.gov/ipeds/datacenter/

National Council of Teachers of English. (2008). The definition of 21st Century Literacies. Retrieved from http://www.ncte.org/governance/literacies

National Telecommunications and Information Administration. (n. d.). University cooperation for advanced Internet development. Retrieved from http://www2.ntia.doc.gov/grantee/university-corporation-for-advanced-Internet-development

NC State Industry Expansion Solutions. (2015). Pros and Cons of Online Education. *NC State White Papers.* Retrieved from https://www.ies.ncsu.edu/resources/white-papers/pros-and-cons-of-online-education/

Neill, M. J. (1977). Some thoughts on reasons, definitions and tasks to achieve functional computer literacy. *SIGCSE Bulletin, 9*(1), 175–177. doi:10.1145/382063.803386

Nemko, M. (2008). America's most overrated product: The Bachelor's degree. *Chronicle of Higher Education.* Retrieved from http://www.chronicle.com/article/americas-most-overrated/19869

Neuendorf, K. A. (2002). *The content analysis guidebook.* Thousand Oaks, CA: Sage.

New Media Consortium. (2017). *NMC horizon report: 2017 higher education edition.* Retrieved from http://cdn.nmc.org/media/2017-nmc-horizon-report-he-EN.pdf

Nonnecke, B., & Preece, J. (2000). Lurker demographics: Counting the silent. In *Proceedings of the SIGCHI Conference on Human Factors in Computing Systems* (pp. 73-80). doi:10.1145/332040.332409

North Central Regional Educational Laboratory. (2001). *Critical Issue: Using Technology to Enhance Literacy Instruction.* Retrieved from http://www.ncrel.org/sdrs/areas/issues/content/cntareas/reading/li300.htm#contacts

Oblinger, D., & Oblinger, J. (2005). Is it age or IT: First steps toward understanding the net generation. *Educating the net generation, 2*(1–2), 20.

Odabaşı, H. F. (2000, May). Social Impact and Technology Literacy. *Paper presented at Education Conference In light of Information Technology (BITE 2000).* Middle East Technical University, Ankara.

OECD. (2016). *Global competency for an inclusive world.* Paris, France.

Ofcom. (2017). About Media Literacy. Retrieved from https://www.ofcom.org.uk/research-and-data/media-literacy-research/media-literacy

Ohler, J. (2013). *Digital Storytelling in the Classroom: New Media Pathways to Literacy, Learning, and Creativity.* Thousand Oaks, CA: Corwin.

Ohler, J. (2006). The World of Digital Storytelling. *Educational Leadership, 63*(4), 44–47.

Once Noticias. (2013). Ventajas y desventajas del uso de la tecnología en niños. Retrieved from www.oncenoticias.tv, https://youtu.be/gXDgyY1RVqY

OneNote Team. (2014a). Introducing OneNote Class Notebooks—a flexible digital framework for teaching and learning. Retrieved from https://blogs.office.com/2014/10/07/introducing-onenote-class-notebooks-flexible-digital-framework-teaching-learning/

OneNote Team. (2014b). OneNote Class Notebook Creator updated with top educator requests and new language support. Retrieved from https://blogs.office.com/2014/12/09/onenote-class-notebook-creator-updated-top-educator-requests-new-language-support/

OneNote. (2013). Bloc de notas de clase de OneNote. Retrieved March 10, 2016 from https://www.onenote.com/class-notebook

Oprah.com. (2011). *Chaz Bono on when he knew he was transgender*. Retrieved from http://www.oprah.com/own-oprahshow/chaz-bonos-on-when-he knew-he-was-transgender-video

Organization for Economic Co-Operation and Development. (2005). *Are students ready for a technology-rich world? What PISA studies tell us*. Paris, France: OECD Publications.

Ozan, O. (2013). Scaffolding in connectivist mobile learning environment. Unpublished Master Thesis, Anadolu University, Social Sciences Institute, Eskişehir.

P21. (2007). Framework for 21ˢᵗ century learning. *Partnership for 21ˢᵗ Century Learning*. Retrieved from http://www.p21.org/our-work/p21-framework

P21. (n. d.). Our vision and mission. *Partnership for 21ˢᵗ Century Learning*. Retrieved from http://www.p21.org/about-us/our-mission

Palaiologou, I. (2016). Children under five and digital technologies: Implications for early years pedagogy. *European Early Childhood Education Research Journal, 24*(1), 5–24. doi:10.1080/1350293X.2014.929876

Palomo, J., & Montalvo, S. (2010). *Plataforma para el apoyo a la docencia basada en la Web 2.0 y la actualidad relevante. E-learning en la enseñanza universitaria. I Jornadas de Innovación y TIC (Tecnologías de Información y Comunicación) Educativas* (pp. 43–46). Madrid, España: JITICE.

Pan, V. L., & Akay, C. (2016). Prospective teachers' and instructors' opinion on mobile communication technology use for anywhere any time lear. Mustafa Kemal University Journal of Graduate School of Social Sciences, 13(34).

Pantelopoulos, A., & Bourbakis, N. G. (2010). A survey on wearable sensor-based systems for health monitoring and prognosis. *IEEE Transactions on Systems, Man and Cybernetics. Part C, Applications and Reviews, 40*(1), 1–12. doi:10.1109/TSMCC.2009.2032660

Papastephanou, M. (2005). Globalisation, Globalism and Cosmopolitanism as an Educational Ideal. *Educational Philosophy and Theory, 37*(4), 533–551. doi:10.1111/j.1469-5812.2005.00139.x

Parker, H. (2013). 'It's a strange thing for a mother to go through': Cher on how she came to terms with Chaz undergoing sex change. *Daily Mail*. Retrieved from http://www.dailymail.co.uk/tvshowbiz/article-2430741/Cher-came-terms-Chaz-undergoing-sex-change.html

Partnership for 21st Century Learning—P21 (2016). Framework for 21ˢᵗ Century Learning. Retrieved from http://www.p21.org/our-work/p21-framework

Partnership For 21st Century Skills, (P21). Framework For 21st Century Learning. Retrieved from http://www.p21.org/about-us/p21-framework

Pearce, K., Barta, K., & Fesenmaier, M. (2015). The Affordances of Social Networking Sites for Relational Maintenance in a Distrustful Society: The Case of Azerbaijan. *Social Media+ Society*, 1(2).

Pelletier, C. (2005). The uses of literacy in studying computer games: Comparing students' oral and visual representations of games. *English Teaching*, 4(1), 40–59. Retrieved from http://education.waikato.ac.nz/journal/english_journal/uploads/files/2005v4n1art3.pdf

Pereira, S., Pereira, L. & Melro, A. (2015). The Portuguese programme one laptop per child: Political, educational and social impact. In *Digital Literacy, Technology and Social Inclusion – Making sense of one-to-one computer programmes around the world* (pp. 29-100). Vila Nova de Famalicão: Edições Húmus.

Pew Research Center. (2016). *Mobile technology fact sheet*. Retrieved from http://www.pewInternet.org/fact-sheets/mobile-technology-fact-sheet/

Piller, I. (2016). *Linguistic diversity and social justice*. Oxford: Oxford University Press. doi:10.1093/acprof:oso/9780199937240.001.0001

Pinto, M., Pereira, S., Pereira, L., & Ferreira, T. (2011). *Educação para os Media em Portugal: experiências, actores e contextos*. Lisboa: ERC.

Plomp, T., Anderson, R. E., & Kontogiannopoulou-Polydorides, G. (Eds.). (1996). *Cross national policies and practices on computers in education*. The Netherlands: Kluwer Academic Publishers. doi:10.1007/978-0-585-32767-9

Potter, J. (2005). Media Literacy (3rd ed.). USA: Sage Pub.

Potter, W. J. (2004). Theory of Media Literacy: A Cognitve Approach. *Sage (Atlanta, Ga.)*.

Prensky, M. (2001). *Digital game-based learning*. New York, NY: McGraw-Hill.

Prensky, M. (2001). Digital natives, digital immigrants. *On the Horizon*, 9(5), 1–6. doi:10.1108/10748120110424816

Price, K. (2006). Web 2.0 and education: What it means for us all. *Paper presented at the 2006 Australian Computers in Education Conference*, Cairns, Australia, October 2-4.

Qu, X., & Stucker, B. (2003). A 3D surface offset method for STL-format models. *Rapid Prototyping Journal*, 9(3), 133–141. doi:10.1108/13552540310477436

Raley, A. B., & Lucas, J. L. (2006, October). Stereotype or success? *Journal of Homosexuality*, 51(2), 19–38. doi:10.1300/J082v51n02_02 PMID:16901865

Randel, J. M., Morris, B. A., Wetzel, C. D., & Whitehill, B. V. (1992). The effectiveness of games for educational purposes: A review of recent research. *Simulation & Gaming*, 23(3), 261–276. doi:10.1177/1046878192233001

Rau, P. L. P., Gao, Q., & Ding, Y. (2008). Relationship between the level of intimacy and lurking in online social network services. *Computers in Human Behavior*, 24(6), 2757–2770. doi:10.1016/j.chb.2008.04.001

Reagan, T. G., & Osborn, T. A. (2001). *The foreign language educator in society: Toward a critical pedagogy*. Routledge.

Redecker, C., Ala-Mukta, K., & Punie, Y. (2010). *Learning 2.0 – The impact of Social Media on Learning in Europe*. Luxembourg: Office for the Official Publications of the European Communities.

Report of Federal Communications Commission in the matter of violent television programming and its impact on children. (n.d.). Retrieved from http://www.c-span.org/pdf/fcc_tvviolence.pdf

Riboni, D., & Bettini, C. (2011). Hybrid reasoning for context-aware activity recognition. *Personal and Ubiquitous Computing, 15*(3), 271–289. doi:10.1007/s00779-010-0331-7

Richardson, W. (2006). *Blogs, Wikis, Podcasts, and other powerful tools for classrooms*. Thousand Oaks, CA: Sage.

Rideout, V. J., & Katz, V. S. (2016). *Opportunity for all? Technology and learning in lower-income families. A report of the Families and Media Project*. New York, NY: The Joan Ganz Cooney Center at Sesame Workshop.

Ridings, C. M., & Gefen, D. (2004). Virtual community attraction: Why people hang out online. *Journal of Computer-Mediated Communication, 10*(1).

Ritzhaupt, A. D., Liu, F., Dawson, K., & Barron, E. B. (2013). Differences in student information and communication technology literacy based on socioeconomic status, ethnicity, and gender: Evidence of a digital divide in Florida schools. *Journal of Research on Technology in Education, 45*(4), 291–307. doi:10.1080/15391523.2013.10782607

Rivoltella, P. (2007). Realidad y desafíos de la educación en medios en Italia. *Comunicar, 28*, 17–24.

Rivoltella, P. (2012). Retrospectivas e tendências da pesquisa em mídia-educação no contexto internacional. In *Cultura Digital e Escola: pesquisa e formação de professores, org. Mónica Fantin e Pier Cesare Rivoltella*. Campinas, SP: Papirus Editora.

Robertson, K. (2013). Preparing ELLs to be 21st-century learners. *Colorin Colorado*. Retrieved from http://www.colorincolorado.org/article/preparing-ells-be-21st-century-learners

Roberts, P. (2012). Bridging east and west—or, a bridge too far? Paulo Freire and the *Tao Te Ching. Educational Philosophy and Theory, 44*(9), 942–958. doi:10.1111/j.1469-5812.2011.00797.x

Roberts, P. (2013). Acceptance, resistance and educational transformation: A Taoist reading of The First Man. *Educational Philosophy and Theory, 45*(11), 1175–1189. doi:10.1080/00131857.2013.772700

Robin, B. (2008). The effective uses of digital storytelling as a teaching and learning tool. In *Handbook of Research on Teaching Literacy Through the Communicative and Visual Arts* (Vol. 2, pp. 429–440). New York, NY: Lawrence Erlbaum Associates.

Roblyer, M. D. (2006). *Integrating educational technology into teaching* (5th ed.). Upper Saddle River, NJ: Pearson Merrill Prentice Hall.

Rochlin, M. (1972). Heterosexual Questionnaire. *Gender and Sexuality Center*. Retrieved from https://www.uwgb.edu/pride-center/files/pdfs/Heterosexual_Questionnaire.pdf

Rogers, Y. (2014, June). New technology, new learning? In *Proceedings of the 2014 conference on Innovation & technology in computer science education* (pp. 1-1). ACM.

Rogers, P. C., Liddle, S. W., Peter, C. H. A. N., Doxey, A., & Brady, I. S. O. M. (2007). A Web 2.0 learning platform: Harnessing collective intelligence. *Turkish Online Journal of Distance Education, 8*(3), 16–33.

Rosales, J. (2013). ¿Qué es OneNote y para qué sirve? *Apuntes de Office*. Apuntesdeoffice.blogspot.mx. Retrieved from http://apuntesdeoffice.blogspot.mx/2013/10/que-es-onenote-y-para-que-sirve.html

RTÜK (Radyo ve Televizyon Üst Kurulu-Radio and Television Supreme Council), Media Literacy Book, Retrieved from https://www.rtuk.gov.tr/duyurular/3788/611/22-09-2014-medya-okuryazarligi-kitabi-sil-bastan.html

Ryan, C., Huebner, D., Diaz, R. M., & Sanchez, J. (2009). Family rejection as a predictor of negative health outcomes in white and Latino lesbian, gay, and bisexual young adults. *Pediatrics, 123*(1), 346–352. doi:10.1542/peds.2007-3524 PMID:19117902

Sabar Ben-Yehoshua, N. (1990). *Qualitative research in teaching and learning*. Givataim: Massada. (in Hebrew)

Sabrina, D. (2016). *Traditional Journalism is Dying: Why the Publishing Industry Must Adapt to Survive*. Retrieved from http://www.huffingtonpost.com/news/content-creation/

Şahinler Albayrak, M. (2015). The impact of Kinect usable 3D virtual reality applications on young learners' vocabulary development in foreign languages vocabulary learning. Unpublished Master Thesis, Fatih University, İstanbul.

Saldanha, A. (2016, December 27). Top 10 fake news forwards that we (almost) believed in 2016. *hindustantimes.com*. Retrieved from http://www.hindustantimes.com/india-news/top-10-fake-news-forwards-that-we-almost-believed-in-2016/story-hL7pnDYwF51M4cNAwgMtrN.html

Salen, K. (2006). Everywhere now: Three dialogues on kids, games, and learning. Retrieved from http://spotlight.macfound.org/images/uploads-participants/everywhere_now_dialogues_salen.pdf

Sanchez, G. (2014). Qué es la tinta electrónica. Retrieved from http://www.gusgsm.com/que_es_la_tinta_electronica

Sauder, K. (2017). If you're disabled in an M. Night Shyamalan film, you are either a villain or a supercrip (mostly a villain though). *Crippled Scholar*. Retrieved from https://crippledscholar.com/category/media-representation-of-disability/

Savolainen, R. (2002). Network competence and information seeking on the Internet: From definitions towards a social cognitive model. *The Journal of Documentation*, *58*(2), 211–226. doi:10.1108/00220410210425467

Scardamalia, M., & Bereiter, C. (2006). Knowledge building: Theory, pedagogy, and technology. In K. Sawyer (Ed.), *Cambridge Handbook of the Learning Sciences* (pp. 97–118). New York: Cambridge University Press. Retrieved from http://ikit.org/fulltext/2006_KBTheory.pdf

Schilder, E., Lockee, B., & Saxon, D. P. (2016). The Challenges of Assessing Media Literacy Education. *Journal of Media Literacy Education*, *8*(1), 32–48.

Scribol. (2015). 20 Beautiful transgender women who make your girlfriend look like a dude. Retrieved from http://scribol.com/pop-culture/celebrities/beautiful-transgender-women/

Sefton-Green, J., Marsh, J., Erstad, O., & Flewitt, R. (2016). Establishing a Research Agenda for the Digital Literacy Practices of Young Children: A White Paper for COST Action IS1410. Retrieved from http://digilitey.eu

Seifert, T. (2015). Pedagogical applications of smartphone integration in teaching: Lecturers, pre-Service teachers and pupils perspectives. *International Journal of Mobile and Blended Learning*, *7*(2), 1–16. doi:10.4018/ijmbl.2015040101

Seifert, T. (2016). Involvement, Collaboration and Engagement–Social Networks through a Pedagogical Lens. *Journal of Learning Design*, *9*(2), 31–45. doi:10.5204/jld.v9i2.272

Serrhini, M. (2015). Online Experimentation: Emerging Technologies and IoT, M. T. Restivo, A. Cardoso and A.M. Lopes (Ed.), BCI Sensor as ITS for Controlling Student Attention in Online Experimentation, Spain: International Frequency Sensor Association Publishing.

Seymour, S. (2008). *Fashionable technology: The intersection of design, fashion, science, and technology*. Springer Publishing Company, Incorporated. doi:10.1007/978-3-211-74500-7

Sheely, S. (2006). Persistent technologies: Why can't we stop lecturing online? In L. Markauskaite, P. Goodyear, and P. Reimann (Eds.), *Who's learning? Whose technology? Proceedings of the 23rd ASCILITE Conference* (pp. 769-774). Sydney: CoCo, University of Sydney.

Sherman, W. R., & Craig, A. B. (1995). Literacy in virtual reality: A new medium. *Computer Graphics*, *29*(4), 37–42. Retrieved from http://portal.acm.org/citation.cfm?id=216887 doi:10.1145/216876.216887

Shilo, R., & Caspi, A. (2011). To climb up the network – Influence of use of social networks in an informal educational framework on identification with a group (electronic version). In I. Eshet-Alkalai, A. Caspi & N. Geri (Eds.), *Book of the Chase Conference for Technological Learning Research, 2011: The learning man in a technological era.* (pp. 239-247). Raanana: The Open University. (in Hebrew) Retrieved from: http://chais.openu.ac.il/chais2011/download/shilo_caspi.pdf

Shoop, M. C. (2009). *Public service employees experience in communities of practice* [Ph.D. dissertation]. Antioch University.

Siemens, G. (2005). Connectivism: A learning theory for the digital age. *International Journal of Instructional Technology and Distance Learning, 2*(1), 3–10.

Silverblatt, A., & Nagaraj, K. V. Kundu, Vedabhyas & Yadav, Anubhuti (n. d.). *Media Literacy, Keys to Interpreting Media Messages.* Retrieved on December 20, 2016 from www.dimle.org

Singare, S., Lian, Q., Wang, W. P., Wang, J., Liu, Y., Li, D., & Lu, B. (2009). Rapid prototyping assisted surgery planning. *Rapid Prototyping Journal, 15*(1), 1923. doi:10.1108/13552540910925027

Singer, J. (2005). The political j-blogger: 'Normalizing' a new media form to fit old norms and practices. *Journalism, 6*(2), 173–198. doi:10.1177/1464884905051009

Singh, J. (2015) From Information Skills for Learning to Media and Information Literacy -A Decade of Transition in South Asia: 2004-2014. In J. Singh, A. Grizzle, S.J. Yess et al. (Eds.), Media and Information Literacy for the Sustainable Development Goals: MILID Yearbook 2015 (pp. 49-58). Gothenburg, Sweden: Nordicom.

Singleton, M. (2015, January 29). The FCC has changed the definition of broadband. *The Verge.* Retrieved from http://www.theverge.com/2015/1/29/7932653/fcc-changed-definition-broadband-25Mbps

Sinha, Pratik (2017, April 15). Killing of one Abu Syed in Bangladesh shared 37000+ times on FB as a Hindu killed by Muslims in West Bengal. *altnews.com.* Retrieved from https://www.altnews.in/killing-one-abu-syed-bangladesh-shared-37000-times-fb-hindu-killed-muslims-west-bengal/

Skrbis, Z., Kendall, G., & Woodward, I. (2004). Locating cosmopolitanism: Between humanist ideal and grounded social category. *Theory, Culture & Society, 21*(6), 115–136. doi:10.1177/0263276404047418

Smith, A. (2010). Technology trends among people of color. *Pew Internet and American Life Project.* Retrieved from http://www.pewInternet.org/2010/09/17/technology-trends-among-people-of-color/

Smith, A., Rainee, L., & Zickuhr, K. (2011, July 19). College students and technology. *Pew Research Center.* Retrieved from http://www.pewinternet.org/2011/07/19/college-students-and-technology/

Smith, J. (2017). Assessing creativity: Creating a rubric to effectively evaluate mediated digital portfolios. *Journalism and Mass Communication Educator, 72*(1), 24–36. doi:10.1177/1077695816648866

Soloway J. (2014). Pilot. *Transparent.* Retrieved from http://www.amazon.com/gp/product/B00I3MPRUK/ref=dv_dp_ep1

Somech, A. (2005). Teachers personal and team empowerment and their relations to organizational outcomes: Contradictory or compatible constructs? *Educational Administration Quarterly, 41*(2), 237–266. doi:10.1177/0013161X04269592

Spectrum, G. (2017). *Gender Spectrum.* Retrieved from https://www.genderspectrum.org/quick-links/trainings/

Squire, K. (2011). *Video games and learning: Teaching and participatory culture in the digital age.* New York, NY: Teachers College Press.

Stahl, G. K., Maznevski, M. L., Voigt, A., & Jonsen, K. (2010). Unraveling the effects of cultural diversity in teams: A meta-analysis of research on multicultural work groups. *Journal of International Business Studies*, *41*(4), 690–709. doi:10.1057/jibs.2009.85

Stanley, L. D. (2003). Beyond access: psychosocial barriers to computer literacy special issue: ICTs and community networking. *The Information Society*, *19*(5), 407–416. doi:10.1080/715720560

State of Tennessee v. Federal Communications Commission and United States of America. (2015).

State University System of Florida Board of Governors. (2013). *Task force on postsecondary online education in Florida: Final report*. Retrieved from http://flbog.edu/about/taskforce/_doc/2013_12_09_Online-Task-Force-Final-Report.pdf

State University System of Florida Board of Governors. (2015). *Online education 2025 strategic plan*. Retrieved from http://OnlineStratePlanning%Committee/2015_11_05%20FINAL_StrategicPlan.pdf

State University System of Florida Board of Governors. (2016). *Implementation schedule and action steps for strategic goals and associated tactics for online education: 2025 strategic plan*. Retrieved from http://flbog.edu/board/advisorygroups/_doc/online/2016_07_24_Implementation _Timeline.pdf

Statista. (n. d.). How frequently do you use the internet to consume or access online press or news content? Retrieved March 8, 2017 from https://www.statista.com/statistics/661910/online-news-usage-frequency-germany/

Statista. (n. d.). Number of monthly active VKontakte users via desktop connections in Russia from December 2012 to December 2014 (in millions). Retrieved March 8, 2017 from https://www.statista.com/statistics/425423/number-of-monthly-active-vkontakte-users/

Statista. (n. d.). Number of persons reading newspapers during their free time in Germany from 2010 to 2015, by frequency (in millions). Retrieved March 8, 2017 from https://www.statista.com/statistics/383150/leisure-newspaper-reading-frequency-germany/

Steakley, L. (2013). Abraham Verghese uses Google Glass to demonstrate how to begin a patient exam. Retrieved from http://scopeblog.stanford.edu/2013/07/25/abraham-verghese-usesgoogle-glass-to-demonstrate-how-to-begin-a-patient-exam/

Steinkuehler, C. A. (2004b). Learning in massively multiplayer online games. In Y. B. Kafai, W. A. Sandoval, N. Enyedy, A. S. Nixon, & F. Herrera (Eds.), *Proceedings of the Sixth International Conference of the Learning Sciences* (pp. 521-528). Mahwah, NJ: Erlbaum.

Steinmetz, K. (2015). Why transgender people are being murdered at a historic rate. *Time.com*. Retrieved from http://time.com/3999348/transgender-murders-2015/

Sternberg, R. J. (2001). What is the Common Thread of Creativity? Its Dialectical Relation to Intelligence and Wisdom. *The American Psychologist*, *56*(4), 360–362. doi:10.1037/0003-066X.56.4.360 PMID:11330237

Stern, M. (2001). Nerds need not apply. *Canadian Business*, *74*(2), 70–74.

Sunrayne, S. (2013). *Profile of a man: Balien Buschbaum*. Retrieved from https://samanthasunrayne.com/2013/07/15/profile-of-a-man-balian-buschbaum/

Süzen, A. A., & Taşdelen, K. (2013). Home automation for disabilities using kinect technology. *SDU International Technologic Science*, *5*(2), 1–10.

Takacs, D. (2002). Positionality, epistemology, and social justice in the classroom. *Social Justice (San Francisco, Calif.)*, *29*(4), 168–181.

Takacs, D. (2003). How does your positionality bias your epistemology? *Thought & Action: The NEA Higher. Education Journal*, 27–28.

Tapscott, D. (2009). *Grown up digital: How the net generation is changing your world.* New York, NY: McGraw-Hill.

Tenekeci, M. E., Gümüşçü, A., & Ağırman, Ö. (2014, February). Interactive Kinect Application for Letter Training. *Paper presented at Academic Information '14 Academic Information Conference Papers*, Mersin University.

The Aspen Institute. (2014). *The Aspen Institution task force on learning and the Internet: Learner at the center of a networked world.* Retrieved from https://assets.aspeninstitute.org/content/uploads/files/content/docs/pubs/Learner-at-the-Center-of-a-Networked-World.pdf

Thoman, E., & Jolls, T. (2003). *Literacy for the 21st Century An Overview & Orientation Guide To Media Literacy Education.* Center for Media Literacy.

Thomas, S. (2008). Transliteracy and new media, In Randy Adams, Steve Gibson e Steffan Füller Arisona, eds., Transdisciplinary Digital Art: Sound, Vision and the New Screen (pp. 101-109). Berlin: Springer-Verlag Berlin Heidelberg.

Thompson, P. (2013). The digital natives as learners: Technology use patterns and approaches to learning. *Computers & Education*, *65*, 12–33. doi:10.1016/j.compedu.2012.12.022

Tierney, R. J., Bond, E., & Bresler, J. (2006). Examining literate lives as students engage with multiple literacies. *Theory into Practice*, *45*(4), 359–367. doi:10.1207/s15430421tip4504_10

Timmerman, M. A. (2000). Learning in the context of a mathematics teacher education course: Two case studies of elementary teachers' conceptions of mathematics, mathematics teaching and learning, and the teaching of mathematics with technology. *Journal of Technology and Teacher Education*, *8*(3), 247–258.

Tiwari, K., & Saini, S. P. S. (2015). Brain controlled robot using neurosky mindwave. *Journal of Technological Advances & Scientific Research*, *1*(4), 328–331.

TMZ. (2015, April 24). I've always had the soul of a woman. Retrieved from http://www.tmz.com/2015/04/24/bruce-jenner-diane-sawyer-interview-woman-transgender/

Tomé, V. (2008). CD-Rom "Vamos fazer jornais escolares": um contributo para o desenvolvimento da Educação para os Média em Portugal [PhD Thesis]. Faculdade de Psicologia e de Ciências da Educação da Universidade de Lisboa, Portugal.

Tomé, V. (2015). Redes sociais online: práticas e percepções de jovens (9-16), seus professores e encarregados de educação. In E. Bévort & V. Reia-Baptista (Eds.), Research on social media: a glocal view. Vitor Tomé (pp. 127-335). Lisbon: RVJ-Editores.

Transathlete.com. (2017). Retrieved from https://www.transathlete.com/policies-college

Trilling, B., & Fadel, C. (2009). *21st century skills: Learning for life in our times. America.* Jossey –Bass.

Tzu, C. (1996). *The book of Chuang Tzu* (M. Palmer & E. Breuilly, Trans.). London: Arkana.

Tzu, C. (1997). *The inner chapters* (D. Hinton, Trans.). Washington, D. C.: Counterpoint.

Tzu, L. (1990). *Tao te ching.* New York: Bantam.

Tzu, L. (1992). *Hua hu ching: The unknown teachings of Lao Tzu* (B. Walker, Trans.). New York: Harper-Collins.

U.S. Department of Education. (2011). *Meeting the nation's 2020 goal: State targets for increasing the number and percentage of college graduates with degrees.* Retrieved from https://www.whitehouse.gov/sites/default/files/completion_state_by_state.pdf

U.S. Department of Education. (2016). Future ready learning: Reimagining the role of technology in education. *2016 National Education Technology Plan*. Retrieved from https://tech.ed.gov/files/2015/12/NETP16.pdf

Umbach, P. D. (2006). How effective are they? Exploring the impact of contingent faculty on undergraduate education. *The Review of Higher Education*, *30*(2), 91–123. doi:10.1353/rhe.2006.0080

UNESCO survey highlights correlation between media violence and youth perception of reality. (n.d.). Retrieved from http://www.unesco.org/bpi/eng/unescopress/98-32e.htm

UNESCO. (1963). Statistics on radio and television: 1950 - 1960. Paris: France. Retrieved from http://unesdoc.unesco.org/images/0003/000337/033739eo.pdf

UNESCO. (1982). Declaração de Grünwald. Retrieved from http://www.UNESCO.org/education/pdf/MEDIA_E.PDF

UNESCO. (1982). *Grunwald Declaration on Media Education*. Retrieved from www.unesco.org/education/pdf/MEDIA_E.PDF

UNESCO. (2007). Paris Agenda or 12 recommendations for media education. Retrieved from http://www.diplomatie.gouv.fr/fr/IMG/pdf/Parisagendafin_en.pdf

UNESCO. (2011) Media and Information Literacy: Curriculum for Teachers. Paris

UNESCO. (2011). *Media and Information Literacy: curriculum for teachers*. Paris: UNESCO.

UNESCO. (2013). *Alfabetização midiática e informacional: currículo para formação de professores / Carolyn Wilson, Alton Grizzle, Ramon Tuazon, Kwame Akyempong e Chi-Kim Cheung*. Brasília: UNESCO, UFTM.

UNESCO. (2013). *Global Media and Information Literacy (MIL). Assessment framework: Country readiness and competencies*. Paris, France. United States Institute for Peace. Retrieved from http://www.buildingpeace.org/forums/how-do-you-define-global-citizenship

UNESCO. (2014). Declaration on Augmented Media and Information Literacy (MIL) in the Digital era. Paris: Unesco. Retrieved from http://www.unesco.org/new/en/communication-and-information/resources/news-and-in-focus-articles/in-focus-articles/2014/paris-declaration-on-media-and-information-literacy-adopted/

UNESCO. (2015). Keystones to foster inclusive Knowledge Societies - Access to information and knowledge, Freedom of Expression, Privacy, and Ethics on a Global Internet- Paris: UNESCO. Retrieved from http://www.unesco.org/new/fileadmin/MULTIMEDIA/HQ/CI/CI/pdf/internet_draft_study.pdf

Unwin, T. (2009). *ICT4D Information and Communication Technology for Development*. Cambridge, UK: Cambridge University Press.

Valentin, E. K. (2001). SWOT analysis from a resource-based view. *Journal of Marketing Theory and Practice*, *9*(2), 54–69. doi:10.1080/10696679.2001.11501891

Vallurupalli, S., Paydak, H., Agarwal, S. K., Agrawal, M., & Assad-Kottner, C. (2013). Wearable technology to improve education and patient outcomes in a cardiology fellowship program-a feasibility study. *Health Technology*, *3*(4), 267–270. doi:10.1007/s12553-013-0065-4

Veiga, A. (2009). *El Chat como herramienta didáctica en la administración de un curso de postgrado. Revista Científica: Teorías, Enfoques y Aplicaciones en las Ciencias Sociales (TEACS), 2(1), Junio, Universidad Experimental de los Llanos Occidentales Ezequiel Zamora*. UNELLEZ.

Vorderer, P., Hartmann, T., & Klimmt, C. (2003). Explaining the enjoyment of playing video games. In *Proceedings of the ACM International Conference Proceeding Series*. Pittsburgh: Carnegie Mellon University.

Vraga, E., & Tully, M. (2015). Media literacy messages and hostile media perceptions: Processing of nonpartisan versus partisan political information. *Mass Communication & Society, 18*(4), 422–448. doi:10.1080/15205436.2014.1001910

Vygotsky, L. (1978). *Mind in Society*. London: Harvard University Press.

Waetjen, W. B. (1993). Technological literacy reconsidered. Retrieved from https://scholar.lib.vt.edu/ejournals/JTE/v4n2/waetjen.jte-v4n2.html

Walter, D. (2015). Microsoft OneNote for beginners: Everything you need to know. *PCWorld*. Retrieved from http://www.pcworld.com/article/2686026/microsoft-onenote-for-beginners-everything-you-need-to-know.html

Walther, J. B. (1992). Interpersonal effects in computer-mediated interaction a relational perspective. *Communication Research, 19*(1), 52–90. doi:10.1177/009365092019001003

Wang, A. T., Sandhu, N. P., Wittich, C. M., Mandrekar, J. N., & Beckman, T. J. (2012). Using social media to improve continuing medical education: A survey of course participants. *Mayo Clinic Proceedings, 87*(12), 1162–1170. doi:10.1016/j.mayocp.2012.07.024 PMID:23141117

Wang, S.-K., Hsu, H.-Y., Campbell, T., Coster, D., & Longhurst, M. (2014). An Investigation of Middle School Science Teachers and Students Use of Technology Inside and Outside of Classrooms: Considering whether digital natives are more technology savvy than their teachers. *Educational Technology Research and Development, 62*(6), 637–662. doi:10.1007/s11423-014-9355-4

Warschaeur, M., & Matuchniak, T. (2010). New technology and digital worlds: Analyzing evidence of access, equity, and outcomes. *Review of Research in Education, 34*(1), 179–225. doi:10.3102/0091732X09349791

Webster-Wright, A. (2009). Reframing professional development through understanding authentic professional learning. *Review of Educational Research, 79*(2), 702–739. doi:10.3102/0034654308330970

Wecker, C., Kohnlet, C., & Fischer, F. (2007). Computer Literacy and Inquiry Learning: When Geekslearn Less. *Journal of Computer Assisted Learning, 23*(2), 133–144. doi:10.1111/j.1365-2729.2006.00218.x

Williams, K. (2003). Literacy and computer literacy: Analyzing the NRC's being fluent with information technology. *The Journal of Literacy and Technology, 3*(1). Retrieved from http://www.literacyandtechnology.org/v3n1/williams.htm

Windham, C. (2005). Educating the Net generation. In *Father Google & Mother IM: Confessions of a Net Gen Learner* (pp. 43-58). EDUCASE.

Wisker, G. (2008). *The postgraduate research handbook* (2nd ed.). Basingstoke: Palgrave. Palgrave Study Guides. doi:10.1007/978-0-230-36494-3

Woodard, B. S. (2003). Technology and the constructivist learning environment: Implications for teaching information literacy skills. *Research Strategies, 19*(3), 181–192. doi:10.1016/j.resstr.2005.01.001

World Economic Forum. (2016). The Global World Information Technology Report: Innovating in the digital Economy.

Wouters, P., van Nimwegen, C., von Oostendorp, H., & van der Spek, E. D. (2013). A meta-analysis of the cognitive and motivational effects of serious games. *Journal of Educational Psychology, 105*(2), 249–265. doi:10.1037/a0031311

Wu, T., Dameff, C., & Tully, J. (2014). Integrating Google Glass into simulation-based training: Experiences and future directions. *Journal of Biomedical Graphics and Computing, 4*(2), 49. doi:10.5430/jbgc.v4n2p49

Yadav, A. (2011). Media Studies in School Curriculum: Obstacles, Challenges and Possibilities. *Journal of Indian Education*.

Yamauchi, Y, & Nakasugi, H. (2003, June). Past Viewer: Development of wearable learning system. *Paper presented at World Conference on Educational Media and Technology*, Honolulu, Hawaii.

Yaniv, H. (2011). The social network as a learning community – Culture of lifelong learning. *MOFET Institute Journal, 46.* (in Hebrew)

Yee, V., David, K., & Patel, J. K. (2017). Here's the Reality About Illegal Immigrants in the United States. *Migrationpolicy.org*. Retrieved from http://www.migrationpolicy.org/article/frequently-requested-statistics-immigrants-and-immigration-united-states

Yetik, U. E., & Keskin, N. Ö. (2016). Use of seamless learning approach in open and distance education. *Journal of Research in Education and Teaching, 5*(1), 98–103.

Yiannopoulos, M. (2015). I Am So Done With The Trans Outrage Brigade: Why I'm Supporting 'Drop The T'. *Breitbart*. Retrieved from http://www.breitbart.com/big-government/2015/11/10/i-am-so-done-with-the-trans-outrage-brigade-why-im-supporting-drop-the-t/

Yıldız, B., Ilgaz, H., & Seferoğlu, S. S. (2010, February). Science and technology policies in Turkey: An overview of development plans from 1963 to 2013. *Paper presented at Akademic informatic* (pp. 10-12).

Yildiz, M. (2002). Analog and digital video production techniques in media literacy education. *National Educational Computing Conference Proceedings*.

Yin, R. K. (2008). *Case study research: Design and methods* (4th ed.). London: Sage Publications.

Yokoyama, O. (1995). Slavic Discourse Grammar and the literary text. in O.T. Yokoyama (ed.), *Harvard Studies in Slavic Linguistics, 3*, 187-212.

Young, H. (2013). The digital language divide: How does the language you speak shape your experience of the Internet? *British Academy for the Humanities and Social Sciences*. Retrieved from http://labs.theguardian.com/digital-language-divide/

Young, A. (2010). *The Scene of Violence: Cinema, Crime, Affect*. New York, NY: Routledge.

Yutang, L. (1948). *The wisdom of Laotse*. New York: Random House.

Zhang, P. H. (2013). *Digital divides and socio-demographic factors: A longitudinal quantitative study of Internet users in U.S. from 2000 to 2010*. Retrieved from ProQuest. (UMI Number: 3556741)

Zickuhr, K., & Smith, A. (2013). Home broadband 2013: Trends and demographic differences in home broadband adoption. *Pew Research Center*. Retrieved from http://www.pewInternet.org/2013/08/26/home-broadband-2013/

Zong, J., & Batalova, J. (2017). *Frequently Requested Statistics on Immigrants and Immigration in the United States*. Retrieved March 9, 2017, from http://www.migrationpolicy.org/article/frequently-requested-statistics-immigrants-and-immigration-united-states

АронсонЭ.УилсонТ.ЭйкертР. (2002). *Социальная психология. Психологические законы поведения человека в социуме*. Санкт-Петербург: прайм-ЕВРОЗНАК.

Берон, Р., & Ричардсон, Д. (1998). *Агрессия*. Санкт-Петербург: Питер.

Брайант, Дж., & Томпсон, С. (2004). *Основы воздействия СМИ*. Москва: Вильяме.

Брушлинская, Л. В. (2002). Криминальное насилие в семье и его трансляция средствами массовой информации. In Е. Е. Пронина (Ed.), *Проблемы медиапсихологии* (pp. 72–86). Москва: РИП Холдинг.

В Азербайджане Саддам убивает после смерти. (2007). Retrieved from http://www.strana.co.il/news/?ID=9787&cat=0

СтароваО. (n.d.). *Средства массовой информации как источник агрессии*. Retrieved from http://psyfactor.org/lib/starova.htm

About the Contributors

Melda N. Yildiz teaches in the School for Interdisciplinary Studies and Education at NYIT. Melda served as a Fulbright Scholar in Turkmenistan and Azerbaijan teaching and conducting research integrating media education in P20 classrooms. Melda co-authored, published, and presented featuring Media and Information Literacy, Instructional Technology, and Global Education. Melda N. Yildiz is global scholar, assessment and curriculum consultant, instructional designer, author, and edupreneur. She is the chair of the Instructional Technology program and associate professor in the School for Interdisciplinary Studies and Education at NYIT. Melda served as a Fulbright Scholar in Turkmenistan (2009) and Azerbaijan (2016) teaching and conducting research integrating new media and technologies in P16 classrooms. Melda worked as a Media Specialist and the director of media services at Northfield Mount Hermon School and taught media literacy and production to grades 9-12. As a teacher educator, she taught Media Literacy Education, Multimedia Production, and Educational Technology to P-16 educators and teacher candidates. She taught as a national faculty at Lesley University, as a contributing faculty to Walden University, as a research fellow at Oxford University, and as a visiting scholar at Abant Izzet Baysal University and Mehmet Akif University. She worked as the director of assessment and accreditation and also as a program reviewer and site visitor for StarTalk: National Security Language Initiative (NSLI). Melda co-authored, published, and presented featuring Media and Information Literacy, Instructional Technology, and Global Education in national and international conferences. She received Ed.D. from University of Massachusetts, Amherst, on Math & Science and Instructional Technology; M.S. from Southern Connecticut State University on Instructional Technology. She majored in Teaching English as a Foreign Language at Bogazici University, in Turkey.

Steven S. Funk is a lecturer in Writing and Critical Media Literacy at Montana State University, Billings (MSUB). He also teaches in Veterans Upward Bound, a college bridge program delivered through Montana State University Northern (MSUN) and Federal TRIO programs. In addition, he serves as a faculty advisor on the MSUB campus Safe Zone initiative. Dr. Funk's research is grounded in Critical Media Literacy, a framework incorporating Media Studies and Critical Pedagogy to further social justice through critical engagement with media. He is currently developing a framework of media analysis called Trans*+ Media Literacy that, in addition to drawing inspiration from Critical Media Literacy, incorporates Feminist and Disabilities Studies to underscore the need for the critical analysis of trans*+ representation in and engagement with media. Named by the American Educational Research Association (AERA) as an "Emerging Scholar" in 2013 for his research in Critical Media Literacy, Dr. Funk has published in *Critical Questions in Education* and *Sexuality and Culture*, and other publications committed to advancing the education of traditionally underrepresented students. Moreover, he serves as a faculty moderator for an online support group hosted by the Gender Spectrum, and as a consultant to the Youth and Gender Media Project, two non-profit organizations committed to increasing awareness of and social justice for trans*+ individuals. Collaborating with his partner, Dr. Jaydi Funk, he is currently analyzing data collected in a large-scale mixed-methods study addressing gender equity in medical practices and media.

Belinha S. De Abreu, Ph.D., is a Media Literacy Educator and serves as an International Expert to the Forum on Media & Information Literacy for UNESCO's Communication & Information Section. Her research interests include media and information literacy education, educational technology, global perspectives, critical thinking, privacy & big data, young adults, and teacher training. Dr. De Abreu's focus is on the impact of learning as a result of media and technology consumed by K–12 students; providing students with viable, real-life opportunities for engaging in various technological environments while in turn encouraging students to be creative and conscious users of technology and media. Dr. De Abreu serves as the Vice President for the National Telemedia Council (NTC). The National Telemedia Council is a national non-profit organization that has been promoting a media-wise, literate, global society since 1953. NTC also produces The *Journal of Media Literacy* for which Dr. De Abreu is a member of the editorial board and has been a guest editor on several occasions. She is also a board member of the Leadership Council for the National Association for Media Literacy Education (NAMLE). Dr. De Abreu's work has been featured in *Cable in the Classroom*, *Civic Media Project*, and various other publications. She is the author of *Mobile Learning through Digital Media Literacy* (Peter Lang, 2017), and the author/ co-editor of *The International Handbook for Media Literacy Education* (Routledge, 2017), and *Global Media Literacy in a Digital Age* (Peter Lang, 2016), *Media Literacy Education in Action: Theoretical and Pedagogical Perspectives* (Routledge, 2014), and the author of *Media Literacy, Social Networking and the Web 2.0 World for the K–12 Educator* (Peter Lang, 2011). Follow @belmedia.

* * *

Kadir Almus is the Vice President for Administrative Affairs and Associate Professor of Educational Leadership at North American University (NAU). Dr. Almus joined NAU in 2012 and worked as the Vice President for Enrollment Management for one year. He then taught at undergraduate and graduate levels in Education Department at NAU for three years. Dr. Almus received his M.Ed. and Ed.D. degrees in Educational Administration and Supervision from University of Houston. Prior to joining NAU, Dr. Almus worked as the Associate Superintendent and Chief Academic Officer of the largest STEM focused charter school network in Texas. During his four-year tenure as Chief Academic Officer, Harmony Public Schools (HPS) has increased to 36 schools with 20,000 students and has become one of the highest academically rated schools in the state, particularly in STEM areas. Prior to serving as Chief Academic Officer, Dr. Almus worked at a number of schools as a school principal for 7 years and as a high school chemistry teacher, science Olympiad team coach, department chair for 6 years. In addition to numerous research articles in educational leadership, STEM education, and educational technology fields, Dr. Almus has also co-authored two high school chemistry textbooks and published various policies, procedures, and guidelines for school governance and operations. In 2006, he served as the founding principal of one of the first-generation T-STEM academies, and since then, STEM education has been one of his main research topics. Dr. Almus was part of a $15 million T-STEM grant awarded by Texas High School Project & Communities Foundation of Texas. He was also involved with federal grants that HPS received, the most recent of those being the CS Replication Grant, totaling $4.8 million from the Department of Education in 2011. Dr. Almus was the Project Director/PI of this grant. In addition to administrative duties at NAU, Dr. Almus also involved in many departmental and committee work such as chairing the General Education Committee, establishing Masters of Education in Educational Leadership program, and serving as graduate programs coordinator in Education Department.

Smadar Bar-Tal Lecture and Staff member of the center for Innovation and Excellence in Teaching art Levinsky College, Israel. Served as Head of the High School Program, at Levinsky College and as Head of the Departments at online environments at the Mofet Institute. Field of specialization: Distance teaching and Learning' organizing and leading conferences, seminars, workshops, meetings and online learning days. Her researches and her development of materials focus on combining technologies in teaching and learning, online discussions and social networks. Smadar teaches courses on digital pedagogy and leads online workshops for novice teachers.

Mary Catherine Boehmer is an English Language Fellow in Baku, Azerbaijan, teaching English and developing English language projects through a grant with the Office of English Language Programs through the U.S. Department of State. She has a B.A. in linguistics and a minor in Russian and Spanish from the University of Mississippi. After graduating in 2007, she spent two years teaching English and American Studies as a Fulbright English Teaching Assistant in Russia before pursuing her M.A in TESOL from Teachers College, Columbia University. There she focused on communicative approaches to language teaching, cross-cultural communication, culturally relevant pedagogy, and technology in education. Since then, she has primarily taught ESL in higher education in the Boston area - with a one-year break to teach at universities in Germany, where she taught English for economics, English for engineering, and English for public relations. She has also taught elementary Russian. She speaks varying degrees of Russian, Spanish, German, and Azerbaijani.

Victoria Brown is the Assistant Provost of eLearning at Florida Atlantic University. She oversees the day-to-day operations of the instructional technology professional development of faculty and provides support for online course development. Dr. Brown's has published articles and book chapters on the cognitive load of multimedia for individuals with attention and intention symptoms, universal design, global literacy, academic integrity, and professional development.

Flory A. Dieck-Assad has a Ph.D. in Finance from Tulane University (2003). Author of the textbook "Financial Institutions" by McGraw-Hill used by all the universities of the country. Invited lecturer in Mexico, Chile, U.S.A., Canada, and Europe and got the "Best Lecture Award" in 2004, 2008, 2010, 2011, 2012, 2013, 2014, 2015, and 2016. She has more than 200 publications in national/international magazines, reviews, and journals. She got the "Prize to Education and Research 2007, 2010, and 2014". Texas A&M University Press published her book: "Energy and Sustainable Development in Mexico" (2008), honored with the "National Romulo Garza Award for the Best Written Book". She is currently a Tenured Professor at Tecnologico de Monterrey. Received the 2013 National Ethics Award in Academic

Teaching, 2015 Professor of the Year, 2015 Distinguished Professor of the Institute of Chartered Accountants of the State of Nuevo Leon, Mexico, and the 2015 National Energy Prize for her contributions to the energy sector. Member of the Mexican National System of Researchers (SNI). Received an award for presenting the Best Academic Project with Social Impact in 2016 for its contribution to improve the welfare of rural communities in Mexico.

Bulent Dogan received his Ed.D. in Curriculum and Instruction with emphasis in Instructional Technology from University of Houston. He has been teaching in Education Department at the North American University (NAU) since 2011. Prior to his current position, he taught classes at St. Philip's College in San Antonio, Texas. Additionally, he also has 6 years of public school teaching and 5 years of school administration experience in San Antonio and Houston area. Dr. Dogan currently teaches Educational Technology courses both at undergraduate and graduate level at NAU. He also serves as field supervisor/college mentor for student teacher candidates as part of NAC-Teacher Certification Program. Dr. Dogan serves as the project director and developer of the "DISTCO" (Digital Storytelling Contests) and "EdTech People" projects. His research interests include educational technology training for school teachers and administrators; the educational uses of digital storytelling in K-12 and higher education; digital storytelling in teacher e-portfolio's; tablets/games in education and social Media in Higher Education, Virtual Reality Applications in Education.

Oris T. Griffin is a professor in the Adult Education/Human Resource Development (AHRD) Program in the Learning Technology and Leadership Education Department at James Madison University. I have been on the faculty for over 26 years. My areas of interest are Diversity, Leadership and Adult Learning. My commitment to student learning is exemplified by my long-term involvement with community service-learning, having served as faculty liaison and a Professor in Residence (PIR) for several inner-city schools in Richmond, VA for over six years, I also served as the Director of the PIR Program for three years.

Turan Guntepe is a research assistant at Giresun University. Her research focuses on information and communication technologies, technologies integration, design of technologies supported learning environments and game based learning environments.

Hui-Yin Hsu is professor and chair of the Teacher Education Department in the School of Interdisciplinary Studies and Education at New York Institute of Technology. She received her Ph.D. in Reading Education and master's degree in Elementary/Early Childhood Education from the Pittsburgh University. Hui-Yin has authored and co-authored over twenty peer-reviewed journal articles and presented over fifty national and international conferences. Hui-Yin concentrates her research interests on using technologies to enhance language and literacy learning. Her professional interests have been in the area of new literacies: the idea of using Information and Communication Technologies (ICTs), teacher professional development, and mobile device to consume and produce information for learning. Dr. Hsu is the Co-PI for the National Science Foundation (NSF, DRK12- 1020091) project. She served on the NYS ELA Common Core State Standards Setting Committee. She is the President of the Chinese American Academic & Professional Society (CAAPS), and serves as program committee and chairs for several internal conferences.

Sevinj Iskandarova is a Ph.D. student at James Madison University, Harrisonburg, VA, the USA. She received her MS.Ed. in Adult Education/Human Resource Development from James Madison University, Harrisonburg, VA, the USA in May 2016. Her main research interests include Human-Computer Interface, Information Technology, International Education, Leadership, Learner-centered Education and Multicultural Education. In 2016, Sevinj received the Graduate College's Outstanding Thesis Award in Education, Social Science, and Humanities. She has advanced experience on the educational system in Caucasus and Central Asia regions. She has presented at more than 30 international conferences, and seminars thought USA, Europe, and Asia.

Lala Jabbarova is an associate professor in the Department of Social and pedagogical psychology at the Baku State University. I graduated from Faculty of Social science and psychology (1997) and received my Ph.D. degree in social psychology from Baku State University in 2002.

Matthew Lewerenz is an assistant professor of applied linguistics at Ashford University and a doctoral candidate in Education with a concentration in applied linguistics at Walden University. His research and publication interests include language education, critical pedagogy, Taoism, and global and cultural studies.

Shahla Naghieva is a Professor of the Foreign Literature Department of the Azerbaijan University of Languages. As a winner of Fulbright Visiting Scholar Program sponsored by the State Department of the USA she did research on literary translation at the East Carolina University, North Carolina for 6 months in 2003-2004, and at George Mason University for 4 months in 2010-2011. She is the author of many scholarly articles and several books. She is also a chairwoman of Sonmaz Mashal Cultural Relations Public Union.

P. Sri Jothi is an Assistant Professor and Head of the Department, in Visual Communication Department, Asan Memorial College of Arts and Science, Chennai, India. Her interdisciplinary research is focused on the Role of Media in Science and Technology Communication for the Development Rural Women. She has published and presented many research papers in national and international journals and in conferences. She handles classes for both UG and PG programmes since 2004 till date. She specialized in, Mass Communication theories, Advertising, Multimedia-2D graphics and animation subjects. Her main areas of research interests include Science Communication, Information Communication Technology, Women Empowerment, Rural Development and Development Communication.

Tami Seifert is currently a lecturer at Kibbutzim College of Education, Tel-Aviv. She has a PhD in Urban Studies and Instructional Design and Technology from Old Dominion University (Virginia, USA) in 2001. She earned both her B.Sc and M.Sc from Tel-Aviv University. Between 2003 and 2005 she completed a post-doctorate from Tel-Aviv University on implementation of handheld computers in education. She served as head of the Department of Educational Computing, the head of Academic ICT and vice-director of the Teacher Training for Graduates Program at Kibbutzim College of Education (2007-2014). Courses Tami has taught in the past five years include: Innovative Technologies in

Education, Online Education, The Design of Online Instruction: From Planning to Assessment, Social Networking in Educational Contexts, Application of Video in Teaching. She promotes and advises digital literacy among faculty so that they can serve as role-models for their own students, helping to bridge the technological gap between generations.

Aakanksha Rajeev Sharma is an educator and researcher working on media literacy. The author is especially interested in looking at media practices of children and youth in developing nations. She is pursuing doctoral research on media literacy education in Indian schools and writes on films, new media, media and information literacy and media education.

Sujatha Sosale is interested in the capacity-building and empowering roles of media and communication in international development. Her projects include the use of information communication technologies for facilitating change, global communication policies and their impact on developing societies, and media representations of social change and public affairs in developing countries. She is an Associate Professor in the School of Journalism and Mass Communication at The University of Iowa.

Vitor Tomé, professional journalist, teacher trainer and researcher, concluded a post-PhD degree in Communication Sciences (2015) and a PhD in Education Sciences (2008). He's currently involved in several research projects, such as "Digital Citizenship Education" (Council of Europe), COST Action "The Digital Literacy and Multimodal Practices of Young Children" (which involves 34 countries), and "Digital Citizenship Education for Democratic Participation" (FCT, Portugal). He has been a lecturer in Portugal, Brazil and Japan, and is the author of several books, book chapters and articles in international scientific journals.

Shiang-Kwei Wang is professor and associate dean of the School of Interdisciplinary Studies and Education, New York Institute of Technology. She received her Ph.D. in Instructional Technology from the University of Georgia, master's degree in M.B.A. at the Yuan-Ze University (Taiwan), and bachelor's degree in Library Science at the TamKang University (Taiwan). Wang has authored or co-authored more than twenty peer-reviewed journal articles and made more than fifty national and international conference presentations. Her professional interests include technology integration in learning settings, the motivational impact of information and communication technologies (ICTs) on learning attitude and performance, mobile learning, as well as the design and development of interactive learning tools. Her work has appeared in Educational Technology Research and Development, Journal of Science Education and Technology, and Tech Trend. Dr. Wang is the PI for the National Science Foundation (NSF, DRK12-1020091) project. She is the program chair of the AERA (American Educational Research Association) Computer and Internet Applications Program Chair and serves on the technology advisory board of the NSTA (National Science Teacher Association).

Index

Purchase Print, E-Book, or Print + E-Book

IGI Global books can now be purchased from three unique pricing formats:
Print Only, E-Book Only, or Print + E-Book. Shipping fees apply.

www.igi-global.com

Recommended Reference Books

ISBN: 978-1-5225-0267-8
© 2016; 477 pp.
List Price: $175

ISBN: 978-1-4666-9519-1
© 2016; 622 pp.
List Price: $235

ISBN: 978-1-5225-0164-0
© 2016; 1,663 pp.
List Price: $1,850

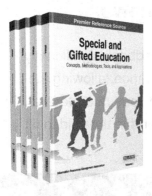

ISBN: 978-1-5225-0034-6
© 2016; 2,429 pp.
List Price: $1,925

ISBN: 978-1-4666-9634-1
© 2016; 866 pp.
List Price: $400

ISBN: 978-1-4666-9680-8
© 2016; 450 pp.
List Price: $300

Looking for free content, product updates, news, and special offers?

Join IGI Global's mailing list today and start enjoying exclusive perks sent only to IGI Global members.
Add your name to the list at **www.igi-global.com/newsletters.**

Publishing Information Science and Technology Research Since 1988

www.igi-global.com   Sign up at www.igi-global.com/newsletters   f facebook.com/igiglobal   t twitter.com/igiglobal

Stay Current on the Latest Emerging Research Developments

Become an IGI Global Reviewer for Authored Book Projects

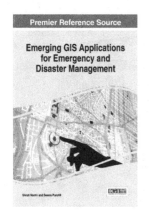

Premier Reference Source

Emerging GIS Applications for Emergency and Disaster Management

Premier Reference Source

Managerial Strategies and Green Solutions for Project Sustainability

Premier Reference Source

Comparative Approaches to Using R and Python for Statistical Data Analysis

Premier Reference Source

Solutions for High-Touch Communications in a High-Tech World

The overall success of an authored book project is dependent on quality and timely reviews.

In this competitive age of scholarly publishing, constructive and timely feedback significantly decreases the turnaround time of manuscripts from submission to acceptance, allowing the publication and discovery of progressive research at a much more expeditious rate. Several IGI Global authored book projects are currently seeking highly qualified experts in the field to fill vacancies on their respective editorial review boards:

Applications may be sent to:
development@igi-global.com

Applicants must have a doctorate (or an equivalent degree) as well as publishing and reviewing experience. Reviewers are asked to write reviews in a timely, collegial, and constructive manner. All reviewers will begin their role on an ad-hoc basis for a period of one year, and upon successful completion of this term can be considered for full editorial review board status, with the potential for a subsequent promotion to Associate Editor.

If you have a colleague that may be interested in this opportunity, we encourage you to share this information with them.

www.igi-global.com

InfoSci®-Books

A Database for Information Science and Technology Research

Maximize Your Library's Book Collection!

Invest in IGI Global's InfoSci®-Books database and gain access to
hundreds of reference books at a fraction of their individual list price.

The InfoSci®-Books database offers unlimited simultaneous users the
ability to precisely return search results through more than 80,000 full-text
chapters from nearly 3,900 reference books in the following academic research areas:

Business & Management Information Science & Technology • Computer Science & Information Technology
Educational Science & Technology • Engineering Science & Technology • Environmental Science & Technology
Government Science & Technology • Library Information Science & Technology • Media & Communication Science & Technology
Medical, Healthcare & Life Science & Technology • Security & Forensic Science & Technology • Social Sciences & Online Behavior

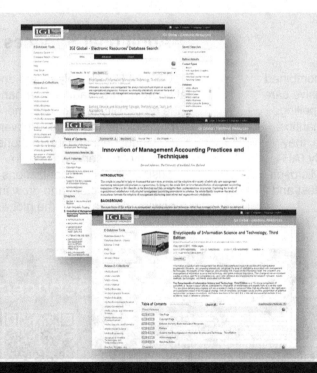

Peer-Reviewed Content:
• Cutting-edge research
• No embargoes
• Scholarly and professional
• Interdisciplinary

Award-Winning Platform:
• Unlimited simultaneous users
• Full-text in XML and PDF
• Advanced search engine
• No DRM

Librarian-Friendly:
• Free MARC records
• Discovery services
• COUNTER4/SUSHI compliant
• Training available

To find out more or request a free trial, visit:
www.igi-global.com/eresources

www.igi-global.com

IGI Global Proudly Partners with

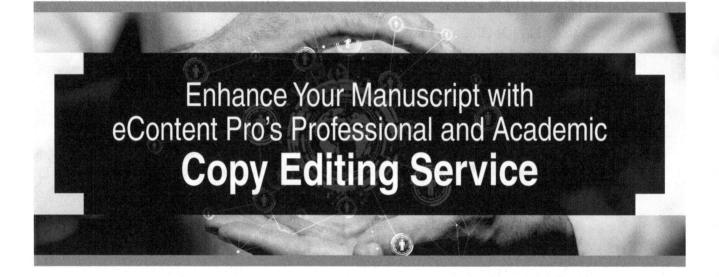

Enhance Your Manuscript with
eContent Pro's Professional and Academic
Copy Editing Service

Expert Copy Editing

eContent Pro copy editors, with over 70 years of combined experience, will provide complete and comprehensive care for your document by resolving all issues with spelling, punctuation, grammar, terminology, jargon, semantics, syntax, consistency, flow, and more. In addition, they will format your document to the style you specify (APA, Chicago, etc.). All edits will be performed using Microsoft Word's Track Changes feature, which allows for fast and simple review and management of edits.

Additional Services

eContent Pro also offers fast and affordable proofreading to enhance the readability of your document, professional translation in over 100 languages, and international marketing services to help businesses and organizations localize their content and grow into new markets around the globe.

IGI Global Authors Save 25% on eContent Pro's Services!

Scan the QR Code to Receive Your 25% Discount

The 25% discount is applied directly to your eContent Pro shopping cart when placing an order through IGI Global's referral link. Use the QR code to access this referral link. eContent Pro has the right to end or modify any promotion at any time.

Email: customerservice@econtentpro.com

econtentpro.com

Information Resources Management Association

Advancing the Concepts & Practices of Information Resources Management in Modern Organizations

Become an IRMA Member

Members of the **Information Resources Management Association (IRMA)** understand the importance of community within their field of study. The Information Resources Management Association is an ideal venue through which professionals, students, and academicians can convene and share the latest industry innovations and scholarly research that is changing the field of information science and technology. Become a member today and enjoy the benefits of membership as well as the opportunity to collaborate and network with fellow experts in the field.

IRMA Membership Benefits:

- **One FREE Journal Subscription**

- **30% Off Additional Journal Subscriptions**

- **20% Off Book Purchases**

- Updates on the latest events and research on Information Resources Management through the IRMA-L listserv.

- Updates on new open access and downloadable content added to Research IRM.

- A copy of the Information Technology Management Newsletter twice a year.

- A certificate of membership.

IRMA Membership $195

Scan code or visit **irma-international.org** and begin by selecting your free journal subscription.

Membership is good for one full year.

www.irma-international.org

www.igi-global.com

Available to Order Now
Order through www.igi-global.com with **Free Standard Shipping**.

The Premier Reference for Information Science & Information Technology

100% Original Content
Contains 705 new, peer-reviewed articles with color figures covering over 80 categories in 11 subject areas

Diverse Contributions
More than 1,100 experts from 74 unique countries contributed their specialized knowledge

Easy Navigation
Includes two tables of content and a comprehensive index in each volume for the user's convenience

Highly-Cited
Embraces a complete list of references and additional reading sections to allow for further research

Included in:

InfoSci®-Books

Encyclopedia of Information Science and Technology Fourth Edition
A Comprehensive 10-Volume Set

Mehdi Khosrow-Pour, D.B.A. (Information Resources Management Association, USA)
ISBN: 978-1-5225-2255-3; © 2018; Pg: 8,104; Release Date: July 2017

For a limited time, receive the complimentary e-books for the First, Second, and Third editions with the purchase of the *Encyclopedia of Information Science and Technology, Fourth Edition* e-book.**

The **Encyclopedia of Information Science and Technology, Fourth Edition** is a 10-volume set which includes 705 original and previously unpublished research articles covering a full range of perspectives, applications, and techniques contributed by thousands of experts and researchers from around the globe. This authoritative encyclopedia is an all-encompassing, well-established reference source that is ideally designed to disseminate the most forward-thinking and diverse research findings. With critical perspectives on the impact of information science management and new technologies in modern settings, including but not limited to computer science, education, healthcare, government, engineering, business, and natural and physical sciences, it is a pivotal and relevant source of knowledge that will benefit every professional within the field of information science and technology and is an invaluable addition to every academic and corporate library.

Scan for Online Bookstore

Pricing Information

Hardcover: **$5,695**   E-Book: **$5,695***   Hardcover + E-Book: **$6,895***

Both E-Book Prices Include:
- *Encyclopedia of Information Science and Technology, First Edition E-Book*
- *Encyclopedia of Information Science and Technology, Second Edition E-Book*
- *Encyclopedia of Information Science and Technology, Third Edition E-Book*

* Purchase the Encyclopedia of Information Science and Technology, Fourth Edition e-book and receive the first, second, and third e-book editions for free. Offer is only valid with purchase of the fourth edition's e-book. Offer expires January 1, 2018.

Recommend this Title to Your Institution's Library: www.igi-global.com/books

www.igi-global.com/infosci-ondemand

InfoSci®-OnDemand

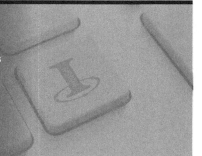

Continuously updated with new material on a weekly basis, InfoSci®-OnDemand offers the ability to search through thousands of quality full-text research papers. Users can narrow each search by identifying key topic areas of interest, then display a complete listing of relevant papers, and purchase materials specific to their research needs.

Comprehensive Service

- Over 81,600+ journal articles, book chapters, and case studies.
- All content is downloadable in PDF format and can be stored locally for future use.

No Subscription Fees

- One time fee of $37.50 per PDF download.

Instant Access

- Receive a download link immediately after order completion!

Database Platform Features:

- Comprehensive Pay-Per-View Service
- Written by Prominent International Experts/Scholars
- Precise Search and Retrieval
- Updated With New Material on a Weekly Basis
- Immediate Access to Full-Text PDFs
- No Subscription Needed
- Purchased Research Can Be Stored Locally for Future Use

"It really provides an excellent entry into the research literature of the field. It presents a manageable number of highly relevant sources on topics of interest to a wide range of researchers. The sources are scholarly, but also accessible to 'practitioners'."

- Lisa Stimatz, MLS, University of North Carolina at Chapel Hill, USA

"It is an excellent and well designed database which will facilitate research, publication and teaching. It is a very very useful tool to have."

- George Ditsa, PhD, University of Wollongong, Australia

"I have accessed the database and find it to be a valuable tool to the IT/IS community. I found valuable articles meeting my search criteria 95% of the time."

- Lynda Louis, Xavier University of Louisiana, USA

Recommended for use by researchers who wish to immediately download PDFs of individual chapters or articles.

www.igi-global.com/e-resources/infosci-ondemand

www.igi-global.com

Printed in the United States
By Bookmasters